Personal Computer Inventory

Use the following list to make an inventory of your computer hardware and software. If you have a problem, or need to provide a serial number or model number to a company's customer service department, the information on this list will save you time and effort.

Computer Brand: . . . .

Computer Model Number: . . . .

Computer Serial Number: . . . .

CPU Type: . . . .

CPU Speed: . . . .

Monitor Brand: . . . .

Monitor Serial Number: . . . .

Operating System/Version Number: . . . .

Hard Disk Size: . . . .

Modem Brand: . . . .

Modem Model: . . . .

Modem Serial Number: . . . .

Amount of Memory (RAM): . . . .

Printer Brand: . . . .

Printer Model Number: . . . .

Printer Serial Number: . . . .

Available Room on Hard Disk: . . . .

Any Special Enhancements? . . . .

Most Frequently Used Software: . . . .

. . . .

. . . .

. . . .

. . . .

The Official

Tech Support
Yellow Pages

CyberMedia®
The Autofix Company

3000 Ocean Park Blvd.
Suite 2001
Santa Monica, CA 90405

Main number: (310) 581-4700
FAX number: (310) 581-4720

http://www.cybermedia.com/

The Official Tech Support Yellow Pages™

Trademarks

Contents

Acknowledgements

In Honor of Seymour Cray.

I would like to acknowledge the work of these people:

Anne Lam, Barbara Cooper, Ben Brown, Bernadette Duffy, Binh Ly, Brad Kingsbury, Bruce B. Barlow, Chi-Ching Chang, Daniel Riddle, David Perry, Dorthea Atwater, Doug Walner, Gary Carlson, Giselle Bisson, Greg Kennedy, Janet Daly, Jean Valdez, Karen Torimaru, Kathy Brady, Kimberly Baer, Lorne Steiner, Mary Wollman Behshid, Melissa Bloom, Patrick Faustino, Sri Chari, Stephanie Haibloom, Susan Petaja, Tiki Barbeau, Unni Warrier, Valerie Behrendt ...as well as the many others who contributed in the effort to produce this book.

Scott Shea

Product Manager,
Tech Support Yellow Pages

Introduction

Thank you for buying The Official Technical Support Yellow Pages. Your purchase ensures that you now have the most up-to-date contact information on hardware and software companies. We list over 2,000 companies, and over 500 user groups nationwide.

All company entries are listed alphabetically and indexed by category, so you can find companies by name, by product or by service.

The Tech Support Yellow Pages is supplied in a searchable online version and a quaint paper version—this handy book.

What the Tech Support Yellow Pages Offers

It's hard to keep track of which product came from what company—especially when you want to get in touch with that company. The Tech Support Yellow Pages is the best way to keep current. What if your computer or software manufacturer moved, merged, got acquired by a bigger company, or changed their name?

Whether you need extra help to learn a specific feature, or want some tips on how to navigate around an alien obstacle in your new software game; or if you need to replace the manual your dog ate for lunch, the Tech Support Yellow Pages provides you with the information at your fingertips and, with your Internet connection, just a mouse click away.

Using the Electronic Technical Support Yellow Pages

The electronic Tech Support Yellow Pages™ is a Windows help file that lists contact information for more than 2,000 hardware and software companies. No more searches, or waiting on hold for information, or trying to contact a company during business hours for information you can retrieve from its World Wide Web site.

You must have an existing Internet connection to access web addresses with the electronic Tech Support Yellow Pages.

Installing the Tech Support Yellow Pages

Use the following steps to install the electronic Tech Support Yellow Pages.

NOTE: If you've previously installed a CyberMedia software product that contains the Tech Support Yellow Pages, you don't have to install it again. The following procedure only applies if you have purchased the Tech Support Yellow Pages as a separate product.

1 Insert the Tech Support Yellow Pages CD in your CD-ROM drive.

2 In Windows Explorer or File Manager, select your CD-ROM drive in the drop-down list, then double-click **Setup.exe**.

3 Follow the instructions in the Setup program.

The installation process adds a TSYP program group and icon to your Windows programs.

Once you have installed the electronic Tech Support Yellow Pages and have established a connection to your existing Internet provider, you can use it to locate company's listing and connect to its World Wide Web site. All you have to do is click a listed web address, and the Tech Support Yellow Pages opens your browser and takes you to that site. For details, follow the steps under "Locating and Accessing Companies" in the next section.

Locating and Accessing Companies

NOTE: If you are using a dial-up service to access the Internet and Windows is not set up to dial in to your Internet connection automatically, you must connect and start your browser application *before* using the linking function of the electronic Tech Support Yellow Pages. Your normal Internet access fees and long distance charges still apply.

To search for a company in Windows 3.1x

1 Start the Tech Support Yellow Pages. (If you purchased the Tech Support Yellow Pages as a separate product, double-click the **TSYP** icon in the program group created during installation.)

The **Technical Support Yellow Pages** window appears. You can browse through the categories or you can search for a specific company.

2 Click the **Search** button. The **Search** window appears.

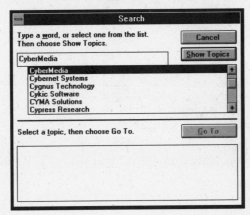

3 Type the letters of the company name until you see the full name in the list.

4 Click the company name.

5 Click the **Show Topics** button. A list of similar names appears in the topics list.

6 Select a topic, then click the **Go To** button.

The window displays information about the selected company. Similar information can be retrieved for thousands of other companies.

7 Do one of the following:

- To find another company, click the **Search** button and repeat steps 1 through 4.

- If the URL for the company's home page appears in green, and you have established a connection to your existing Internet provider, click the URL to open your browser and connect with the company's home page.

To search for a company in Windows 95

1 Start the Tech Support Yellow Pages. (If you purchased the Tech Support Yellow Pages as a separate product, double-click the **TSYP** icon in the program group created during installation.)

The **Technical Support Yellow Pages** window appears. You can browse through the Hardware, Software, and Services categories, or you can search for a specific company.

2 Click the Search button. The **Help Topics** dialog box appears:

3 Type the letters of the company name until you see the full name in the list.

4 Click the company name.

5 Click the **Display** button.

The help window displays with information about the selected company. Similar information can be retrieved for thousands of other companies.

6 Do one of the following:

- To find another company, click the **Search** button and repeat steps 1 through 3.
- If the URL for the company's home page appears in green, and you have established a connection to your existing Internet provider, click the URL to open your browser and connect with the company's home page.

About the Tech Support Yellow Pages Listings

While we have made every effort to verify that the names, addresses, and phone numbers in the Tech Support Yellow Pages are correct, this type of information is subject to constant change. If you have any corrections or additions, please send them to us; we gladly welcome them.

E-mail: vendors@cybermedia.com

FAX: (310) 581-4720 Attention: Technical Publications

How this Manual is Organized

Following this "Introduction" is a "Troubleshooting" section full of basic advice to help you with common problems. Next is the "User Groups Directory"—listing over 500 user groups in the United States and other countries worldwide. The "Company Names (A–Z)" section contains over 2,000 company listings organized alphabetically. Following the company listings is a glossary with basic computer terms and an index that lists companies by name and by category.

If you know the specific name of the company you're looking for, you can look it up directly in "Company Names (A–Z)." If you're browsing for a company in a specific category—for example, Printers—you can look it up in the category section of the index.

Troubleshooting

Look for our mascot, "Bugsy™" in First Aid™ 95 Deluxe.

This troubleshooting section of the Technical Support Yellow Pages is part of CyberMedia's effort to put essential problem-solving information at your fingertips so you can help yourself. This chapter does the following:

- Gives you advice for maximum computing productivity.

- Provides you with problem-solving checklists, tips and troubleshooting procedures.

- Tells you how to prevent problems before they happen to you.

Some of these suggestions may seem elementary. But don't be fooled. Experienced computer professionals know—mostly from their own bitter, amusing, embarrassing, and/or enlightening experiences—that you cannot troubleshoot effectively unless you start from scratch. So try these suggestions. They could save you a lot of time, money, and red faces.

So even if you think you know it all, take a quick look through this chapter. Chances are you'll learn something new. We did!

Our "Top Ten" List to Avoid Panic

Here's the top ten things to do instead of panicking—Do these things first!

If you're having a problem with your computer, don't panic! Use the following checklist to help get back to work:

1   When did the computer start acting like this?

2   What happened immediately before your problem started?

3   Have you checked all the connections and on/off switches?

4   Is anything new or different—for example:

   • Did you install a new program, or add something to an existing program?

   • Did you just add a new or different hardware device, such as a printer or modem?

5   Did you change the settings, or configuration, for a program?

6   Has anyone else used the computer who might have made changes?

7   Have you checked for virus activity?

8   Are you running out of room on your hard disk?

9   Does your hard disk need defragmentation?

10 Do you have enough memory for the program you're running? (If you are using Windows 95, 8MB is barely adequate for many programs.)

Monitor Problems: Nothing on the Screen

If your monitor is blank, or acting badly, use the following suggestions:

1   Turn your monitor and computer off.

2   Check the power plug for the monitor.

3   Check the cable connecting the computer to the monitor. Make sure the plug is connected securely.

4   When you know the connections are secure, turn on the monitor first, then the computer.

5   Adjust the darkness and contrast controls on the monitor to make sure they haven't been turned off accidentally.

6   If your monitor has a degaussing switch, give it a try. (Check the monitor's manual for details.)

7   If these suggestions don't work, try the monitor with a different but compatible computer. If it works, the problem could be with the video card in your computer.

Printing Problems: Nothing on the Page

Has your printer been printing OK, but now doesn't? Try these tips:

1 Turn the printer and computer off and then on.

2 If it is not printing at all, chances are that a connection has come loose.

   • Check your cables and all the printer settings.

   • Make sure the printer is not offline.

   • Do the printer's self-test. If that works, the problem is with the connection or the computer.

3 If it is printing odd characters, there are several possibilities:

   • Your cable connection might be slightly loose.

   • You have installed new software that is giving the wrong instructions.

4 Make sure you haven't made any other configuration adjustments to the printer.

5 Try printing with a different software program.

6 Your printer driver may need updating -- especially if you have a new program.

7 Are you out of toner, ink, or ribbon?

   If you are using a laser printer, remove the toner cartridge, rock it gently from side to side, and replace. That should give you a few more pages until you have a chance to replace the cartridge.

Can't Find the File: Nothing on the Disk

Can't find the file you KNOW is on your hard disk somewhere but you can't find it when you need it? Or your word processing program is saying it can't find a file it needs to work properly?

Try using a utility such as First Aid 95 or First Aid 95 Deluxe to locate the file, or try these tips to help:

1   In Windows 95, run Windows Explorer.

2   Choose Find from the Tools menu, and enter the name of the file you are looking for. Be sure that you select your root directory. If the search is only taking place in one folder, for example, your Windows folder, chances are you won't find it.

3   In Windows 3.1, use the Search command on the Program Manager's or File Manager's File menu and follow the same instructions as for Windows Explorer.

4   Can't remember the name of the file? If you have Microsoft Office, use the Find command on the Open File dialog box. You can specify some text that you know is in the file.

Advanced Troubleshooting

Troubleshooting Windows 3.1x and Windows 95 Problems

Use the following steps to solve general software configuration problems in Windows 3.1.

Eliminating DOS Startup Problems

If you have DOS 6.x, restart your computer. When the screen says "Starting MS DOS," press the F8 function key. This causes the computer to prompt you to say Yes or No to each command line in the CONFIG.SYS and AUTOEXEC.BAT files. By loading and running Windows without these settings, and repeating this process until you have added back each command line, you can either identify the problem, or eliminate configuration settings or memory resident programs from consideration.

The following lines in the CONFIG.SYS and AUTOEXEC.BAT must be loaded, so when these lines appear, be sure to press (Y)es or the Enter key when prompted.

CONFIG.SYS

```
dos=
himem.sys
emm386.exe
files=
buffers=
```

You may also have to load the following files:

- Your CD ROM driver, only if the CD ROM is part of the problem.
- IFSHLP, only if the network is part of the problem and you're using Windows for Workgroups.
- A SCSI device driver (ASPI4DOSs, USPI24), only if you have a SCSI controller.

AUTOEXEC.BAT

```
path
prompt
set temp
```

You may also have to load the following files:

- Network drivers, only if the network is part of the problem.
- MSCDEX driver, only if the CD ROM is part of the problem.

Set Temp Statement

If your `set temp` statement is set to the DOS directory, or a directory other than `TEMP`, it is advisable for you to change it so the computer uses a directory named `TEMP` for its temporary file management. You can create and assign this directory at the C:> prompt without rebooting your computer, using the following steps:

1   Create the temp directory if one does not exist. From the C:> prompt, type the following to create the temp directory:

```
md temp
```

2   Press Enter.

3   Tell DOS to use this as the temporary directory by typing the following line at the C:> prompt:

```
set temp=c:\temp
```

4   Press Enter again.

5   To confirm that the setting is in effect, type `set` and press Enter. The message you see should confirm the temporary directory is set to "temp".

6   Now you need to edit the autoexec.bat file to do the same thing. Use the following steps:

7   At the C:> prompt, type the following:

```
edit autoexec.bat
```

The AUTOEXEC.BAT file opens in your DOS text editor.

8   Use your arrow key to move down to the end of the existing command lines, and press Enter to start a new line.

9   Type the following:

```
set temp=c:\temp
```

10 Press Enter.

11 To save the file and exit, hold down the ALT key and press the F key.

12 Press the X key.

13 Respond to the question by pressing the Y (Yes) key to save the file before exiting.

Win.INI File Editing

The next step is to look at the WIN.INI file in the Windows Directory. This file contains all the instructions Windows uses to start and run.

Although you can do this in Windows using Sysedit, (or another text editing tool), you might want to edit it in DOS, or another text editor or word processing program.

1   To edit in DOS using the current DOS text editor, type the following:

    ```
    edit c:\windows\win.ini
    ```

2   Press Enter. The win.ini file loads in the DOS editor.

3   The win.ini file is divided into sections identified by [square brackets]. Look for the first section, called [`windows`].

4   To troubleshoot a Windows problem, you are going to put a semi-colon (;) in front of the first character in some of the command lines in this section. This causes Windows to skip this instruction when loading, and is called "remarking out" the line. (In DOS, you type REM in front of a command in the CONFIG.SYS or AUTOEXEC.BAT files to do the same thing.) Put the semicolon in front of any line that starts with the following commands:

    ```
    load=

    run=
    ```

    When you have done this, the commands will look like the following:

    ```
    ;load=

    ;run=
    ```

5   To save the file and exit, hold down the ALT key and press the F key.

6   Press the "X" key.

7   Respond to the question in the box by pressing "Y" to save the file before exiting.

Start Windows

The next step is to start Windows and see what is loading into memory at startup.

1   In Windows 3.1, type `win/s`

    OR: In Windows for Workgroups (3.11) type `win/d:sxvf`.

2   When you see the Windows logo, press and hold the shift key until the hourglass becomes an arrow.

3   Press CTRL + ESC to view the task list. If there is anything other than Program Manager open, close it.

Isolating Program Conflicts

You may need to isolate a memory-resident program or device driver that is interfering with the proper operation of your computer.

To isolate the memory resident or another device driver:

1 Exit Windows

2 Restart Windows using a command that prevents the enhanced memory sections in Windows from loading:

   - In Windows 3.1, type `win/s`

   - In Windows for Workgroups (3.11) type `win/d:sxvf`.

3 If the problem reappears, look in your Startup Group (task list) and isolate which of those listed are involved.

4 If the problem doesn't reappear, continue.

5 Exit Windows, then restart as normal.

Editing Your SYSTEM.INI File

If the problem reappears, edit your SYSTEM.INI file.

1 In the section [386Enh], add the following command lines:

```
SystemROMBeakPoint=FALSE

EMMExclude=A000-FFF

VirtualHDIRQ=FALSE

32BitDiskAccess=FALSE
```

2 If the problem reappears, then you know there is a conflict with one or more of the devices in the load= and/or run= line.

3 If the problem does *not* reappear, re-edit your WIN.INI file, and take out the semi-colon (;) from in front of the `run=` and `load=` lines in the [windows] section.

Starting Windows 95 in Safe Mode

When troubleshooting Windows 95 problems, you can start in Safe Mode by pressing the F5 key when you see the "Starting Windows 95" message on your screen. This allows Windows to start up with a generic set of drivers and no programs loaded into memory.

Even if you can not run your usual programs in Safe Mode, this method does give you limited use of your computer running Windows 95. The fact that you can start and run Windows 95 in Safe Mode is important information for a tech support technician to know.

Viewing the Windows 95 Task List

With Windows 95 running, you can load the Task List by pressing the Ctrl, Alt, and Delete keys. The Task List shows you what applications and memory-resident programs are running.

1   With Windows 95 running, press Ctrl, Alt, and Delete keys.

    The Task List dialog box displays a list of active programs.

2   Review the programs. You can highlight any of them and click the End Task button to close them.

3   Close a program and continue running Windows. If the problem doesn't reoccur after you have closed a program, that program may have been causing your problem. When you identify the offending program, you can contact Technical Support for that program's company and get help in running it without causing further problems in Windows.

What to do When Your PC Crashes: Don't Panic

When your computer suddenly stops working and closes down or restarts, it's called "crashing."

A computer crashes when:

- Its memory is overloaded
- The active program can't find an essential file
- The program encounters an unexpected error.

Depending on what type of computer system you have, and what software you are running, the crash can be caused by something very simple, or very complicated. Let's look at the simple things first.

1 Write down all of the error messages you received and what you were doing prior to the crash.

2 Run a virus scan, especially of the memory and boot files.

3 Locate a **clean** boot disk that has the same version of DOS as your hard drive. Use that to boot up your computer if it won't boot on its own.

4 Obtain and use a data recovery tool and a drive analysis tool. Use the CHKDSK and SCANDISK commands in DOS to check your hard disk.

5 Use your most recent backup of your system (if you have one).

6 Make copies of any system files before making changes to them.

7 Remain by your computer when you call for technical support. Be sure to have paper and pen ready.

8 Let the technician know what the error message was and if the error can be reproduced. This can be very helpful in resolving the crash.

9 If you have already tried Ctrl + ALT + Delete, try turning the machine off, waiting 10-20 seconds, and then turning it back on.

In addition, First Aid 95 or First Aid 95 Deluxe can be used to help solve—and prevent—these problems.

General Health Care for You and Your PC

Protecting Yourself

It's easy to get carried away while working on your computer. We do it all the time! Whether you're working on your accounts, writing a novel, or surfing the 'Net, hours can fly by while you are absorbed in what's happening on the screen.

Meanwhile, you ignore your body telling you to take a break, and rest your eyes, wrists, and back. If you keep it up, you may find that you need medical help for eye or muscle strain.

Avoid these problems by using common sense precautions in your computer practices. Here are some basics:

Get the Right Furniture

After you have spent so much on equipment, perhaps you feel that buying computer furniture is more than you can afford. But if you think about the hours you may spend at your keyboard, proper ergonomics is essential.

- Make sure your computer desk is at the right height. It should be comfortable to lean your elbow or part of your forearm on the desk while using your mouse.
- Use a wrist rest while typing. This helps prevent strain on your wrists and arms.
- Get a comfortable chair with arm rests. Again, this helps not only your back and neck, but your arms and wrists.
- Position the monitor at eye level. Use a small desktop stand to raise it to eye level if you have to.

Use the Right Lighting

- If you can, position your room lighting where it illuminates your reading or reference material, but doesn't throw a glare on the screen.
- If you are near a window, position the monitor away from the window so the daylight glare doesn't make it difficult to see the screen.
- Resist the temptation to work in the dark with just the monitor on. This is hard on your eyes. Having a light beside or behind the monitor relaxes your eye.

Use the Right Monitor

- Try to buy a monitor that lets you see without squinting. Shop around before deciding on a monitor.

Use the Right Input Devices

- Although the mouse and keyboard that come with your computer may be fine, be aware that there are dozens of alternatives, including trackballs, ergonomically designed keyboards, pen input devices, and other add-ons to make computing more comfortable and fun.

Don't Forget to Take Breaks!

- Although that 50th game may be the one you'll win, be sure to take frequent breaks. Stretch your fingers, arms, and back. Walk around, breathe some fresh air.
- While working, take brief breaks from looking at the screen, and let your eyes focus on other things at different distances than your computer screen.

Caring for Your Computer

Your computer system has three common physical enemies...dust, heat, and electricity. Unfortunately, none are avoidable. However, you can help prolong the life of your computer.

- Purchase a surge protector that has a peak of 200 volts.
- Keep your computer in a moderate temperature environment.
- Make sure the main chip in your processor has a fan or heat sink.
- Provide an additional fan for systems with multiple internal components (that is, more than one hard drive).
- Don't block any air vents on your system, especially your monitor.
- Don't place your computer near heating vents or in direct sunlight.
- Keep pets away. Their shedding hair adds to the dust that infiltrates the inside of your computer, and it can cause ventilation problems for the internal circuits.
- Dust your computer. **Do not use a dust mop or a vacuum.** A can of static-free compressed air (available at camera shops, stereo centers, and computer stores) can be used to blow out disk drives, vents, the fan on the power supply, the keyboard, and inside your computer.
- Clean the ball of your mouse with denatured alcohol and a cotton swab.
- Shake off the dust from your mouse pad every now and again.
- Always unplug your computer in an electrical storm.
- Avoid plugging and unplugging components while the system is on.

Checklist for Technical Support

If you have to call technical support, be sure to collect a full inventory. This will save you a lot of time. If you don't have the information, the technician may have to take time to collect the information, or it may take longer to solve your problem.

If you filled out the Computer Inventory form on the inside cover, you can use that information too.

1 Name and model number of your computer system.

2 Name and model of your monitor and any other external components.

3 If you can, have a report of all the software and drivers installed on your system. If you have First Aid 95 Deluxe, you can use that report. Otherwise, look for another system information utility and have a printout of that information.

4 Write down exactly what was happening when you encountered the problem. Especially include any error messages, unusual sounds, or other behavior you noticed just before the problem occurred.

5 Make sure you have checked all the connections and gone through the items on our "top ten" list before you call Tech Support.

User Groups Directory

Countries

Australia

Bundaberg PC Users Group Inc.
63 Enterprise St.
Bundaberg QLD 4670

Melbourne PC User Group
P.O. Box 283
South Melbourne VIC 3205
http://www.melbpc.org.au

PC Users Group
P.O. Box 42
Belconnen ACT 2616
http://www.pcug.org.au/pcug/
welcome.htm

Personal Computing Support Group
G.P.O Box 2402
Melbourne VIC 3001

Queensland Railway Institute Compute
P.O. Box 1819
Gladstone QLD 4680

Victorian Osborne User Group Inc.
P.O. Box 169
Camberwell VIC 3124

Yarra Valley Computer Users Group
P.O. Box 359
Lilydale Victoria 3140
http://netspace.net.au/~adrian_o/
yvcug.html

Canada

Alberta

Northern Alberta PC Users Group
P.O. Box 33131 Glenwood Postal Outlet
Edmonton AB T5P 4V8

British Columbia

Big Blue and Cousins
P.O. Box 5309 Station B
Victoria BC V8R 6S4
http://www.IslandNet.com/~bigblue/

Healthcare Computer Users Group
8415 Granville St. #149
Vancouver BC V6P 4Z9

Kelowna Computer Users Group
55, 1101 Cameron Ave.
Kelowna BC V1Y 8V9

Nanaimo PC Users Group Home Page, The
http://bbs.sd68.nanaimo.bc.ca:8001/SD68B
BS/PUBLIC/NANPCUG/welcome.html

Vanouver FoxPro UG Computer Society
200-1177 W. Broadway
Vancouver BC V6H 1G3

Vancouver PC Users Society
625 - 810 West Broadway
Vancouver BC V5Z 4C9

Vancouver Regional Freenet Association
411 Dunsmuir St. 2nd Fl.
Vancouver BC V6B 1X4

Manitoba

Winnipeg PC User Group
P.O. Box 3149
Winnipeg MB R3C 4E6
http://www.wpcusrgrp.org

Nova Scotia

Halifax Area Personal Computer Society
P.O. Box 29008
Halifax NS B3L 4T8
http://ccn.cs.dal.ca/Technology/HAPCS/
HAPCS_Home.html

Ontario

Kawartha Computer Club, The
P.O. Box 1321
Peterborough ON K6J 7H5

Ottawa-Orleans Personal Systems Club
981 Gulf Place
Ottawa ON K1K 3X9

Ottawa PC Users Group, The
164 Laurier Ave.
Ottawa ON K2G 1S6

Ottawa Valley Computer Club
164 Laurier Ave.
Pembroke ON K8A 2J2

Personal Computer Club of Toronto
P.O. Box 5429 Station A
Toronto ON M5W 1N6

Quebec

Caribou Club, The
P.O. Box 1826
Schefferville QC G0G 2T0

Japan

AEGIS Society, The
Minami Hirao 1-6 Imazato
Nagaokakyo-shi Kyoto-fu 617

New Zealand

New Zealand PC Association
P.O. Box 14-163
Kilbirnie-Wellington   6030

Russia

International Computer Club
Proyezd Serova, 4 'Znanie' Building
Moscow   101813

Windows User Association
Moscow State University Lenin's Hills
Moscow   119899

South Africa

Adelaide PC Users Group Inc.
P.O. Box 2541
Kent Town SA 5071
http://www.iss.net.au/APCUG/

Multimedia User Group of South Africa
P.O. Box 42402
Fordsburg   2033

United Kingdom

Project User Group LTD., The
P.O. Box 95, Bushey
Watford   WD2 1EG

UK dBase User Group
3 Marborough Rise
Camberley Surrey GU15 2ED

Notes ....
....
....
....
....
....
....

United States

User Groups are organized alphabetically by state and name.

Alaska

Alaska Computer Society
P.O. Box 240945
Anchorage AK 99524-0945

Polar PC User Group
P.O. Box 72934
Fairbanks AK 99707

Up and Running Windows Users Group
7302 Huntmen Circle Unit A
Anchorage AK 99518

Alabama

Birmingham IBM PC User Group
P.O. Box 19248
Birmingham AL 35219-9248

Cullman PC Users Group
P.O. Box 1494
Cullman AL 35056-1494

Huntsville PC User Group
P.O. Box 16013
Huntsville AL 35802

Montgomery PC Users Club
3505 McGehee Rd.
Montgomery AL 36111

Notes..
....
....
....
....

Arkansas

Arkansas/Oklahoma PC Users Group
1816 Vicksburg St.
Fort Smith AR 72901-8567

Central Arkansas PC Users Association
P.O. Box 24064
Little Rock AR 72221
http://www.aristotle.net/~cbailey/
capcua.ht

Conway PC Users Group, Inc.
P.O. Box 10442
Conway AR 72033
http://www.intellinet.com/~tcw/cpcug.htm

Jonesboro User Group
P.O. Box 838
State University AR 72467

Monticello Area Computer Users Group
Rt. 4 Box 134B
Monticello AR 71655

NW Arkansas Microcomputer User Group
Rt. 4 Box 376
Springdale AR 72762-9307

Rogers PC Users Group
P.O. Box 1251
Bentonville AR 72712

Twin Lakes Computer Users Group
Rte 5-Box 127
Mountain Home AR 72653

Notes ....
....
....
....
....

Arizona

Bisbee (Computer) Users Group
P.O. Box 5012
Bisbee AZ 85603-5012

Computer Booters of Sun Lakes
10925 E. Chestnut Dr.
Sun Lakes AZ 85248
http://www.eas.asu.edu/~cpd/hal/
schmpage.html

Computer Club of Green Valley
GVR-Desert Hills Center P.O. Box 586
Green Valley AZ 85622

Computer Using Graphic Artists
P.O. Box 16712
Tucson AZ 85712-6712
http://members.gnn.com/dwhitby/
index.htm

Computers West (IBM-UG)
12302 Aurora Dr.
Sun City West AZ 85375-1965

Gilbert PC Users Group
3355 E. Renee Dr.
Phoenix AZ 85024

Healthcare PC Users Group
4727 E. Bell Rd. Suite 45-202
Phoenix AZ

Internet Users Group International
c/o Arizona State University Engineering
Computer Services MAIL-STOP 5206
Tempe AZ 85287-5206

Leisure World Computer Club
875 Leisure World
Mesa AZ 85206-2411

Phoenix PC Users Group
5515 N. 7th St. Suite 5-101
Phoenix AZ 85014
http://www.phoenixpcug.org

Sierra Vista IBM PC Users Group
4616 Gardner St.
Sierra Vista AZ 85635
http://www.primenet.com/~tomheld/
svpcug.htm

Sonoran Internet Users Group
3640 West Eastham Lane
Tucson AZ 85741
http://siug.rtd.com

South Mountain User Group
P.O. Box 50002
Phoenix AZ 85076
http://aztec.asu.edu/smug/smughome.html

Tucson Computer Society
P.O. Box 1489
Tucson AZ 85702
http://www.azstarnet.com/public/
nonprofit/tcs/home.htm

Tucson IBM PC Club
5702 E. 8th St.
Tucson AZ 85711

Notes ....
....
....
....
....
....
....
....
....
....
....
....
....
....
....
....

California

Antelope Valley Internet Dialers
http://www.avid.org
http://www.smartlink.net/~scvpcg

Antelope Valley Microcomputer User Group
P.O. Box 2942
Lancaster CA 93539
http://pages.prodigy.com/CA/scota
/scota6.html

Associates, The
2104 Olga St.
Oxnard CA 93030-2238

Association of Database Developers
998 -- 61st St.
Oakland CA 94608-2308

BayTalk Computer Users Group
4529 18th St.
San Francisco CA 94114

Berkeley PC/Compatibles User Group
1145 Walnut St.
Berkeley CA 94707

California Southland DPMA
P.O. Box 1965
Newport Beach CA 92659

Central Coast Computer Club
4168 Glenview Dr.
Santa Maria CA 93455-3315

Central Orange County Computer Club
2000 Main St
Huntington Beach CA 92464

Channel Islands PC Users Group
P.O. Box 5025
Oxnard CA 93031

Coast PC Users Group
Box 299
The Sea Ranch CA 95497-0299
http://www.mcn.org/MenComNet/
Community/clubs/GPC/pchome.htm

Color America, Inc.
MS DOS/Win Users Group
1466 Spruce Tree Dr.
Diamond Bar CA 91765

Community Computer Club
1950 9th St.
La Verne CA 91750

Computer Experts of Northern California
15 Tamal Vista Lane
Kentfield CA 94904-1005

Computer Genealogy Society of San Diego
P.O. Box 370357
San Diego CA 92137-0357

Computer Rooters
9491 Lake Natoma Dr.
Orangevale CA 95662

Cross-Platform User Group
12201 Texas Ave.
Los Angeles CA 90025

CSUF DPMA
19602 Crestknoll Dr.
Yorba Linda CA 92686

Diablo Valley PC Users Group
P.O. Box 8040
Walnut Creek CA 94596-8040
http://www.hooked.net/users/rmwood/
dvpc.html

Edwards Air Force Base
AFFTC\FMC 1 South Rosamond Blvd.
Building 1, Room 103
Edwards Air Force Base CA 93523

Eel Valley Floppy Disk Gang
P.O. Box 397
Hydesville CA 95547

Fallbrook PC Users Group
1537 Knollpark Lane
Fallbrook CA 92028

Fresno PC Users Group
6751 North Blackstone Ave. #395
Fresno CA 93710-3500
http://www.cybergate.com/fpcug/

FOG International Computer Users
P.O. Box 1030
Dixon CA 95620

Glendora Seniors Computer Club
c/o La Fetra Center 333 E. Foothill Blvd.
Glendora CA 91740

Gold Country PC Users Group
P.O. Box 5575
Auburn CA 95603

Golden Gate Computer Society
P.O. Box 151696
San Rafael CA 94915-1696
http://www.ggcs.org

Goleta DeskTop Publishing Users Group
P.O. Box 2450
Goleta CA 93118-2450
http://www.troutcom.com/gdtpug

Greater South Bay PC Users Group
(GSBUG)
P.O. Box 6950
Torrance CA 90504-0050

Hi-Desert Computer Society
2119 Penny Lane
Rosamond CA 93560-6132

Home Savings of America PC Users Group
4900 Rivergrade Rd. Suite 6055
Irwindale CA 91706

Hughes PC UG
5452 W. 96th St.
Los Angeles CA 90045

IBM & Compatibles User Group, The
P.O. Box 87770
San Diego CA 92138-7770

IBM Humboldt Users Group
P.O. Box 6721
Eureka CA 95502

IBM PC Club - San Jose
NO5/C154 555 Bailey Avenue
San Jose CA 95141

Inland Empire Computer Group
P.O. Box 5281
San Bernadino CA 92412-5281

Inner City Computer Society, Los Angeles
P.O. Box 1023
Hawthorne CA 90251-1023
http://host.scbbs.com/~iccs

JW Construction
28966 Via La Rueda
Murrieta CA 92563

Kern Independent PC Users Group
P.O. Box 2780
Bakersfield CA 93303
http://www.kern.com/kipug.html

Lake Wildwood Computer Club
18540 Jayhawk Dr.
Penn Valley CA 95946

Long Beach IBM Users Group
4156 Woodruff Ave. Suite 517
Lakewood CA 90713

Long Beach IBM Users Group
4156 Woodruff Ave. Suite 517
Lakewood CA 90713

Los Angeles Computer Society
P.O. Box 661189
Los Angeles CA 90006-9589
http://solar.rtd.utk.edu/~mtaylor/focus/
main.htm

Microlink PCUG of Southern California
22 Creek Rd. Suite 25
Irvine CA 92714
http://members.aol.com/mlink01/mlink/
mlweb.htm

Mid-Valley PC Users Group
7323 Katherine Ave.
Van Nuys CA 91405

Modesto PC Users Group
P.O. Box 5122
Modesto CA 95352-5122
http://www.ainet.com/mpcug

Monterey Bay Users Group-PC
177 Webster St. #A354
Monterey CA 93940

Napa Valley PC Users Group
3539 Lowrey Court
Napa CA 94558-5210
http://nvpcug.org/~nvpcug

Nevada County PC User Group
P.O. Box 162227
Sacramento CA 95816-2227

North Bay Users Group
315 Nevada St.
Vallejo CA 94590

North Orange County, ACAD
1980 Byrd Court
Placentia CA 92670

North Orange County Computer Club
P.O. Box 3616
Orange CA 92665
http://www.citivu.com/noccc/index.html

Oakmont PC Users Group
330 Miramounte Way
Santa Rosa CA 95409

Orange Coast IBM PC User Group
1500 Adams Ave. #105
Costa Mesa CA 92626

Orange County Computer Society
1221 N. State College Blvd. #20
Anaheim CA 92806

Orange County Corel Association
1980 Byrd Ct.
Placentia CA 92670
http://www.members.gnn.com/judyunger/
corel.htm

Orange County IBM PC Users Group
P.O. Box 1779
Brea CA 92622

Palmia Computer Club
21455 Monterey
Mission Viejo CA 92692

Pasadena IBM Users Group
711 E. Walnut St. #306
Pasadena CA 91101

Peninsula Apple User Group
4 Cragmont Court
San Mateo CA 94403

Peninsula PC User Group
1400 El Camino Real #108
S. San Francisco CA 94080

Peninsula Computer Club
222 Laurel St. #310
San Carlos CA 94070-2363

PC Clone User Group
2440 16th St. #301
San Francisco CA 94103

PC Clubhouse
P.O. Box 3127
Hayward CA 94540-3127
http://www.pcc.org

**PC Computer Club of Leisure World
PC User Group**
3421-3G Calle Azul
Laguna Hills CA 92653

PC Tech User Group
2440 - 16th St. Suite 301
San Francisco CA 94103

PC Users Group of the Redwoods
P.O. Box 5055
Santa Rosa CA 95402
http://sonic.net/pcugr

R&W IBM PC Users Group
2076 San Gabriel
Clovis CA 93611

Ripon PC User Group
1146-7th St.
Ripon CA 95366

Riverside IBM Computer Club
7860 Live Oak Dr.
Riverside CA 92509-5339

**Sacramento Microcomputer User
Group**
P.O. Box 161513
Sacramento CA 95816

Sacramento PC Users Group
P.O. Box 162227
Sacramento CA 95816-2227
http://sacpcug.org

San Bernadino PC User Group
CSU, San Bernadino Dept of Accounting and
Finance
San Bernadino CA 92407-2397

San Diego Computer Society
P.O. Box 81444
San Diego CA 92138-7770
http://www.sdcs.org

San Diego Q&A Plus
3541 Altadena Ave.
San Diego CA 92105-3612

**San Gabriel Valley Tandy Users
Group**
P.O. Box 6818
Burbank CA 91510

San Francisco Computer Society
485-36th Ave.
San Francisco CA 94121

San Francisco PC Users Group
744 Harrison St.
San Francisco CA 94107
http://www.sfpcug.org/~group

San Jose IBM PC Club
6723 Landerwood Lane
San Jose CA 95120

San Luis Obispo PC Users Group
2100 Andre Ave
Los Osos CA 93402
http://s283456.thegrid.net/slobytes

Santa Barbara PC Users
462 S. San Marcos Rd.
Santa Barbara CA 93111-2726
http://www.silcom.com/sbpcug

Santa Clarita Valley PC Group
18727 Nadal St.
Canyon Country CA 91351

Seniors Computer Group
5710 Baltimore Dr. Suite 435
La Mesa CA 91942-1698

Silicon Valley Computer Society
2464 El Camino Real Suite 190
Santa Clara CA 95051-3097
http://www.svcs.org

Silicon Valley PAF Users Group
4417 Pitch Pine Court
San Jose CA 95136-2410
http://www.rahul.net/svpafug

Simi Valley Computer User Group
P.O. Box 3498
Simi Valley CA 93093

Solano Community College User Group
P.O. Box 475
Fairfield CA 94533-0047

Sonoma Valley Computer Group
P.O. Box 216
Vineburg CA 95487

Stanford Palo Alto PC Users Group
P.O. Box 3738
Stanford CA 94309
http://www.mediacity.com/~spaug

State Microcomputer Forum
410 24th St.
Sacramento CA 95816

Synergistic Computer User Group
877 S. Victoria Ave. Suite 201
Ventura CA 93003

Technical User Group Network (TUG-NET)
3926 Community Ave.
La Crescenta CA 91214

Temecula Valley Computer User Group
27636 Ynez Rd. L7-254
Temecula CA 92591

Thousand Oaks PC Club
P.O. Box 6981
Thousand Oaks 91359 CA

Tule Fog PC Users Group, Inc.
P.O. Box 1373
Visalia CA 93279
North County PC Users Group
P.O. Box 647
Vista CA 92085

UCLA PC Users Group
P.O. Box 661189
Los Angeles CA 90066

University Computer Association
982 North Batavia St. B11
Orange CA 92667

USC Microcomputer User Group
Commons Bldg. Suite 5/830 Childs Way
Los Angeles CA 90007

Valley Computer Club, The
P.O. Box 6008
Burbank CA 91510-6008

Valley IBM Compatible Users Group
8901 Eton Ave. #16
Canoga Park CA 91304

Valley IBM Compatible Users Group
8901 Eton Ave. #16
Canoga Park CA 91304

Valley West dBase Users Group, Inc.
P.O. Box 8291
Calabasas CA 91372

Ventura County Windows Publishing UG
1873 Dewayne Ave.
Camarillo CA 93010-3819

Westside PC Users Group
P.O. Box 4520
Culver City CA 90231

WINNERS - Windows Users
P.O. Box 9274
Newport Beach CA 92658-9274

Yuba Sutter PC Users Group
1747 Live Oak Blvd. #J-253
Yuba City CA 95991

Colorado

Alpha Micro Users Society
619 Florida Ave.
Longmont CO 80501

Chaffee County Computer Club
P.O. Box 7
Poncha Springs CO 81242

Colorado Senior Network Users Group
2982 Whileaway Cir W
Colorado Springs CO 80917

Colorado Springs PC Users Group
P.O. Box 1028
Colorado Springs CO 80901

Computer Users Group of Greeley
3950 W. 12th St. Suite 30
Greeley CO 80634-2547

Electric Locksmith PC Users Group
P.O. Box 15217
Colorado Springs CO 80935-5217
American Society of Women Accountants
P.O. Box 2234
Denver CO 80202

Front Range PC Users Group
305 W. Magnolia #152
Fort Collins CO 80521
http://www.omn.com/frpcug

IBM Computer Connection Users Group
3370 Rain Drop Ave.
Colorado Springs CO 80917

Mile High Computer Resource Organization
(MICRO)
8175A Sheridan Blvd. #201
Arvado CO 80003

PC Users Group of Colorado
P.O. Box 944
Boulder CO 80306
http://aescon.com/boulder/pc-club/index.ht

Pikes Peak Computer Applications Society
c/o Brad Logan 1011 N. Murray Blvd.
Lake George CO 80915
http://rainbow.rmii.com/~nuvo/ppcompas.ht

Pikes Peak Programmers Group
8955 Aragon Dr.
Colorado Springs CO 80920

Windows on the Rockies User Group
634 East Ridge Glen Way
Highlands Ranch CO 80126

Connecticut

Business & Prof. Micro Users Group
(BP/MUG)
P.O. Box 271468
West Hartford CT 06127-1468
http://www.bpmug.org

Central Connecticut PC (PCjr) Group
781 Main St.
Coventry CT 6238

Connecticut IBM PC Users Group
P.O. Box 291
New Canaan CT 6840
http://kiwi.futuris.net/cpcug

Danbury Area Computer Society
7 Academy Rd.
Oxford CT 6478
http://www.danbury.lib.ct.us/org/dacs/
index.htm

Hartford User Group Exchange, Inc.
P.O. Box 380027
East Hartford CT 6138

New York LAN Association
4 Moody Lane
Danbury CT 6811

PC Users Group of Connecticut, The
P.O. Box 545
Trumbull CT 6611
http://www.tpcug-ct.org

Delaware

Delaware Shore Users Group
1 Shipcarpenter Square
Lewes DE 19958

District of Columbia

Association of PC User Groups, Inc.
1730 M St., N.W. Suite 700
Washington DC 20036

Florida

Alachua Cty Computer Users Group
3334 NW 4th St.
Gainesville FL 32609

Amelia Island PC Users Group
P.O. Box 1213
Fernandina Beach FL 32035

Boca Raton Computer Society, Inc.
P.O. Box 273421
Boca Raton FL 33427-3421
http://www.emi.net/~brcs/index.html

Brevard Users Group
P.O. Box 372111
Satellite Beach FL 32937-2111

Broward Personal Computer Association
P.O. Box 119554
Ft. Lauderdale FL 33339

Central Florida Computer Society
P.O. Box 948019
Maitland FL 32751

Central Florida FoxPro Users Group
2400 Falkner Rd.
Orlando FL 32810
http://www.worldramp.net/foxpro

Charlotte County PC Users Group
2280 Aaron St. Suite 3
Port Charlotte FL 33952

Computer Society of West Florida, The
6230 Vicksburg Dr.
Pensacola FL 32503

Crystal River Users Group
P.O. Box 2108
Crystal River FL 34423-2108

Englewood Computer Users Group, The
502-1/2 Estada
Englewood FL 34223
http://www.flnet.com/~crosby/eug.html

EpSuncoast Users Group
1237 79 St.,S
St. Petersburg FL 33707

Fairways Computer Club
1874 Inverary Dr.
Orlando FL 32826

Florida Association of Computer User
6039 Cypress Gardens Blvd. Suite 185
Winter Haven FL 33884
http://members.gnn.com/bkoslow/
facug.htm

**Ft. Lauderdale ACM Siggraph
Professional**
c/o Metro Link Inc.
4711 North Powerline Road
Ft. Lauderdale FL 33309
http://flsig.org/ftl

**Ft. Lauderdale Computer Users
Group Inc.**
8461 NW 31st Place
Sunrise FL 33351-8904

Ft. Lauderdale PC Computer Society
4239 NW 76th Ave.
Hollywood FL 33024

**Greater Orlando Computer User
Group**
113 Chutney Dr.
Orlando FL 32825-3607

Greater Tampa Bay PC Users Group
P.O. Box 501
Brandon FL 33509-0501
http://www.cftnet.com/members/gtbpcug

Haines City Computer Club
915 Hill Dr.
Haines City FL 33844

Hernando Computer Club
P.O. Box 6392
Spring Hill FL 34606
http://innet.com/~hernando/index.html

Hogtown Hackers
4623 NW 13 Ave.
Gainesville FL 32605-4534

**IBM PC Medical Users Group/
Department of Anesthesiology**
P.O. Box 100254
Gainesville FL 32610

Lake Henry Computer Club
P.O. Box 6392
Spring Hill FL 34606

Marion Computer & BBS Users Group
P.O. Box 6941
Ocala FL 34478-6941
http://www.cfcc.cc.fl.us/mcbug/
mcbug.htm

Miami PC User Group
4651 Sheridan St. Suite 300
Hollywood FL 33021

Microcomputer Users Group, The
1801 Vancouver Dr.
Clearwater FL 34616-1743

North Florida Computer Society
P.O. Box 58
Hilliard FL 32046

Palm Beach PC Users Group
319 Sequoia Dr.
Palm Beach Gardens FL 33419

Pasco Area Computer Users Group
P.O. Box 1582
Dade City FL 33526-1582

Pasco Compats, The
7330 Jenner Ave.
New Port Richey FL 34655

Perdido Bay Users Group
5463 Grande Lagoon Court
Pensacola FL 32507

PC Business Users Group of Naples
P.O. Box 285
Naples FL 33939-0285

PC Forum of City of Miami Employees
City of Miami, Audits
300 Biscayne Way
Suite 309
Miami FL 33131-2207

PC Rams Computer Club
2919E North Military Trail, #362
West Palm Beach FL 33409
http://yonder.com/pcrams

PC Users Group of Jacksonville
P.O. Box 47197
Jacksonville FL 32247-7197

Pinellas IBM PC User Group
5100 Dover St NE
St Petersburg FL 33703

Polk IBM PC Users Group Inc
P.O. Box 5694
Lakeland FL 33807-5694
http://www.Concentric.net/~Egenie4u/florida.html

Port St. Lucie Computer Society
2 Don Quixote Court
Port St. Lucie FL 34952-2314

Ridge Area Computer Club
2060 N. US Hwy. 27, #251
Lake Wales FL 33853-6802

Sarasota PC Users Group
P.O. Box 15889
Sarasota FL 34277-1889
http://www.spcug.org

South Florida Windows Users Group
Dania City Hall - Attn: Vern Johnson 100 West Dania Beach Blvd.
Dania FL 33004

South Polk County PC Users Group
815 N. Lake Reedy Blvd.
Frostproof FL 33843

Southwest Florida PC & Internet Users
2431 Malaya Court S
Port Charlotte FL 33983

Southwest Florida PC Users Group
1519 Reynard Dr.
Fort Myers FL 33919
http://www.olsusa.com/pcug/index.html

Space Coast PC User Group
460 Monaco Dr.
Indialantic FL 32903

Sun City Center PC Users Group
3022 SR 674 Box #174
Ruskin FL 33570
http://www.icubed.net/sccpcug/default.htm

Tallahassee PC Users Group
4125 Chelmsford Rd.
Tallahassee FL 32308

Tampa Bay Computer Society
1510 Barry St. Unit J-2
Clearwater FL 34616-4427

Tampa Bay Netware Users Group
P.O. Box 7702
Clearwater FL 34618-7702

Tampa IBM PC Club
3104 W Martin Luther King Blvd. L201
Tampa FL 33607

Tampa PC User Group, Inc.
P.O. Box 3492
Tampa FL 33601-3492

Tri-County Computer User Group, Inc.
P.O. Box 7414
Port St. Lucie FL 34985-7414
http://www.meadwood.com/tccugweb.htm

Univ. of South Florida PC User Group
4202 E. Fowler Ave. SVC 4010
Tampa FL 33620-3190

Vero Beach Computer Group
1432 21st St. Suite B
Vero Beach FL 32960

West Pasco Clones Computer Club
3501 Sarazen Dr.
New Port Richey FL 34655-2025

Womens MAC & PC User Group
201 Greencove
Venice FL 34292
http://www.acun.com/~wpcug

Word Processing Users Group
7958 SW 105 Place
Miami FL 33173

Zolfo Computer Users Group
Rt. 2, Box 20
Zolfo Springs FL 33890

Georgia

Atlanta IBM Employees PC Club
3073 Batesville Rd.
Woodstock GA 30188

Atlanta PC Users Group
P.O. Box 28788
Atlanta GA 30358
http://www.mindspring.com/~atlpcug

CSRA Computer Society, Inc.
P.O. Box 284
Augusta GA 30903
http://www.augusta.net/csra_users

Dublin/Laurens County Computer Club
Route 7 Box 29
Dublin GA 31021-9707

Kings Bay Computer Club
P.O. Box 1748
Kingsland GA 31548-1748

Landings Computer Society
3 Magnolia Crossing
Savannah GA 31411

Metro Atlanta Computer Club
3391 Bryan Way
Marietta GA 30060

Mountain Computer User Group, Inc.
P.O. Box 474
Young Harris GA 30582
http://www.yhc.edu/mcug

Online Atlanta Society
42 Lethea St.
Atlanta GA 30315

Perry, Georgia PC User Group
98 Knightsvue Place
Warner Robins GA 31093

Usr/Info/Group
P.O. Box 95805
Atlanta GA 30347-0805

Warner Robins Users Group Inc
218 Madrid St
Warner Robins GA 31093

Hawaii

Hawaii PC Users Group
P.O. Box 22967
Honolulu HI 96823
http://members.gnn.com/PhilSharp/index.htm

Hawaii State PC Users Group
2520 Jasmine St.
Honolulu HI 96816

TROA Users Group
61 Kai One Place
Kailua HI 96734

Iowa

Central Iowa Computer User Group, The
P.O. Box 672
Ankeny IA 50021
http://george.ecity.net/~ciacug

DuBuque Users Group/D_BUG
P.O. Box 3332
DuBuque IA 52004-3332

Hawkeye PC Users Group
P.O. Box 2592
Iowa City IA 52244-2592
http://members.gnn.com/lbielicke/
hpcug.htm

Quad-Cities Computer Society
P.O. Box 2456
Davenport IA 52809-2456

Idaho

Boise Internet User Group
http://198.60.253.50

Idaho PC Users Group
P.O. Box 9136
Boise ID 83707

Illinois

Association of Personal Computer Users
9063 N. Clifton Ave.
Niles IL 60714

Binary Chautauqua Society
307 W. Jackson
Petersburg IL 62675

Bloomington/Normal Computer Users Group
P.O. Box 1058
Bloomington IL 61702-1058

CACHE
117 W. Harrison Suite 640-C176
Chicago IL 60605

CACHE
117 W. Harrison Suite 640-C176
Chicago IL 60605

Central Illinois PC User Group
3032 Griffiths
Springfield IL 67202

Chicago Area Computer Hobbyists
601 S. LaSalle Suite C176
Chicago IL 60605-1790

Chicago Computer Society
P.O. Box 247
Wauconda IL 60084-0247
http://www.ccs.org

COMMON
401 North Michigan Ave.
Chicago IL 60611
http://205.217.130.14/

Common People Using Computers UG, The
126 Greenwood Cemetery Rd.
Danville IL 61832

Computers Are Easy Users Group
P.O. Box 2727
Glen Ellyn IL 60138

Corporate Assn. for Microcomputer Prof.
950 Skokie Boulevard Suite 310
Northbrook IL 60062-4018

Fox Valley Computer Society
P.O. Box 188
South Elgin IL 60177

Fox Valley Computer User Group
P.O. Box 28
North Aurora IL 60542

IBM User Group of Madison County
2405 Sanford Ave.
Alton Il 62002

Ill Academy of Engineers Anglers & Computer Buffs
3105 Newmark Civil Eng Bldg MC-250/205
North Mathe
Urbana IL 61801

New Wave Computer User Group, Inc.
10234 S. Champlain Ave.
Chicago IL 60628

No. Illinois Computer Owners League
7611 Bloomingdale
Elmwood Park IL 708/453-25

Northern Illinois PC User roup
P.O. Box 7236
Romeoville IL 60441

Peoria Computer Club
P.O. Box 758
Peoria IL 61602

QUASAR
308 Westgate Dr.
Aurora IL 60506

Sandwich Computer Users Group
P.O. Box 23
Sandwich IL 60548

Springfield Pet Users Group
P.O. Box 9035
Springfield IL 62794-9035

Sterling Computer Users Group
P.O. Box 827
Sterling IL 61081

Western Illinois Programmers and Users Group
RR 5 Box 75
Quincy IL 62301-9314

Indiana

ACUTE, Inc.
8060 Knue Rd., Suite 127
Indianapolis IN 46250-1524

Elkhart PC Users Group
P.O. Box 13
Elkhart IN 46515-0013

Indianapolis Computer Society
5309 Graceland Ave
Indianapolis IN 46208-2517
http://www.otisnet.com/ics/ics.html

Northeastern Indiana PC Club, The
4422 Bridgetown Run
Fort Wayne IN 46804

Southside Computer Club
2181 Horizon Blvd.
Greenwood IN 46143

Southwest Indiana PC Users Group
P.O. Box 6364
Evansville IN 47719

Kansas

Topeka PC Users Club
P.O. Box 1279
Topeka KS 66601

Wichita PC Users Group, Inc.
P.O. Box 781200
Wichita KS 67278

Kentucky

Bluegrass IBM PC Users Group
686 Sheridan Dr.
Lexington KY 40503-1726
Central Kentucky Computer Society
1300 New Circle Rd. Suite 105
Lexington KY 40505

Bowling Green Area MS-DOS Users Group, The
P.O. Box 20384
Bowling Green KY 42103

Kentucky-Indiana PC Users Group
291 N. Hubbards Lane Suite B-26, #318
Louisville KY 40207

Powell County PC Users Group
c/o Compserve Limited P.O. Box 399
Stanton KY 40380-0399

Louisiana

Acadiana Microcomputer Users Group
P.O. Box 51142
Lafayette LA 7050

Atchafalaya Computer Club
P.O. Box 3128
Morgan City LA 70381

Cajun Clickers Computer Club
P.O. Box 83053
Baton Rouge LA 70791
http://www.intersurf.com/~cars/
index3.html

Chalmette Computer Users Group
P.O. Box 1515
Chalmette LA 70044
http://www.sstar.com/ccug

Crossroads Computer Club
P.O. Box 1564
Alexandria LA 91309-1564

New Orleans PC Club
P.O. Box 8364
Metairie LA 70011-8364

Northwest Louisiana PC User Group
945 Dudley Dr.
Shreveport LA 71104

Page Computer Users Group, Inc.
P.O. Box 7703
Alexandria LA 71306-7703

PC Club of Western Louisiana
1202 Anderson Dr.
Leesville LA 71446

Massachusetts

BCS Visual Basic & Component Software
30 Clark St.
Holden MA 1520

BCS Zitel
27 Howland Rd.
West Newton MA 2165

Boston Computer Society
101 First Ave. Suite 2
Waltham MA 2154
http://www.bcs.org

I.B.M. PC Users Group/Sub-group of BCS
188 Needham St., Suite 230
Newton MA 2164

Pioneer Valley Computer Club
P.O. Box 87
Westfield MA 1086

Pioneer Valley PC User Group
117 W. Orange Rd.
Orange MA 1364

Worcester Computer Society, Inc.
181 West St.
East Douglas MA 1516

Maryland

Capital Area PC Club
13231 Hathaway Dr.
Silver Spring MD 20906

Capital PC User Group, Inc.
51 Monroe St. Plaza East Two
Rockville MD 20850
http://cpcug.org

Central Maryland Microcomputer Users Group
3709 Old Baltimore
Olney MD 20832

Chesapeake PC Users Group
2315B Forest Dr.
Annapolis MD 21401

Columbia-Baltimore PC Users Group
P.O. Box 125
Columbia MD 21045-0125
http://millkern.com/cbug

Communal Computing
6931 Arlington Rd. Suite 505
Bethesda MD 20814-5235

Computer Users of Baltimore
P.O. Box 23510
Baltimore MD 21203
http://www.cub.org

Hagerstown Users Group
1136 Sunnyside Dr.
Hagerstown MD 21742-3044

MDE PC Users Group
2500 Borening Highway
Baltimore MD 21224

Washington Area Midrange (FOCUS)
c/o K.B.Soni Systems Management
Associates 12023 Blackberry Terrace
North Potomac MD 20878
http://solar.rtd.utk.edu/~mtaylor/wam/
index.html

Maine

Downeast Computer Society
P.O. Box 384
Deer Isle ME 4627

Kennebec Valley Computer Society
RFD 1, Box 53
Augusta ME 4330

Maine DOS Users Group
P.O. Box 8578
Portland ME 4101

Portland Area Computer Club
10 Trundy Rd.
Cape Elizabeth ME 1407

Richmond Computer Society
4 Myrtle St.
Richmond ME 4357

Michigan

Ann Arbor Computer Society
http://ic.net/~hibbitts/aacs

Delta DOS Users Group
1415 Michigan Ave.
Gladstone MI 49837

Detroit Area Network Users Group, The
9241 Niver
Allen Park MI 48101
http://www.danug.org

Factory Computer UG of SW MI
2901 Hubbard Rd.
Ann Arbor MI 48105-2467

Flint Area Computer Enthusiasts
P.O. Box 69
Flint MI 48501

Jackson Area PC Users Group
P.O. Box 1808
Jackson MI 49204

Midland Computer Club
P.O. Box 132
Midland MI 48642

Northern Computer Users Group
409 West H St.
Iron Mountain MI 49801

Saginaw Valley Computer Assn.
577 Mackinaw Rd.
Saginaw MI 48604

Southeastern Michigan Computer Org.
P.O. Box 707
Bloomfield Hills MI 48303-0707

Sterling Heights Computer Club
P.O. Box 385
Sterling Heights MI 48311

Users Personal Computer Organization
P.O. Box 45
East Lansing MI 48826-0045

Minnesota

Compunuts
Worthington MN
http://www.rconnect.com/compunut/index

Twin Cities PC User Group
2850 Metro Dr. Suite 250
Bloomington MN 55425
http://freenet.msp.mn.us/science/
computer/tcpc.html

Missouri

Gateway Underground of R:Base Users Network
12462 Cinema Lane
St. Louis MO 63127-1334

Joplin Region PC Users Group
613 Main
Joplin MO 64801

Kansas City IBM PC User Group
221 E 63rd St.
Kansas City MO 64113

St. Louis User Group for the PC
P.O. Box 69099
St. Louis MO 63169-0099

Mississippi

Jackson County PC Users Group
2803 Ingalls Ave.
Pascagoula MS 39567
http://www.datasync.com/jcpcug

Mississippi State Microcomputer Users
Group/MSU Co
P.O. Drawer CS
Mississippi State MS 39762

Oxford Computer Club User Group
P.O. Box 1408
University MS 38677

Montana

Montana Power Company WP UG
40 East Broadway
Butte MT 59701-9394

Nebraska

Omaha Computer Users Group
4817 Magnolia St.
Omaha NE 68137

New Hampshire

Pemi-Baker Computer Group
RFD #2 Box 399
Plymouth NH 3264

Raymond PC Users Group
P.O. Box 412
Raymond NH 03077-0412

Seacoast IBM Users Group
98 Loche Rd.
Hampton NH 3042

New Jersey

Amateur Computer Group of New Jersey
P.O. Box 135
Scotch Plains NJ 7076
http://www.intac.com/acgnj

Association of PC Professionals
c/o N.B.C. Associates Inc. 808 Richard
Cherry Hill NJ 8034

Brookdale Computer Users Group
116 South Lake Dr.
Red Bank NJ 07701-5353
http://www.monmouth.com/
community_web/non_profits/bcug/

Central Jersey Computer Club
c/o Hal Vogel 19 Neptune Lane
Willingboro NJ 8046

CentraState Computer Users Group
87 Bernice Dr.
Freehold NJ 7728
http://www.cybercom.com/~intutor/
ccug.ht

Computer Club of Ocean County
737 Pacific Ave
Beachwood NJ 08722-4619

Garden State Computer Users Group
89 Stratford Rd
Tinton Falls NJ 7724

New Jersey PC User Group
P.O. Box 14
Paramus NJ 07653-0014

PC 101, Inc.
8 Mustang Trail
Warren NJ 7059

PC Users Group of South Jersey, The
P.O. Box 427
Cherry Hill NJ 8003

Philadelphia HUB PC Users Group
16 W. Judith Dr.
Blue Anchor NJ 8037

Princeton PC Users Group
P.O. Box 291
Rocky Hill NJ 8553
http://pluto.njcc.com/~jda-ir/ug/ppcug.html

South Jersey FoxPro Developers UG
705 Birchfield Dr.
Mt. Laurel NJ 8054

South Jersey IBM PC Users Group
P.O. Box 1117
Ocean City NJ 08226-1117
http://net2.intserv.com:80/~sjibmpc

Nevada

Elko Computer User Group
P.O. Box 1525
Elko NV 89801

Las Vegas PC Users Group
316 Bridge Ave. Box 240
Las Vegas NV 89101

Southern Nevada PC Users Group
1905 Villa De Conde
Las Vegas NV 89102

Sun City Summerlin Computer Club
P.O. Box 33613
Las Vegas NV 89133
http://www.scscc.com

New Mexico

Windows Information Forum
1805 Vassar Dr. SE
Albuquerque NM 87106

New York

Buffalo IBM PC User Group, Inc
P.O. Box 609
Amherst NY 14226-0609
http://www.bibmug.org/general.htm

C++ and C SIG (NYPC)
P.O. Box 679
Spring Valley NY 10977

Capital District Computer Enthusiasts
987 Kings Rd.
Schenectady NY 102301
http://members.gnn.com/jpasquini/
        cdcehome.htm

Central New York PC User Group, Inc
Teall Station PO Box 6411
Syracuse NY 13217-6411
http://www.cnypcug.org

Centralized PC Users
69-03 62 Rd.
Middle Village NY 11379

Creative Computing Club
153 East 57 St., #8-G
New York NY 10022

Endicott IBM Club/IBM Microcompter Club
9 Deborah Dr.
Apalachin NY 13732

Federations Human Servics PC UG
225 Rabro Dr. East
Hauppauge NY 11788

Finger Lakes Users Group
P.O. Box 92
Canandaigua NY 14424

FROG Computer Society
350 Chili Ave
Rochester NY 16411.3

Gotham New York PC Corp.
40 Wall St. Suite 2124
New York NY 10005-1301

Governors Island Computer User Group
Building 110 P.O. Box 34
Governors Island NY 10004

Greater Rochester Fidonet Assn.
3176 Elmwood Ave.
Rochester NY 14618-2096

Hudson Valley Personal Computing Club
P.O. Box 6057
Kingston NY 12401

ICON User Group
ATTN: Presdent Tom Engel c/o Brentwood
Public Library 2nd Avenue and 4th Street
Long Island NY 11717
http://www.li.net/~arcspark/iconclub.htm

Leatherstocking Computer Users Club
P.O. Box 1284
Oneonta NY 13820-5284

Long Island Computer Association, Inc. (LICA)
P.O. Box 71
Hicksville NY 11802
http://www.li.net/~lipcug/

Long Island Computer Society
P.O. Box 2440
Patchogue NY 11772

Long Island PC Users Group
659 Stratford Rd.
Baldwin NY 11510-1031

Mid-Hudson Computer User Group, Inc
14 Sherwood Place
Hyde Park NY 12538

Mohawk Valley PC User Group, Inc.
P.O. Box 586
Marcy NY 13403
http://www.borg.com/~mvpcug

New York Amateur Computer Club, Inc.
P.O. Box 3442 Church St. Station
New York NY 10008

New York Personal Computer User Group
40 Wall St. #2124
New York NY 10005-1301
http://www.catalog.com/cgibin/var/nypc/index.htm

OPUS Computer User Group
43 Bobann Dr.
Nesconset NY 101767

PC Rockland User Group
32 Smith Ave
South Nyack NY 10960

Picture City PC Programmers Club
237 Fitzhugh St.
Rochester NY 14608

Queensborough IBM PC Users Group
53-32 213th St.
Bayside NY 11364

Rockland PCUG
9 Chestnut Grove Court
New City NY 10956-2713

Software W Group, The
158 Cambon Aven
St. James NY 11780-3042

Smithtown Computer Info. Source UG
100 Central Rd.
Smithtown NY 11787-1696

Suffold - NYSSCPA - CUDP
383 Second Ave.
Massapequa Park NY 11762

Syracuse Microcomputer Club
P.O. Box 753
Syracuse NY 13205-0753

Telecom Rochester
8000 Victor-Pittsford Rd. Suite 129
Victor NY 14564

Warwick Valley PC Users Group
5 Second St.
Warwick NY 10990
http://www.wvtv.com/~wvpcug

Westchester PC Users Group
P.O. Box 349
White Plains NY 10602-0349
http://www.wpcug.org

Western New York Fox User Group
112 Brenridge Dr.
East Amherst NY 14051

North Carolina

Asheville PC Users Group
34 Park Ave.

Computer Club of Seven Lakes
2097 S. Seven Lakes
West End NC 27376

Foothills PC User Group
3133 28th Ave. Dr. NE
Hickory NC 28601-7731

Forsyth Computer Club
4032 Yarborough Ave.
Winston-Salem NC 27106

Hendersonville Area Computer Society
P.O. Box 208
Hendersonville NC 28793

Macon Users Group
356 Hickory Knoll Ridge
Franklin NC 28734

Metrolina NetWare Users Group
P.O. Box 35375
Charlotte NC 28235-5375

Personal Computer Club of Charlotte
380 Tulake Dr.
Concord NC 28027
http://www.chem.uncc.edu/pccc/index.htm

Seven Lakes Computer Club
104 Sweetbriar Court 1187 Seven Lakes North
West End NC 27376

Tri-County PC Users Group
Rt 2 Box 408
Grifton NC 28530

Triad Computer Club
3103 Collier Dr.
Greensboro NC 27403

Triangle Computer Society
P.O. Box 3588
Chapel Hill NC 27515
Asheville NC 28803

Triangle Midrange Users Group (TMUG)
P.O. Box 19003
Raleigh NC 27619-9003
http://www.webbuild.com/~jholcomb/ tmug.

Western North Carolina Novell UG
P.O. Box 1252
Asheville NC 28802

North Dakota

Wahpeton IBM-PC User Group
311 N. 6th St.
Wahpeton ND 58075

Ohio

Akron Canton PC Users Group
P.O. Box 2151
Akron OH 44309

Canton Alliance Massilion User Group
P.O. Box 36492
Canton OH 44735-6492
http://members.gnn.com/jeff41/camug.htm

Cincinnati PC Users Group
P.O. Box 42256
Cincinnati OH 45242
http://www.cincypcug.org

Cincinnati Tri-State Users Group
44 Dow Court
Fairfield OH 45013
http://www.iac.net/~jferree/cintug.html

Columbus Computer Society, The
P.O. Box 163336
Columbus OH 43216-3336

Computer Erie Bay User Group
P.O. Box 1461
Sandusky OH 44870-1461

Dayton Microcomputer Assn., Inc.
P.O. Box 4005
Dayton OH 45401
http://www.dma.org

Greater Cleveland PC User Group
3150 Payne Ave
Cleveland OH 44114
http://www.gcpcug.org

Newark Area Computer Club
1373 Howell Dr. North
Newark OH 43055-1737

Northeast Ohio PC Club
P.O. Box 81281
Cleveland OH 44181
http://www.en.com/users/dsieg

Northeast Ohio PC Users Group, The
P.O. Box 81281
Cleveland OH 44181-0281

Ohio State University PC User Group
1971 Neil Ave.
Columbus OH 43210

Southeast Ohio Computer Society
P.O. Box 1120
Cambridge OH 43725-6120

Toledo PC Users Group
P.O. Box 13085
Toledo OH 43613-3085

Western Reserve IBM & Compatible PC
5796 Sarah NW
Warren OH 44483

Oklahoma

OKC-PC Users Group
P.O. Box 12027
Oklahoma City OK 73157-2027

Oklahoma City PC Users Group
P.O. Box 12027
Oklahoma City OK 73157-2027
http://www.inthenet.com/pcugwww.htm

Oklahoma Computer Society
701 S. Wicklow, #506
Stillwater OK 74074

PC Business Users Group
7431 S Fulton Ave.
Tulsa OK 74136

Tulsa Computer Society
Box 3211
Tulsa OK 74101
http://www.galstar.com/~tcs

World of Windows User Group
6100 South Yale Ave.
Tulsa OK 74136

Oregon

Eugene PC Users Group, Inc.
P.O. Box 11436
Eugene OR 97440

Oregon Cavemens User Group
P.O. Box I
Cave Junction OR 97523

Portland PC Users Group
921 SW Morrison Suite 545
Portland OR 97205
http://odin.cc.pdx.edu/~psu01435/
ppcug30.html

Rogue Area Computer Club (RACC)
1358 Willow Court
Grants Pass OR 97527

Pennsylvania

Central Pennsylvania IBM PC Association
P.O. Box 197
State College PA 16804-0197
http://news.third-wave.com/cpipc

Computer Users of Erie
P.O. Box 1975
Erie PA 16507

DELCHUG (Del Ches Users Group)
P.O. Box 299
Lionville PA 19353

Exton PC Council, Inc (EPIC)
310 N. High St.
West Chester PA 19380

Harrisburg PC Users Group
6301 Grayson Rd. #155
Harrisburg PA 17111
http://hug.leba.net/pc

Lehigh Valley Computer Group
Allentown PA
http://www.lvcg.org
Lancaster Microcomputer Users Group
14 Safe Harbor Village
Conestoga PA 17516

Lower Bucks Users Group (LUG)
P.O. Box 397
Croydon PA 19021-0959
http://pluto.njcc.com/~jda-ir/ug/lug.html

Philadelphia Area Computer Society
La Salle University 1900 W. Olney Avenue
Philadelphia PA 19141

Pittsburgh Area Computer Club
P.O. Box 6440
Pittsburgh PA 15212

Professional PC Users Group of Pittsburgh
P.O. Box 23116 4th Ave Station
Pittsburgh PA 15222

Quarryville Library Information Computer
29 Kinsey Lane
New Providence PA 17560

SUN Area Computer User Group, The
RR1, Box 668

Susquehanna Valley Computer Users
721 Picnic Lane
Selinsgrove PA 17870
Millmont PA 17845

Union County Computer Club, The
RR1, Box 668
Millmont PA 17845

White Rose IBM Computer Enthusiasts
P.O. Box 54
York PA 17405

Rhode Island

NUWC ASECC Users Group
24 Glenn Dr.
West Warwick RI 02893-2105

Providence Chapter PC User Group
3595 Post Rd. Apt #22208
Warwick RI 2886
http://ids.net/~louissn/ribcs.html

Providence Satellite, Boston Computer Society
4 Teakwood Lane
Barrington RI 02806-3217

South County Computer Users Group
c/o Chuck Jacques
P.O. Box 493
Wakefield RI 2880

South Carolina

Anderson Computer User Group
110 Blake Dr.
Townville SC 29689

Charleston Computer Club
14 Sussex Rd.
Charleston SC 29407
Greenville SC 29609

Hilton Head Island Computer Club
16 Forest Dr.
Hilton Head Island SC 29928
http://www.hhisland.com/hhicc/hhic.htm

Keowee Key Computer Club
24 Lash Up Lane
Salem SC 29676

Orangeburg Computer Club
P.O. Box 474
Orangeburg SC 29116

Palmetto Personal Computer Club, Inc.
P.O. Box 2046
Columbia SC 29202
http://www.scsn.net/biz/ppcc

Piedmont Users Group
P.O. Box 4725
Greenville SC 29608

Spartanburg IBM PC Users Group
P.O. Box 6074
Spartanburg SC 29304

Upstate IBM-PC Users Group
P.O. Box 16478

South Dakota

Sioux Falls IBM and PC Compatibles Users Group
P.O. Box 89701
Sioux Falls SD 57105

Tennessee

CorelDraw User Group of Nashville
2340 Bill Rice Ranch Rd.
Murfreesboro TN 37129-4554

Cumberland Microcomputer Users Group
P.O. Box 151
Cookeville TN 38503

East Tennessee PC Users' Group
P.O. Box 52504
Knoxville TN 37950-2504
http://solar.rtd.utk.edu/~mtaylor/etug.html

Memphis PC Users Group, Inc.
P.O. Box 241756
Memphis TN 38124-1756

Murfreesboro Area Computer Hobbyists
P.O. Box 8114
Murfreesboro TN 37133-8114

Music City PC Users Group
488 Saddle Dr.
Nashville TN 37221

Nashville Area PC Users Group
488 Saddle Dr. Suite 200
Nashville TN 37221

Nashville Clippers Developers Assoc.
488 Saddle Dr.
Nashville TN 37221

Nashville Windows Users Group
853 Long Hunter Court
Nashville TN 37217

Oak Ridge PC Users Group
1345 Oak Ridge Turnpike Suite 291
Oak Ridge TN 37830

Plateau PC Users Group
P.O. Box 3787
Crossville TN 38557-3787

Rutherford Computer Users Group
8660 Bradybille Pike
Murfreesboro TN 37130
http://www.hotcc.com/users/charliep/
welcome.htm

Smokey Mountain Computer Users Group
P.O. Box 4445
Sevierville TN 37862-4445

Texas

Alamo PC Organization
P.O. Box 65180
San Antonio TX 78265-5180
http://www.alamopc.org

Association of Personal Computer Users Group
4020 McEwen Suite 105
Dallas TX 75244-5019

Central Texas PC Users Group, Inc
P.O. Box 10169
Austin TX 78766-1169
http://www.ctpcug.com

Dallas-Fort Worth Users Group
309 Lincolnshire
Irving TX 75061

Fort Worth PC Users Group, Inc.
P.O. Box 1476
Fort Worth TX 76101-1476

Golden Triangle PC Club
5770 Clint Lane
Beaumont TX 77713-9531
http://www.ih2000.net/ira/gtpcc.htm

Houston Area League PC Users, Inc.
1200 Oak Blvd. Suite 106
Houston TX 77056
http://www.hal-pc.org

Longview Computer Users Group
P.O. Box 150071
Longview TX 75615

Microcomputer Study Group, SPE Dallas Section
9424 Hunters Creek
Dallas TX 75243-6108

Mid-Cities PC User Group
P.O. Box 54141
Hurst TX 76054

North Dallas PC Users Group
735 Scottsdale Dr.
Richardson TX 75080

North Texas PC Users Group, Inc.
P.O. Box 780066
Dallas TX 75378-0066
http://www.ntpcug.org

Sr. Education & Community Svc. UG
Tarrant County Junior College
701 Wayland Drive
Arlington TX 76012-2034

Southwest IBM PC Users Group
P.O. Box 870236
Dallas TX 75287-0236

Southwest International PC Club
6516 Camino Fuente
El Paso TX 79912-2406

State Bar of Texas Computer UG
1018 Preston St., Republic
Houston TX 77002

Temple Area PC Club, The
4506 Old Howard Rd.
Temple TX 76504

Tyler Computer Club
4928 Richmond Rd.
Tyler TX 75703

Utah

Southern Utah Computer Users Group
1242 S. 450 West
Cedar City UT 84720
http://tcd.net/~shack

Utah Computer Society (Utah Blue Chips)
P.O. Box 510811
Salt Lake City UT 84151
http://www.ucs.org

Utah Valley PC User Group
P.O. Box 1834
Provo UT 84603
http://www.xmission.com/~uvpcug/
          index.ht

Virginia

Advanced Systems User Group
3613 Rose Lane
Annandale VA 22003

America OnLine
8619 Westwood Center Dr. Suite 200
Vienna VA 22182

DOS Umbrella, The
330 W. Brambleton #912

Hampton Roads Internet Association
P.O. Box 1725
Williamsburg VA 23187-1725
http://www.hria.org

Middle Peninsula Computer Users Group
P.O. Box 192
Gloucester VA 23061
http://www.inna.net/mpcug/mpcug.html

National Capital Tandy Computer UG, Inc
P.O. Box 949
Arlington VA 22216-0949

Northern Neck Computer Users Group
P.O. Box 1213
Kilmarnock VA 22482

SYDTRUG, Inc.
P.O. Box 75
Panania NSW 2213
Norfolk VA 23510

Tidewater Users Group
P.O. Box 9874
Virginia Beach VA 23450-2453

Virginia Beach Users Group
4084 Peridot Dr.
Virginia Beach VA 23456

Washington Area Computer User Group
30 Fendall Ave.
Alexandria VA 22304-630

Washington

Boeing Employees Computing Society
P.O. Box 3707 Mail Stop 8L-35
Seattle WA 98124

Fifth Corner PC Users Group
2100 Alabama Suite W-14
Bellingham WA 98226

Lower Columbia IBM PC Users Group
P.O. Box 978
Long Beach WA 98631

Mason Middle School Community UG
2812 N. Madison St.
Tacoma WA 98407-

Olympia Microcomputer Users Group
5939 54th Way SE
Lacey WA 98513

Pacific NW IBM PC User Group
P.O. Box 3363
Bellevue WA 98009

Pacific Northwest PC Users Group
P.O. Box 3363
Bellevue WA 98009-2211
http://www.halcyon.com/seasigi

Peninsula Microcomputer Club
1380 Huckle Dr.
Bremerton WA 98311

Puget Sound Netware Users Group
P.O. Box 81083
Seattle WA 98105

Tacoma Area PC Users Group
5510 Orchard St. West Suite B-1425
Tacoma WA 98467

Tacoma Open Group for Microcomputers
1808 Lenore Dr.
Tacoma WA 98406-1920

Wisconsin

Capitol City Clipper Club
6227 Wood Circle East
Middleton WI 53562

Central Wisconsin Computer Society, Inc.
c/o J.R. Dairy Supply 410 East Main Street
Auburndale WI 54412

Chips N Dips (Computer Club)
620 South 76th St
Milwaukee WI 53214

Computer People Unlimited User Group
P.O. Box 1677
Milwaukee WI 53203-1677

Eau Claire Area PC Users Group
P.O. Box 1369
Eau Claire WI 54702

FVTC PC Users Group
P.O. Box 2277 M/S 318-1825 N. Bluemound Drive
Appleton WI 54913

Fox Valley Technical College PC Users Grp
P.O. Box 2277 Mail Room 318
Appleton WI 54913-2277

Johnson Controls IBM PC Users Group
507 E Michigan St
Milwaukee WI 53202

Madison PC Users Group
P.O. Box 2598
Madison WI 53701-2598
http://mpcug.com

Milwaukee Area IBM PC Users Group
P.O. Box 2121
Milwaukee WI 53201-2121
http://www.execpc.com/~pc-users

Milwaukee Heath Users Group
13325 W. Burleigh 11
Brookfild WI 53005

Northland Microcomputer Users Group
804 23rd Ave., E.
Superior WI 54880-3750

Rapid River PC Users Group, Inc.
6848 Highway 34
Rudolph WI 54475-9531

Southeast Wisconsin Windows Users
P.O. Box 26765
Wauwatosa WI 53226-0765

West Virginia

3 Rivers PC-SIG
8 Aqua Isles Court
Parkersburg WV 26104

Boot Hills PC Users Group
P.O. Box 686
Wheeling WV 26003

Huntington PC Users Group
P.O. Box 2173
Huntington WV 25722-2173

Southeast Virginia Computer Group
http://www.exis.net/umbrella/svcg.htm

Wyoming

Sheridan Microcomputer Users Group
P.O. Box 6282
Sheridan WY 82801-1682
http://wave.sheridan.wy.us/smug

Notes...
....
....
....
....

Miscellaneous

A

Association of Corporate Computing Professionals
http://ccnet4.ccnet.com/~accp

B, C

Campus Novell User Group
gopher://tuna.berkeley.edu:577/1

Coconet PC Users Group

E

Etowah County Computer Users Group
http://www.gadsden.net/eccug/

F

Fremont-Union City-Newark PC Users

G

Gateway Users International
http://www.mcs.com/~brooklyn/home.html

Global Network Academy Web Users
http://
uugna.mit.edu:8001uugnatechwebgroup.ht
ml

I

Internet Surfers of Central Utah Users
http://www.itsnet.com/home/isocu/
isocu.ht

L

Launceston Computer Group, Inc.
http://www.vision.net.au/~chuck/lcg/index.

M

Mid America Computer Enthusiasts
http://www.fn.net/~phein/mace.htm

Mountain Home Internet Users Group
http://netnow.micron.net/~miug

P

PC Minnesota Users Group
http://www.pcmug.org/BillR

Personal Computer Huntington Users Group
http://www.eve.net:80/~ddunford/pchug

R

Rocky Mountain Internet Users Group
http://internet-plaza.net/rmiug/index.html

S

San Fernando Valley Midrange Users

South Jersey Internet Users Group
http://acy1.digex.net:80/~sjiug

Southern Maine Internet Users Group
http://www.biddeford.com/SMUG

Sydney PC Users Group
http://www.ozemail.com.au/sydpcug

Personal User Group List

Use this page to add the names and
addresses of other user groups.

Notes...

....
....
....
....
....
....
....
....
....
....
....
....
....
....
....
....
....
....
....
....
....
....
....
....
....
....
....
....
....
....
....
....
....
....

Notes...

....
....
....
....
....
....
....
....
....
....
....
....
....
....
....
....
....
....
....
....
....
....
....
....
....
....
....
....
....
....
....
....
....
....

Company Names (A–Z)

1776
8632 S Sepulveda Blvd. Ste. 203
Los Angeles, CA 90045
Main:......................................310-215-1776
Tech. Support:......................310-215-1776
Sales:....................................310-215-1776
Customer Service:..................310-215-1776
Tech. Support FAX:................310-216-1107
E-Mail:............................info@1776soft.com
Web: www.1776soft.com

20th Century Fox Home Entertainment
10201 W. Pico Blvd.
Los Angeles, CA 90067
Main:......................................310-369-3900
FAX:.......................................310-369-3318
Web: www.tcfhe.com

2500 AD Software, Inc.
PO Box 480
Buena Vista, CO 81211
Main:......................................719-395-8683
Tech. Support:.......................719-395-2475
Sales:....................................800-843-8144
Customer Service:..................800-843-8144
Tech. Support FAX:................719-395-8206
FAX:.......................................719-395-8206
Web: www.2500ad.com

3 Com Switching Division
80 Central St.
Box Borough, MA 01719
Main:......................................508-864-1400
Customer Service:..................508-264-1400
FAX:.......................................508-264-1418
BBS:.......................................508-670-9015

NOTES...
....
....
....
....
....
....
....
....

3Com Corp.
PO Box 58145
Santa Clara, CA 95052-8145
Main: 408-764-5000
Tech. Support:......................800-876-3266
Sales:....................................310-348-8110
Customer Service:..................800-876-3266
Tech. Support FAX: 408-764-5001
CompuServe:................GO ASKTHREECOM
E-Mail:..............................info@3com.com
BBS:.......................................408-980-8204
FTP: ftp.3com.com
Web: www.3com.com

3D/Eye, Inc.
700 Galleria Pkwy Ste. 400
Atlanta, GA 30339
Main: 800-469-6514
Tech. Support:......................800-469-6514
Sales:....................................800-946-9533
E-Mail:.........................webmaster@eye.com
BBS:.......................................607-266-7100
Web: www.eye.com

3M Private Network Products
6801 RiverPl. Blvd.
Austin, TX 78769
Main: 512-984-3400
Customer Service:..................800-426-8688
Tech. Support FAX: 800-626-0329

3NAME3D
1202 W. Olympic Blvd. Ste. 101
Santa Monica, CA 90404
Main: 310-314-2171
Sales:....................................800-993-4621
FAX: 310-314-2181
E-Mail:...................................info@ywd.com
Web: www.ywd.com

3RD Dimension Technologies, Inc.
31225 La Baya Dr. Ste. 107
Westlake Village, CA 91362
Main: 800-455-3558
FAX: 818-865-8213
BBS:.......................................818-865-0496
Web: www.3dt.net/3d-art/

7th Level
1110 E Collins Blvd. Ste. 122
Richardson, TX 75081
Main:......................................214-437-4858
Tech. Support:........................214-437-4858
Sales:....................................214-437-4858
Customer Service:...................214-437-4858
Tech. Support FAX:.................214-437-2717
CompuServe:...............................GO SEVEN
America Online:......................Keyword Seven
E-Mail:..........................support@7thlevel.com
FTP: ftp.7thlevel.com
Web: www.7thlevel.com

A & D Computer
211 South St.
Milford, NH 03055-3743
Main:.....................................603-672-4700
E-Mail:............................amiga@mv.mv.com
BBS:......................................603-673-2788

A & G Graphics Interface
51 Gore St.
Cambridge, MA 02141
Main:.....................................617-492-0120
Sales:....................................617-492-0120
FAX:......................................617-492-2133
CompuServe:.............................. 74774,273
E-Mail:.................. customvc@world.Std.com

AA Computech
28170 Crocker Ave. Ste. 105
Valencia, CA 91355
Main:.....................................805-257-6801
Tech. Support:........................805-257-6804
Sales:....................................800-360-6801
FAX:......................................805-257-6805
E-Mail:..............................bob@scvnet.com
BBS:......................................805-257-6805
Web: www.scbnet.com/telbobs

ABC LaserJet, Inc.
3050 Holcomb Bridge Rd.
Norcross, GA 30071
Main: 800-438-7745
Tech. Support:........................ 770-416-0009
FAX: 770-448-6253
Web: www.atl.mindspring.com/~ribbons
   /index.html

ABL Electronics
10942 Beaverdam Rd.
Hunt Valley, MD 21030
Main: 800-726-0610
Tech. Support:........................ 410-584-2700
Sales:.................................... 800-726-0610
Tech. Support FAX: 401-584-2790
E-Mail:.........................sales@ablcables.com
BBS: 410-560-1198

ABT CORP.
361 Broadway Ste. 400
New York, NY 10013
Main: 212-219-8945
Tech. Support:........................ 212-219-2448
Sales:.................................... 800-477-6532
Customer Service:................... 800-477-4752
Tech. Support FAX: 212-219-0484
FAX: 212-219-3597
BBS: 212-219-3597

ACC Computer Peripherals
Acc Technology Group
7 Whatney
Irvine, CA 92718-2608
Main: 714-454-2441
Tech. Support:........................ 714-454-2441
Sales:.................................... 800-234-7811
Customer Service:................... 714-454-2441
Tech. Support FAX: 714-454-8527
E-Mail:.......techsupport@acctechnology.com
BBS: 714-470-1759

ACE Software
22611 Markey Court Unit 113
Sterling, VA 20166-6903
Main:....................................703-450-1980
Tech. Support:........................703-450-2318
Sales:...................................800-346-9413
Customer Service:..................800-346-9413
Tech. Support FAX:................703-450-9786
America Online:............mstilt7714@aol.com
E-Mail: ....support@aecsoft.com
Web: www.aecsoft.com

ACS Communications, Inc.
10 Victor Square
Scotts Valley, CA 95066
Main:....................................800-538-0742
Tech. Support:........................800-995-5500
Sales:...................................800-995-5500
Tech. Support FAX:...............408-438-7730
FAX:....................................408-438-2745

ADC Kentrox
14375 NW Science Park Dr.
Portland, OR 97229
Main:....................................503-643-1681
Tech. Support:........................800-733-5511
Customer Service:..................800-733-5511
Tech. Support FAX:................503-641-3341
E-Mail: ....info@kentrox.com
BBS:....................................503-643-1681
FTP: ftp.kentrox.com
Web: www.kentrox.com

ADC Telecommunications
12501 Whitewater Dr.
Minneapolis, MN 55343
Main:....................................612-938-8080
Tech. Support:...............800-366-3891-3475
Sales:...................................800-366-3891
Customer Service:..........800-3663891-3000
Tech. Support FAX:................612-946-3237
E-Mail: ....technical@adc.com
Web: www.adc.com

ADDSoft, Inc.
11850 Nicholas St. Ste. 120
Omaha, NE 68154
Sales:.................................. 800-229-0559
FAX: 402-491-4152
CompuServe:............................ 76301,3204
E-Mail:.......... 76301,3204@compuserve.com

ADI Systems, Inc.
2115 Ringwood Ave.
San Jose, CA 95131
Main: 800-228-0530
Tech. Support:........................ 408-944-0100
FAX: 408-944-0300
Web: www.adi-online.com

AG Group
2540 Camino Diablo Ste. 200
Walnut Creek, CA 94596
Main: 510-937-7900
Tech. Support FAX: 510-937-2479
CompuServe:............................ 74431,2500
E-Mail:............................info@aggroup.com
FTP: ftp.aggroup.com
Web: www.aggroup.com

AIS
180 Clossen Ave.
Elk Grove Village, IL 60067
Main: 800-950-1100
Tech. Support:........................ 847-593-2626
Tech. Support FAX: 847-593-2790
BBS:....................................... 847-593-2789

ALPS Electric (USA), Inc.
3553 N First St.
San Jose, CA 95134
Main: 800-825-2577
Tech. Support:........................ 800-449-2577
Sales:.................................... 800-449-2577
Customer Service:................... 800-950-2577
BBS:....................................... 408-432-6424
Web: www.alps.com

ALR - Advanced Logic Research
9401 Jeronimo
Irvine, CA 92718
Main:......................................800-444-4257
Tech. Support:.........................800-257-1230
Sales:....................................714-458-1952
Customer Service:...................714-458-1952
Tech. Support FAX:.................714-581-9240
FAX: 714-458-0532
E-Mail:....................................sales@alr.com
Web: www.alr.com

AM Communications
1900 AM Dr.
Quakertown, PA 18951-9004
Main:......................................215-536-1354
Tech. Support FAX:.................215-536-1475

AMCC
6195 Lusk Blvd.
San Diego, CA 92121-2793
Main:......................................619-450-9333
Sales:....................................800-755-2622
Tech. Support FAX:.................619-450-9885
E-Mail:.........................compinfo@amcc.com
Web: www.amcc.com

AMD
Tech. Support:.........................408-325-8028
Sales:....................................800-863-9436
E-Mail: ....admin@nexgen.com
BBS:......................................408-955-1839
FTP: ftp.nexgen.com
Web: www.nexgen.com

AMP, Inc.
PO Box 3608
Harrisburg, PA 17105-3608
Main:......................................717-986-7777
Tech. Support:.........................800-866-2104
Sales:....................................800-522-6752
Customer Service:...................800-526-0721
FAX: 717-986-7575
Web: www.amp.com

AMT International
2393 Qume Dr.
San Jose, CA 95131
Main: 408-432-1790
Tech. Support:.........................408-432-0552
Sales: 408-432-1790
Tech. Support FAX: 408-383-9047
BBS: 408-944-9801

ANA Technolgy
10499 Bradford Rd.
Littleton, CO 80127
Main: 303-973-6722
Tech. Support FAX: 303-973-7092
FAX: 303-973-7092
E-Mail:..................custsvc@anatech.ingr.com
Web: www.scanners.com

ANDATACO
10140 Mesa Rim Rd.
San Diego, CA 92121
Main: 800-334-9191
Tech. Support:.........................619-453-9809
Sales:....................................619-453-9191
FAX: 619-453-9294
E-Mail:..............................cs@andataco.com
Web: www.andataco.com

APT Communications, Inc.
9607 Dr. Perry Rd.
Ijamsville, MD 21754
Main: 301-874-3307
Tech. Support:.........................800-842-0626
Sales:.....................................800-842-0626
Tech. Support FAX: 301-871-5255
E-Mail:........................support@aptcom.com
Web: www.aptcom.com

ARSoftware Corp.
Applied Research
8201 Corporate Dr. Ste. 1110
Landover, MD 20785-2230
Main: 301-459-3773
FAX: 301-459-3776
E-Mail:...ars@ari.net
Web: www.ari.net/ars

ASCOM Timeplex Corp.
400 Chestnut Ridge Rd.
Woodcliff Lake, NJ 07675
Main:......................................800-776-2677
Tech. Support:.........................201-391-1111
Sales:......................................201-391-1111
Customer Service:...................201-391-1111
Tech. Support FAX:.................201-573-6470
FAX:..201-573-6470
Web: www.timeplex.com

ASP Computer Products, Inc.
1021 N Wolfe Rd.
Sunnyvale, CA 94086
Main:......................................408-746-2965
Tech. Support:...............408-746-2965 #534
Sales:......................................800-445-6190
Customer Service:............800-445-619-0459
Tech. Support FAX:.................408-738-4702
BBS:..408-749-8240
Web: www.asp.net

AST Research, Inc.
16215 Alton Pkwy.
PO Box 57005
Irvine, CA 92619
Main:......................................714-727-4141
Tech. Support:.........................800-727-1278
Sales:......................................800-723-2278
Customer Service:...................800-876-4278
Tech. Support FAX:.................714-727-9355
E-Mail: ....web.support@ast.com
BBS:..817-230-6850
FTP: ftp.ast.com
Web: www.ast.com

AT&T Paradyne
8545 126th Ave. NPO Box 2826
Largo, FL 34649-2826
Main:......................................813-530-2000
Tech. Support:.........................800-237-0016
Sales:......................................800-243-4977
Customer Service:...................800-237-0016
Tech. Support FAX:.................813-530-2453
E-Mail: ....hba@www.att.com
BBS:..813-532-5254
Web: www.att.com

AT&T Wireless Services
10230 NE Points Dr.
Kirkland, WA 98033
Main: 206-803-4000
Web: www.airdata.com

ATI Technologies, Inc.
33 Commerce Valley Dr. E
Thorn Hill, ONT L3T 7N6
Canada
Main: 905-882-2600
Tech. Support:.......................905-882-2626
Sales:.....................................905-882-2600
Customer Service:..................905-882-2600
Tech. Support FAX: 905-882-0546
FAX: 905-882-2620
CompuServe:.............................74740,667
BBS:.......................................905-764-9404
FTP: ftp.atitech.ca
Web: www.atitech.ca

AUSCAN Software Unlimited
8 Springmount Ave.
Toronto, ONT MBH 2Y4
Canada
Main: 416-665-4037
E-Mail:................................rjp@interlog.com
Web: www.interlog.com/~rjp/auscan.html

AVA Instrumentation
19 Horseshoe Court
Scotts Valley, CA 95066
Main: 408-336-2281
Tech. Support FAX: 408-336-5049
FAX: 408-336-5049
E-Mail:.........................avasales@aimnet.com
Web: www.aimnet.com/~avasales

Abaco Software
6 Trafalgar Square
Nashua, NH 03063
Main: 603-883-1818
Tech. Support:.......................603-883-1818
Sales:.....................................603-883-1818
Customer Service:..................603-883-1818
Tech. Support FAX: 603-883-2019

Accent Software International
PO Box 914
Exton, PA 19341-0906
Main:.......................................800-535-5256
FAX: 800-535-5257
CompuServe:............................. 7477,4264

Access Softek, Inc.
2550 9th St. Ste. 206
Berkeley, CA 94710
Sales: 800-386-4272
FAX: 510-848-0608
E-Mail:...............................info@softek.com
Web: users.lanminds.com/~softek/index.html

Access Software
4750 Wyley Post Way
Building 1, Ste. 200
Salt Lake City, UT 84116
Main:....................................800-800-4880
Tech. Support:.......................801-359-2900
Sales: 801-359-2900
Customer Service:..................800-800-4880
Tech. Support FAX:................801-596-9128
E-Mail: ....tech@acces.com
BBS:......................................801-359-2968
FTP: ftp.access.com
Web: www.access.com

Accolade
5300 Stevens Creek Blvd. Ste. 500
San Jose, CA 95129
Main:....................................408-296-8400
Tech. Support:.......................408-296-8400
Sales: 800-245-7744
Customer Service:..................408-296-8400
Tech. Support FAX:................408-246-0231
FAX: 408-246-0321
CompuServe:.........................GO GAMAPUB
America Online:...............Keyword Accolade
E-Mail: ....techelp@accolade.com
BBS:......................................408-296-8800
Web: www.accolade.com

NOTES..
....
....

Accton Technology Corp.
1962 Zanker Rd.
San Jose, CA 95112
Main: 408-452-8900
Tech. Support:.......................800-926-9288
Sales:....................................800-926-9288
Customer Service:..................800-926-9288
Tech. Support FAX: 408-452-8988
BBS: 408-452-8828
Web: www.accton.com

Acer America
2641 Orchard Pkwy.
San Jose, CA 95134
Main: 408-432-6200
Tech. Support:.......................800-445-6495
Sales: 800-733-2237
Customer Service:..................800-637-7000
Tech. Support FAX: 408-922-2933
CompuServe: ....GO ACER
America Online:......................Keyword Acer
BBS: 408-428-0140
FTP: ftp.acer.com
Web: www.acer.com/aac/index.htm

Acius
20883 Stevens Creek Blvd.
Cupertino, CA 95014
Main: 408-252-4444
Tech. Support:.......................408-252-4444
Sales:....................................408-252-4444
Customer Service:......... 408-252-4444 #252
Tech. Support FAX: 408-252-7765
FAX: 408-252-0831
CompuServe: .... GO ACIUS
FTP: ftp.dnai.com\pub\acius\us_intl
Web: www.aci-4d.com

Acma Computers, Inc.
47988 Fremont Blvd.
Fremont, CA 94538
Main: 510-623-1212
Sales:....................................800-786-6888
Tech. Support FAX: 510-623-0818
E-Mail:............................sales@acma.com
BBS: 510-651-0629
Web: www.acma.com

Acme Electric Corp.
9962 Route 446
Cuba, NY 14727
Sales: 800-325-5848
FAX: 716-968-3948

Actel Corp.
955 E Arques Ave.
Sunnyvale, CA 94086-4533
Main: 408-739-1010
Tech. Support: 800-262-1060
Sales: 800-228-3532
Customer Service: 408-739-1010
Tech. Support FAX: 408-739-1540
Web: www.actel.com

Activision
11601 Wilshire Blvd. Ste. 300
West Los Angeles, CA 90025
Main: 310-473-9200
Tech. Support: 310-479-5644
Sales: 800-477-3650
Customer Service: 310-479-5644
Tech. Support FAX: 310-479-7355
CompuServe: 76004,2122
America Online: .... Keyword Activision
E-Mail: ....support@activision.com
BBS: 310-479-1335
Web: www.activision.com

Ad Lib Inc.
50 Staniford St. Ste. 800
Boston, MA 02114
Main: 418-529-9676
Sales: 800-463-2686
Customer Service: 800-463-2686
FAX: 418-529-1159

NOTES...
....
....
....

Adaptec, Inc.
691 W. Milpitas Blvd.
Milpitas, CA 95035
Main: 408-945-8600
Tech. Support: 408-934-7274
Sales: 408-945-8600
Customer Service: 800-959-7274
Tech. Support FAX: 408-262-2533
FAX: 408-262-2533
CompuServe: .... GO ADAPTEC
E-Mail: ....support@adaptec.com
BBS: 408-945-7727
FTP: ftp.adaptec.com
Web: www.adaptec.com

Adaptive Software Corporation
125 Pacifica Ste. 250
Irvine, CA 92718
Main: 714-789-7300
Tech. Support: 714-789-7311
Sales: 800-598-1222
Customer Service: 714-789-7316
Tech. Support FAX: 714-789-7320
E-Mail: .... sales@adaptiv.com
Web: www.adaptiv.com

Addison-Wesley Longman
2725 Sand Hill Rd.
Menlo Park, CA 94025
Main: 415-854-0300
Tech. Support FAX: 415-853-2591
Web: www.aw.com

Addtron Technology
Delta Products
10200 W. 75th St. Ste. 111A
Shawnee Mission, KS 66204
Main: 913-789-7120
Tech. Support: 800-998-4646
FAX: 913-789-7103
BBS: 510-770-0272
Web: www.addtron.com

Adobe Systems

333 W San Carlos St.
San Jose, CA 95110
Main:.....................................408-975-6000
Tech. Support:.......................408-975-6466
Customer Service:..................408-975-6000
Tech. Support FAX:................408-975-6651
CompuServe:......................... GO DPTVEND
E-Mail:......................comments@frame.com
BBS:.....................................408-975-6729
FTP: ftp.frame.com
Web: www.frame.com

Adobe Systems, Inc.

1585 Charleston Rd.
PO Box 7900
Mountain View, CA 94039-7900
Main:.....................................415-961-4400
Sales:....................................800-833-6687
Customer Service:..................800-628-2320
Tech. Support FAX:................415-961-3769
CompuServe:........................GO ADOBEAPP
America Online:....................Keyword Adobe
BBS:.....................................206-623-6984
FTP: ftp.adobe.com
Web: www.adobe.com

Adtech Co.

1571 Whitmore Ave.
Ceres, CA 95307
Main:.....................................800-326-6548
Tech. Support:.......................408-954-8038
Tech. Support FAX:................209-541-1401

Advanced Computer Communication

340 Storke Rd.
Santa Barbara, CA 93117
Main:.....................................800-444-7854
Tech. Support:.......................800-666-7308
Sales:....................................805-685-4455
Customer Service:..................800-666-7308
Tech. Support FAX:................805-685-4465
E-Mail:.......................................info@acc.com
BBS:.....................................805-562-8825
Web: www.acc.com

Advanced Computer Innovations

30 Burncoat Way
Pittsford, NY 14534-2216
Main: 716-383-1939
Tech. Support:.......................716-383-1939
FAX: 716-383-8428

Advanced Concepts, Inc.

4129 N Port Washington Ave.
Milwaukee, WI 53212
Main: 414-963-0999
Tech. Support:.......................414-963-0999
Sales:....................................414-963-0999
Customer Service:..................414-963-0999
Tech. Support FAX: 414-963-2090
CompuServe: 72623,3273
E-Mail:........................advcon@execpc.com
BBS: 414-963-9990

Advanced Digital Information Corp.

PO Box 97057
Redmond, WA 98073
Main: 206-881-8004
Tech. Support:.......................206-883-4357
Sales:....................................800-336-1233
Customer Service:..................206-881-8004
Tech. Support FAX: 206-881-2296
E-Mail:.......................................info@adic.com
BBS: 206-883-3211
Web: www.adic.com

Advanced Gravis Computer Technology, Ltd.

3750 N Fraser Way Ste. 101
Burnaby, BC V5J 5E9
Canada
Main: 604-431-5020
Tech. Support:.......................604-431-1807
Sales:....................................800-257-0061
Customer Service:..................800-663-8558
Tech. Support FAX: 604-431-5155
FAX: 604-431-5155
E-Mail:...............................tech@gravis.com
BBS: 604-431-5927
Web: www.gravis.com

Advanced Micro Devices (AMD)

1 AMD Pl.
PO Box 3453
Sunnyvale, CA 94088-3453
Main:.....................................800-538-8450
Tech. Support:........................800-222-9323
Sales: 408-732-2400
Customer Service:...................408-749-5703
Tech. Support FAX:.................408-749-5299
E-Mail: ....hwsupt@brahms.amd.com
BBS:......................................408-749-4659
Web: www.amd.com

Advanced Microelectronics

ITD
1080 River Oaks Dr. Ste. A-250
Jackson, MS 39208
Main:.....................................601-960-3600
Sales: 601-932-7620
Customer Service:...................601-932-7620
Tech. Support FAX:.................601-932-7621
E-Mail: ....design@aue.com
FTP: ftp.aue.com
Web: www.aue.com

Advanced RISC Machines Inc.

Advance RISC Machines, Ltd.
985 University Ave. Ste. 5
Los Gatos, CA 95030
Main:.....................................408-399-5199
Tech. Support FAX:.................408-399-8854
E-Mail: ....support@arm.com
Web: www.arm.com

Advanced Storage Concepts

10713 Ranch Rd. 620 N. Ste. 305
Austin, TX 78726
Main:.....................................512-335-1077
FAX:......................................512-335-1078
E-Mail: .... sales@advstor.com
Web: www.eden.com/~asc/

Advanced Technologies International

ATI
361 Sinclair-Frontage Rd.
Milpitas, CA 95035
Main: 408-942-1780
Tech. Support FAX: 408-942-1260

Advanced Visual Systems Inc.

300 Fifth Ave.
Waltham, MA 02154
Main: 617-890-4300
Tech. Support FAX: 617-890-8287
E-Mail:................................... info@avs.com
Web: www.avs.com

Advantest America

Advantest Corp (Japan)
1100 Busch Pkwy.
Buffalo Grove, IL 60089
Main: 847-634-2552
Tech. Support FAX: 847-634-2872

Aerotron-Repco Systems, Inc.

2400 Sand Lake Rd.
Orlando, FL 32809
Main: 800-950-5633
Tech. Support:........................ 407-856-1953
FAX: 407-856-1960
E-Mail:..................sales@aerotron-repco.com
Web: www.aerotron-repco.com

Agile Networks

1300 Massachusetts Ave.
Boxborough, MA 01719
Main: 800-286-9526
Tech. Support FAX: 508-263-5111
E-Mail:...................................info@agile.com
Web: www.agile.com

Ahead Systems, Inc.
4114 Clipper Court
Fremont, CA 94538
Main:.....................................510-623-0900
Sales: 510-623-0900
Tech. Support FAX:................510-623-0960
E-Mail: ....ahead@ix.netcom.com
BBS:.....................................510-623-0961

Ahearn Soper Co., Inc.
540 N Commercial St.
Manchester, NH 03101-1107
Main:.....................................603-647-2700
Tech. Support:........................603-647-2700
Customer Service:..................603-647-2700
Tech. Support FAX:................603-647-2724

Aicom Corp.
2381 Zanker Rd. Ste. 160
San Jose, CA 95131
Main:.....................................408-577-0370
Tech. Support FAX:................408-577-0373
BBS:.....................................408-577-0372

Aim Tech Corp.
20 Trafalgar Sq.
Nashua, NH 03063-1973
Main:.....................................800-289-2884
Tech. Support:........................800-801-2884
FAX: 603-883-5582
E-Mail: .... support@aimtech.com
BBS:.....................................603-598-8402
Web: www.aimtech.com

Air Technology
4699 Old Ironsides Dr. Ste. 400
Santa Clara, CA 95054
Main:.....................................800-848-8649
Tech. Support:........................408-748-8649
FAX: 408-748-0161
E-Mail: ....staff@aim.com
BBS:.....................................408-748-0161
Web: www.aim.com

NOTES...
....
....
....

Aladdin Software Security, Inc.
Aladdin Knowledge Systems, Ltd.
350 5th Ave. Ste. 6614
New York, NY 10118
Main: 800-223-4277
Tech. Support:........................800-223-4277
Sales:....................................800-223-4277
Customer Service:..................800-223-4277
Tech. Support FAX: 212-564-3377
FAX: 212-564-3377
E-Mail:...............................sales@us.aks.com
FTP: ftp.aks.com
Web: www.aks.com

Aladdin Systems
165 Westridge Dr.
Watsonville, CA 95076
Main: 408-761-6200
Tech. Support:........................408-761-6200
Sales:....................................408-761-6200
Customer Service:..................408-761-6200
Tech. Support FAX: 408-761-6206
CompuServe: .... GO ALADDIN
America Online:.................. Keyword Aladdin
E-Mail:...............cust.service@aladdinsys.com
FTP: ftp.aladdinsys.com
Web: www.aladdinsys.com

Alcom Corp.
1616 N Shoreline Blvd.
Mountain View, CA 94043
Main: 415-694-7000
Sales:....................................415-694-7000
Tech. Support FAX: 415-694-7070
CompuServe: ....GO ALCOM
E-Mail:...............................sales@alcom.com
BBS: 415-694-7091
Web: www.alcom.com

Aldridge Co., The
2500 City West Blvd. Ste. 575
Houston, TX 77042
Main: 713-953-1940
Tech. Support:........................713-953-1940
Sales:....................................800-548-5019
Tech. Support FAX: 713-953-0806
E-Mail:.............................dlac@aldridge.com
Web: www.aldridge.com

Aliance Electronics
9410 Owensmouth Ave.
Chatsworth, CA 91311
Main:....................................818-718-8667
Tech. Support:........................800-431-8124
FAX:......................................818-718-8667
Web: www.ora.usa.com

Alias Research, Inc.
110 Richmond St. E
Toronto, ONT M5C 1P1
Canada
Main:....................................800-447-2542
Tech. Support FAX:................416-362-0630
Web: www.aw.sgi.com

Alias Wavefront
Santa Barbara, CA
Main:....................................805-962-8117
Tech. Support:........................800-255-7781
Tech. Support FAX:................805-963-0782
FAX:......................................805-963-0410
E-Mail: ....webmaster@aw.sgi.com
Web: www.alias.com

Alisa Systems, Inc.
221 E Walnut St. Ste. 175
Pasadena, CA 91101
Main:....................................818-792-9474
Tech. Support:........................800-992-5472
Sales:....................................800-628-3274
Tech. Support FAX:................818-792-4068
BBS:......................................818-683-8479
Web: www.alisa.com

All Computer Warehouse
224 S 5th Ave.
City of Industry, CA 91746
Main:....................................818-369-4181
Tech. Support:........................800-755-1953
Sales:....................................800-775-1953
FAX:......................................818-961-7462
E-Mail: ....alcomp@alcomp.com

Allegro New Media
16 Passaic Ave., Building 6
Fairfield, NJ 07004-3835
Main: 201-808-1992
Tech. Support:........................201-808-1992
Sales:....................................201-808-1992
Customer Service:...................201-808-1992
Tech. Support FAX: 201-808-2645
FAX: 201-808-2645
E-Mail:.....................nygy14ef@prodigy.com
Web: www.allegronm.com

Allen Communications
Times Mirror
5 Triad Center, Fifth Floor
Salt Lake City, UT 84180
Main: 800-325-7850
Tech. Support:........................800-515-2626
Tech. Support FAX: 801-799-7378
FAX: 801-537-7805
E-Mail:...........................info@allencom.com
BBS:......................................801-799-7382
Web: www.allencom.com

Allied Telesyn International
950 Kifer Rd.
Sunnyvale, CA 94086
Main: 800-424-4282
Tech. Support:........................800-428-4835
Sales:....................................800-424-4284
Customer Service:...................800-424-5012
Tech. Support FAX: 408-736-0292
CompuServe:.............................. GO ALLIED
E-Mail:..........................ati_sales@centr.com
Web: www.alliedtelesyn.com

Alpha Software
168 Middlesex Turnpike
Burlington, MA 01803
Main: 617-229-2924
Sales:....................................800-451-1018
Customer Service:...................617-229-2924
Tech. Support FAX: 617-272-4876
CompuServe:...............................GO ALPHA
BBS:......................................617-229-2915
Web: www.alphasoftware.com

Alpha Technologies
3767 Alpha Way
Bellingham, WA 98226
Main:......................................360-647-2360
Tech. Support FAX:................360-733-8690
BBS:.......................................360-671-4936
Web: www.alpha-us.com

Alphatronix
4022 Stirup Creek Dr. Ste. 315
Durham, NC 27703
Main:......................................919-544-0001
FAX: 919-544-4079
Web: www.alphatronix.com

Alta Technology
9500 South, 500 West
Sandy, UT 84070-6655
Main:......................................801-539-0852
Tech. Support FAX:................801-254-2020
E-Mail: ....support@altatech.com
Web: www.xmission.com/~altatech/

Altera Corp.
2610 Orchard Pkwy.
San Jose, CA 95134-2020
Main:......................................408-894-7900
Tech. Support:......................800-800-3753
Customer Service:..................800-767-3753
Tech. Support FAX:................408-954-0348
FAX: 408-894-7979
CompuServe:........................... GO ALTERA
E-Mail: .... sos@altera.com
BBS:.......................................408-954-0104
FTP: ftp.altera.com
Web: www.altera.com

Altex Electronics, Inc.
11342 IH-35 N
San Antonio, TX 78233
Main:......................................210-637-3200
Tech. Support:......................512-349-8795
Sales:....................................800-531-5369
Tech. Support FAX:................210-637-3264
E-Mail: .... support@altex.com
BBS:.......................................512-637-3264
Web: www.altex.com

Alto Group/Candence Design Systems Inc.
555 N Matilda Ave.
Sunnyvale, CA 94086
Main: 415-574-5800
Tech. Support:........................408-523-4677
Customer Service:..................408-733-1595
Tech. Support FAX: 408-523-4601
Web: www.altagroup.com

Altra
520 West Cedar St.
Rawlins, WY 82301
Main: 800-445-6778
Customer Service:..................800-726-6153
Web: www.altra.com

Amber Wave Systems
42 Nagog Park
Acton, MA 01720
Main: 508-266-2900
Tech. Support FAX: 508-266-1159
E-Mail:........................ info@amberwave.com
FTP: ftp.amberwave.com
Web: www.amberwave.com

AmegaByte!
5001 Garrett Ave.
Beltsville, MD 20705
Main: 800-834-7153
Sales:....................................301-937-1640
FAX: 301-937-1658
E-Mail:..............................amega@globe.net

Ameri Data Inc.
10200 51St. Ave. N
Minneapolis, MN 55442
Main: 612-557-2500
Tech. Support:........................203-294-5800
Sales:....................................612-557-2500
Customer Service:..................800-873-2827
Tech. Support FAX: 203-269-9021
FAX: 612-557-6949
BBS: 203-758-3858
Web: www.ameridata.com

America Online
8619 Westwood Center Dr.
Vienna, VA 22182-2220
Main:.......................................703-448-8700
Sales: 800-827-6364
FAX:..703-883-1509
E-Mail: ....info@aol.com
BBS:..800-827-5808
FTP: ftp.aol.com
Web: www.aol.com

Americal Group
PO Box 16388
North Hollywood, CA 91615
Main:.......................................818-765-3040
Tech. Support:.........................818-765-3040
Sales: 818-288-8025
Customer Service:...................818-765-3040
Tech. Support FAX:.................818-765-3887
BBS:..818-765-3887

American Business Systems
315 Littleton Rd.
Chelmsford, MA 01824
Main:.......................................508-250-9600
Tech. Support FAX:.................508-250-8027
E-Mail: ....sales@abs-software.com
Web: www.abs-software.com

American Chemical Society
1155 16th St. NW
Washington, DC 20036
Main:.......................................202-872-4378
FAX:..202-452-8913
FTP: FTP: acs.org
Web: www.acs.org

American Computer Hardware
2205 S Wright St.
Santa Ana, CA 92705-5315
Main:.......................................714-549-2688
Tech. Support:.........................800-447-1237
Tech. Support FAX:.................714-662-0491

American Covers
102 West 12200 S
PO Box 987
Draper, UT 84020
Main: 801-553-0600
Tech. Support:.........................800-228-8987
Sales:......................................800-553-0600
Customer Service:...................800-228-8987
Tech. Support FAX: 801-553-1212

American Digital Cartography, Inc.
3003 West College Ave.
Appleton, WI 54914
Main: 414-733-6678
FAX: 414-734-3375
E-Mail:....................................info@adci.com

American Fundware
Flagship Group
1385 S Colorado Blvd. Ste. 400
Denver, CO 80222
Main: 303-756-3030
Tech. Support:.........................800-227-7575
Tech. Support FAX: 303-756-3514
BBS:..303-879-6850

American Megatrends, Inc. (AMI)
6145-F Northbelt Pkwy.
Norcross, GA 30071-2906
Main: 770-246-8600
Tech. Support:.........................770-246-8645
Sales:......................................800-828-9264
Customer Service:...................770-246-8645
Tech. Support FAX: 770-246-8791
E-Mail:...support@american.megatrends.com
BBS:..770-246-8782
Web: www.megatrends.com

American Research Corp. (ARC)
602 Monterey Pass Rd.
Monterey Park, CA 91754
Main: 800-346-3272
Tech. Support FAX: 818-284-4213
BBS:..818-284-8836

American Ribbon Co.
2895 W Prospect Rd.
Ft. Lauderdale, FL 33309
Main:......................................800-327-1013
Tech. Support:........................305-733-4552
Tech. Support FAX:................954-733-0319
BBS:.......................................954-733-0319

Amherst -Merritt International
5565 Red Bird Center Dr. Ste. 150
Dallas, TX 75237
Main:......................................214-339-0753
BBS:.......................................214-339-1313

Amiga-Crossing
PO Box 12A
Cumberland Center, ME 04021
Main:......................................800-498-3959
Sales:.....................................207-829-3959
FAX: 207-829-3522
E-Mail: ....amiga-x@tka.com

Amiga Technologies GmbH (English)
Web: www.amiga-tech.com

Amiga Video Solutions
1568 Randolph Ave.
St. Paul, MN 55105
Main:......................................612-698-1175
FAX: 612-224-3823
E-Mail: ....wohno001@maroon.tc.umn.edu
BBS:.......................................612-698-1918

Amigability Computers
PO Box 572
Plantsville, CT 06479
Main:......................................203-276-8175
E-Mail: ....caldi@pcnet.com

Amka
15328 E Valley Blvd.
City of Industry, CA 91746
Main:......................................818-369-2121
Tech. Support:........................818-369-2121
Tech. Support FAX:................818-961-0482

Analog Devices
Norwood, MA
Main: 617-329-4700
Web: www.analog.com

Anawave Software, Inc.
Main: 714-250-7262
Customer Service:................... 714-250-7263
E-Mail:..................webmaster@anawave.com
Web: www.anawave.com

Anco Corp.
140 N Palm St.
Brea, CA 92821
Main: 714-992-9000
Tech. Support FAX: 714-992-1672

Andrew Corp.
10500 W. 153rd St.
Orland Pk., IL 60462
Main: 708-349-3300
Tech. Support:....................... 800-826-3739
Sales:..................................... 800-328-2696
Customer Service:................... 800-328-2696
Tech. Support FAX: 708349-5673
E-Mail:.............................. info@andrew.com
Web: www.andrew.com

Angia Corp.
441 East Bay Blvd.
Provo, UT 84606
Main: 801-371-0488
Tech. Support:....................... 800-998-0555
Sales:..................................... 800-877-9159
Customer Service:................... 800-877-9159
Tech. Support FAX: 801-374-1476
FAX: 801-373-9847
E-Mail:............................... sales@angia.com
BBS: 801-373-7807
FTP: ftp.angia.com
Web: www.angia.com

NOTES ....
....
....
....

Animated Voice Corp.
PO Box 819
San Marcos, CA 92079
Main:.....................................619-744-8190
Tech. Support:........................619-744-8190
FAX:.......................................619-744-8903

Annex Telecommunications
14126 Sherman Way Ste. 207
Van Nuys, CA 91405-5633
Main:.....................................818-779-5646
Sales: 800-462-6639
E-Mail: ....ggooden@annex.com
Web: www.annex.com

Anritsu America, Inc.
365 W. Passaic St.
Rochelle Park, NJ 07662
Main:.....................................201-843-2690
Tech. Support:........................201-337-1111
FAX:.......................................201-843-2665
BBS:.......................................201-337-1033

Ansoft Corp.
Four Station Square Ste. 660
Pittsburgh, PA 15219-1119
Main:.....................................412-261-3200
Tech. Support FAX:.................412-471-9427
E-Mail: ....info@ansoft.com
Web: www.ansoft.com
Web: www.azron.com

Answer Software
20045 Stevens Creek Blvd.
Cupertino, CA 95014
Main:.....................................408-253-7515

Antec Inc.
2859 Bayview Dr.
Fremont, CA 94538
Main:.....................................510-770-1200
Tech. Support:........................510-770-1200
Sales: 510-770-1200
Customer Service:...................510-770-1200
Tech. Support FAX:.................510-770-1288
Web: www.antec-inc.com

Antex Electronics Corp.
16100 S Figueroa St.
Gardena, CA 90248
Main: 800-338-4231
Tech. Support:........................310-532-3092
Customer Service:................... 800-338-4231
Tech. Support FAX: 310-532-8509
E-Mail:...........................antexnews@aol.com
BBS:.......................................310-768-3947
Web: www.antex.com

Anthem Electronics
1160 Ridder Park Dr.
San Jose, CA 95131
Main: 408-453-1200
Tech. Support FAX: 408-441-4504

Aperture Technologies
100 Summit Lake Dr.
Valhalla, NY 10595
Main: 800-346-6828
Tech. Support:........................914-769-7800
FAX: 914-769-8951
E-Mail:............................info@aperture.com
Web: www.aperture.com

Apertus Technologies
2 Penn Plaza
New York, NY 10121
Main: 212-279-8400
FAX: 212-967-8368
BBS:.......................................212-967-8368

Apex Software Corp.
4516 Henry St.
Pittsburgh, PA 15213
Main: 412-681-4343
Tech. Support:........................412-681-4738
Sales:....................................800-858-2739
Tech. Support FAX: 412-681-4384
CompuServe:................................GO APEX
E-Mail:...............................info@apexsc.com
BBS:.......................................412-681-4370
Web: www.apexsc.com

Apex Voice Communications, Inc.
15250 Ventura Blvd. 3rd Floor
Sherman Oaks, CA 91403
Main:.....................................800-727-3970
Tech. Support:.......................818-379-8400
Tech. Support FAX:.................818-379-8410

Apiary Systems
10201 W. Markham Ste. 101
Little Rock, AR 72205
Sales:....................................501-221-3600
FAX: 501-221-7412

Apogee
1901 S. Bascom Ste. 325
Campbell, CA 95008
Main:....................................408-369-9001
FAX: 408-369-9018
E-Mail: .... info@apogee.com

Apogee Technologies
1851 University Pkwy.
Sarasota, FL 34243
Main:....................................813-355-6121
E-Mail: .... apogee@cup.portal.com

Apple Cambridge
Web: www.cambridge.apple.com

Apple Computer, Inc.
1 Infinite Loop
Cupertino, CA 95014-2084
Main:....................................408-974-4897
Sales:....................................408-996-1010
FAX: 408-862-7602
Web: dev.info.apple.com

Apple Computer-Newton Systems Group
1 Infinite Loop
Cupertino, CA 95014
Main:....................................408-996-1010
Tech. Support:.......................800-767-2775
Customer Service:..................800-776-2333
BBS:......................................408-996-0275
Web: www.apple.com

Apple Information
1 Infinite Loop
Cupertino, CA 95014
Main: 408-996-1010
Sales:.................................... 800-769-2775
Web: www.info.apple.com

Apple Island
Main: 354-162-4800
FAX: 354-162-4818
E-Mail:...........................jonpall@apple.is
Web: www.apple.is/

Application Techniques, Inc.
10 Lomar Park Dr.
Pepperell, MA 01463
Main: 508-433-5201
Tech. Support:....................... 508-433-8464
Sales:.................................... 800-433-5201
Customer Service:.................. 508-433-8464
Tech. Support FAX: 508-433-8466
E-Mail:..................... support@pizazz-us.com

Applied Automated Engineering
65 S Main St.Building C
Pennington, NJ 08534
Main: 609-737-6800
FAX: 609-737-9570
Web: www.aae.com

Applied Computer Sciences, Inc.
11807 Northcreek Pkwy S Ste. 102
Bothell, WA 98011
Tech. Support:....................... 206-486-2722
Tech. Support FAX: 206-485-4776

Applied Computer Systems, Inc.
3060 Johnstown-Utica Rd.
Johnstown, OH 43031
Main: 800-237-5465
Tech. Support:....................... 800-237-5465
Tech. Support FAX: 614-892-4838
CompuServe: 72170,3703

Applied Creative Technology, Inc.
2626 Lombardy Ln. Ste. 107
Dallas, TX 75225
Main:....................................800-433-5373
Tech. Support:.........................214-358-4800
Tech. Support FAX:.................214-352-2281

Applied Information Systems, Inc.
100 Europa Dr. Ste. 555
Chapel Hill, NC 27514
Main:....................................800-334-5510
Tech. Support:.........................919-942-7801
Tech. Support FAX:.................919-493-7563
E-Mail:......................................info@ais.com
BBS:...919-493-7563
Web: www.ais.com

Applied Innovation
5800 Innovation Dr.
Dublin, OH 43016
Main:....................................800-247-9482
Sales:....................................800-247-9482
Customer Service:...................614-798-2000
FAX:......................................614-798-1770
Web: www.aiinet.com

Applied Medical Informatics
NFT
2681 Parley's Way Ste. 204
Salt Lake City, UT 84109-1630
Main:....................................801-464-6200
Tech. Support:.........................801-464-6200
Sales:....................................801-464-6200
Customer Service:...................801-464-6200
Tech. Support FAX:.................801-464-6201
E-Mail:..........................info@ami-med.com
Web: www.ami-med.com

Applied Microsystems
5020 148th Ave. NE
Redmond, WA 98073-9702
Main:....................................800-426-3925
Tech. Support FAX:.................206-883-3049
E-Mail:...........................support@amc.com
Web: www.amc.com

Applied Multimedia, Inc.
89 Northill St.
Stamford, CT 06907
Main: 203-3480108

Applied Testing and Technology
59 North Santa Cruz Ave. Ste. U
Los Gatos, CA 95030
Main: 408-399-1930
Tech. Support FAX: 408-399-1931
E-Mail:.............................aptest@aptest.com
Web: www.aptest.com

Arachnae Management, Ltd.
225 E Beaver Creek Rd. Ste. 230
Richmond Hill, ONT L4B 3P4
Canada
Main: 905-771-6166
Tech. Support:.........................905-771-6166
Sales:......................................905-771-6166
Customer Service:...................905-771-6166
Tech. Support FAX: 905-771-6170
E-Mail:.........................ppv@arachnae.com
Web: www.arachnae.com

Arcada-Seagate Software
37 Skyline Dr. Ste. 1101
Lake Mary, FL 32746
Main: 407-333-7500
Tech. Support:.........................407-333-7600
Sales:......................................800-327-2232
Customer Service:...................800-327-2232
Tech. Support FAX: 407-333-7750
FAX: 407-333-7730
CompuServe:...........................GO ARCADA
E-Mail:.........................support@arcada.com
BBS:...407-444-9979
FTP: ftp.arcada.com
Web: www.arcada.com

NOTES ....
....
....
....
....

Arista Enterprises
125 Commerce Dr.
Hauppauge, NY 11788
Main:.....................................516-435-0200
Tech. Support:.......................800-274-7824
Sales:....................................516-435-0200
Customer Service:..................800-274-7824
Tech. Support FAX:................516-435-4545
CompuServe:...........................74404,3334
America Online:..............Keyword Cfcstacey

Arlington Computer Products
851 Commerce Ct.
Buffalo Grove, IL 60089
Main:.....................................847-541-6694
Tech. Support:.......................708-541-6583
Customer Service:..................708-541-6333
Tech. Support FAX:................708-541-6881

Arlington Computer Products, Inc.
1970 Carboy
Mt. Prospect, IL 60056
Main:.....................................847-541-6333
Tech. Support:.......................847-228-1470
Sales:....................................800-548-5105
Customer Service:..................800-548-5105
FAX:......................................847-541-6881
BBS:.....................................708-228-0516

Armadillo Brothers
753 E. 3300 South
Salt Lake City, UT 84116
Main:.....................................801-484-2791
E-Mail:..................... b.bray@genie.geis.com

Artecon
630 S El Camino Real
Carlsbad, CA 92009
Main:.....................................619-931-5500
Tech. Support FAX:................619-931-5527
E-Mail:............................sales@articon.com
Web: www.articon.com

NOTES...
....
....
....
....

Artel Video Systems, Inc.
600 Nickerson Rd.
Marlborough, MA 01752
Main: 800-225-0228
Tech. Support:.......................508-787-3500
Customer Service:..................508-787-3500
FAX: 508-787-3060

Artemus/Computer Sciences Corp.
3702 Pender Dr. Ste. 300
Fairfax, VA 22030
Main: 703-277-1085
Sales:....................................800-477-6648
FAX: 703-277-1053
E-Mail:........................info@artemus-intl.com
BBS: 800-777-7100
Web: www.artemus-intl.com

Artic Technologies International
55 Park St. Ste. 2
Troy, MI 48083
Main: 810-588-7370
BBS: 810-588-1424

Artisoft
2202 N Forbes Blvd.
Tucson, AZ 85745
Main: 520-670-7100
Tech. Support:.......................520-670-7000
Sales:....................................800-846-9726
Customer Service:..................800-846-9726
Tech. Support FAX: 520-670-7101
BBS: 520-884-8648
Web: www.artisoft.com

Asante Technologies
821 Fox Ln.
San Jose, CA 95131
Main: 408-435-8388
Tech. Support:.......................800-622-7464
Sales:....................................800-566-6680
Customer Service:..................800-566-6680
Tech. Support FAX: 408-432-6018
CompuServe: ....GO ASANTE
E-Mail:........................techpubs@asante.com
BBS: 408-432-1416
FTP: ftp.asante.com
Web: www.asante.com

AskSam Systems
PO Box 1428
Perry, FL 32347
Main:....................................904-584-6590
Tech. Support:........................904-584-6590
Sales:..................................800-800-1997
Customer Service:...................904-584-6590
Tech. Support FAX:.................904-584-7481
CompuServe:...........................GO ASKSAM
E-Mail: ....janie@asksam.com
BBS:..................................904-584-8287
Web: www.asksam.com

Aspen Systems Inc.
4026 Youngfield St.
Wheat Ridge, CO 80033-3862
Main:....................................303-431-4606
Tech. Support FAX:.................303-431-7196
E-Mail: ....aspen@aspsys.com
Web: www.aspsys.com

Asymetrix, Corp.
110 110th Ave. NE Ste. 700
Bellevue, WA 98004-5840
Main:....................................206-462-0501
Tech. Support:........................206-637-1600
Sales:..................................800-448-6543
Customer Service:...................206-637-1500
Tech. Support FAX:.................206-455-3071
CompuServe:........................ GO ASYMETRIX
E-Mail: ....support@asymetrix.com
BBS:..................................206-451-1173
FTP: ftp.asymetrix.com
Web: www.asymetrix.com

Atari Corp.
455 S. Mathilda Ave.
Sunnyvale, CA 94089
Main:....................................408-328-0900
FAX:....................................408-328-0909
Web: www.atari.com

Attachmate Corporation
3617 131st Ave. SE
Bellevue, WA 98006
Main: 206-644-4010
Tech. Support:........................800-688-3270
Sales:..................................206-426-6283
Tech. Support FAX: 206-747-9924
FAX: 206-747-9924
Customer Service:...................800-426-6283
CompuServe:................... GO ATTACHMATE
E-Mail:...................support@attachmate.com
BBS:..................................206-649-6660
FTP: gopher://gopher.attachmate.com/
Web: www.attachmate.com

Attain Corp.
48 Grove St.
Summerville, MA 02144
Main: 617-776-1110
Tech. Support:........................617-776-2711
Sales:..................................800-925-5615
Customer Service:...................617-776-1110
Tech. Support FAX: 617-776-1626
E-Mail:...........................support@attain.com
Web: www.attain.com

Attest Systems, Inc.
165 North Redwood Dr. Ste. 150
San Rafael, CA 94903-1969
Main: 415-491-7800
Tech. Support:........................415-491-7811
Sales:..................................800-471-4277
Customer Service:...................415-491-7800
Tech. Support FAX: 415-491-7805
FAX: 415-491-7805
CompuServe:................................GO GASP
America Online:................Keyword Attestsys
E-Mail:........................info@attest-gasp.com
BBS:..................................415-491-7807
Web: www.attest-gasp.com/

Atwater Consulting
12700 Park Central Dr. Ste. 400
Dallas, TX 75251
Main: 214-233-9296
Web: www.mindpath.com

Auspex Systems
5200 Great America
Santa Clara, CA 95054
Main:......................................408-986-2000
Tech. Support:......................800-328-7739
Tech. Support FAX:................408-986-2020
BBS:......................................408-492-0909
Web: www.auspex.com

Austin Computer Systems
10300 Metric Blvd.
Austin, TX 78758
Main:......................................800-752-1577
Tech. Support:......................800-752-4171
Sales:...................................800-752-1577
Customer Service:..................800-752-1577
FAX:......................................512-454-1357
E-Mail:..............sales@ccmail.ipctechinc.com
BBS:......................................512-454-1357
Web: www.austindirect.com

Austin-Hayne Corp.
2000 Alameda De Las Pulgas Ste. 242
San Mateo, CA 94403
Main:......................................415-610-6800
Tech. Support:......................415-809-9920
Sales:...................................800-809-9920
Customer Service:..................415-809-9920
Tech. Support FAX:................415-655-3820
FAX:......................................415-655-3820
Web: www.austin-hayne.com

Autodesk, Inc.
111 McInnis Pkwy.
San Rafael, CA 94903
Main:......................................415-507-5000
Tech. Support:......................415-507-5000
Sales:...................................800-435-7771
Customer Service:..................800-538-6401
Tech. Support FAX:................415-507-5100
FAX:......................................415-507-5100
CompuServe:............................GO ADESK
America Online:................Keyword Autodesk
BBS:......................................415-507-5921
FTP: ftp.autodesk.com
Web: www.autodesk.com

Automap, Inc.
1309 114th Ave. SE Ste. 110
Bellevue, WA 98004-6999
Main: 800-564-6277
Sales:..................................800-564-6277
FAX: 206-455-3667

Automata, Inc.
1200 Severn Way
Sterling, VA 20166-8904
Main: 703-450-2600
Tech. Support FAX: 703-450-5871
E-Mail:......................... sales@automata.com
Web: www.automata.com

Automated Programming Technologies, Inc.
30100 Telegraph Rd. Ste. 402
Bingham Farms, MI 48025-9939
Main: 810-540-9877
Tech. Support FAX: 810-540-0403
E-Mail:......................... support@aptnet.com
Web: www.aptnet.com

AutoSig Systems
PO Box 16505
Irving, TX 75016
Main: 800-843-9235
Tech. Support:...................... 214-258-8033
Sales:..................................800-843-9235
Customer Service:.................. 800-843-9235
Tech. Support FAX: 214-258-1412
BBS: 214-258-1412

Avalan Technology, Inc.
PO Box 6888
Holliston, MA 01746
Main: 508-429-6482
Tech. Support:...................... 800-441-2281
Sales:..................................508-429-6482
Customer Service:.................. 508-429-6482
Tech. Support FAX: 508-429-3179
FAX: 508-429-3179
CompuServe: .... GO AVALAN
E-Mail:........................ tsupport@avalan.com
BBS: 508-429-3671
FTP: FTP: avalan.com
Web: www.avalan.com

Avanti Technology
13492 Research Blvd. Ste. 120-271
Austin, TX 78750
Main:......................................512-335-1168
Customer Service:...................512-335-1168

Avantos Performance Systems
5900 Hollis St. Ste. A
Emeryville, CA 94608
Main:......................................510-654-4600
Tech. Support:........................510-654-4727
Sales:.....................................800-262-6867
Customer Service:...................510-654-4600
Tech. Support FAX:................510-654-1276
FAX:..510-654-1276
CompuServe:......................... GO AVANTOS
America Online:................. avantos@aol.com
E-Mail:............................... avantos@aol.com
BBS:.......................................510-654-1521
Web: www.avantos.com

Avery International
20955 Pathfinder Rd.
Diamond Bar, CA 91765-4000
Main:......................................800-252-8379
Tech. Support:........................214-389-3699
Sales:.....................................800-252-8379
Customer Service:...................800-252-8379
Tech. Support FAX:................800-862-8379
FAX:..909-594-4876
CompuServe:............................... GO AVERY
Web: www.averydennison.com

Avnet Inc.
Main:......................................800-231-4266
Web: www.avnet.com

Award Software International
777 E Middlefield Rd.
Mountain View, CA 94043
Main:......................................415-968-3400
Tech. Support:........................510-440-3740
Sales:.....................................415-968-3400
Tech. Support FAX:................415-968-0594
FAX:..415-968-0274
BBS:.......................................415-968-0249
Web: www.award.com

Axil Computer Inc.
3151 Coronado Dr.
Santa Clara, CA 95054
Main: 800-284-2945
Customer Service:................... 408-486-5976
FAX: 408-654-5718
E-Mail:....................................info@axil.com
Web: www.axil.com

Ax-Systems
130 Pelham Rd. Ste. 3C
New Rochelle, NY 10805
Sales:..................................... 914-633-5127
FAX: 914-633-5146
CompuServe:........................... 715-60,1754
Web: super.sonic.net/ann/delphi/max

Azron, Inc.
4330 La Jolla Village Dr. Ste. 270
San Diego, CA 92122
Main: 619-450-0200
Tech. Support:........................ 609-550-0203
Sales:..................................... 619-450-0200

Aztech New Media Corp.
1 Scarsdale Rd.
Don Mills, ONT M3B 2R2
Canada
Main: 800-494-4787
Sales:..................................... 416-449-4787
Tech. Support FAX: 416-680-8125
FAX: 416-449-1058
CompuServe:............................ 70722,241
E-Mail:............................. anmc@hookup.net
Web: www.aztech.com

B & B Electronics Manufacturing Co.
707 Dayton Rd.
PO Box 1040
Ottawa, IL 61350-9973
Main: 815-433-5100
FAX: 815-434-7094
E-Mail:............................. sales@bb-elec.com
BBS:....................................... 815-434-2927
FTP: FTP: //ftp.bb-elec.com/bb-elec/
Web: www.bb-elec.com

BASF
9 Oak Park Dr.
Beford, MA 01730-1471
Main:......................................617-271-4000
Tech. Support:........................800-225-3326
Sales:.....................................800-356-9006
Customer Service:..................800-356-9006
Tech. Support FAX:................617-275-3069
Web: www.basf.com

BBN Domian
150 Cambridge Park Dr.
Cambridge, MA 02140
Main:......................................617-873-5000
Tech. Support:........................617-873-4020
Sales:.....................................800-331-2266
Customer Service:..................800-772-8737
Tech. Support FAX:................617-873-4020
E-Mail:......................bbn/support@bbn.com
Web: www.bbndomian.com

BBN Planet
Web: www.bbnplanet.com

BC Soft
Sales:.....................................468-657-9190
FAX:......................................468-656-6772

BCAM International
1800 Walt Whitman Rd.
Melville, NY 11747
Main:......................................516-752-3568
Sales:.....................................516-752-3550
Customer Service:..................516-752-3550
Tech. Support FAX:................516-752-3506
E-Mail:............74103,2413@compuserv.com
BBS:......................................516-752-3550

BDT Products
17152 Armstrong Ave.
Irvine, CA 92714
Main:......................................714-660-1386
Tech. Support:........................714-263-6376
Sales:.....................................714-660-1386
Customer Service:..................714-660-1386
BBS:......................................714-263-6378
Web: www.bdt.com

BE Software
1631 NW Johson St.
Portland, OR 97209
E-Mail:......................... info@inflor.com
Web: www.besoft.com

BG Micro Inc.
PO Box 280298
Dallas, TX 75228
Main: 214-271-5546
Tech. Support:........................ 214-271-9834
Sales:.................................... 214-271-5546
Customer Service:................... 214-271-5546
Tech. Support FAX: 214-271-2462
FAX: 214-271-2462
E-Mail:...................bgmicro@ix.netcom.com
BBS: 214-271-2462
Web: www.bgmicro.com

BGL Technology Corp.
1006 W 104th Ave.
Northglenn, CO 80234
Main: 303-451-5005
Tech. Support:........................ 303-404-3397
Sales:.................................... 303-404-3397
Customer Service:................... 303-404-3397
Tech. Support FAX: 303-451-5227
FAX: 303-404-3760
BBS: 303-404-3611

BIX - Byte Information Exchange
1 Phoenix Mill Ln.
Peterborough, NH 03458
Main: 617-491-6642
Tech. Support:........................ 617-354-4137
Sales:.................................... 800-695-4775
Customer Service:................... 800-232-2983
Tech. Support FAX: 603-924-2603
E-Mail:................................editors@bix.com
Web: www.bix.com

BJW Computer Solutions
38 Avondale Dr.
Riverview, NB E1B 1C2
Canada
Sales:.................................... 506-454-4717
E-Mail:..............................BJWall@msn.com

BLAST, Inc.
PO Box 808
Pittsboro, NC 27312
Main:......................................800-242-5278
Tech. Support:........................919-542-3007
Tech. Support FAX:.................919-542-0161
E-Mail: .... sales@blast.com
BBS:......................................919-542-9039
Web: www.blast.com

BSDI
5575 Tech Center Dr. Ste. 110
Colorado Springs, CO 80918
Main:......................................719-593-9445
Tech. Support:........................800-487-2738
Sales: 800-776-2734
Customer Service:...................800-800-4273
Tech. Support FAX:.................719-598-4238
E-Mail: ....bsdi-info@bsdi.com
Web: www.bsdi.com

BTG Inc.
1945 Old Gallows Rd.
Vienna, VA 22182
Main:......................................703-556-6518
Customer Service:...................800-899-6200
Tech. Support FAX:.................703-714-7000
FAX:......................................703-556-9290
E-Mail: ....webmaster@btg.com
Web: www.btg.com

B.Y.O.B.: Build Your Own Business
7285 Franklin Ave.
Los Angeles, CA 90046
Main:......................................213-850-5394
Tech. Support:........................602-941-5602
Sales: 602-941-4789
Tech. Support FAX:.................213-874-5646

Baker & Taylor Entertainment
8501 Telfair Ave.
Sun Valley, CA 91352
Main:......................................818-768-2900
FAX:......................................818-768-4858

Baler Software/TechTools
Applied Cellular Technology
3-I Taggart Dr.
Nashua, NH 03060
Main: 603-888-8400
Tech. Support:........................ 603-888-8400
Sales:................................... 800-501-2677
Customer Service:.................. 603-888-8400
Tech. Support FAX: 603-888-8413
FAX: 603-888-8413
CompuServe:.......................GO TECHTOOLS
E-Mail:......................support@techtools.com
BBS:.. 603-888-8411
Web: www.techtools.com

Bancroft-Whitney
Main: 800-313-9339
E-Mail:......................mcarton@bancroft.com
Web: www.bancroft.com

BancTec Technologies
3701 S.Thomas Rd.
Oklahoma City, OK 73179
Main: 405-686-6200
Tech. Support FAX: 405-686-6366
E-Mail:............................ bti@soonernet.com
Web: www.bti-ok.com/bti/index.html

Bandy Inc.
201 International Rd.
Garland, TX 75042
Main: 214-272-5455
Tech. Support:........................ 214-272-5455
Sales:..................................... 214-272-5455
Customer Service:.................. 214-272-5455
Tech. Support FAX: 214-272-5613
FAX: 214-272-5613
E-Mail:......................... bandyinc@onram.net
Web: www.11rampages.onram.net/~bandyinc/

Banner Blue Software
39500 Stevenson Pl. Ste. 204
Fremont, CA 94539
Main:.............,....................510-794-6850
Tech. Support:........................510-794-6850
Sales:.....................................510-794-6850
Customer Service:...................510-794-6850
Tech. Support FAX:................510-794-9152
FAX: 510-794-9152
CompuServe:...........................:...... 71333,3713
Web: www.familytreemaker.com

Banyan Systems, Inc.
120 Flanders Rd.
Westborough, MA 01581
Main:....................................800-828-2404
Tech. Support:..............508-898-1000-1520
Sales:.....................................818-265-1828
Customer Service:...................800-222-6926
Tech. Support FAX:................800-932-9226
FAX: 508-898-1755
CompuServe:......................GO BAN FORUM
BBS:......................................508-898-1810
Web: www.banyan.com

Barr Systems
4131 NW 28th Ln.
Gainesville, FL 32614-7015
Main:....................................800-227-7797
Tech. Support:........................352-491-3100
Customer Service:...................800-227-7797
Tech. Support FAX:................352-491-3141
E-Mail: ....sales@barrsys.com
BBS:......................................352-491-3148
Web: www.barrsys.com

Baseline Software
PO Box 1219
Sausalito, CA 94966
Main:....................................800-829-9955
Tech. Support:........................415-332-7763
Tech. Support FAX:.................415-332-8032
FAX: 415-332-8032
E-Mail: ....info@baselinesoft.com
BBS:......................................415-332-8039
Web: www.baselinesoft.com/people/infosec

Basic Needs
118 State Pl. Ste. 202
Escondido, CA 92029
Main: 619-738-7020
Tech. Support:.......................800-633-3703
Sales:.....................................619-738-7020
Customer Service:...................800-633-3703
Tech. Support FAX: 619-738-0515
FAX: 619-738-0515

Bay Networks, Inc.
4401 Great America Pkwy.
Sant Clara, CA 95054
Main: 800-231-4213
Sales:....................................800-822-9638
FAX: 800-786-3228
CompuServe: ....GO BAYNET
E-Mail:................ answers@baynetworks.com
Web: www.baynetworks.com

Bay Technical Associates
200 N 2nd St.
PO Box 387
Bay St. Louis, MS 39520
Main: 800-523-2702
Tech. Support:........................601-467-4551
Sales:....................................800-523-2702
Customer Service:...................800-523-2702
Tech. Support FAX: 601-467-4551
BBS: 601-467-4551

Bear River Associates, Inc.
505 14th St., 6th floor
Oakland, CA 94612
Main: 510-824-5300
Tech. Support:........................510-644-9788
CompuServe: ....GO EEARIBER
E-Mail:............................info@bearriver.com
Web: www.bearriver.com

Bear Rock Technologies Corp.
4140 Mother Lode Dr. Ste. 100
Shingle Springs, CA 95682
Main: 916-672-0244
Sales:....................................800-232-7625
FAX: ....:.916-672-1103
Web: www.bearrock.com

Belkin Components
1303 Walnut Pkwy.
Compton, CA 90220
Main:.....................................310-898-1100
Tech. Support:........................310-898-1100
Sales:.....................................310-898-1100
Customer Service:...................310-898-1100
Tech. Support FAX:.................213-898-1111
Web: www.belkinc&msn.com

Bell Atlantic Corp.
1500 Maccorkle Ave.
Charleston, WV 25314
Main:.....................................800-621-9900
Tech. Support:........................703-974-3000
Sales:.....................................800-621-9900
Customer Service:...................800-621-9900
Tech. Support FAX:.................800-903-1122
Web: www.bell'atl.com

Bennet-Tec Information Systems
50 Jericho Turnpike
Jericho, NY 11753
Sales:.....................................516-997-5596
FAX:.......................................516-997-5597
E-Mail: .... controls@bennett-tec.com
Web: www.bennet-tec.com/

Bentley Systems
690 Pennsylvania Dr.
Exton, PA 19341
Main:.....................................610-458-5000
Sales:.....................................800-236-8539
Customer Service:...................800-236-8539
Tech. Support FAX:.................610-458-1060
FAX:.......................................610-458-1060
E-Mail: .... info@bentley.com
Web: www.bentley.com

Berg Electronics
825 Old Trail Rd.
Etters, PA 17319
Main:.....................................717-938-6711
Tech. Support:........................717-938-1753
Sales:.....................................800-237-2374
Tech. Support FAX:.................717-938-7604
Web: www.bergelect.com

Berkeley Systems Design
2095 Rose St.
Berkeley, CA 94709
Main: 510-540-5535
Tech. Support:........................510-540-5535
Sales:.....................................510-540-5535
Customer Service:...................510-540-5535
Tech. Support FAX: 510-540-5630
E-Mail:..............................tech@berksys.com
Web: www.berksys.com

Best Computers Supplies
690 Kresge Ln. Ste. 101
Sparks, NV 89431
Main: 800-544-3472
Sales:.....................................800-544-3472
Customer Service:...................800-544-3472
Tech. Support FAX: 800-829-4881
FAX: 702-331-5352
E-Mail:.........................bestcomsup@aol.com

Best Data Products
21800 Nordoff St.
Chatsworth, CA 91311
Main: 818-773-9600
Tech. Support:........................818-773-9600
Sales:.....................................818-773-9600
Customer Service:...................818-773-9600
Tech. Support FAX: 818-717-1721
CompuServe:........................GO BEST DATA
America Online:...............bestdata@aol.com
E-Mail:.........................admin@bestdata.com
BBS:......................................818-773-3943
Web: www.bestdata.com

Best Power Technology
General Signal
N246
PO Box 280
Necedah, WI 54646
Main:.................................608-565-7200
Tech. Support:.......................800-356-5737
Sales:...............................800-356-5794
Customer Service:...................608-565-2100
Tech. Support FAX:.................608-565-2221
FAX: 800-487-6813
E-Mail:.tech.support@bestpower.gensig.com
BBS:...608-565-7424
Web: www.bestpower.com

BestWare
300 Roundhill Dr.
Rockaway, NJ 07866
Main:.................................800-322-6962
Tech. Support:.......................800-322-6962
FAX: 201-586-8885
CompuServe:................................ GO MYOB
America Online:....................Keyword MYOB
E-Mail: ....njcustserv@bestware.com
Web: www.bestware.com

Better Business Systems
7949 Woodly Ave.
Van Nuys, CA 91406
Main:.................................818-376-1558
Tech. Support:.......................818-407-5111
Sales:...............................800-829-9991
Customer Service:...................818-376-1558
Tech. Support FAX:.................818-376-1581

Bible Research Systems
2013 Wells Branch Pkwy. Ste. 304
Austin, TX 78728
Main:.................................800-423-1228
Tech. Support:.......................512-251-7541
Customer Service:...................800-423-1228
Tech. Support FAX:.................512-251-4401
CompuServe:............................ 72203,2004
E-Mail: ....bible@brs-inc.com
Web: www.brs-inc.com/bible

Big Top Productions
548 Fourth St.
San Francisco, CA 94107
Main: 415-978-5363
Sales:...................................800-900-7529
FAX: 415-978-5353
Web: www.bigtop.com

Bill White Software Creations
3117 Raymond Dr.
Atlanta, GA 30340
Sales:................................ 800-242-4775
FAX: 713-524-6398
CompuServe: 73612,3477
FTP: ftp.is.net/pub/csm/
Web: www.destek.net/cybermkt/blwhite.htm

Biscom
321 Billerica
Chelmsford, MA 01824
Main: 800-477-2472
Customer Service:...................508-250-8355
BBS: 508-250-4795
Web: www.biscom.com

Bitstream
215 First St.
Cambridge, MA 02142
Main: 617-497-6222
Tech. Support:.......................617-497-7514
Sales:................................... 800-522-3668
Customer Service:...................800-223-3176
Tech. Support FAX: 617-828-0784
E-Mail:........................... sales@bitstream.com
Web: www.bitstream.com

Black Ice Software, Inc.
113 Route 122
Amherst, NH 03031
Sales:....................................603-673-1019
FAX: 603-672-4112
BBS: 603-673-6617

Blizzard Entertainment
PO Box 18077
Irvine, CA 92713
Main:....................................714-955-1380
Tech. Support:........................714-955-1382
Sales:....................................800-953-7669
CompuServe:........................... 74537,2505
America Online:..............Keyword Blizzrdent

Blossom Software Corp.
1 Kendall Square, Building 600
PO Box 9171
Cambridge, MA 02139
Main:....................................617-738-1516
E-Mail:......................support@blossom.com

Blue Lance Software, Inc.
1700 W Loop S Ste. 1100
Houston, TX 77027
Main:....................................713-680-1187
Tech. Support FAX:.................713-622-1370
CompuServe:........................... 71333,1526
E-Mail:.........................sales@bluelance.com

Blue Ocean Software
15310 Amerly Dr. Ste. 250
Tampa, FL 33647
Main:....................................813-977-4553
Tech. Support FAX:.................813-979-4447
CompuServe:......................... GO NOVUSER
BBS:....................................813-979-4447
Web: www.blueocean.com

Blue Sky Software Corp.
7777 Fay Ave.
La Jolla, CA 92037
Main:....................................619-551-2485
Tech. Support:........................619-551-5680
Sales:....................................800-677-4946
Tech. Support FAX:.................619-551-2486
FAX:....................................614-551-2486
E-Mail:............................. info@bluesky.com
Web: www.bluesky.com

Blue Star Marketing
2312 Central Ave. NE
Minneapolis, MN 55418
Main: 800-950-8884
Tech. Support:........................ 612-788-3711
FAX: 612-788-3442
E-Mail:...........................sales@blue-star.com
Web: www.blue-star.com

Blyth Software, Inc.
989 E. Hillsdale Blvd. Ste. 400
Foster City, CA 94404
Main: 415-571-0222
Tech. Support:........................ 415-570-2220
Sales:................................... 800-346-6647
FAX: 415-571-1132
CompuServe:........................... 713-33,2525
E-Mail:...........................us_sales@bylth.com
Web: www.bylth.com

Boca Research, Inc.
1377 Clint Moore Rd.
Boca Raton, FL 33487-2722
Main: 407-997-6227
Tech. Support:........................ 407-241-8088
Sales:................................... 407-997-6227
Customer Service:.................. 407-241-8088
Tech. Support FAX: 407-994-5848
CompuServe:................................GO BOCA
E-Mail:................................support@boca.org
BBS:................................... 407-241-1601
FTP: ftp.boca.org
Web: www.boca.org

Bofo Technologies
62 Mountain Rd.
Pleasantville, NY 10570
Main: 914-747-4201
Sales:................................... 800-552-9157
FAX: 914-747-9115

Bokler Software
1570 Pacheco Ste. E-4
Santa Fe, NM 87505
Sales: 505-984-2226
FAX: 505-989-5089
E-Mail: .... info@bokler.com
FTP: ftp.bokler.com
Web: www.bokler.com/bokler

Books That Work
2300 Geng Rd., Building 3, Ste. 100
Palo Alto, CA 94303-0930
Main:.....................................415-326-4280
Tech. Support:.......................415-617-9663
Sales: 800-242-4546
Customer Service:.................415-843-4440
Tech. Support FAX:................415-812-9700
BBS:......................................415-326-2913
Web: www.btw.com

Border Network Technologies, Inc.
20 Toronto St. Ste. 400
Toronto, ONT M5C 2B8
Canada
Main:.....................................416-368-7157
Tech. Support FAX:................416-368-7789
E-Mail: .... info@border.com
Web: www.border.com

Borland International
100 Borland Way
Scotts Valley, CA 95066
Main:.....................................408-431-1000
Tech. Support:.......................800-841-8180
Sales: 408-431-1000
Customer Service:.................408-461-9000
Tech. Support FAX:................408-657-0816
CompuServe:.........................GO BORLAND
E-Mail: .... customer-support@borland.com
BBS:......................................408-431-5096
FTP: ftp.borland.com/pub/techinfo/
Web: www.borland.com

Bottom Line Distribution
4544 S Lamar Ste. B100
Austin, TX 78745
Main: 512-892-4070
FAX: 512-892-4455
Web: www.blol.com

Bradly Corporation
Two Executive Dr.
Chelmsford, MA 01824
Main: 506-937-3700
Sales:...................................800-366-2372
FAX: 506-453-2462

Brainstorm Technologies, Inc.
24 Thorndike St
Cambridge, MA 02141
FAX: 617-492-9126

Bravo Communications, Inc.
1310 Tully Rd. Ste. 107
San Jose, CA 95122
Main: 408-297-8700
Tech. Support:.......................408-297-8700
Sales:...................................800-366-0297
Customer Service:.................408-297-8700
Tech. Support FAX: 408-297-8701
E-Mail:............ bravobravo@usa.pipeline.com

Bristol Technology, Inc.
241 Ethan Allen Highway
Ridgefield, CT 06877
Main: 203-438-6969
Tech. Support FAX: 203-438-5013
E-Mail:................................info@bristol.com
Web: www.bristol.com

Broderbund Software, Inc.
500 Redwood Blvd.
PO Box 6121
Novato, CA 94948-6121
Main:......................................415-382-4400
Tech. Support:........................415-382-3000
Sales:....................................800-521-6263
Customer Service:..................800-521-6263
Tech. Support FAX:.................415-382-4419
FAX:.......................................415-382-4419
CompuServe:.....................................GO BB
America Online:..................bbund@aol.com
E-Mail:................ support@broderbund.com
BBS:.......................................415-883-5889
Web: www.broderbund.com

Brother International Corp.
200 Cottontail Ln.
Somerset, NJ 08875
Main:......................................908-356-8880
BBS:.......................................201-469-4415
Web: www.brother.com.

Bryant Software
PO Box 102216
Benver, CO 80250
Main:......................................303-733-3116
Customer Service:..................303-733-3116
Tech. Support FAX:.................303-777-2876
E-Mail:..........................support@bryant.com
Web: www.bryant.com

Buffalo, Inc.
2805 19th St. SE
Salem, OR 97302-1520
Main:......................................800-345-2356
Tech. Support:........................503-585-4174
Tech. Support FAX:.................503-585-4505
E-Mail:............................sales@buffing.com
BBS:.......................................503-585-5797
Web: www.buffinc.com

Bug Bee
121 Freeport Rd.
Pittsburgh, PA 15238
Main:......................................412-828-5480
Sales:....................................800-851-3780
FAX:.......................................412-828-8987

Building Block Software
49 Waltham St.
Lexington, MA 02173
Main:....................................617-860-9091
Tech. Support:........................617-860-9091
Tech. Support FAX:...............617-860-9066
CompuServe:.............................. 70471,734
E-Mail:............ 70471,734@compuserve.com
Web: www.icp.com/buildingblock

Bull Inc.
300 Concord Rd.
Billerica, MA 01821
Main:................................... 508-294-6000
Tech. Support:........................208-967-5000
Sales:....................................508-294-5600
Customer Service:..................208-967-5000
Web: www.wang.com

Bulldog Computers
851 Commerce Ct.
Buffalo Grove, IL 60089
Main:................................... 800-438-6039
Tech. Support:........................847-541-2394
Tech. Support FAX:...............708-541-6988

Bus-Tech, Inc.
Storage Tech
129 Middlesex Turnpike
Burlington, MA 01803
Main:................................... 617-272-8200
FAX:...................................... 617-272-0342
BBS:.......................................617-273-2392
Web: www.bustech.com

Business Forecast Systems, Inc.
68 Leonard St.
Belmont, MA 02178
Main:................................... 617-484-5050
Tech. Support FAX:................617-484-9219
CompuServe:............................. 76773,1634
E-Mail:.......... 76773,1634@compuserve.com
Web: ourworld.compuserve.com/homepages
   /forecasepro

BusTek Corp.
4151 Burton Dr.
Santa Clara, CA 95054-1564
Main:.....................................408-492-9090
Tech. Support:........................408-654-0760
Sales: 408-492-9090
Tech. Support FAX:.................408-492-1542
FAX: 408-492-1542
E-Mail: ....techsup@buslogic.com
BBS:.......................................408-492-1984
Web: www.buslogic.com

Byte/Wide Software
PO Box 1778
DeLand, FL 32721
Main:.....................................904-738-4923
Tech. Support FAX:.................904-736-7635
Web: www.totcon.com/bytewide

Bytex Corp.
4 Technology Dr.
West Borough, MA 01581-1760
Main:.....................................508-480-0840
Tech. Support:........................508-480-0840
Sales: 800-232-9839
Customer Service:............800-227-114-5260
FAX: 508-366-7977
BBS:.......................................508-481-5111

C-Cor Electronics
60 Decibel Rd.
State College, PA 16801
Main:.....................................800-233-2267
Tech. Support:........................814-238-2461
Tech. Support FAX:.................814-238-4065

C-Lab/DigiDesign
Avid Technology, Inc.
3401-A Hillview Ave.
Palo Alto, CA 94304
Main:.....................................415-842-7900
Tech. Support:........................415-842-6699
Sales: 800-333-2137
Customer Service:..................415-842-6699
Tech. Support FAX:.................415-856-4275
FAX: 609-514-1818
Web: www.digidesign.com

CABLIExpress
500 E Brighton Ave.
Syracuse, NY 13210
Main: 315-476-3000
Sales:.....................................315-476-3000
Customer Service:..................315-476-3100
FAX: 315-476-3034
E-Mail:............techsupport@cablexpress.com

CAD & Graphics Computers
1175 Chess Dr. Ste. C
Foster City, CA 94404
Main: 800-288-1611
Tech. Support FAX: 415-378-6414

CAW
323 Lee Pl.
Ellmore, NY 11710
Main: 516-781-2799
Sales:.....................................800-303-9111

CD Connection
5805 State Bridge Rd.
Duluth, GA 30155
Main: 770-446-1332
Tech. Support:........................800-344-8426
Sales:.....................................800-344-8426
Customer Service:..................800-344-8426
Tech. Support FAX: 770-446-9164
FAX: 800-344-8426
BBS: 770-446-5535

CD Technology
762 San Aleso Ave.
Sunnyvale, CA 94086
Main: 408-752-8500
Tech. Support:........................408-752-8500
Sales:.....................................408-752-8500
Customer Service:..................408-752-8500
Tech. Support FAX: 408-752-8501
CompuServe: 71762,3512

CE Software, Inc.
1801 Industrial Circle
West Des Moines, IA 50265
Main:.....................................515-221-1801
Tech. Support:........................515-221-1803
Sales: 800-523-7638
Customer Service:..................800-523-7638
FAX:......................................515-221-2694
America Online:...........Keyword CE Software
E-Mail: ....sales@cesoft.com
FTP: ftp.cesoft.com
Web: www.cesoft.com

CGI Systems, Inc.
1301 Lindenwood Dr. Ste. 215
Malvern, PA 19355
Main:.....................................800-722-1866
Tech. Support:........................914-735-5030
Sales: 610-993-8082
Tech. Support FAX:................914-735-2231
FAX:......................................610-993-8125
BBS:......................................914-735-2231

CH Products
970 Park Center Dr.
Vista, CA 92083
Main:.....................................619-598-2518
Tech. Support:........................619-598-2518
Sales: 800-624-5804
Customer Service:..................800-624-5804
Tech. Support FAX:................619-598-2524
E-Mail: ....tech@chproducts.com
BBS:......................................619-598-3224
Web: www.chproducts.com
Web: www.cyrix.com

CIE America, Inc.
2701 Dow Ave.
Tustin, CA 92680
Main:.....................................800-877-1421
BBS:......................................714-573-2645
Web: www.citoh.com

CMS Enhancements
1051 S East St.
Anaheim, CA 92805
Main: 714-517-0915
Sales:....................................800-555-1671
Customer Service:..................800-555-1671
FAX: 714-445-5365

CNet Technology, Inc.
2199 Zanker Rd.
San Jose, CA 95131
Main: 408-954-8000
Tech. Support:........................408-954-8800
Sales:....................................408-954-8800
Customer Service:..................408-954-8800
Tech. Support FAX: 408-954-8866
FAX: 408-954-8866
E-Mail:............................support@cnet.com
BBS:......................................408-954-1787
Web: www.cnet.com.tw

CPU
1120 Kaibab
Flagstaff, AZ 86001
Main: 602-779-3341
Tech. Support FAX: 602-779-5998
BBS:......................................602-779-5998

CSS Laboratories, Inc.
1641 McGaw Ave.
Irvine, CA 92714
Main: 714-852-8161
Tech. Support:........................800-966-2771
Sales:....................................714-852-8161
Customer Service:..................800-966-2771
Tech. Support FAX: 714-852-9212
BBS:......................................714-852-9231

CTX International
20470 Walnut Dr.
Walnut, CA 91789
Main: 909-595-6146
Tech. Support:........................800-888-2120
Sales:....................................909-598-8094
Customer Service:..................800-888-2017
FAX: 909-595-6293
BBS:......................................214-242-8730
Web: www.ctxintl.com

CXR
Microtel International
2040 Fortune Dr.
San Jose, CA 95131
Main:...................................800-537-5762
Customer Service:.................408-435-8520
Tech. Support FAX:................408-435-5556
FAX: 408-435-1276

CYMA Solutions
330 W. University Dr. Ste. 7
Tempe, AZ 85281
Main:...................................800-292-2962
Tech. Support:.......................602-831-2607
Tech. Support FAX:................602-303-2969
BBS:....................................602-345-5703

Caci Products
Caci, Inc.
3333 N Torrey Pines Ct.
La Jolla, CA 92037
Main:...................................619-457-9681
Tech. Support:.......................619-455-6300
Tech. Support FAX:................619-457-1184
Web: www.paciasl.com

Cadco
2363 Merritt Dr.
Garland, TX 75041
Main:...................................800-877-2288
Tech. Support:.......................214-271-3651
Tech. Support FAX:................214-271-3654
BBS:....................................214-271-3654

Cadkey, Inc.
4 Griffin Rd. N
Windsor, CT 06095-1511
Main:...................................203-298-8888
Customer Service:..........203-298-8888 #830
FAX: 860-298-6590
BBS:....................................203-298-6405

Caere Corp.
100 Cooper Court
Los Gatos, CA 95030
Main:...................................408-395-7000
Tech. Support:.......................408-395-8319
Sales:.................................800-535-7226
FAX:...................................408-354-2743
BBS: 408-395-1631
Web: www.caere.com

California Microwave Network Systems
California Microwave
4000 Greenbriar Ste. 100-A
Stafford, TX 77477
Main: 713-263-6500
Tech. Support FAX: 713-263-6400

California Software Products
525 N Cabrillo Park Dr., 3rd Floor
Santa Ana, CA 92701
Main: 714-973-0440
Tech. Support:.......................714-973-0440
Sales:.................................800-841-1532
Tech. Support FAX: 714-558-9341
FAX: 714-558-9341
CompuServe: 74644,3140
BBS: 714-558-9341

Caligari Corporation
1935 Landings Dr.
Mountain View, CA 94043
Main: 800-351-7620
Tech. Support:.......................800-351-7620
Customer Service:..................415-390-9600
FAX: 415-390-9755
Web: www.calgari.com

Calliope Media
1526 Cloverfield Blvd.
Santa Monica, CA 90404
Main: 310-829-1100
FAX: 310-829-7044
E-Mail:...........................magic@calliope.com
Web: www.calliope.com

Cambridge Soft Corp.
875 Massachusetts Ave.
Cambridge, MA 02139
Main:......................................617-491-2200
Tech. Support FAX:.................617-491-7203
FAX:...617-491-8208
CompuServe:.............................. 76070,615
America Online:.................Keyword Camsoft
E-Mail: ....support@camsoft.com
Web: www.camsci.com

Cambrix Publishing, Inc.
9304 Deering Ave.
Chatsworth, CA 91311
Main:......................................818-993-4274
Tech. Support:........................818-993-4274
Tech. Support FAX:.................818-993-6201
CompuServe:.......................... 102466,2622
E-Mail: ....askcambrix@aol.com
Web: www.movieweb.com

Cameo Network
1920 W Corporate Way
PO Box 61022
Anaheim, CA 92803-6122
Main:......................................714-533-8910
Tech. Support FAX:.................714-533-8642
BBS:..714-533-8642

Camintonn Z-RAM
22 Morgan
Irvine, CA 92718-2022
Main:......................................714-454-1500
Tech. Support:.................714-454-1500-347
Sales: 800-368-4726
Customer Service:............714-454-1500-347
Tech. Support FAX:.................714-830-4726
FAX:..714-830-4726

Campbell Services Inc.
21700 NorthWestern Hwy. 10th Floor
Southfield, MI 48075
Main: 810-559-5955
Tech. Support:........................ 810-559-5955
Sales: 810-559-5955
Customer Service:.................. 810-559-5955
Tech. Support FAX: 810-559-1034
CompuServe:............................GO ONTIME
E-Mail:........................support@ontime.com
BBS:...................................... 810-559-6434
Web: www.ontime.com

Canary Communications Inc.
1851 Zanker Rd.
San Jose, CA 95112-4610
Main: 408-453-9201
Sales:..................................... 800-883-9201
Tech. Support FAX: 408-453-0940
BBS:....................................... 408-453-0940

Canoga Perkins
21012 Lassen St.
Chatsworth, CA 91311
Main: 818-718-6300
Tech. Support:........................ 818-718-6300
Sales:..................................... 818-718-6300
Customer Service:.................. 800-360-6642
Tech. Support FAX: 818-718-6312
FAX: 818-718-6312
E-Mail:.............................fiber@canoga.com
Web: www.canoga.com

Canon Computer Systems
2995 Red Hill Ave.
Costa Mesa, CA 92626-5048
Main: 714-438-3000
Tech. Support:........................ 800-423-2366
Sales:..................................... 800-848-4123
Customer Service:.................. 714-438-3391
Tech. Support FAX: 800-922-9068
CompuServe:............................ GO CANON
E-Mail:............................pr@ccsi.canon.com
Web: www.ccsi.canon.com

Canon USA - Printer Division
1 Canon Plaza
Lake Success, NY 11042
Main:......................................516-488-6700
Tech. Support:......................516-488-6700
Sales:...................................800-221-3333
Customer Service:..................800-221-3333
Tech. Support FAX:................516-328-4369
FAX: 516-328-4409
CompuServe:............................ GO CANON
E-Mail: ....info@cusa.canon.com
Web: www.usa.canon.com

Capital Equipment Corp.
900 Middlesex Turnpike
Billerica, MA 01821
Main:......................................800-234-4232
Tech. Support:......................508-663-2002
Sales:...................................800-234-4232
Customer Service:..................800-234-4232
Tech. Support FAX:................508-663-2626
E-Mail: ....info@cec488.com
Web: www.cec488.com

Capstone
INTRACORP
501 Brickell Key Dr. Ste. 600
Miami, FL 33131
Main:.....................................305-373-7700
Tech. Support:......................305-373-3770
Sales:...................................305-373-7700
Customer Service:..................305-373-7700
Tech. Support FAX:................305-577-9875
CompuServe:........................GO CAPSTONE
America Online:.............. Keyword Capstone
E-Mail:...........................Info@intracorp.com
FTP: ftp.gate.net/pur/users/intracor
Web: www.intracorp.com

Cardinal Technologies
1827 Freedom Rd.
Lancaster, PA 17601
Main: 717-293-3000
Tech. Support:........................ 717-293-3124
Sales: 717-293-3049
Customer Service:.................. 717-293-2605
Tech. Support FAX: 717-293-3043
FAX: 717-293-3055
E-Mail:.........................techs@cardtech.com
BBS: 717-293-3074
Web: www.cardtech.com

Carnegie Group
Five PPG Pl.
Pittsburgh, PA 15222
Main: 800-284-3424
Tech. Support FAX: 412-642-6906
E-Mail:................................... info@cgi.com
Web: www.cgi.com

Castelle
3255-3 Scott Blvd.
Santa Clara, CA 95054
Main: 408-496-0474
Tech. Support:........................ 408-496-0474
Customer Service:.................. 408-496-0474
Tech. Support FAX: 408-492-1338
CompuServe: ....GO CASTELLE
BBS: 408-496-1807
Web: www.castelle.com

Catenary Systems
470 Belleview
St. Louis, MO 63119
Sales:.................................... 314-962-7833
FAX: 314-962-8037
E-Mail:......................... victor@catenary.com
Web: www.catenary.com/victor

Cawthon Software Group
24224 Michigan Ave.
Dearborn, MI 48124-1897
Main:......................................313-565-4000
Tech. Support:.......................313-565-4000
Tech. Support FAX:................313-565-4001
FAX:.......................................313-565-4001
E-Mail: ....support@chipchat.com
Web: www.chipchat.com

Cayman Systems
100 Maple St.
Stoneham, MA 02180
Main:......................................617-279-1101
Tech. Support:.......................617-279-1101
Sales: 800-473-4776
Customer Service:..................617-279-1101
Tech. Support FAX:................617-438-5560
FAX:.......................................617-438-5560
E-Mail: ....info@cayman.com
BBS:......................................617-494-9270
FTP: ftp.cayman.com
Web: www.cayman.com

Central Data Inc.
Champagne, IL
Main:......................................800-482-0315
Tech. Support:.......................800-482-0315
Sales: 800-482-0315
Customer Service:..................800-482-0315
Tech. Support FAX:................217-359-6904
E-Mail: ....sales@cd.com
FTP: ftp.cd.com
Web: www.cd.com

Central Design Systems Inc.
223 River St. Ste. C
Santa Cruz, CA 95060
Main:......................................408-458-2600
Tech. Support:.......................408-458-2600
Sales: 408-327-9800
Customer Service:..................408-458-2600
Tech. Support FAX:................408-458-2664
E-Mail: ....info@cendes.com
Web: www.cendes.com

Central Point Software
Symantec
10201 Torre Ave.
Cupertino, CA 95014-2132
Main: 408-253-9600
Tech. Support:.......................800-491-2764
Sales: 800-278-6657
Customer Service:................800-441-7234
Tech. Support FAX: 800-554-4403
CompuServe:........................GO SYMANTEC
America Online:............Keyword Symantec
BBS:.......................................503-984-5366
Web: www.symantec.com

Central Technologies, Inc.
387 Zachary Ave. Building 103
Moorpark, CA 93021
Main: 805-532-9165
Tech. Support:.......................805-532-9171
Sales:...................................800-838-6423
Customer Service:................805-532-9171
Tech. Support FAX: 805-532-9174
FAX: 805-532-9174
E-Mail:.......................sales@centraltech.com
BBS:.......................................805-532-9181
Web: www.centraltech.com

Century Software
5284 South Commerce Dr. Ste. C 134
Salt Lake City, UT 84107
Main: 801-268-3088
Tech. Support:.......................801-268-3088
Sales:...................................800-877-3088
Customer Service:................800-877-3088
Tech. Support FAX: 801-268-0642
FAX: 801-268-2772
CompuServe:..........................GO CENTURY
E-Mail:...............................sales@censoft.com
BBS:.......................................801-266-0330
FTP: ftp.censoft.com
Web: www.censoft.com

Cerfnet
PO Box. 919014
San Diego, CA 92191-9014
Main: 800-876-2373
Sales:...................................619-455-3900
FAX: 619-455-3990

Cerveau Inc.
1213 Saint Catherine St. E
Montreal, PQ H2L 2H1
Canada
Main:.....................................514-525-7776
Sales: 514-525-7776
Customer Service:...................514-525-7776
FAX: 514-525-8570

Charles River Analytics
55 Wheeler St.
Cambridge, MA 01238
Main:....................................617-491-3474
Tech. Support:........................617-491-3474
Sales: 617-491-3474
Customer Service:...................617-491-3474
Tech. Support FAX:................617-868-0780
CompuServe:............................ GO SESAME
America Online:.......... Keyword openSesame
E-Mail: ....sales@cra.com
Web: www.opensesame.com

Chase Research, Inc.
545 Marriott Dr. Ste. 100
Nashville, TN 37210
Main:....................................615-872-0770
Tech. Support:........................615-872-0770
Sales: 800-242-7387
Tech. Support FAX:................615-872-0771
FAX: 615-872-0771
E-Mail: ....support@chaser.com
BBS:.....................................615-872-0771
FTP: ftp.chaser.com
Web: www.chaser.com

Chatcom, Inc.
9600 Topanga Canyon Blvd.
Chatsworth, CA 91311
Main:....................................818-709-1778
Tech. Support:........................800-282-2428
Sales: 800-456-1333
FAX: 818-882-9134
Web: www.jlchatcom.com

CheckMark Software
724 Whalers Way
Builidng "H"
Fort Collins, CO 80525
Main: 970-225-0522
Tech. Support:........................970-225-0387
Sales:.....................................800-444-9922
Customer Service:...................800-444-9922
Tech. Support FAX: 970-225-0611
FAX: 970-225-0611
E-Mail:.....................checkmark@fortnet.com
Web: www.checkmark.com

Cheetah Computer Systems, Inc.
3928 S Broadway
Tyler, TX 75701
Main: 903-581-7272
Tech. Support:........................214-757-3001
Sales:.....................................800-243-3824
Customer Service:...................800-243-3824

Cheyenne Software
3 Expressway Plaza
Roslyn Heights, NY 11577
Main: 516-465-4000
Tech. Support:........................800-243-9832
Sales:.....................................800-243-9462
Customer Service:...................516-465-4000
Tech. Support FAX: 516-465-5115
CompuServe: ....GO CHEYENNE
BBS: 516-465-3900
FTP: ftp.cheyenne.com
Web: www.cheyenne.com

Chi Corp.
31200 Carter St.
Solon, OH 44139
Main: 800-828-0599
Sales:.....................................216-349-8605
FAX: 216-349-8609
Web: www.goshen.net/chi/chi.html

Chi/Cor Information Management Inc.
300 S Wacker Dr.
Chicago, IL 60606
Main:......................................800-448-8777
Tech. Support:.......................312-322-0150
Tech. Support FAX:.................312-322-0161
FAX:.......................................312-322-0161
E-Mail: ....chicor1@aol.com
BBS:......................................312-322-0161

Chicago Computer Works
1362 N. Cleveland Ave.
Chicago, IL 60610
Main:.....................................312-280-9378

Children's Software Revue
44 Main St.
Flemington, NJ 08822
Main:.....................................908-284-0404
Customer Service:..................415-382-1818
Tech. Support FAX:.................908-284-0405
FAX:.......................................415-382-1717
Web: www.microweb.com/pepsite/Revue/revue

Chinon America
615 Hawaii Ave.
Torrance, CA 90503
Main:.....................................310-533-0274
Tech. Support:.......................310-533-0274
Sales:.....................................310-533-0274
Customer Service:..................310-533-0274
Tech. Support FAX:.................310-533-1727
BBS:......................................310-320-4160

Chipcom Corp. (3 Com)
118 Turnpike Rd.
Southborough, MA 01772
Main:.....................................800-228-9930
Tech. Support:.......................508-460-8900
Sales:.....................................408-980-8204
Customer Service:..................800-638-3260
BBS:......................................508-460-8950
Web: www.chipcom.com

Chips & Technologies, Inc.
3050 Zanker Rd.
San Jose, CA 95134
Main: 408-434-0600
Tech. Support:.......................408-894-2085
Sales:.....................................408-434-0600
Customer Service:..................408-434-0600
BBS:......................................408-526-2260
Web: www.chips.com

Chuck Stuart
2204 Camp David
Mesquite, TX 75149-1920
E-Mail:..................... cstuart@metronet.com
FTP: ftp.apexsc.com/pub/cgvb/coop/cstuart
Web: www.apexsc.com/vb/ftp/coop/cstuart

Cincinnati Microwave Escort Store
5200 Ertel Field Rd.
Cincinnati, OH 45249
Sales:..................................... 800-433-3487
Customer Service:.................. 513-489-5400
E-Mail:..................... webmaster@cnmw.com
Web: www.cnmw.com

Ciprico, Inc.
2800 Campus Dr. Ste. 60
Plymouth, MN 55441
Main: 800-727-4669
Tech. Support:....................... 800-727-4669
Sales:..................................... 800-727-4669
Customer Service:.................. 800-727-4669
FAX: 612-551-4002
BBS:...................................... 612-551-4002

Circuit Technology
E-Mail:.................. Webmaster@halcyon.com
Web: www.halcyon.com/sverne/home.html

Cirrus Logic
3100 W Warren Ave.
Fremont, CA 94538
Main: 510-623-8300
FAX: 510-252-6020
Web: www.cirrus.com

Cisco Systems
170 W. Tasman
San Jose, CA 95134
Main:......................................800-553-6387
BBS:......................................714-752-8389
Web: www.cisco.com

Citadel Systems Inc.
1300 Post Oak Blvd., 9th Floor
Houston, TX 77023
Main:......................................800-962-0701
Tech. Support:.........................800-962-0701
Sales:.....................................800-962-0701
Customer Service:....................800-962-0701
Tech. Support FAX:.................713-686-6495
FAX:......................................713-686-6495
CompuServe:...........................73541,2014
America Online:...............Keyword CitadelCS
E-Mail:.........................contact@citadel.com
FTP: ftp.citadel.com
Web: www.citadel.com

Citel America
1111 Park Centre Blvd. Ste. 4707
Miami, FL 33169
Main:......................................305-621-0022
Tech. Support:.........................305-621-0022
Sales:.....................................305-621-0022
Customer Service:....................305-621-0022
Tech. Support FAX:.................305-621-0766
E-Mail:.................citel4u@1x.net.com.com
Web: www.emi.net/~asp/citel

Citizen America
2450 Broadway Ste. 600
Santa Monica, CA 90404-3060
Main:......................................310-453-0614
Tech. Support:.........................310-453-0614
Sales:.....................................815-455-4050
Customer Service:....................310-453-0614
Tech. Support FAX:.................310-453-2814
BBS:......................................310-603-0699
Web: www.citizen-america.com

Citrix Systems, Inc.
210 University Dr. Ste. 700
Coral Springs, FL 33071
Main: 800-437-7503
Tech. Support:........................ 305-755-0559
BBS: 954-346-9004
Web: www.citrix.com

Claris Corp.
5201 Patrick Henry Dr.
PO Box 58168
Santa Clara, CA 95052-8168
Main: 408-987-7000
Tech. Support:........................ 408-727-9004
Sales:..................................... 800-554-8554
Customer Service:................... 408-727-8227
Tech. Support FAX: 408-987-7447
FAX: 408-987-7574
CompuServe: .... GO CLARIS
America Online:.....................claris@aol.com
BBS: 408-987-7421
FTP: ftp.claris.com
Web: www.claris.com

Clark Development Co.
3950 S 700 E Ste. 303
Murray, UT 84157
Main: 801-261-1686
Tech. Support:........................ 801-261-1686
Sales:..................................... 800-356-1686
Customer Service:................... 800-356-1686
Tech. Support FAX: 801-261-8987
FAX: 801-261-8987
E-Mail:.............................sales@saltair.com
BBS: 801-261-8976
Web: www.pcboard.com

Classic Software
Sales:..................................... 313-913-8075
FAX: 313-914-4087

Clear Software, Inc.
199 Wells Ave.
Newton, MA 02159
Main:......................................617-765-6755
Tech. Support:.....................617-965-5019
Sales:...................................800-338-1759
Customer Service:..................617-765-6755
Tech. Support FAX:................617-965-5310
FAX:......................................617-965-5310
CompuServe:........................GO CLEARSOFT
E-Mail: ....techsup@clearsoft.com
BBS:.....................................617-232-5406
Web: www.clearsoft.com

Clearpoint Enterprises, Inc.
25 Birch St. Ste. B-41
Milford, MA 01748
Main:......................................508-473-6111
Tech. Support:.......................508-473-6111
Sales:...................................800-253-2778
Customer Service:..................800-253-2778
Tech. Support FAX:................508-473-0112
FAX:......................................508-473-0112
E-Mail: .... clearpt@world. Std.com
Web: www.ultranet.com/~memory

Cleo Products Group
Interface Systems, Inc.
4203 Galleria Dr.
Loves Park, IL 61111
Main:......................................815-654-8110
Tech. Support:.......................800-233-2536
Sales:...................................800-233-2536
Customer Service:..................800-233-2536
Tech. Support FAX:................815-654-8294
FAX:......................................815-654-8294
E-Mail: ....cleo@interaccess.com
BBS:.....................................815-654-8173
Web: www.rock.cleo.com

Cliffs Notes
4851 S 16th St.
Lincoln, NE 68512
Main: 402-423-5050
Tech. Support:......................402-421-8324
Sales:...................................800-228-4078
Customer Service:..................800-228-4078
Tech. Support FAX: 800-826-6831
CompuServe:........................ 71344,3404
America Online:..................clifftsts@aol.com
E-Mail:.....................techsupport@cliffs.com

Cloud 9 Interactive
1101 Colorado Ave.
Santa Monica, CA 90401
Main: 310-319-5364
FAX: 310-319-5371
E-Mail:........................... cloud9inc@aol.com
Web: www.cloud9int.com

Coastcom Corp.
1151 Harbor Bay Pkwy.
Alameda, CA 94502-6511
Main: 800-433-3433
Tech. Support:.......................800-385-4689
Sales:...................................510-523-6000
Customer Service:..................800-433-3433
Tech. Support FAX: 415-523-6150
FAX: 510-623-6150
Web: www.coastcom.com

Coda Music Technologies
6210 Bury Dr.
Eden Prairie, MN 55346
Main: 800-843-2066
Tech. Support:.......................612-937-9703
Sales:...................................800-843-2066
Customer Service:..................800-843-2066
Tech. Support FAX: 612-937-9760
FAX: 612-937-9760
CompuServe:........................... 75300,3727
America Online:....................codatech@.com
E-Mail:............................. codatech@aol.com
Web: www.codamusic.com

Codenoll Technology
1086 N Broadway
Yonkers, NY 10701
Main:......................................914-965-6300
Tech. Support:.........................914-965-6300
Sales: 914-965-6300
Customer Service:....................914-965-6300
Tech. Support FAX:..................914-965-9811
FAX:.......................................914-965-9811
BBS:.......................................914-965-1972

Cogent Data Technologies
640 Mullis St.
Friday Harbor, WA 98250
Main:......................................360-378-2929
Tech. Support:.........................360-378-2929
Sales: 800-426-4368
Customer Service:....................360-378-2929
Tech. Support FAX:..................360-378-2882
CompuServe:.......................... 713-33,1507
E-Mail: ....sales@cogentdata.com
FTP: ftp.pipex.net
Web: www.cogentdata.com

Cognitech Corp.
500 Sugar Mill Rd. Ste. 240-A
Atlanta, GA 30350
Main:......................................770-518-4577
Tech. Support:.........................770-518-5010
Sales: 800-947-5075
Customer Service:....................770-518-3285
Tech. Support FAX:..................770-518-9137
FAX: 770-518-4588
CompuServe:.......................... 72662,3417
E-Mail: ....sharkware@sharkware.com
BBS:.......................................770-518-7617

Cognitive Technology Corp.
9 El Camino Dr.
Corte Madera, CA 94925
Main: 415-925-2323
Tech. Support:.........................415-925-2323
Sales:.....................................415-925-2323
Customer Service:....................415-925-2323
Tech. Support FAX: 415-461-4010
FAX: 415-461-4010
CompuServe: 76600,1623
E-Mail:............................... ctc@ocr.com
FTP: ftp.ocr.com
Web: www.ocr.com

Colorado Memory Systems/Hewlett-Packard
800 S Taft Ave.
Loveland, CO 80537-9929
Main: 970-669-8000
Tech. Support:.........................970-635-1500
Sales:.....................................970-635-1500
Customer Service:....................970-635-1500
Tech. Support FAX: 970-635-0650
FAX: 970-667-0997
BBS: 970-635-0650
FTP: ftp.hp.com/pub/information_storage
  /hp-colorado

Colorgraphic Communications Corp.
5980 Peachtree Rd.
Atlanta, GA 30341
Main: 770-455-3921
Tech. Support:.........................770-455-3921
Sales:.....................................770-455-3921
Customer Service:....................770-455-3921
Tech. Support FAX: 770-458-0616
FAX: 770-458-0616
CompuServe: 76620,3631
E-Mail:..............................tech@colorgfx.com
BBS: 770-452-8238
Web: www.colorgfx.com

Columbia Data Products
First Aid Supply Co.
1070-B Riner Dr.
Altamonte Springs, FL 32714
Main:......................................407-869-6700
Tech. Support:........................407-869-6700
Tech. Support FAX:.................407-862-4725
E-Mail: ....cdpi@cdpi.com
BBS:.......................................407-862-4725
Web: www.cdp.com

Columbia House
1221 Ave. of the Americas
New York, NY 10020-1090
Main:......................................212-596-2703
Customer Service:...................212-596-2701
FAX:.......................................212-596-2740

Columbia University Kermit Software
612 West 115th St.
New York, NY 10025-7799
Tech. Support:........................900-555-5595
Customer Service:...................212-854-5126
FAX:.......................................212-663-8202
E-Mail: .... kermit-support@columbia.edu
Web: www.columbia.edu/kermit

Comcab
PO Box 44027
Pittsburg, PA 15205
Main:......................................800-533-0415
Sales: 800-533-0415
FAX:.......................................412-922-7523

ComData
7900 N Nagle Ave.
Morton Grove, IL 60053
Main:......................................800-255-2570
Tech. Support:........................847-470-2570
Sales: 847-470-9600

Command Software Systems
1061 E Indiantown Rd. Ste. 2500
Jupiter, FL 33477
Main: 800-423-9147
Tech. Support:........................407-575-3200
Tech. Support FAX: 407-575-3026
CompuServe:...............................GO FPROT
E-Mail:............. support@commandcom.com
BBS:.......................................407-575-1281
FTP: ftp.command.com
Web: www.commandcom.com

Command Technology Corp. (CTC)
1040 Marina Village Pkwy.
Alameda, CA 94501-1041
Main: 800-648-6700
Sales:.....................................800-336-3320
Tech. Support FAX: 510-521-0369
E-Mail:............................ctcinquiry@aol.com
BBS:.......................................510-769-6826

Common Ground Software
Hummingbird Communication
480 San Antonio Rd.
Mountain View, CA 94040
Main: 415-917-7300
Sales:.....................................800-598-3821
Tech. Support FAX: 415-917-7310
E-Mail:.................info@commonground.com
Web: www.commonground.com

Commvision
510 Logue Ave.
Mountain View, CA 94043
Main: 415-254-9300
Tech. Support:........................415-254-9355
Sales: 415-254-9300
Customer Service:................... 800-832-6526
E-Mail:..............jlillywhite@commvision.com
BBS:.......................................415-254-9305
Web: www.commvision.com

Comp Utopia
205 Hallene Rd.
Warwick, RI 02886
Main:.......................................401-732-5588
Customer Service:...................800-444-3683
FAX: 401-732-5518
E-Mail: ....postmaster@computopia.com
Web: www.computopia.com

Compaq Computer Corp.
20555 State Highway 249
Houston, TX 77070-2698
Main:.......................................713-370-0670
Tech. Support:.......................800-652-6672
Sales:....................................800-345-1518
Customer Service:...................800-345-1518
Tech. Support FAX:................713-514-1743
E-Mail: ....support@compaq.com
BBS:.......................................713-518-1418
Web: www.compaq.com

Compaq Networking
Compaq Corp.
8404 Easters Blvd.
Irving, TX 75063
Main:.......................................800-544-5255
Tech. Support:.......................214-929-6984
Tech. Support FAX:................800-386-2172
BBS:.......................................214-929-4882
Web: www.compaq.com

Compatible Systems Corp.
PO Drawer 17220
Boulder, CO 80308
Main:.......................................800-356-0283
Tech. Support:.......................303-444-9532
Tech. Support FAX:................303-444-9595
E-Mail: ....info@compatible.com
BBS:.......................................303-443-0845
Web: www.compatible.com

Compex, Inc.
4051 E La Palma,
Anaheim, CA 92807
Main: 714-630-7302
Tech. Support:........................714-630-5451
Sales:.....................................800-279-8891
Tech. Support FAX: 714-630-6521
BBS: 714-630-2570
Web: www.cpx.com

Compression Labs, Inc.
2860 Junction Ave.
San Jose, CA 95134
Main: 408-435-3000
Tech. Support:........................800-767-2254
Sales:.....................................800-225-5254
Customer Service:..................800-225-5254
FAX: 408-922-5412
BBS: 408-922-5429
Web: www.clix.com

Compton's New Media
1 Athenaeum St.
Cambridge, MA 02142
Main: 617-494-1200
Tech. Support:........................423-670-2020
Sales:.....................................800-227-5609
Customer Service:..................800-227-5609
Tech. Support FAX: 617-494-1219
FAX: 617-494-1219
E-Mail:.........................support@softkey.com
Web: www.softkey.com

CompuAdd Corp.
12337 Technology Blvd.
Austin, TX 78727
Main: 800-627-1901
Tech. Support:........................512-250-1489
Sales:.....................................800-456-3660
Tech. Support FAX: 800-999-9901
FAX: 512-250-2060
BBS: 512-250-3226

CompuData Translators, Inc.
8816 A. Reseda Blvd.
Northridge, CA 91324
Main:.....................................213-387-4477
Tech. Support:.........................818-700-9090
Tech. Support FAX:..................818-700-1500

Compulink Management Center, Inc.
370 S Crenshaw Blvd. Ste. E106
Torrance, CA 90503
Main:.....................................310-212-5465
Tech. Support:.........................310-212-5465
Sales:....................................310-212-5465
Customer Service:....................310-212-5465
Tech. Support FAX:..................310-212-5064
CompuServe:......................GO COMPULINK
E-Mail:..........75162,2305@compuserve.com
BBS:......................................310-212-5850
Web: www.laserfiche.com

CompuServe, Inc.
5000 Arlington Centre Blvd.
Columbus, OH 43220
Main:.....................................614-457-8600
Sales:....................................800-345-1518
Web: www.compuserve.com

Compu-Teach
16541 Redmond Way Ste. 137-C
Redmond, WA 98052
Main:.....................................206-885-0517
Tech. Support:.........................206-885-0517
Sales:....................................800-448-3224
Customer Service:....................206-885-0517
Tech. Support FAX:..................206-883-9169
E-Mail:...................cmpteach@wolfenet.com
Web: www.wolfenet.com/~cmpteach

CompuAdd Corp.
12337 Technology Blvd.
Austin, TX 78727
Main:.....................................800-627-1901
Tech. Support:.........................512-250-1489
Sales:....................................800-456-3660
Tech. Support FAX:..................800-999-9901
FAX:......................................512-250-2060
BBS:......................................512-250-3226

CompUSA, Inc.
15167 Business Ave.
Dallas, TX 75244
Main: 800-932-2667
Tech. Support:.........................214-702-0055
Tech. Support FAX: 214-888-5743
BBS:......................................214-702-0300

ComputAbility Consumer Electronics
7271 N. 51st Blvd.
PO Box 17882
Milwaukee, WI 53217
Main: 800-558-0003
Tech. Support:.........................800-558-0003
Sales:....................................800-558-0003
Customer Service:....................800-558-0003
Tech. Support FAX: 414-357-7814
FAX: 414-357-7814

Computational Logic
1717 W. 6th St. Ste. 290
Austin, TX 78703-4776
Main: 512-322-9951
Tech. Support FAX: 512-322-0656
Web: www.cli.com

Compu-Teach
16541 Redmond Way Ste. 137-C
Redmond, WA 98052
Main: 206-885-0517
Tech. Support:.........................206-885-0517
Sales:....................................800-448-3224
Customer Service:....................206-885-0517
Tech. Support FAX: 206-883-9169
E-Mail:...................cmpteach@wolfenet.com
Web: www.wolfenet.com/~cmpteach

Computer & Control Solutions
1510 Stone Ridge Dr.
Stone Mountain, GA 30083
Main: 800-782-3525
Tech. Support:.........................404-491-1046
Tech. Support FAX: 770-493-7033

Computer Advantage
7370 Hickman Rd.
Des Moines, IA 50322
Main:.......................................515-252-6167
E-Mail: ....number1@netins.net

Computer Aided Business Solution
607-19th St.
Golden, CO 80401
Main:.......................................303-279-1868
Tech. Support FAX:.................303-279-5305
Web: www.cabs.com

Computer & Control Solutions
1510 Stone Ridge Dr.
Stone Mountain, GA 30083
Main:.......................................800-782-3525
Tech. Support:........................404-491-1046
Tech. Support FAX:.................770-493-7033

Computer Associates
1 Computer Associates Plaza
Islandia, NY 11788-7000
Main:.......................................516-342-5224
Tech. Support:........................516-342-5466
Sales:......................................800-225-5224
Customer Service:...................800-773-5445
Tech. Support FAX:.................516-342-5734
CompuServe:.................................... GO CAI
Web: www.cai.com

Computer Bank
7701 NW 56th St.
Miami, FL 33166
Main:.......................................800-222-8324
Tech. Support:........................305-477-7140
Tech. Support FAX:.................305-477-7342
BBS:..305-599-9586

Computer Buddy Co.
4000 Moorpark Ste. 222
San Jose, CA 95117
Main: 408-985-5570
Tech. Support:........................ 800-808-7706
Sales:...................................... 800-808-7706
Customer Service:................... 800-808-7706
Tech. Support FAX: 408-985-5580
FAX: 408-985-5580
E-Mail:............. buddy@computerbuddy.com
Web: www.computerbuddy.com

Computer Concepts
18001 Bothell-Everett Hwy. Ste. O
Bothell, WA 98012
Main: 206-481-3666

Computer Discount Warehouse
1020 E Lake Cook Rd.
Buffalo Grove, IL 60089
Tech. Support:........................ 800-383-4239
Sales:...................................... 800-233-4426
Customer Service:................... 847-465-6000
Tech. Support FAX: 847-465-6800
BBS: 847-291-1737

Computer Dynamics Sales
7640 Telham Rd.
Greenville, SC 29615
Main: 864-627-8800
Tech. Support FAX: 864-675-0106
E-Mail:.........................sales@cdynamics.com

Computer Friends
14250 NW Science Park Dr.
Portland, OR 97229
Main: 800-547-3303
Tech. Support:........................ 506-626-2291
Tech. Support FAX: 503-643-5379
E-Mail:.........................cfriends@teleport.com
Web: www.teleport.com/~cfriends/

Computer Innovations, Inc.
1129 Board St.
Shrewsbury, NJ 07702
Main:......................................800-922-0169
Tech. Support:........................908-542-5920
FAX:.......................................908-542-6121
E-Mail: .... sales@starpower.com
Web: www. Starpower.com

Computer Language Research
2395 Midway Rd.
Carrollton, TX 75006
Main:......................................800-327-8829
Web: www.clr.com

Computer Link
6573 Middlebelt
Garden City, MI 48135
Main:......................................313-522-6005
FAX:.......................................313-522-3119
E-Mail: ....clink@m-net.arbornet.org

Computer Mail Order (CMO)
2400 Reach Rd.
Williamsport, PA 17701
Tech. Support:........................800-221-4283
Sales: 800-221-4283
Tech. Support FAX:.................717-327-1217
FAX:.......................................717-327-1217
BBS:.......................................717-327-9952
Web: www.newmmi.com

Computer Mindware Corp.
36 Trinity Pl.
E. Hanover, NJ 07936
Sales: 201-884-1123
FAX:.......................................201-884-1666
CompuServe:............................ 76115,2564

Computer Network Technology
6500 Wedgewood Rd
Maple Grove, MN 55311
Main:......................................612-550-8000
FAX:.......................................612-797-6800
Web: www.cnt.com

Computer Parts Express
Main: 602-872-0893
E-Mail:.............................mac@netzone.com
Web: www.netzone.com/~mac/parts_express.html

Computer Peripherals, Inc.
ACC Technology Group
7 Whatney
Irvine, CA 92718
Main: 800-854-7600
Tech. Support:........................714-454-2441
Tech. Support FAX: 714-454-8527
BBS:.......................................714-470-1759

Computer Power, Inc.
124 W Main St.
High Bridge, NJ 08829
Main: 908-638-8000
Tech. Support:........................908-638-8000
Customer Service:...................908-638-8600
Tech. Support FAX: 908-638-4931
BBS:.......................................908-638-4931

Computer Sciences Corp./Artemus
Computer Sciences Corp.
3702 Pender Dr. Ste. 300
Fairfax, VA 22030
Main: 703-277-1085
Sales:......................................800-477-6648
FAX: 703-277-1053
E-Mail:.........................info@artemis-intl.com
BBS:.......................................800-777-7100
Web: www.artemis-intl.com

Computer Solutions, NW
PO Box 192
Benzonia, MI 49616
Main: 616-325-2540
Tech. Support:........................616-325-2540
Sales:......................................800-327-2540
FAX: 616-325-2505

Computer Station Corp.
6611 Bissonnet Ste. 112
Houston, TX 77074
Main:......................................713-777-3464
Tech. Support:.........................713-777-3464
Tech. Support FAX:.................713-777-3431

Computer Support Corp.
15926 Midway Rd.
Dallas, TX 75244-2123
Main:......................................214-661-8960
Tech. Support:.........................214-661-8960
Sales:......................................214-661-8960
Customer Service:...................214-661-8960
Tech. Support FAX:.................214-661-5429
CompuServe:............................ 74777,3434
BBS:.......................................214-404-8652
Web: www.ridethewave.com/arts&letters

Computer System Advisers
300 Tice Blvd.
Woodcliff Lake, NJ 07675
Main:......................................201-391-6500
Tech. Support:.........................800-361-0528
Sales:......................................800-361-0528
Customer Service:...................201-391-6500
Tech. Support FAX:.................201-391-2210
E-Mail: ....postmaster@silverrun.com
Web: www.silverrun.com

Computer System Products, Inc.
14305 21st Ave. N
Plymouth, MN 55447
Main:......................................612-476-6866
Tech. Support:.........................800-422-2537
Sales:......................................800-422-2537
Customer Service:...................800-422-2537
Tech. Support FAX:.................612-475-8457
E-Mail: ....info@csp.com
Web: www.csp.com

Computer Tyme
411 N Sherman, Ste. 300
Springfield, MO 65802
Main: 800-548-5353
Tech. Support:........................ 417-866-1222
Sales:...................................... 417-866-1222
Tech. Support FAX: 417-866-1665
Web: www.ctyme.com

Computers International, Inc.
5415 Hixson Pike
Chattanooga, TN 37343
Main: 615-843-0630

Computone Corp.
1100 North Meadow Pkwy.
Roswell, GA 30076
Main: 800-241-3946-280
Tech. Support:................. 770-475-2725-250
Sales:.............................. 770-475-2725-230
Customer Service:........... 800-241-3946-280
FAX: 770-664-1510
E-Mail:................. support@computone.com
BBS: 770-343-9737
Web: www.computone.com

CompuTrend
1306-1308 John Reed Ct.
City of Industry, CA 91745
Main: 818-333-5121
Tech. Support:........................ 818-333-5176
Tech. Support FAX: 818-369-6803
Web: www.premio.pc.com

Compuware Corp.
31440 N. Western Highway
Farmington Hills, MI 48334-2564
Main: 810-737-7300
FTP: ftp.compuware.com
Web: www.compuware.com

Comtech Publishing, Ltd.
PO Box 12340
Reno, NV 89510
Main:..................................702-825-9000
Tech. Support:.......................702-825-9000
Sales:.................................800-456-7005
Tech. Support FAX:................702-825-1818
CompuServe:............................. 70724,561
E-Mail:..............................tae@accutek.com
Web: www.accutek.com/comtech

Concentric Data Systems, Inc.
Wall Data
110 Turnpike Rd.
Westboro, MA 01581
Main:...................................800-325-9035
Tech. Support:.......................508-366-1122
FAX:....................................508-366-2954

Connect Tech, Inc.
727 Speedvale Ave. W
Guelph, ONT N1K 1E6
Canada
Main:...................................519-836-1291
Tech. Support:.......................519-836-4878
E-Mail:.................support@connecttech.com
BBS:....................................519-836-5848
FTP: ftp.connecttech.com
Web: www.connecttech.com

Connectix
2655 Campus Dr.
San Mateo, CA 94403
Main:...................................415-571-5100
Tech. Support:.......................800-950-5880
Sales:.................................800-950-5880
Customer Service:...................800-950-5880
Tech. Support FAX:................415-571-5195
CompuServe:..................... GO CONNECTIX
America Online:.............. connectix@aol.com
E-Mail:..........................info@connectix.com
Web: www.connectix.com

Conner Peripherals
Seagate
MS 4309, 3081 Zanker Rd.
San Jose, CA 95134-2128
Main: 408-456-3019
Tech. Support:.......................800-426-6637
Sales:.................................800-626-6637
Customer Service:...................800-537-2248
BBS:....................................408-456-4415
Web: www.conner.com

Connors Communications
30 W 21st St.10th Floor
New York, NY 10010-1209
Main: 212-995-2200
E-Mail:...................... connerscom@aol.com
Web: www.connors.com

Conrac Corp.
730 E. Cypress
Monrovia, CA 91016
Main: 818-303-0095
Tech. Support FAX: 818-303-5484

Consumer Electronics Shows
2500 Wilson Blvd.
Arlington, VA 22201-3834
Main: 703-907-7600
Customer Service:...................703-907-7676
FAX: 703-907-7602
Web: www.eia.org/cema

Control Memory Factory
1450 Koll Cir. Ste. 107
San Jose, CA 95112
Main: 408-437-1122
Tech. Support:.......................408-437-1186
Tech. Support FAX: 408-437-1278

Control Technology, Inc.
7608 N Hudson
Oklahoma City, OK 73116
Main: 405-840-3163
Tech. Support FAX: 405-848-0489

Copia International, Ltd.
1342 Avalon Ct.
Wheaton, IL 60187
Main:......................................708-682-8898
Tech. Support:........................708-682-8898
Sales:....................................800-689-8898
FAX:.....................................708-665-9841
E-Mail:..........................copia@copia.com
BBS:.....................................708-665-9841
FTP: ftp.copia.com
Web: www.copia.com

Core Technology Corp.
7435 Westshire Dr.
Lansing, MI 48917
Main:......................................517-627-1521
Sales:....................................800-338-2117
Customer Service:...................517-627-1531
Tech. Support FAX:.................517-627-8944
BBS:.....................................517-627-1011
Web: www.ctc-core.com

Corel Systems, Inc.
1600 Carling Ave.
Ottawa, ONT K1Z 8R7
Canada
Main:......................................613-728-8200
Tech. Support:........................613-728-1010
Sales:....................................613-728-8200
Customer Service:...................800-772-6735
BBS:.....................................613-728-4752
FTP: ftp.corel.ca/pub/
Web: www.corel.com

CoStar
599 W Putnam Ave.
Greenwich, CT 06830-6092
Main:......................................203-661-9700
Tech. Support:........................203-661-9700
Sales:....................................800-426-7827
Customer Service:...................800-426-7827
Tech. Support FAX:.................203-661-1540
CompuServe:.............................75300,2225
America Online:...................Keyword CoStar
E-Mail:...........................support@costar.com
BBS:.....................................203-661-6292
Web: www.costar.com

Cougar Mountain Software
7180 Potomac Dr. Ste. D
Boise, ID 83704
Main: 208-375-4455
Tech. Support:........................800-727-0656
Sales:....................................800-388-3038
Customer Service:...................208-375-4455
Tech. Support FAX:...............208-375-4460
BBS: 208-323-9011
Web: www.cougarmtn.com

Cracchiolo & Feder, Inc.
4400 E Broadway Ste. 312
Tucson, AZ 85711
Main: 520-327-1357
Tech. Support FAX:...............520-321-7456
BBS: 520-327-7456

Cray Communications, Inc.
Cray Electronics
9020 Junction Dr.
Annapolis Junction, MD 20701
Main: 800-227-3134
Tech. Support FAX:...............301-317-7270
E-Mail:..........................info@craycom.com
BBS: 301-317-7116
Web: www.craycom.com

Creative Equipment International
5555 W. Flagler St.
Miami, FL 33134
Main: 305-266-2800
Sales:....................................800-378-3057
FAX: 305-261-2544

Creative Labs
1901 McCarthy Blvd.
Milpitas, CA 95035
Main: 408-428-6600
Tech. Support:........................405-742-6622
Sales:....................................800-998-1000
Customer Service:...................800-998-5227
Tech. Support FAX:...............405-742-6633
FAX: 405-624-6780
CompuServe: ....GO BLASTER
BBS: 405-742-6660
FTP: ftp.creativelabs.com
Web: www.creativelabs.com

Creative Multimedia
225 SW Broadway Ste. 600
Portland, OR 97205
Main:......................................503-241-4351
Tech. Support:........................503-241-1530
Sales: 800-262-7668
Customer Service:...................503-241-4351
Tech. Support FAX:.................503-241-4370
FAX:.......................................503-2414370
E-Mail: ....713-33,3143@compuserve.com
BBS:.......................................503-241-1573
FTP: ftp.creativemm.com
Web: www.creativemm.com

Crescent- Division of Progress Software
Progress Software
14 Oak Park
Bedford, MA 01730
Main:......................................800-352-2742
Tech. Support:........................617-280-3000
FAX:.......................................617-280-4025
CompuServe:............................ 70662,2065
BBS:.......................................617-280-4221
Web: www.crescent.progress.com

CrossComm Corp.
450 Donald Lynch Blvd.
Marlboro, MA 01752
Main:......................................800-388-1200
Tech. Support:........................800-388-9877
BBS:.......................................508-481-4216

Crossley Group, The
PO Box 921759
Norcross, GA 30092
Main:......................................770-751-3703
FAX:.......................................770-751-3704
BBS:.......................................770-751-0155

Crosswise
105 Locust St. Ste. 301
Santa Cruz, CA 95060
Main:......................................408-459-9060
Tech. Support FAX:.................408-426-3859
E-Mail: .... support@crosswise.com
FTP: ftp.crosswise.com
Web: www.crosswise.com

Crystal Works
534 Shennandoah
DeSoto, TX 75115
Main: 214-223-4074
FAX: 214-223-8711
E-Mail:......... 713-33,3372@compuserve.com

Cubix Corp.
2800 Lockheed Way
Carson City, NV 89706
Main: 702-888-1000
Tech. Support:........................ 702-888-1000
Sales:..................................... 800-829-0550
Customer Service:................... 800-829-0551
Tech. Support FAX: 702-888-1001
FAX: 702-888-1001
BBS:....................................... 702-888-1003
Web: www.cubix.com

Current Logic Systems
48025 Fremont Blvd.
Fremont, CA 94538
Main: 800-468-4629

Curtis by Rolodex
Rolodex
225 Secaucus Rd.
Secaucus, NJ 07094
Main: 201-422-0240
Tech. Support:........................ 800-727-7656
Sales:..................................... 201-422-0240
Customer Service:................... 800-727-7656
Tech. Support FAX: 201-422-0254

Curtis, Inc.
418 W County Rd. D
St. Paul, MN 55112
Main: 612-631-9512
Tech. Support:........................ 612-631-9512
Sales:..................................... 800-245-3171
Customer Service:................... 800-245-3171
Tech. Support FAX: 612-631-9508
BBS:....................................... 612-631-9508

CyberCorp, Inc.
1019 Old Monrovia Rd Ste. 337
Huntsville, AL 35806
Main:.....................................615-425-6994
CompuServe:............................ GO WINAP E
E-Mail: .... sales@cybercorp.com
FTP: ftp.cybercorp.com
Web: www.cybercorp.com

CyberMedia, Inc.
3000 Ocean Park Blvd. Ste. 2001
Santa Monica, CA 90405
Main:.....................................310-581-4700
Tech. Support:.......................310-581-4710
Sales:...................................310-581-4700
Customer Service:..................310-581-4700
Tech. Support FAX:................310-581-4737
FAX: 310-581-4720
CompuServe:..................... GO CYBERMEDIA
America Online:...........Keyword Cybermedia
E-Mail: ....support@cybermedia.com
BBS:......................................310-581-4724
FTP: ftp.cybermedia.com
Web: www.cybermedia.com

Cybernet Systems
727 Airport Blvd.
Ann Arbor, MI 48108
Main:.....................................313-668-2567
Tech. Support FAX:................313-668-8780
E-Mail: ....heidi@cybernet.com
Web: www.cybernet.com

Cyborn Software
140 Ernest Rd, Kensington
Johannesburg, 2094, South Africa
Main:.....................................271-162-6056
FAX: 271-161-6425
E-Mail: .... borising@iafrica.com
Web: www.pcb.co.za/users/borising/cyborg.htm

Cygnus Support
1937 Landings Dr.
Mountain Veiw, CA 94043
Main: 415-903-1400
Sales:.................................... 415-903-1400
Customer Service:.................. 415-903-1400
FAX: 415-903-0122
E-Mail:.............................. info@cygnus.com
FTP: ftp.cygnus.com
Web: www.cygnus.com

Cykic Software
123 Camino De La Reina Ste. N200
San Diego, CA 92108
Main: 619-220-7970
Tech. Support FAX: 619-220-7959
E-Mail:.............................cykic@cykic.com
Web: cykic.com

Cypress Research
2901 Tasman Dr. Ste. 208
Santa Clara, CA 95054
Main: 408-486-7900
Tech. Support FAX: 408-486-7952

Cypress Semiconductor
3901 N. First St.
San Jose, CA 95134
Main: 408-943-2600
Tech. Support:....................... 408-943-2600
Sales:.................................... 800-293-2311
Tech. Support FAX: 408-943-2843
FAX: 408-943-2843
E-Mail:....................... cyapps@cypress.com
BBS: 408-943-2954
Web: www.cypress.com

Cyrix
2703 N Central Expy.
Richardson, TX 75080
Main: 214-968-8388
Tech. Support:....................... 800-462-9749
Sales:.................................... 800-462-9749
Customer Service:.................. 800-462-9749
Tech. Support FAX: 214-968-8070
E-Mail:................... tech_support@cyrix.com
BBS: 214-968-8610

DBS/Griffin Technologies
PO Box 1982
Lawrence, KS 66044
Sales: 913-832-2070
FAX:................................913-832-8787
CompuServe:............................ 71141,3624

DC Productions
218 Stockbridge Ave.
Kalamazoo, MI 49001
Main:....................................616-373-1985
Sales: 800-932-7763
E-Mail: ....dcpro!chetw@heifetz.msen.com

DCD Corp.
Sales: 800-457-3015
Customer Service:..................612-544-7077
Web: www.dcdcorp.com

DD&TT Enterprise
5680 Rickenbacker Rd.
Bell, CA 90201
Main:....................................213-780-0099
Tech. Support:........................213-780-0099
Sales: 213-780-0099
Customer Service:..................213-780-0099
Tech. Support FAX:................213-780-0419

DDC Publishing
275 Madison Ave.
New York City, NY 10016
Main:....................................212-986-7300
Tech. Support:........................212-986-7300
Sales: 800-528-3897
Customer Service:..................800-528-3897
Tech. Support FAX:................212-986-7302

DEC (Digital Equipment Corp.)
111 Powder Mill Rd.
Maynard, MA 01754
Main: 508-493-5432
Tech. Support:........................800-354-9000
Sales:...................................800-344-4825
Customer Service:...................800-354-9000
Tech. Support FAX: 508-493-6244
BBS:.....................................508-496-8800
FTP: ftp.pc.digital.com
Web: www.pc.digital.com

DFI (Diamond Flower Inc.)
135 Main Ave.
Sacramento, CA 95838-2041
Main: 916-568-1234
Tech. Support:........................916-568-1234
Sales:...................................916-568-1234
Customer Service:...................916-568-1234
Tech. Support FAX: 916-568-1233
E-Mail:..............................info@dfiusa.com
BBS:.....................................908-390-4820
Web: www.dfiusa.com

DFL Software, Inc.
1712 Ave Rd.
PO Box 54616
Toronto, ONT M5M 4N5
Canada
Sales:...................................416-789-2223
FAX: 416-789-0204
CompuServe:............................ 74723,3321

DIGI International
2450 Edison Blvd.
Twinsburg, OH 44087
Main: 800-782-7428
Tech. Support:........................800-782-7728
Sales:...................................800-782-7428
Customer Service:...................800-782-7428
Tech. Support FAX: 216-963-4745
FAX: 216-425-2460
BBS:.....................................216-912-4800
FTP: ftp.digi.com
Web: www.digi.com

DRA
1276 N. Warson Rd.
St. Louis, MO 63132-1806
Main:.....................................314-432-1100
Sales: 800-325-0888
E-Mail: ....sales@dra.com
Web: www.dra.com

DSP Development Corp.
One Kendall Square
Cambridge, MA 02139
Main:.....................................617-577-1133
Tech. Support FAX:.................617-577-8211
E-Mail: ....dspdev@world. Std.com
BBS:.....................................617-577-8211
Web: www.dadisp.com

DSP Group
3120 Scott Blvd.
Santa Clara, CA 95054
Main:.....................................408-986-4300
Tech. Support:........................408-986-4428
Sales: 408-986-4300
Customer Service:..................408-986-4300
Tech. Support FAX:.................408-986-4323
Web: www.dspg.com

DTK Computer
770 Epperson Dr.
City of Industry, CA 91748
Main:.....................................818-810-0098
Tech. Support FAX:.................818-810-0090
BBS:.....................................818-854-0797

DacEasy
17950 Preston Rd. Ste. 800
Dallas, TX 75252
Main:.....................................214-248-0205
Tech. Support:........................214-248-0205
Sales: 800-322-3279
Customer Service:..................800-322-3279
Tech. Support FAX:.................214-713-6331
FAX: 214-248-0850
BBS:.....................................214-931-6617

Dalco Electronics
275 Pioneer Blvd.
Springboro, OH 45066
Main: 800-445-5342
Tech. Support:........................513-743-8042
Tech. Support FAX: 513-743-9251
CompuServe: ....GO DA
BBS: 513-743-2244
Web: www.dalco.com

Daly Technologies Ltd.
1040 Marsh Rd.
Menlo Park, CA 94025
Main: 800-876-3267
Tech. Support:........................415-321-5471
Sales:....................................415-321-9500
Customer Service:..................415-617-4600
BBS: 415-688-0213
Web: www.gupta.com

Dantz Development Corp.
4 Orinda Way Building C
Orinda, CA 94563
Main: 510-253-3000
Tech. Support:........................510-253-3050
Sales:....................................510-253-3000
Customer Service:..................510-253-3000
Tech. Support FAX: 510-253-9099
FAX: 510-253-9099
E-Mail:............................. info@dantz.com
FTP: ftp.dantz.com
Web: www.dantz.com

Darim Co., Ltd.
3460 Wilshire Blvd. Ste. 1114
Los Angeles, CA 90010
Main: 800-432-8905
FAX: 213-637-1705
Web: darvision.kaist.ac.kr

Dart Communications
61 Albany St.
Cazenovia, NY 13035
Sales:....................................315-655-1024
FAX: 315-655-1025
E-Mail:...............................sales@dart.com
FTP: ftp.dart.com
Web: www.dart.com

Data Access Corp.
14000 SW 119th Ave.
Miami, FL 33186
Main:.....................................305-238-0012
Tech. Support:........................305-232-3142
Sales:....................................800-451-3539
FAX:......................................305-238-0017
CompuServe:.................GO DACCESS.COM
E-Mail: ....slsinfo@daccess.com
Web: www.daccess.com

Data-Cal Corp.
531 E Elliot Rd. Ste. 145
Chandler, AZ 85225
Main:.....................................800-223-0123
Tech. Support:........................602-545-8089
FAX:......................................602-545-8090

Data Fellows
4000 Moonpark Ave. Ste. 207
San Jose, CA 95117
Main:.....................................408-244-9090
Tech. Support FAX:................408-244-9494
FAX:......................................408-244-9494
E-Mail: ......,.................. info@datafellows.com
FTP: ftp.datafellows.com
Web: www.datafellows.fi

Data General Corp.
4400 Computer Dr.
Westboro, MA 01580
Main:.....................................508-898-4051
Sales: 800-328-2436
FAX:......................................508-898-2684
Web: www.dg.com

Data Interface Systems Corp.
11130 Jollyville Rd. Ste. 300
Austin, TX 78759-4895
Main:.....................................800-351-4244
Tech. Support:........................512-346-5641
Sales: 800-351-4244
Customer Service:...................512-346-5641
Tech. Support FAX:................512-346-4035
E-Mail: ....info@di3270.com
BBS:......................................512-346-7045
Web: www.di3270.com

Data Pro
5439 Beaumont Center Blvd. Ste. 1050
Tampa, FL 33634
Main: 813-885-9459
Tech. Support:........................813-888-5847
Customer Service:..................800-237-6377
FAX: 813-882-8143
E-Mail:............................support@dpro.com
BBS:......................................813-888-8892
Web: www.dpro.com

Data Race
12400 Network Blvd.
San Antonio, TX 78249
Main: 210-263-2060
Tech. Support:........................210-262-2010
Sales:....................................210-263-2118
Tech. Support FAX: 210-263-2111
FAX: 210-263-2075
BBS:......................................210-263-2096
Web: www.datarace.com

Data Techniques, Inc.
340 Bowditch St. Ste. 6
Burnsville, NC 28714
Sales:....................................800-955-8015
FAX: 704-682-0025
BBS:......................................704-682-4356

Datacom Technologies, Inc.
11001 31st Pl. W
Everett, WA 98204
Main: 206-355-0590
Tech. Support FAX: 206-290-1600
BBS:......................................206-290-1600

DataCom Warehouse
1720 Oak St.
PO Box 301
Lakewood, NJ 08701
Main: 800-456-6246
FAX: 908-363-4823
Web: www.warehouse.com

DataEase International, Inc.
7 Cambridge Dr.
Trumbull, CT 06611
Main:......................................800-243-5123
Tech. Support:........................203-374-8000
Tech. Support FAX:.................203-374-2020

Datamar Systems
6969 D Corte Santa Fe
San Diego, CA 92101
Main:......................................800-223-9963
Tech. Support:........................619-452-7986
Tech. Support FAX:.................619-452-3990
BBS:.......................................619-452-3990

Datapoint Corp.
8400 Datapoint Dr.
San Antonio, TX 78229-8500
Main:......................................210-593-7900
Tech. Support:........................800-733-1500
Sales:.....................................210-593-7683
Tech. Support FAX:.................210-593-7920
Web: www.datapoint.com

Dataproducts Corp.
1757 Tapo Canyon Rd.
Simi Valley, CA 93063
Main:......................................805-578-4000
Tech. Support:........................805-578-4000
Sales:.....................................805-578-4000
Customer Service:..................805-578-4000
Tech. Support FAX:.................805-578-4001
FAX: 805-578-4001
BBS:.......................................818-887-3816
Web: www.dpc.com

Dataquest, A Dun & Bradstreet Co.
251 River Oaks Pkwy
San Jose, CA 95134-1913
Main:......................................408-468-8000
FAX: 408-954-1780
Web: www.dataquest.com

DataTimes Corp.
14000 Quail Springs Pkwy. Ste. 450
Oklahoma City, OK 73134
Main: 405-751-6400
Tech. Support:........................405-751-6400
Customer Service:..................800-642-2525
Tech. Support FAX: 405-755-8028
Web: www.enews.com/clusters/datatimes

Dataviews
Dynatech Corp..
47 Pleasant St.
North Hampton, MA 01060
Main: 413-586-4144
Tech. Support FAX: 413-586-3805
E-Mail:...............................info@dvcorp.com
Web: www.dvcorp.com

DataViz
55 Corporate Dr.
Trumbull, CT 06611
Main: 800-733-0030
Tech. Support:........................203-268-0030
FAX: 203-268-4345
E-Mail:...............................info@dataviz.com
Web: www.dataviz.com

DataWiz
1500 Fashion Island Blvd. Ste. 209
San Mateo, CA 94404
Main: 415-571-1300
Tech. Support FAX: 415-574-2336
Web: www.datawiz.com

Dauphin Technology
800 East NW HWY Ste. 950
Palatine, IL 60067
Main: 847-358-4406
FAX: 847-358-4407

Davidson & Associates, Inc.
19840 Pioneer Ave.
Torrance, CA 90503
Main:......................................310-793-0600
Tech. Support:........................800-556-6141
Sales:.....................................800-545-7677
Customer Service:..................800-545-7677
Tech. Support FAX:................310-793-0601
FAX:.......................................310-793-0601
America Online:.............. Keyword Davidson
E-Mail:................................sales@davd.com
BBS:.......................................310-793-9966
Web: www.davd.com

DayStar Digital
5556 Atlanta Hwy.
Flowery Branch, GA 30542
Main:......................................770-967-2077
FAX:.......................................770-967-3018
E-Mail:........................support@daystar.com
FTP: ftp.//daystar.com
Web: www.daystar.com

Daytimer
2855 Campus Dr.
San Mateo, CA 94403
Main:......................................800-535-4242
Sales:.....................................415-572-6260
Web: www.daytimer.com

Decision Ware, Inc.
27 School St.
Weston, MA 02193
Main:......................................617-899-8200
FAX:.......................................617-891-3729
E-Mail:.................... dwl@theworld. Std.com

Decisioneering, Inc.
Sales:.....................................303-449-5177
FAX:.......................................303-449-1442

DecisionOne
50 E Swedeford Rd.
Frazer, PA 19355
Main:......................................610-296-6000
FAX:.......................................610-296-2910
Web: www.decisionone.com

Dell Computer Corp.
2214 W Braker lane Ste. D
Austin, TX 78758-4053
Main: 512-338-4400
Tech. Support:........................ 800-624-9896
Sales:..................................... 800-879-3355
Customer Service:.................. 800-624-9897
Tech. Support FAX: 512-728-3589
CompuServe:................................ GO DELL
America Online:....................... Keyword Dell
E-Mail:........................... support@us.dell.com
BBS:....................................... 512-728-8528
FTP: ftp.us.dell.com
Web: www.us.dell.com

DeLorme
PO Box 298
Freeport, ME 04032
Main: 207-865-4171
Tech. Support:........................ 207-865-7098
Sales:..................................... 207-865-1234
Customer Service:.................. 800-452-5931
Tech. Support FAX: 207-865-9291
FAX: 207-865-9291
CompuServe:............................ 72030,2146
America Online:..........Keyword Delormemap
E-Mail:............................. info@delorme.com
BBS:....................................... 207-865-3545
Web: www.delorme.com

Delphi Internet
1030 Mass. Ave.
Cambridge, MA 02139
Main: 617-491-3393
Tech. Support:........................ 800-544-4005
Sales:..................................... 800-695-4005
Customer Service:.................. 800-544-4005
E-Mail:............................. service@delphi.com
Web: www.delphi.com

Delrina Technology
Symantec Corp
6320 San Ignacio Ave.
San Jose, CA 95119-1209
Main:......................................408-363-2345
Tech. Support:.......................416-443-4390
Sales: 800-268-6082
Customer Service:..................800-441-7234
FAX: 408-363-2340
CompuServe:.......................GO SYMANTEC
America Online:...............Keyword Symantec
E-Mail: .... support@delrina.com
BBS:......................................416-441-2752
FTP: ftp.delrina.com
Web: www.delrina.com

Desaware
5 Town & Country Village Ste. 790
San Jose, CA 95128
Sales: 408-377-4770
FAX: 408-371-3530
E-Mail: .... 74431,3534@compuserve.com

Develcon Electronics
856 51 St. E
S Saslatoon, SK F7K 5C7
Canada
Main:......................................800-667-9333
Tech. Support:........................306-933-3300
Sales: 306-933-3300
Customer Service:..................800-667-3333
FAX: 306-931-1370
E-Mail: ....info@develcon.com
BBS:......................................306-931-1370

Devont Software, Inc.
10407 Sand Pass Ste. 2112
Houston, TX 77064
E-Mail: .... jimtyson@ix.netcom.com
BBS:.......................................713-955-9867

devSoft, Inc.
PO Box 13821
Research Triangle Pk, NC 27709
Sales: 919-493-5805
FAX: 919-493-5805
E-Mail: ....devsoft@aol.com
Web: www.dev-soft.com/devsoft

DiagSoft
5615 Scotts Valley Dr.
 Ste. 140
Scotts Valley, CA 95066
Main: 408-438-8247
Tech. Support:......................408-438-8247
Sales:....................................408-438-8427
Customer Service:..................408-438-8427
Tech. Support FAX: 415-341-2859
FAX: 408-438-7113
E-Mail:....................webmaster@diasoft.com
BBS: 408-438-8997
Web: www.diagsoft.com

Diamond Data Management
740 N Pilgrim Pkwy
Elm Grove, WI 53122
Main: 414-786-9000

Diamond Flow (Southeast), Inc.
2210 NW 92nd Ave.
Miami, FL 33172
Main: 305-477-1988
Tech. Support FAX: 305-594-0607

Diamond Head Software, Inc.
Ocean View Ctr.
707 Richard St. Ste. 630
Honolulu, HI 96813
Sales:....................................808-545-2377
FAX: 808-545-7042
Web: www.dhs.com

Diamond Multimedia Systems
2880 Junction Ave.
San Jose, CA 95134-1922
Main: 408-325-7000
Tech. Support:......................408-325-7100
Sales:....................................408-325-7100
Customer Service:..................408-325-7100
Tech. Support FAX: 408-325-7171
CompuServe: ....GO DMNDONLINE
America Online:...............diamond@aol.com
E-Mail:...............techsup@diamondmm.com
BBS: 408-325-7175
FTP: ftp.diamondmm.com
Web: www.diamondmm.com

Diaquest, Inc.
1440 San Pablo Ave.
Berkeley, CA 94702
Main:.....................................510-526-7167
Tech. Support FAX:.................510-526-7073
FAX:.......................................510-526-7073
E-Mail: .... sales@diaquesst.com
BBS:......................................510-526-7073
Web: www.diaquest.com

Digi-dat Corp.
8580 Dorsey Run Rd.
Jessur, MD 20794
Tech. Support:........................301-498-0200
Tech. Support FAX:.................301-498-0771
FAX:......................................301-498-0971
BBS:......................................301-498-0771

Digi International
11001 Bren Rd. East
Minnetonka, MN 55343
Main:.....................................800-782-7428
Sales:....................................800-344-4273
Customer Service:...................216-425-0723
FAX:......................................612-912-4952
BBS:......................................612-943-0550
FTP: ftp.digibd.com
Web: www.digi.com

Digiboard, International
11001 Bren Rd. E
Minatonka, MN 55343
Main:.....................................800-344-4273
Tech. Support:........................612-922-8055
Tech. Support FAX:.................612-922-4287
FAX:......................................612-912-4991
BBS:......................................612-922-4287
Web: www.dgii.com

Digicom Systems, Inc.
188 Topaz St.
Milpitas, CA 95035
Main:.....................................800-833-8900
Tech. Support:........................408-262-1277
Tech. Support FAX:.................408-262-0550
FAX:......................................408-262-1277
Web: www.digicomsys.com

Digilog
Numerex Corp.
2360 Maryland Rd.
Willow Grove, PA 19090
Main: 215-830-9400
FAX: 215-830-9444
E-Mail:.......................... digilog@digilog.com
Web: www.digilog.com

Digimation, Inc.
150 James Dr. East Ste. 140
St. Rose, LA 70087
Main: 504-468-7898
Tech. Support:........................ 504-468-3372
Sales:..................................... 800-854-4496
FAX: 504-468-5494
Web: www.digimation.com

Digital Alchemy
1100 Troy Hill Rd.
Pittsburgh, PA 15212
Main: 412-321-1010
FAX: 412-321-1011
E-Mail:.......................joel@digalchemy.com
Web: www.digalchemy.com

Digital Arts
1321 N. Walnut
Bloomington, IN 47807-5206
Main: 812-330-0124
FAX: 812-330-0126

Digital Audio Labs
13705 26th Ave. North Ste. 102
Plymouth, MN 55441
Main: 612-559-9098
Tech. Support FAX: 612-559-0124
FAX: 612-559-0124
E-Mail:.......................info@digitalaudio.com
Web: www.digitalaudio.com

Digital Castle
4046 Hubbel Ave. Ste. 155
Des Moines, IA 50317-4434
Main: 515-266-5098
E-Mail:............................. sheep@netins.net

Digital Corporate Research
130 Lynton Ave.
Palo Alto, CA 94301
Main:......................................415-853-2100
FAX: 415-853-2104
E-Mail: ....webmaster@src.dec.com
Web: www.research.digital.com

Digital Entertainment
7400 49th Ave. North
New Hope, MN 55428
Main:......................................612-535-8333
Customer Service:...................612-531-8330
FAX: 612-533-2156

Digital Equipment Corp. (DEC)
111 Powder Mill Rd.
Maynard, MA 01754-2571
Main:......................................508-493-5432
Tech. Support:........................508-493-5111
Sales: 800-344-4825
Customer Service:...................800-354-9000
Tech. Support FAX:.................508-493-7374
BBS:..508-493-8780
FTP: ftp.pc.digital.com
Web: www.dec.com/home.html

Digital Instrumentation Technology
127 Eastgate Dr. Ste. 20500
Los Alamos, NM 87544
Main:......................................505-662-1459
Tech. Support FAX:.................505-662-0897
FAX: 505-662-0897
Web: www.dit.com

Digital Link
217 Humboldt Ct
Sunnyvale, CA 94089
Main:......................................800-441-1142
Tech. Support:........................408-745-4200
Sales: 408-745-4166
Customer Service:....................408-745-4200
FAX: 408-745-6250
E-Mail: ....info@dl.com or sales.dl.com
BBS:..408-745-6250
Web: www.dl.com

Digital Products, Inc.
411 Waverley Oaks Rd.
Waltham, MA 02154-9409
Main: 800-243-2333
Tech. Support:........................617-647-1234
FAX: 617-647-4474
CompuServe: 76366,2245
E-Mail:.......................salesinfo@digprod.com
BBS: 617-647-5959
FTP: ftp.digprod.com
Web: www.digprod.com

Directnet Corp.
3232 McKinney Ave. Ste. 820
Dallas, TX 75204
Main: 214-953-1050
FAX: 214-953-3121
Web: www.directnet.net

DIRECTWAVE Inc.
4260 E Brickell St.
Ontario, CA 91761
Main: 909-390-8099
Tech. Support:........................800-840-1889
Sales:.....................................800-840-1889
Customer Service:...................800-840-1889
Tech. Support FAX: 909-390-8061
E-Mail:.................. drctwave@ix.netcom.com
BBS: 909-390-8052
Web: www.directwave.com

Discis Knowledge Research, Inc.
90 Sheppard Ave. East
7th Floor
Toronto, ONT M2N 3A1
Canada
Main: 416-250-6537
FAX: 416-250-6540
E-Mail:..................... discis@goodmedia.com
Web: www.goodmedia.com/discis

Disney Computer Software
500 S Buena Vista St.
Burbank, CA 91521-8404
Main:......................................800-228-0988
Tech. Support:........................800-228-0988
Sales:...................................800-228-0988
Customer Service:...................800-228-0988
Tech. Support FAX:.................818-846-0454
CompuServe:............................. GO DISNEY
America Online:.................. disney@aol.com
E-Mail:.............................. disneysoft@.com
BBS:.....................................818-567-4027
FTP: ftp.disney.com
Web: www.disney.com

Disston Ridge Software & Consulting
4915 22nd Ave. North
St. Petersburg, FL 33710
Main:......................................813-323-0961
Sales:...................................800-277-0799
Customer Service:...................800-788-0787
FAX:.....................................813-327-0822
CompuServe:............................. 70441,544
BBS:.....................................813-327-0822

Distinct Software
12900 Saratoga Ave.
Saratoga, CA 95070
Main:......................................408-366-8933
Tech. Support:........................408-366-0153
E-Mail:............................ mktt@distinct.com
BBS:.....................................408-366-0169
Web: www.distinct.com

Distributed Processing Technology (DPT)
PO Box 1864
Maitland, FL 32751
Main:......................................407-830-5522
Tech. Support:........................407-830-5522
Sales:...................................800-322-4378
Customer Service:...................407-830-5522
Tech. Support FAX:.................407-260-5366
E-Mail:............................ techsupp@dpt.com
BBS:.....................................407-830-1070
FTP: ftp.dpt.com
Web: www.dpt.com

Diversified Technology
112 E State St.
Ridgeland, MS 39157
Main: 800-443-2667
Tech. Support FAX: 601-856-2888

Doceo Publishing, Inc.
One Meca Way
Norcross, GA 30093
Main: 770-564-5545
Sales:....................................770-564-5545
FAX: 770-564-5528
CompuServe:............................. 73541,523
E-Mail:................................ info@doceo.com
Web: www.doceo.com

DocuMagix Inc.
2880 Zanker Rd.
San Jose, CA 95134-2122
Main: 800-362-8624
Customer Service:................... 408-434-1001
Tech. Support FAX: 408-434-0915
CompuServe:....................GO DOCUMAGIX
E-Mail:............... documagix@ix.netcom.com
Web: www.documagix.com

Docunetworks
Docunet
12861 Industrial Park Blvd.
Plymouth, MN 55441
Main: 612-550-9552
Customer Service:................... 800-936-2863
FAX: 612-550-1615
E-Mail:................. wnm@docunetworks.com
BBS:....................................612-550-0622
FTP: ftp.docunetworks.com
Web: www.docunetworks.com

Dolch Computer Systems
3178 Laurel View Court
Fremont, CA 94538
Main: 800-538-7506
Sales:....................................510-661-2220
Tech. Support FAX: 510-490-2360
BBS:....................................510-490-3269
Web: www.dolch.com

Dolphin Systems, Inc.
13584 Kennedy Rd. N.
Inglewood, ONT L0N 1K0
Canada
Sales:.......................................905-838-2896
FAX: 905-838-0649
E-Mail: ....stephenc@idirect.com
Web: www.dolphinsys.com

Dragon Systems, Inc.
320 Nevada St.
Newton, MA 02160
Main:.....................................617-965-5200
Tech. Support:........................617-965-7670
Sales:.....................................800-825-5897
Customer Service:...................800-825-5897
Tech. Support FAX:.................617-527-4576
E-Mail: ....support@dragonsys.com
BBS:..617-332-7371
Web: www.dragonsts.com

Dundas Software, Ltd.
202-4800 Dundas St. W.
Etobicoke, ONT M9A 1B1
Canada
Sales:.....................................800-463-1492
FAX: 416-239-2183
E-Mail: ....dundas@dundas.com
Web: www.dundas.com

Durand Communications Network
Sales:.....................................805-961-8700
FAX: 805-961-8701
E-Mail: ....sales@durand.com
Web: www.durand.com

Duxbury Systems, Inc.
435 King St.
PO Box 1504
Littleton, MA 01460
Main: 508-486-9766
Tech. Support:........................508-486-9766
Sales:.....................................508-486-9766
Customer Service:...................508-486-9766
Tech. Support FAX: 508-486-9712
FAX: 508-486-9712
E-Mail:.............................sales@duxsys.com
BBS: 617-7675964
Web: www.world. Std.com/~duxbury

Dycam, Inc.
9414 Eton Ave.
Chatsworth, CA 91311
Main: 818-998-8008
Tech. Support FAX: 818-998-7951
America Online:...................Dycam@aol.com
BBS: 818-998-1088
Web: www.dycam.com

Dyna Micro, Inc.
48434 Milmont Dr.
Fremont, CA 94538
Main: 510-438-0233
Tech. Support FAX: 510-353-2020
E-Mail:...................addonics@as400new.com
Web: www.addonics.com

Dynalink Technologies, Inc.
PO Box 593
Beaconfield, PQ H9W 5V3
Canada
Main: 514-489-3007
Tech. Support FAX: 514-489-3007
E-Mail:.............................peter02@ibm.com

Dynatech Communications
Dynatech Corp.
12650 Darby Brooke Ct.
Woodbridge, VA 22192
Main: 703-494-1400
FAX: 703-494-1920
Web: www.dynatech.com

EDP Systems Services, Inc.
19905 Scriber Lake Rd.
Lynnwood, WA 98036
Main:......................................206-771-3796
Tech. Support:........................800-827-4055
Sales:.....................................800-827-4055
Customer Service:...................800-827-4055
FAX:......................................206-778-3702

EDS
5400 Legacy Dr.
Plano, TX 75024-3199
Main:......................................214-605-6000
Sales:.....................................800-566-9337
Tech. Support FAX:.................214-604-3562
E-Mail:......................................info@eds.com
Web: www.eds.com

EFI Electronics Corp.
2415 South 2300 W
Salt Lake City, UT 84119
Main:......................................801-977-9009
Tech. Support:........................800-877-1174
Sales:.....................................801-977-9009
Customer Service:...................800-877-1174
Tech. Support FAX:.................801-977-0200
Web: www.efinet.com

EIZO Nanao Technologies, Inc.
Nanao Corp.
23535 Telo Ave.
Torrance, CA 90505
Main:......................................310-325-5202
Tech. Support:........................310-325-5202
Sales:.....................................800-800-5202
Customer Service:...................800-800-5202
Tech. Support FAX:.................310-530-1679
BBS:.......................................310-325-4744
Web: www.traveller.com/nanao/

ELF Communications
27 Perry St.
Somerville, MA 02143
Main:......................................617-629-2323
E-Mail:......................................info@elf.com
Web: www.elf.com/elf/home.html

ELF Software Co.
210 W. 10th St.
New York, NY 10025
Sales:.....................................800-309-8669
E-Mail:......................................elfsoft@aol.com
Web: users.aol.com/elfsoft/elfsoft.htm

ENSONIQ Corp.
155 Great Valley Pkwy.
Malvern, PA 19355-0735
Main: 610-647-3930
Web: www.ensoniq.com

EPE Technologies
Square D
1660 Scenic Ave.
Costa Mesa, CA 92626
Main: 714-557-1636
Tech. Support FAX: 714-457-1103

EPS Technologies, Inc.
10069 Dakota Ave.
PO Box 278
Jefferson, SD 57038
Main: 800-447-0921
Tech. Support:........................800-526-4258
FAX: 605-966-5482
E-Mail:....................epttech@ix.netcom.com
BBS:.......................................605-966-5482

ESCOM
E-Mail:................................ studio@escom.nl
Web: www.escom.nl

Eagle Data Protection, Inc.
350 S. 400 E Ste. 101
Salt Lake City, UT 84111
Main: 801-363-7300
Sales:.....................................800-909-3141
Tech. Support FAX: 801-538-0200
CompuServe:...............................GO PIRACY
E-Mail:.....................support@eagledata.com
Web: www.eagledata.com

Eagle Electronics
1233 E Colorado St.
Glendale, CA 91205
Main:.......................................800-992-3191
Tech. Support:.......................818-244-3191
Tech. Support FAX:................818-244-0466

Earth Channel Communications, LLC
4405 International Blvd. Ste. B112
Norcross, GA 30093
Main:.......................................800-888-1032
FAX: 770-564-0021
E-Mail: .... exhibit@earthchannel.com
Web: www.earthchannel.com

Eastern Language
33 E 300N Ste. 4
Provo, UT 84601
Main:.......................................801-377-4558
Tech. Support FAX:................801-377-2200
E-Mail: ....easternl@itx.com

Eastham & Associates, Inc.
9100 SW Freeway Ste. 139
Houston, TX 77074
Main:.......................................800-543-3256
Tech. Support FAX:................713-270-6445

Eastman Kodak Co.
901 Elmgrove Rd.
Rochester, NY 14653
Main:.......................................800-243-8811
Tech. Support:.......................800-344-0006
Sales:.....................................716-781-7888
Customer Service:..................800-344-0006
Web: www.kodak.com

Edimax Computer
3350 Scott Blvd. Building 15
Santa Clara, CA 95054
Main:.......................................800-652-6776
Tech. Support:.......................408-988-6092
Sales:.....................................408-496-1105
Tech. Support FAX:................408-980-1530
Web: www.edimax.com

Edmark Corporation
PO Box 97021
Redmond, WA 98073
Main: 206-556-8400
Tech. Support:.......................206-556-8480
Sales:.....................................206-556-8400
Customer Service:..................800-320-8379
Tech. Support FAX: 206-556-8430
E-Mail:..........................pctech@edmark.com
Web: www.edmark.com/

Educational Assistance, Ltd.
PO Box 3021
Glen Ellyn, IL 60138
Main: 630-690-0010
Tech. Support FAX: 630-690-0565
FAX: 630-690-0565

EDUCOM
1112 16th St. NW Ste. 6000
Washington, DC 20036
Main: 202-872-4200
FAX: 202-872-4318
E-Mail:.............................info@educom.edu
Web: www.educom.edu

EDUCORP
7434 Trade St.
San Diego, CA 92121
Main: 619-693-4030
Tech. Support:.......................619-536-9999
Sales:.....................................800-843-9497
Customer Service:..................800-843-9497
Tech. Support FAX: 619-536-2345
FAX: 619-536-2345
E-Mail:........................service@educorp.com
BBS: 801-375-2548
Web: www.gtm.com

Egghead Software
22705 East Mission
Liberty Lake, WA 99019
Main: 509-922-7031
FAX: 509-921-7936
Web: www.egghead.com

Eicon Technology Corp. (USA)
81 Main St. Ste. 412
White Plains, NY 10601-1711
Main:......................................914-946-3270
Tech. Support:.......................914-946-3270
Sales:...................................914-946-3270
Customer Service:..................914-946-3270
FAX:......................................914-946-3430
BBS:......................................214-239-3304
Web: www.eicon.com

Elan Computer Group, Inc.
888 Villa St. 3rd Floor
Mountain View, CA 94041
Main:......................................415-964-2200
Tech. Support FAX:................415-964-8588
BBS:......................................415-964-8588
Web: www.elan.com

Elco Computers
229 S Raymond Ave.
Alhambra, CA 91803
Main:......................................818-284-7018
Tech. Support:.......................818-284-7018
Sales:...................................818-284-3281
Customer Service:..................818-284-7018
Tech. Support FAX:................818-284-4871
BBS:......................................818-284-4871

Electric Magic Co.
209 Downey St.
San Francisco, CA 94117-4421
Main:......................................415-759-4100
Sales:...................................800-987-2001
Tech. Support FAX:................415-566-6615
Web: www.emagic.com

Electronic Arts Inc.
1450 Fashion Island Blvd.
San Mateo, CA 94404
Main: 415-571-7171
Tech. Support:.......................415-572-2787
Sales:...................................800-245-4525
Customer Service:..................800-572-2787
Tech. Support FAX: 415-286-5080
CompuServe:............................ 76,004,237
America Online:.................elecarts@aol.com
E-Mail:............................. support1@ea.com
FTP: ftp.ea.com
Web: www.ea.com

Electronic Form Systems
Veneer Graphics
1555 Valwood Pkwy. Ste. 150
Carrollton, TX 75006-6828
Main: 800-367-6373
Tech. Support:.......................800-934-7728
Sales:...................................800-327-8829

Elementrix Technology
850 Third Ave. 10th Floor
New York, NY 10022
Main: 212-888-8879
Tech. Support FAX: 212-935-3882
E-Mail:......................support@elementrixco.
Web: www.elementrix.co.il

Elgar Corp.
9250 Brown Deer Rd.
San Diego, CA 92121
Main: 800-733-5427
Tech. Support:.......................619-458-0250
Tech. Support FAX: 619-458-0267
E-Mail:.................................sales@elgar.com
BBS:......................................619-458-0267

EliaShim, Inc.
Eliashim, LTD
1 SW 129th Ave. Ste. 105
Pembroke Pines, FL 33027
Main: 954-450-9611
FAX: 954-450-9612
E-Mail:........................ support@eliashim.com
BBS:......................................954-450-9614
Web: www.eliashim.com

Elsa, Inc.
2150 Trade Zone Blvd. Ste. 101
San Jose, CA 95131
Main:.....................................408-935-0350
FAX: 408-935-0370
E-Mail: .... support@elsa.com
BBS:.......................................408-935-0380
Web: www.elsa.com

Emerald Intelligence
3850 Research Park Dr. Ste. E
Ann Arbor, MI 48108
Main:.....................................313-663-9600
FAX: 313-663-9626
E-Mail: .... info@emeraldi.com

Emerald Technologies
10500 W. 153rd St.
Orland Pk, IL 60462
Main:.....................................800-776-6174
Tech. Support:........................800-826-3739
Sales:....................................800-328-2696
Tech. Support FAX:.................708-349-5673
FAX: 708-873-2966
BBS:......................................206-487-1065

Eminent Domain Software
413 Gale St. East Entrance
Laredo, TX 78041
Sales:....................................800-246-5757
FAX: 210-729-0011
E-Mail: .... easalgad@icsi.net

Emulex Corp.
PO Box 6725
Costa Mesa, CA 92626
Main:.....................................800-442-7563
Tech. Support:........................714-662-5600
Tech. Support FAX:................714-241-0792
FAX: 714-513-8269
BBS:......................................714-241-0792
Web: www.emulex.com

Emurph Inc.
PO Box 12800
Englewood Cliffs, NJ 07632
Main: 201-816-2000
Tech. Support:....................... 800-243-0000
Customer Service:.................. 800-243-0000
FAX: 800-448-4026
BBS: 201-772-4612
Web: www.goldstar.co.kr

Enable Software, Inc.
313 Ushers Rd.
Ballston Lake, NY 12019
Main: 800-888-0684
Tech. Support:....................... 518-877-8600
FAX: 518-877-3337
BBS: 518-877-6316

Encore Computer Corp.
6901 West Sunrise Blvd.
Ft Lauderdale, FL 33313-4499
Main: 305-587-2900
Sales:.................................... 800-933-6267
Tech. Support FAX: 305-797-5793
Web: www.encore.com

Enhance Memory Products
18730 Oxnard St.
Tarzana, CA 91356
Main: 818-343-3066
Tech. Support:....................... 818-343-3066
Sales:.................................... 818-343-3066
Customer Service:.................. 800-343-0100
Tech. Support FAX: 818-343-1436
Web: www.enhancememory.com

Enhance Security Products
18730 Oxnard St.
Tarzana, CA 91356
Main: 818-343-3066
Tech. Support:....................... 818-343-3066
Sales:.................................... 818-343-3066
Customer Service:.................. 800-343-0100
Tech. Support FAX: 818-343-1436
Web: www.enhancememory.com

Enhanced Systems, Inc.
6961 Peachtree Industrial Blvd.
Norcross, GA 30092
Main:......................................770-662-1503
FAX:.......................................770-242-1630
E-Mail: .... mittle@esisys.com
Web: www.esisys.com

Envelope Manager Software
PSI Systems, Inc.
247 High St.
Palo Alto, CA 94301-1041
Main:......................................415-321-2640
Tech. Support FAX:.................415-321-0356
CompuServe:........................... 102437,1643
America Online:............. dazzleplus@aol.com
BBS:.......................................415-324-9027
Web: www.envmgr.com
Web: www.evertech.com

Environmental Systems Research Institute, Inc.
380 New York St.
Redlands, CA 92373
Tech. Support:........................909-793-3774
Sales: 800-447-9778
Tech. Support FAX:.................909-792-0960
CompuServe:.................................. GO ESRI
E-Mail: ....info@esri.com
Web: www.esri.com

Envisions Solutions Technology
47400 Seabridge Dr.
Fremont, CA 94538
Main:......................................510-661-4300
Tech. Support:........................510-661-4311
Customer Service:..................800-933-7226
FAX:.......................................510-438-6709
BBS:.......................................510-438-6716
Web: www.envisions.com

EPSON America, Inc.
Seiko
20770 Madrona Ave.
Torrance, CA 90503
Main: 800-338-2349
Tech. Support:........................ 800-922-8911
Customer Service:................... 800-289-3776
CompuServe:.............................. GO EPSON
BBS:...................................... 310-782-4231
FTP: ftp.epson.com
Web: www.epson.com

Equinox Sytems
1 Equinox Way
Sunrise, FL 33351
Main: 305-746-9000
Tech. Support:........................ 954-746-9000
Sales:..................................... 954-746-9000
Customer Service:................... 954-746-9000
Tech. Support FAX: 954-746-9191
FAX: 954-746-9101
E-Mail:....................... support@equinox.com
BBS:...................................... 954-746-0282
FTP: ftp.equinox.com
Web: www.equinox.com

Ergo Computing, Inc.
1 Intercontinental Way
Peabody, MA 01960
Main: 508-535-7510
Tech. Support:........................ 800-633-1922
Sales:..................................... 800-633-1925
Customer Service:................... 800-633-1925
Tech. Support FAX: 508-535-9551
FAX: 508-535-7512
CompuServe:............................... GO ERGO
E-Mail:...........support@ergo-computing.com
BBS:...................................... 508-535-7228
FTP: ftp.ergo-computing.com
Web: www.ergo-computing.com

ErgoSoft
763-B Foothill Blvd. Ste. 128
San Luis Obispo, CA 93405-1617
Sales:..................................... 805-546-3760
E-Mail:................................ergosoft@aol.com

Ergotron, Inc.
1181 Trapp Rd.
Eagan, MN 55121
Main:....................................800-888-8458
Tech. Support:.......................612-681-7600

eSoft, Inc.
15200 E Girard Ave. Ste. 3000
Aurora, CO 80014
Main:....................................303-699-6565
Web: www.esoft.com

Esprit
2115 Ringwood Ave.
San Jose, CA 95131
Main:....................................800-937-7748
Tech. Support:.......................408-954-9900
Sales:...................................800-937-7748
Customer Service:..................800-937-7748
Tech. Support FAX:................408-954-9800
Web: www.adi-online.com

Essex Systems, Inc.
One Central St.
Middleton, MA 01949
Main:....................................800-672-8272
Tech. Support:.......................508-750-6200
Sales:...................................508-750-6200

Eurosource AB
Brattberg Gamla Skola
LOS, HA S-820 50
Sweden
Sales:...................................466-571-0620
FAX:....................................466-571-0620
E-Mail:..............................f0002@ljusdal.se
FTP: ftp.ljusdal.se/eurosource
Web: www.ljusdal.se/esource/

Everex Systems, Inc.
FPG
5020 Brandin Ct
Fremont, CA 94538
Main: 800-821-0806
Tech. Support:.......................510-498-4411
Tech. Support FAX: 510-683-2186
BBS: 510-226-9694
Web: www.everex.com

Evergreen Software Tools, Inc.
15444 NE 95th St. Ste. 244
Redmond, WA 98052-2547
Main: 206-881-5149
Tech. Support:.......................206-881-5149
Sales:...................................800-929-5194
Customer Service:..................800-929-5194
Tech. Support FAX: 206-883-7676
E-Mail:..................................sales@esti.com
Web: www.esti.com

Evergreen Systems, Inc.
120 Landing Ct. Unit A
Novato, CA 94945
Main: 415-897-8888
Tech. Support FAX: 415-897-6158
CompuServe: ....GO EVERSYS
E-Mail:.......................support@eversys.com
BBS: 415-898-9398
Web: www.eversys.com

Evergreen Technologies
8601 Dunwoody Pl. Ste. 420
Atlanta, GA 30350
Main: 800-329-2777
Customer Service:.................. 800-329-2777
FAX: 770-992-6357
Web: www.imnet.com

Evergreen Technologies Corp.
806 NW Buchanan
Corvallis, OR 97330
Main: 800-733-0934
Tech. Support:.......................541-757-7341
Sales:...................................541-757-0934
FAX: 541-757-7350
E-Mail:.........................sales@evertech.com

Evolution Computing, Inc.
437 S 48th St. Ste. 106
Tempe, AZ 85281
Main:.....................................602-967-8633
Tech. Support:.......................602-967-8633
Sales: 800-874-4028
Customer Service:..................800-874-4028
Tech. Support FAX:................602-968-4325
FAX:.....................................602-968-4325
CompuServe:.......................GO EVOLUTION
America Online:..... Keyword easycad/fastcad
BBS:.....................................602-967-8636
Web: www.evcomp.com/evcomp

Ex Machina, Inc.
11 E 26th St.16th Floor
New York, NY 10010-1402
Main:.....................................212-843-0000
Tech. Support:.......................800-843-3883
Tech. Support FAX:................212-843-0029
E-Mail: .... techsupport@exmachina.com
Web: www.nyweb/exmachina/

Exabyte
1685 38th St.
Boulder, CO 80301
Main:.....................................303-442-4333
Tech. Support:.......................800-445-7736
Sales: 800-774-7172
Customer Service:..................800-392-2983
Tech. Support FAX:................303-417-7890
FAX:.....................................303-714-5520
E-Mail: ....support@exabyte.com
BBS:.....................................303-417-7100
FTP: ftp.exabyte.com
Web: www.exabyte.com

Excelltech
113 W 3rd St.
Yankton, SD 57078
Tech. Support:.......................605-665-5811
FAX:.....................................605-665-8324

Excite Inc.
1091 N. Shoreline Blvd.
Mountain View, CA 94043
Main: 415-943-1200
Tech. Support FAX: 415-943-1299
E-Mail:................................info@excite.com
Web: www.excite.com

Executive Software
701 North Brand Blvd. 6th floor
Glendale, CA 91203
Main: 818-547-2050
Tech. Support:........................ 800-829-6468
Sales:..................................... 800-829-6468
Customer Service:................... 800-829-6468
Tech. Support FAX: 818-545-9241
FAX: 818-545-9241
CompuServe:.........................GO EXECSOFT
E-Mail:.....................infodesk@executive.com
Web: www.execsoft.com

Exide Electronics
8509 Six Forks Rd.
Raleigh, NC 27615
Main: 919-872-3020
Sales:..................................... 800-554-3448
Tech. Support FAX: 800-753-9433
FAX: 800-753-9433
E-Mail:................................info@exide.com
Web: www.exide.com

Experdata
10301 Toledo Ave. S
Bloomington, MN 55437
Main: 612-831-2122
Tech. Support FAX: 612-835-0700
BBS:...................................... 612-835-0700

Expersoft
6620 Mesa Ridge Rd. Ste. 100
San Diego, CA 92121
Main:.....................................619-546-4100
Tech. Support:.......................800-316-7858
Sales:....................................800-366-3054
Customer Service:..................800-316-7858
Tech. Support FAX:................619-546-4410
FAX: 619-546-4110
E-Mail: ....rberzle@expersoft.com
Web: www.expersoft.com

Expervision
930 Thompson Pl.
Sunnyvale, CA 94086
Main:.....................................408-523-0900
Tech. Support:.......................408-523-0914
Tech. Support FAX:................408-523-0909
E-Mail: .... support@expervision.com
BBS:.....................................408-523-0910
FTP: ftp.expervision.com
Web: www.expervision.com

Extended Systems, Inc.
5777 North Meeker Ave.
Boise, ID 83713
Main:.....................................208-322-7575
Tech. Support:.......................800-235-7576
Sales:....................................800-235-7576
Customer Service:..................800-235-7576
Tech. Support FAX:................406-585-3606
CompuServe:............................ 71075,2510
E-Mail: ....info@extendsys.com
BBS:.....................................208-327-5020
FTP: ftp.extendsys.com
Web: www.extendsys.com

Express Systems
2101 Fourth Ave. Ste. 303
Seattle, WA 98121-2314
Main: 206-728-8300
Tech. Support:........................ 206-728-8300
Sales:................................... 800-321-4606
Customer Service:.................. 800-321-4606
Tech. Support FAX: 206-728-8301
FAX: 206-728-8301
E-Mail:................ info@express/systems.com
BBS: 206-881-9770
Web: www.express-systems.com

FCR Software
222 Third St. Ste. 3130
Cambridge, MA 02142
Main: 617-494-1300
Tech. Support:........................ 617-494-1300
Sales:................................... 617-494-1300
Tech. Support FAX: 617-494-9592
FAX: 617-494-9592
E-Mail:.. info@fcr.com
Web: www.fcr.com/homepage.html

FTG Data Systems
8381 Katella Ae
Stanton, CA 90680
Main: 714-995-3900
Tech. Support:........................ 800-962-3900
Sales:................................... 800-962-3900
Customer Service:.................. 800-962-3900
FAX: 714-995-3989
CompuServe: 74774,3142
BBS: 714-995-3946

FTP Software, Inc.
100 Brickstone Square
North Andover, MA 01810
Main: 508-685-4000
Tech. Support:........................ 800-382-4387
Sales:................................... 800-282-4387
Tech. Support FAX: 508-794-4484
FAX: 508-794-4488
CompuServe: .... GO PCVENJ
E-Mail:...............................support@ftp.com
BBS: 508-659-6240
FTP: ftp.com
Web: www.ftp.com

FWB Software

1555 Adams Dr.
Menlo Park, CA 94025
Main:......................................415-325-4392
Tech. Support:.......................415-833-4580
Sales:...................................415-833-4616
Customer Service:..................415-833-4616
Tech. Support FAX:................415-833-4662
FAX:....................................415-833-4653
CompuServe:...............................GO FWB
America Online:..................fwbinc@aol.com
E-Mail: ....infor@fwb.com
FTP: ftp.fwb.com
Web: www.fwb.com

Fabius Software Systems

24000 Alicia Pkwy. Ste. 17-353
Mission Viejo, CA 92691
Main:....................................800-632-2487
FAX:.....................................714-888-1681
CompuServe:..........................102004,1642
Web: www.fabius.com

Facet Corp.

4031 W Plano Pkwy. Ste. 205
Plano, TX 75093
Main:....................................214-985-9901
Tech. Support:.......................214-985-9901
Sales:...................................214-985-9901
Customer Service:..................214-985-9901
Tech. Support FAX:................214-612-2035
FAX:....................................214-612-2035
CompuServe:.............................74602,362
E-Mail: ....support@facetcorp.com
Web: www.facetcorp.com

Fairchild Data

350 N Hayden Rd.
Scottsdale, AZ 85257
Main:....................................800-247-9489
Tech. Support:.......................602-949-1155
Sales:...................................800-247-9489
Customer Service:..................800-247-9489
Tech. Support FAX:................602-941-0023
FAX:....................................602-941-0023
BBS:....................................602-941-0023

Faircom Corp.

4006 W Broadway
Columbia, MO 65203
Main: 800-234-8180
Tech. Support:.......................573-445-3828
Sales:...................................800-234-8180
Customer Service:..................800-234-8180
Tech. Support FAX: 314-445-9698
FAX: 573-445-9698
CompuServe:.........................GO FAIRCOM
E-Mail: ....faircom@crf.net
BBS:....................................314-445-6318
Web: www.faircom.com

FairPoint Technologies

133 S. Center Ct. Ste. 1000
Morrisville, NC 27560
Sales:...................................800-645-5913
FAX: 919-460-7606

Falco Data Products, Inc.

440 Potrero Ave.
Sunnyvale, CA 94086-4117
Main: 408-745-7123
Tech. Support:.......................408-745-7123
FAX: 408-745-7860

Falcon Software Inc.

One Hollis St.
Wellesley, MA 02181
Main: 617-235-1767
Tech. Support:.......................617-235-1767
Sales:...................................617-235-1767
Customer Service:..................617-235-1767
Tech. Support FAX: 617-235-7026
FAX: 617-235-7026
E-Mail:..........falconinfo@falconsoftware.com
Web: www.falconsoftware.com/falconweb

Farallon
2470 Mariner Square Loop
Alameda, CA 94501
Main:.....................................510-814-5100
Customer Service:...................510-814-5000
FAX: 510-814-5023
CompuServe:............................ 75410,2702
America Online:.................Keyword Farallon
E-Mail: .... info@farallon.com
BBS:......................................510-596-9023
Web: www.farallon.com

Fargo Electronics Inc.
7901 Flying Cloud Dr.
Eden Prairie, MN 55344
Main:.....................................612-941-9470
Tech. Support:........................612-941-0050
Tech. Support FAX:................612-941-1852
E-Mail: ....webmaster@fargo.com
BBS:......................................612-942-7958
Web: www.fargo.com

Fastcomm Communications Corp.
45472 Holiday Dr..
Sterling, VA 20166
Main:....................................800-521-2496
Tech. Support:........................800-282-9642
FAX: 703-787-4625
E-Mail: ....info@fastcomm.com
FTP: ftp.fastcomm.com
Web: www.fastcomm.com

Faulkner Information Services
114 Cooper Ctr.7905 Browning Rd.
Pennsauken, NJ 08109-4319
Main:....................................800-843-0460
Tech. Support:........................800-843-0460
Sales: 800-843-0460
Customer Service:...................800-843-0460
Tech. Support FAX:................609-662-6634
E-Mail: ....faulkner@faulkner
BBS:......................................609-662-0905
Web: www.faulkner.com

Fax of America Corp.
2554 Brir Trail
Schaumburg, IN 60173
Main: 800-342-3299
Tech. Support:....................... 800-342-3299
Sales:................................... 800-342-3299
Customer Service:.................. 800-342-3299

Fel Computing Inc.
10 Main St.
PO Box 72
Williamsville, VT 05362
Main: 800-639-4110
Tech. Support:....................... 800-639-4110
Sales:................................... 800-639-4110
Customer Service:.................. 800-639-4110
Tech. Support FAX: 802-348-7124
FAX: 802-348-7124
E-Mail:................................... sales@fel.com
Web: www.fel.com

Fellowes
1789 Norwood Ave.
Itasca, IL 60143
Main: 800-945-4545
Tech. Support:....................... 800-448-1184
Tech. Support FAX: 805-237-6267
E-Mail:.................................jbarrett@fix.net
BBS: 805-237-6266
Web: www.fellowes.com

Fibermux Corp.
21415 Plummer St.
Chatsworth, CA 91311
Main: 818-709-6000
Sales:................................... 818-709-6000
Customer Service:.................. 818-709-6000
Tech. Support FAX: 818-709-1556

Ficomp
3015 Advance Ln
Colmar, PA 18915
Main: 215-997-2600
Tech. Support FAX: 215-997-2609

Firefox, Inc.
2099 Gateway Pl. Seventh Floor
San Jose, CA 95110-1017
Main:.....................................408-467-1100
Tech. Support:........................408-467-1111
Sales:.....................................800-230-6090
Customer Service:...................800-230-6090
Tech. Support FAX:.................408-467-1105
FAX:......................................408-467-1105
E-Mail: ....sales@firefox.com
BBS:......................................408-232-1190
FTP: ftp.firefox.com
Web: www.firefox.com

First Byte
3000 Ocean Park Blvd. Ste. 2001
Santa Monica, CA 90405
Main:......................................310-581-4700
Tech. Support:........................310-581-4710
Tech. Support FAX:.................310-581-4720
E-Mail: ....support@cybermedia.com
BBS:......................................310-789-4916
Web: www.cybermedia.com

First Computer Systems, Inc.
6000 Live Oak Pkwy. Ste. 107
Norcross, GA 30093
Main:......................................800-325-1911
Tech. Support:........................770-441-1911
Tech. Support FAX:.................770-441-1856
E-Mail: ....support@fcsnet.com
BBS:......................................770-441-1856
Web: www.fcsnet.com

First International Computer
980A Mission Ct.
Fremont, CA 94539
Main:......................................510-252-7777
Tech. Support:........................510-252-7777
Customer Service:...................800-342-2636
Tech. Support FAX:.................510-252-8888
BBS:......................................510-252-7750
Web: www.fic.com.tw/

FirstMark Technologies, Ltd.
16 Concourse Gate Ste. 300
Ottawa, ONT K2E 7S8
Canada
Main: 613-723-8020
Tech. Support:........................613-723-8020
Tech. Support FAX: 613-723-8048
FAX: 613-723-8048
E-Mail:...................firstmark@ott.hookup.net
Web: www.hookup.net/~firstmrk/

Fitnesoft, Inc.
11 East 200 North   Ste. 204
Orem, UT 84057
Main: 801-221-7777
Tech. Support:........................801-221-7708
Sales:....................................801-221-7777
Customer Service:...................801-221-7777
Tech. Support FAX: 801-221-7707
FAX: 801-221-7707
CompuServe:.............................GO LFORM
E-Mail:........................lifeform@fitnesoft.com
Web: www.fitnesoft.com

Flashpoint, Inc.
125 Cambridge Park Dr.
Cambridge, MA 02140
Main: 800-352-7478
FAX: 617-576-7572
E-Mail:..........................rfields@flashpt.com
Web: www.flashpt.com

FlipTrack Learning Systems
2055 Army Trail Rd.
Addison, IL 60101
Main: 708-628-0500
Tech. Support:........................708-628-0500
Sales:....................................800-424-8668
Customer Service:...................708-628-0500
Tech. Support FAX: 708-628-0550
FAX:......................................708-628-0550
E-Mail:..........73173,2237@compuserve.com
Web: www.oootraining.com

Flytech Technology (USA), Inc.
3008 Scott Blvd.
Santa Clara, CA 95054
Main:.....................................408-727-7373
Tech. Support FAX:................408-727-7375
BBS:.....................................408-727-7375

Focus Electronics, Inc.
4523 13th Ave.
Brooklyn, NY 11219
Main:.....................................718-436-4646
Tech. Support:........................718-871-7600
Sales:....................................800-223-3411
Customer Service:...................718-436-4646
Tech. Support FAX:................718-438-4263
E-Mail:.............focuscom@gramercy.ios.com

Focus Enhancements
800 W. Cummings Park Ste. 4500
Woburn, MA 01801
Main:.....................................800-538-8865
Tech. Support:........................617-937-5500
Sales:....................................800-538-8866
FAX:.....................................617-938-7741
Web: www.shore.net/~focus

Folio Corp.
Read & Elsvier
5072 N. 300 W
Provo, UT 84604
Main:.....................................800-543-6546
Tech. Support:........................801-375-3700
Tech. Support FAX:................801-229-6790
BBS:.....................................801-229-6668
Web: www.folio.com

Force
825 Park St.
Christiansburg, VA 24073
Main:.....................................540-382-0462
Tech. Support FAX:................540-381-0392
Web: www.force.inc@bev.net

Foresight Resources Corp.
Softdesk, Inc.
10725 Ambassador Dr.
Kansas City, MO 64153
Main: 800-231-8574
Tech. Support:...................... 816-891-1040
Tech. Support FAX: 816-891-8018
CompuServe: 76004,1602
Web: www.softdesk.com

Fotec, Inc.
151 Mystic Ave.
Medford, MA 02155
Main: 617-396-6155
Tech. Support:...................... 617-396-6155
Sales:................................... 800-537-8254
Tech. Support FAX: 617-241-8616
FAX: 617-396-6395
E-Mail:................................ info@fotec.com
BBS: 617-241-8616
Web: www. Std.com/fotec

FourGen Software, Inc.
115 NE 100 St.
Seattle, WA 98125
Main: 206-522-0055
Tech. Support:...................... 800-333-4436
Sales:................................... 800-333-4436
Customer Service:.................. 800-333-4436
FAX: 206-522-0053
E-Mail:............................info@fourgen.com
Web: www.fourgen.com

Fractal Design Corp.
PO Box 2380
Aptos, CA 95001
Main: 408-688-8800
Tech. Support:...................... 408-688-8800
Sales:................................... 800-297-2665
Customer Service:.................. 800-297-2665
Tech. Support FAX: 408-688-2845
FAX: 408-688-8836
CompuServe: ....GO GUGRPA
America Online:....................Keyword Fractal
E-Mail:.............................. cs@fractal.com
FTP: ftp.fractal.com
Web: www.fractal.com

Franklin Electronic Publishers
1 Franklin Plaza
Burlington, NJ 08016-4907
Main:......................................609-386-2500
Tech. Support:........................609-386-2500

Franklin Computing Group, Inc.
Sales:....................................215-243-2250
FAX:......................................215-243-2253
E-Mail:..........................info@franklin.win.net

Franklin Quest Technologies
2200 W Pkwy. Blvd.
Salt Lake City, UT 84119
Main:......................................800-877-1814
Tech. Support:........................801-975-9999
Tech. Support FAX:.................801-978-1133
CompuServe:............................ 71333,3662
America Online:......... FranklnsuptAOL.com
BBS:......................................801-977-1991

Frontier Technologies Corp.
10201 N Port Washington Rd.
Mequon, WI 53092
Main:.....................................414-241-4555
Sales:....................................800-929-3054
Tech. Support FAX:.................414-241-7084
FAX:......................................414-241-7084
E-Mail: ....info@frontiertech.com
BBS:......................................414-241-7084
Web: www.frontiertech.com

Fujikura America, Inc.
100 Galleria Pkwy. NW Ste. 1400
Atlanta, GA 30339
Main:.....................................770-956-7200
FAX:......................................770-956-9854
BBS:......................................770-956-9854

Fujitsu America, Inc.
3055 Orchard Dr.
San Jose, CA 95134-2022
Main: 408-432-1300
Tech. Support:........................ 408-894-3950
Sales:.................................... 800-626-4686
Customer Service:................... 800-626-4686
FAX: 408-432-1318
BBS:...................................... 408-432-1318
Web: www.fujitsu.com

Fulcrum Technologies, Inc.
785 Carling Ave.
Ottawa, ONT K1S 5K4
Canada
Main: 613-238-1761
FAX: 613-238-7695
Web: www.fulcrum.com

Funk Software, Inc.
222 Third St.
Cambridge, MA 02142
Main: 617-497-6339
Tech. Support:........................ 617-497-6339
Customer Service:................... 800-828-4146
Tech. Support FAX: 617-547-1031
FAX: 617-547-1031
CompuServe:............................ GO FUNK
E-Mail:............................. support@funk.com
FTP: FTP: //www.funk.com/pub/
Web: www.funk.com

Future Soft Engineering, Inc.
12012 Wickchester Ln. Ste. 600
Houston, TX 77079
Main: 713-496-9400
Sales: 713-496-9400
Tech. Support FAX: 713-496-1090
BBS:...................................... 713-588-6870
Web: www.fse.com/fsehome.html

Futurus
3295 River Exchange Dr. Ste. 450
Norcross, GA 30092
Main: 770-242-7797
Tech. Support:........................ 770-825-0379
Tech. Support FAX: 770-242-7221
CompuServe:..........................GO FUTURUS

G.E. Capital Computer Rental Services
6875 Jimmy Carter Blvd. Ste. 3200
Norcross, GA 30071
Main:.....................................800-437-3687
Tech. Support:........................800-437-3687
Sales:....................................800-437-3687
Customer Service:...................800-437-3687
Tech. Support FAX:................770-623-9336
FAX: 770-623-9336
E-Mail: ....tms.smorgan@capital.ge.com
BBS:..415-341-2651
Web: www.ge.com/capital/techmanage

GBC/Globelle
2052 Corte Del Nogal
Carlsbad, CA 92009
Main:.....................................800-366-6655
Customer Service:...................800-229-2296
FAX: 619-431-2505

GDT Softworks
4664 Lougheed Highway Ste. 188
Burnaby, BC V5C 6B7
Canada
Main:......................................604-2919121
Tech. Support:.........................604-2993379
Sales:.....................................800-6636222
Tech. Support FAX:..................604-4733600
FAX: 604-4733699
E-Mail: ....info@gdt.com
Web: www.gdt.com

GE Capital
31111 Huntwood Ave.
Hayward, CA 94404
Main:.....................................800-553-2255
BBS:.......................................415-341-2651
Web: www.gecapital.com

GE Computer Service
6875 Jimmy Carter Blvd., Ste. 3200
Norcross, GA 30071
Main:.....................................770-246-6200
FAX: 800-277-3885
Web: www.gec.com

GNN Hosting Service
Vienna, CA
Main: 800-879-6882
Customer Service:...................703-918-2147
E-Mail:.............................. info@gnnhost.com
Web: www.gnnhost.com

GNWC Wire, Cable & Network Products
1401 Brook Dr.
Downers Grove, IL 60515
Main: 800-468-2121
Tech. Support:........................708-627-1777
Sales:.....................................800-468-2121
Tech. Support FAX: 708-932-4342
BBS: 708-932-4342

GTM Software
293 E. 950 S
Orem, UT 84658
Main: 801-235-7000
Tech. Support:........................800-733-0383
Tech. Support FAX: 801-235-7099

GVC Technologies, Inc.
400 Commonsway
Rockaway, NJ 07866
Main: 800-289-4821
Tech. Support:........................201-586-8686
Tech. Support FAX: 201-586-3308
BBS: 201-579-2702
Web: www.matcorp.com

GW Instruments
35 Medford St.
Somerville, MA 02143
Main: 617-625-4096
Tech. Support FAX: 617-625-1322

GW MicroDDA
725 Airport No. Office Park
Ft Wayne, IN 46825
Main: 219-489-3671
Tech. Support FAX: 219-489-3671
BBS: 219-489-5281

Gaitronics
400 E Wyomissing
Mohnton, PA 19540
Main:......................................800-492-1212
Tech. Support:......................800-882-1980
Sales:....................................800-882-1980
Customer Service:................800-882-1980
Tech. Support FAX:...............703-641-3297
FAX:......................................713-641-3297
BBS:......................................215-374-1474

Galacticomm, Inc.
4101 SW 47th Ave., Ste. 101
Ft Lauderdale, FL 33314
Main:......................................305-583-5990
Tech. Support:......................305-583-5990
Sales:....................................800-328-1128
Customer Service:................800-328-1128
Tech. Support FAX:...............305-583-7846
FAX:......................................305-583-7848
BBS:......................................305-583-7846
Web: www.gco.com

Gametek
2999 NE 191st St., 5th Floor
Aventura, FL 33180
Main:......................................305-935-3995
Tech. Support:......................800-439-3995
Sales:....................................800-426-3835
Customer Service:................800-927-4263
Tech. Support FAX:...............305-932-8651
FAX:......................................910-229-1635
Web: www.gametek.com

Gandalf Technologies, Inc.
130 Colonande Rd. North
Nepean, ONT K2E 7M4
Canada
Main:......................................613-274-6500
Tech. Support:......................800-426-3253
Sales:....................................800-426-3253
Customer Service:................800-426-3253
Tech. Support FAX:...............613-274-6501
Web: www.gandalf.ca/

Gates/Arrow Distributing
39 Hellhem Dr.
Greenville, SC 29615
Main:......................................800-322-2421
Tech. Support:......................800-332-2315

Gates/Arrow Distributing
Arrow Electronics
1502 Crocker Ave.
Hayward, CA 94544
Main:......................................800-851-8880
Tech. Support:......................800-332-2315

Gateway 2000
610 Gateway Dr. PO Drawer 2000
North Sioux City, SD 57049
Main:......................................800-846-2000
Tech. Support:......................800-846-2301
Sales:....................................800-846-4208
Customer Service:................800-846-2000
CompuServe:........................GO GATEWAY
America Online:............... Keyword Gateway
BBS:......................................605-232-2224
Web: www.gateway2000.com

Geac Computer Corp. Ltd.
45 McIntosh Dr.
Markham, ONT L3R 8C7
Canada
Main:............................905-475-7733-415
Tech. Support FAX: 617-969-1928
FAX: 905-475-7799
E-Mail:...................................info@geac.com
Web: www.geac.com

General Signal Networks
13000 Mid Atlantic Blvd.
Mt. Laurel, NJ 08054
Main:......................................800-368-3261
Tech. Support:......................703-644-9000
BBS:......................................703-644-9011

General Technology Corp.
205 Hallene RdUnit 6A
Warwick, RI 02886
Main:......................................408-732-5588
Tech. Support:.........................408-732-5588
Sales:....................................408-732-5588
Customer Service:...................408-732-5588
FAX:......................................408-732-5518

General Technology, Inc.
415 Pineda Ct.
Melbourne, FL 32940
Main:......................................800-274-2733
Tech. Support:.........................407-242-2733
Tech. Support FAX:.................407-254-1407
E-Mail:...........................gentecinc@aol.com

Genesis Integrated Systems
9200 Nike RdBuilding 105
Maple Plain, MN 55359
Main:......................................800-325-6582
Sales:....................................800-325-6582
Customer Service:...................800-325-6582
FAX:......................................612-446-1387

Genicom Enterprising Service Solutions
Genicom
1100 Venture Ct.
Carrollton, TX 75006
Main:......................................214-386-2000
Tech. Support FAX:.................214-386-2885
BBS:......................................214-386-2159

GEnie On Line Service
401 N Washington St.
Rockville, MD 20850-1785
Main:......................................800-638-9636
Tech. Support:.........................301-517-3600
Sales:....................................800-638-9636
Customer Service:...................800-638-9636
Tech. Support FAX:.................301-517-3600
FAX:......................................301-517-3600
E-Mail:........................feedback@genie.com
Web: www.genie.com

Genoa Technology
5401 Tech Circle
Moor Park, CA 93021
Main: 805-531-9030
Tech. Support:.........................805-531-9030
Sales:....................................805-531-9030
Customer Service:...................805-531-9030
Tech. Support FAX: 805-531-9045
Web: www.gentech.com/

Genovation Inc.
17741 Mitchell N
Irvine, CA 92714
Main: 714-833-3355
Tech. Support:.........................714-833-3355
Sales:....................................800-822-4333
Customer Service:...................714-833-3355
Tech. Support FAX: 714-833-0322
FAX:......................................714-833-0322
E-Mail:.......................mail@genovation.com
BBS:......................................714-442-0826
Web: www.genovation.com

Genus Microprogramming, Inc.
1155 Dairy Ashford St. Ste. 200
Houston, TX 77079
Main: 713-870-0737
Tech. Support:.........................713-870-0557
Sales:....................................713-870-0737
Customer Service:...................800-227-0918
Tech. Support FAX: 713-870-0288
FAX:......................................713-870-0288
CompuServe: 75300,2051
E-Mail:.......... 75300,2051@compuserve.com
BBS:......................................713-870-0601

Geocomp Corp.
10 Craig Rd.
Acton, MA 01720
Main: 800-822-2669
Tech. Support:.........................508-635-0012
Tech. Support FAX: 508-635-0266

George Lucas Educational Foundation
PO Box 3494
San Rafael, CA 94912
Main:....................................415-662-1600
FAX:......................................415-662-1605
E-Mail: ....edutopia@glef.org
Web: www.glf.org

Georgens Industries
3346 Industrial Ct
San Diego, CA 92121
Main:....................................619-481-8114

Gibson Research Corp.
27071 Cabot Rd Ste. 105
Laguna Hills, CA 92653
Main:....................................800-736-0637
Tech. Support:........................714-348-7100
Sales: 800-736-0637
Customer Service:..................800-736-0637
Tech. Support FAX:................714-348-7110
FAX:......................................714-348-7110
CompuServe:.........................GO GRCCORP
E-Mail: ....offices@grc.com
BBS:......................................714-348-7117

Giga Trend Inc.
2234 Rutherford Rd.
Carlsbad, CA 92008
Main:....................................619-931-9122
Tech. Support:........................619-931-9122
Sales: 800-743-4442
Customer Service:..................800-743-4442
Tech. Support FAX:................619-931-9959
E-Mail: .... emailbackup@gigatrend,com
BBS:......................................619-931-9469
FTP: ftp.gigatrend.com
Web: www.gigatrend.com

Gigasoft, Inc.
696 Lantana
Keller, TX 76248
Sales: 817-431-8470
FAX:......................................817-431-9860

Gigatek Memory Systems
1989 Palomar Oaks Way
La Costa, CA 92009
Main: 619-438-9010
FAX: 619-438-5519

Ginger Cat, The
32300 NW Hwy 205
Farmington Hills, MI 4833-41501
Main: 810-932-5771
Sales:...................................800-448-0601
FAX: 810-932-8829

Glare Guard (division of OCLI)
Optical Coating Laboratory, Inc.
2789 Northpoint Pkwy
Santa Rosa, CA 95407-7397
Main: 707-525-7582
Sales:...................................800-545-6254
FAX: 707-525-7595
E-Mail:...............................jsalyers@ocli.com

Glenayre Technologies, Inc.
4800 River Green Pkwy.
Duluth, GA 30136
Main: 770-623-4900
Sales:...................................770-623-4900
Customer Service:..................770-623-4900
Tech. Support FAX: 770-495-7139
FAX: 770-495-7139
E-Mail:......................support@gentech.com
Web: www.glenayre.com/

Global Village Communication
1144 E Arques Ave.
Sunnyvale, CA 94086
Main: 408-523-1000
Tech. Support:......................404-984-8088
Sales:...................................800-736-4821
Tech. Support FAX: 770-984-9956
America Online:.............Keyword GlobalVPC
E-Mail:.............pcsupport@globalvillage.com
BBS:.....................................770-984-9926
Web: www.globalvillag.com/

Globalink, Inc.
9302 Lee Highway 4th Floor
Fairfax, VA 22031
Main:.....................................703-273-5600
Tech. Support:.......................703-934-2734
Sales:....................................703-273-5600
Customer Service:..................703-273-5600
Tech. Support FAX:................703-273-3866
FAX: 703-273-3866
CompuServe:............................... 75352,635
E-Mail: ....info@globalink.com
BBS:.....................................703-273-6502
Web: www.globalink.com

Globe Manufacturing Sales, Inc.
1159 Rt 22
Mountainside, NJ 07092
Main:.....................................800-227-3258
Tech. Support:.......................201-232-7301
Sales:....................................908-232-7301
Customer Service:..................800-227-3258
Tech. Support FAX:................908-232-4729
FAX: 908-232-4729
E-Mail: ....georgenoll@msn.com
BBS:.....................................908-232-4729
Web: www.akshamping.com

Go Software, Inc.
31 Sherborne Rd.
Savannah, GA 31419
Sales: 912-925-4048
FAX: 912-927-0214
Web: www.netpath.com/~gosoft

Gold Disk, Inc.
2475 Augustine Dr.
Santa Clara, CA 95052
Main:....................................408-982-0200
Tech. Support:.......................905-602-5292
Sales:....................................800-982-9888
Customer Service:..................905-602-0395
Tech. Support FAX:................905-602-0393
E-Mail: ....tech@golddisk.com
BBS:.....................................905-602-7534
Web: www.golddisk.com

Golden Bow Systems
PO Box 3039
San Diego, CA 92163
Main: 800-284-3269
Tech. Support:.......................619-298-0901
Sales:....................................800-284-3269
Tech. Support FAX: 619-298-9950
FAX: 619-298-9950

Goldmine Software
17383 Sunset Blvd. Ste. 301
Pacific Palisades, CA 90272
Main: 310-454-6800
Tech. Support:.......................310-459-1222
Sales:....................................310-454-6800
Customer Service:..................800-654-3526
Tech. Support FAX: 310-459-8222
CompuServe: ....GO GOLDMINE
BBS: 310-459-3443
FTP: ftp.goldminesw.com
Web: www.goldminesw.com

GolfWeb
10001 North De Anza Blvd. Ste. 220
Cupertino, CA 95014
Main: 408-342-0440
Tech. Support:.......................408-342-0466
Sales:....................................408-342-0460
Tech. Support FAX: 408-342-0455
FAX: 408-342-0455
E-Mail:.......................golfweb@golfweb.com
Web: www.golfweb.com

Gould Fiber Optics Division
1121 Benfield Blvd.
Millersville, MD 21108
Main: 800-544-6853
Tech. Support:.......................800-544-6853
Sales:....................................800-544-6853
Customer Service:..................800-544-6853
Tech. Support FAX: 410-987-1201
FAX: 410-987-1201
E-Mail:..........................gouldfiber@aol.com

Grand Junction Networks - Cisco Systems Inc.
47281 Bayside Pkwy.
Freemont, CA 94538
Main:.....................................510-252-0726
Sales: 800-553-6387
FAX:.......................................510-252-0915
Web: www.grandjunction.com

Graphics Development International
20-A Pimentel Court Ste. B
Novato, CA 94903
Main:.....................................415-382-6600
Tech. Support:...............415-382-6600 #204
Sales: ....415-382-6600 #202
Customer Service:..........415-382-6600 #205
Tech. Support FAX:.................415-382-0742
FAX:.......................................415-382-0742
E-Mail: ....gdisoft@ijs.com
BBS:......................................415-382-9287
FTP: ftp.ljs.com
Web: www.gdisoft.com

Graphics Unlimited, Inc.
3000 2nd St. N
Minneapolis, MN 55411
Main:.....................................612-588-7571
Tech. Support:.......................612-520-2345
Tech. Support FAX:.................612-588-8783
BBS:......................................612-588-8783
Web: www.visi.com/~gu

Graphix Zone Inc.
42 Corp Park Ste. 200
Irvine, CA 92714
Main:.....................................714-833-3838
Sales: 714-833-3838
FAX:.......................................714-833-3990
E-Mail: ....starpress@dnai.com
Web: www. Starpress.com/starpress

Great Circle Software, Inc.
23161 Ventura Blvd. Ste. 204
Woodland Hills, CA 91364
Sales: 818-222-2771
FAX:.......................................818-222-2752
E-Mail: ....maplib@gcsmaps.com
Web: www.caprica.com/~gcsmaps/maplib.html

Great Plains Software, Inc.
1701 SW 38th St.
Fargo, ND 58103
Main: 800-456-0025
Tech. Support:.......................701-281-0550
Tech. Support FAX: 701-282-4826

Green Egg Software
500 Clyde Ave.
Mountain View, CA 94043
Main: 415-969-7047
Tech. Support:.......................415-969-7066
Sales: 415-969-7047
Customer Service:..................415-969-7047
Tech. Support FAX: 415-696-8936
FAX: 415-969-0118
E-Mail:........................info@systemsplus.com

Greenleaf Software, Inc.
16479 Dallas Pkwy. Ste. 570
Dallas, TX 75248
Main: 800-523-9830
Tech. Support:.......................214-248-2561
Tech. Support FAX: 214-248-7830
CompuServe:.......................GO GREENLEAF
E-Mail:.........................gleaf@onramp.net
BBS:.....................................214-2503778
Web: www.gleaf.com/~gleaf

Greenview Data Inc.
2773 Holyoke Lane
Ann Arbor, MI 48103
Main: 313-996-1300
Tech. Support:.......................800-458-3348
Sales:....................................800-458-3348
Customer Service:..................800-458-3348
Tech. Support FAX: 313-996-1308
FAX: 313-996-1308
CompuServe:.............................GO VEDIT
BBS:......................................313-996-1304

Griffin Technologies/DBS
PO Box 1982
Lawrence, KS 66044
Sales:....................................913-832-2070
FAX: 913-832-8787
CompuServe:............................ 71141,3624

Grolier Educational Corp.
Sherman Turnpike
Danbury, CT 06816
Main:.....................................203-797-3500
FAX: 203-797-3285
Web: www.grolier.com

Grolier Interactive
Sherman Turnpike
Danbury, CT 06816
Main:.....................................203-797-3530
Tech. Support:........................800-356-5590
Customer Service:...................800-285-4534
Tech. Support FAX:.................203-797-3130
FAX: 203-797-3835
BBS:.....................................203-797-6872
Web: www.grolier.com/gep/cust_desk
  /techsupt.htm

Group 1 Software, Inc.
4200 Parliament Pl. Ste. 600
Lanham, MD 20706-1844
Main:.....................................301-731-2300
Tech. Support:........................800-578-8324
Sales:....................................800-368-5806
Customer Service:...................800-367-6950
Tech. Support FAX:.................301-918-0462
FAX: 301-731-0360
E-Mail:.....................................info@g1.com
BBS:.....................................301-918-0835
Web: www.g1.com

Group Logic, Inc.
1408 N Fillmore Ste. 10
Arlington, VA 22201
Main:.....................................703-528-1555
Tech. Support:........................703-528-1555
Sales:....................................800-476-8781
Customer Service:...................800-476-8781
Tech. Support FAX:.................703-528-3296
E-Mail: ....info@grouplogic.com
Web: www.grouplogic.com

Gryphon Software
7220 Trade St. Ste. 120
San Diego, CA 92121-2325
Main: 619-536-8815
Tech. Support FAX: 619-536-8932
CompuServe: 73140,3010
America Online:.............. Keyword Griffin sw
Web: www.gryphonsw.com

Gtek, Inc.
PO Box 2310
Bay St. Louis, MS 39521-2310
Main: 800-282-4835
Tech. Support:........................ 601-467-8048
Tech. Support FAX: 601-467-0935
E-Mail:.................................spot@gtek.com
BBS: 601-466-0506
Web: www.gtek.com

Guideware Corp.
2483 Old Middlefield Way Ste. 224
Mountain View, CA 94043
Main: 415-969-6851
BBS: 415-969-3862

Guyana Crest Technologies
1160 Ridder Park Dr.
San Jose, CA 95131
Main: 800-726-5267
Tech. Support:........................ 408-452-2267
Tech. Support FAX: 408-436-0348
BBS: 703-960-8509
FTP: ftp.mcdy.com
Web: www.mcdy.com

H Co. Computer Products
16812 Hale
Irvine, CA 92714
Main: 800-726-2477
Tech. Support:........................ 714-842-8292
Tech. Support FAX: 714-833-3389
BBS: 714-542-8648
Web: www.ocnet.net\hco

HAL Computer Systems Inc.
Fujitsu
1315 Dell Ave.
Campbell, CA 95008
Main:....................................408-379-7000
Tech. Support:........................800-425-0329
Sales: 800-425-0329
Customer Service:...................800-425-0329
Tech. Support FAX:.................408-379-5022
FAX:......................................408-341-6903
Web: www.hal.com

HD Computer
1196 Kern Ave.
Sunnyvale, CA 94086
Main:....................................800-347-0493
Tech. Support:........................800-676-0164
Sales: 800-347-0493
Customer Service:...................800-347-0493
Tech. Support FAX:.................408-720-1967
FAX:......................................408-720-1967
E-Mail: .... HD@sc.hdcomputer.com
Web: www.hdcomputer.com

HREF Tools Corp.
c/o Shine & Co.
9 E.40th St.
New York, NY 10016
Sales: 800-365-9533
E-Mail: ....info@href.com
Web: www.href.com

HT Electronics
55 W Hoover Ste. 9
Mesa, AZ 85210
Main:....................................800-448-2031
Tech. Support:........................602-464-7840
Tech. Support FAX:.................602-464-9856
Web: www.hte@neta.com

HT Electronics
422 S. Hillview Dr.
Milipitas, CA 95035
Main:....................................408-934-7700
FAX:......................................408-934-7717

HT Electronics
211 Lathrop Way Ste. A
Sacramento, CA 95815
Main: 916-925-0900
FAX: 916-925-2829

Halcyon Software
1590 La Pradera Dr.
Campbell, CA 94008
Sales:....................................408-378-9898
FAX: 408-378-9935
E-Mail:....................................info@vbix.com
Web: www.vbix.com

Hamilton Laboratories
21 Shadow Oak Dr.
Sudbury, MA 01776-3165
Main: 508-440-8307
Tech. Support:........................508-440-8307
Sales:....................................508-440-8307
Customer Service:...................508-440-8307
Tech. Support FAX: 508-440-8308
FAX: 508-440-8308
E-Mail:............................hamilton@bix.com

Hantronix
10080 Buvv Rd.
Cupertino, CA 95014
Main: 408-252-1100
Tech. Support:........................800-776-4472
Tech. Support FAX: 408-252-1123

Harmony Computers
1801 Flatbush Ave.
Brooklyn, NY 11210
Main: 800-441-1144
Tech. Support:........................718-692-2828
FAX: 718-692-4535

HarperCollins
10 E 53rd St.31st Floor
New York, NY 10022
Main:.....................................212-207-7000
Tech. Support:........................800-424-6234
Sales:...................................212-207-7000
Customer Service:..................800-242-7737
FAX:.....................................717-941-1599
Web: www.harpercollins.com

Harris Computer Systems
2101 W. Cypress Creek Rd.
Ft. Lauderdale, FL 33309
Tech. Support FAX:................954-977-5580
Web: www.csd.harris.com

Harris Corp.
1025 W Nasa Blvd.
Melbourne, FL 32919
Main:....................................800-442-7747
Tech. Support FAX:................407-242-4071
FAX:....................................407-727-9344
E-Mail:..........................sfeustal@harris.com
Web: www.harris.com

Harris Digital Telephone Systems
300 Bel Marin Keys Blvd.
Novato, CA 94949
Main:....................................415-382-5000
Sales:...................................800-223-5174
Customer Service:..................800-444-7434
Tech. Support FAX:................415-382-5410
FAX:....................................415-883-1626
E-Mail:...........................info@dts.harris.com
Web: www.harris.com

Harris Semiconductors
PO Box 883
Florida, CA 32902-0883
Main:...........................800-442-7747 #700
Sales:...................................407-727-9207
Customer Service:..................407-724-7000
FAX:....................................407-724-7800
E-Mail:...........................centapp@harris.com
Web: www.semi.harris.com

Harvard Business Computers
PO Box 265
Harvard, IL 60033
Main: 815-943-7684
Tech. Support:....................... 815-943-7684
Tech. Support FAX: 815-943-7679
BBS: 815-943-7679

Hauppauge Computer Works, Inc.
91 Cabot Ct.
Hauppauge, NY 11788-3706
Main: 800-443-6284
Tech. Support:....................... 516-434-1600
Sales:................................... 800-443-6284
Customer Service:.................. 800-443-6284
Tech. Support FAX: 516-434-3198
E-Mail:........................sale@hauppauge,com
BBS: 516-434-8454
Web: www.hauppauge.com/hcw/index.htm

Haven Tree Software Ltd.
PO Box 470
Fineview, NY 13692
Main: 613-544-6035
Tech. Support:....................... 613-544-6035
Sales:................................... 613-544-6035
Customer Service:.................. 800-267-0668
Tech. Support FAX: 613-544-9632
FAX: 613-544-9632
E-Mail:................... tech-sup@haventree.com
BBS: 613-544-9632
Web: www.haventree.com

Hayes Microcomputer Products
5835 Peachtree Corners E
Norcross, GA 30092
Main: 800-377-4377
Tech. Support:....................... 770-441-1617
Sales:................................... 770-441-1617
Customer Service:.................. 770-441-1617
Tech. Support FAX: 770-441-1617
CompuServe: .... GO HAYES
E-Mail:....................techsupport@hayes.com
BBS: 800-874-2937
FTP: ftp.hayes.com
Web: www.hayes.com

Headbone Interactive
1520 Bellevue Ave.
Seattle, WA 98122
Main:......................................800-267-4709
Tech. Support:.........................206-325-3885
FAX:..206-323-0188
E-Mail: ....info@headbone.com
Web: www.headbone.com

Heartbeat Software
315 Bacon St.
Waltham, MA 02154
Main:,....................................617-891-3323
FAX:..617-891-3345
E-Mail: ....rexdean@heartbeat.com
Web: www.hbs.kidsrule.com

Heartland Computer Products
PO Box 2468
Ames, IA 50010
Main:......................................515-233-1632
BBS:.......................................515-292-8216

Helios Systems
1996 Lundy Ave.
San Jose, CA 95131
Main:......................................408-432-0292
Customer Service:...................408-432-0292
Tech. Support FAX:.................408-943-1309
BBS:.......................................408-321-8998

Helix Software Company, Inc.
4709 30th St.
Long Island, NY 11101
Main:......................................800-451-0551
Tech. Support:.........................718-392-3735
Sales: 718-392-3100
Tech. Support FAX:.................718-392-4212
CompuServe:...............................GO HELIX
E-Mail: ....sales@helixsoftware.com
BBS:.......................................718-392-4054
FTP: ftp.helixsoftware.com
Web: www.helixsoftware.com

Help Desk Institute
Softbank Exposition & Conference Co.
1755 Telstar Dr. Ste. 101
Colorado Springs, CO 80920-1017
Main: 800-248-5667
Tech. Support FAX: 719-528-4250
Web: www.helpdeskInst.com/

Hercules
3839 Spinnaker Ct.
Fremont, CA 94538
Main: 510-623-6030
Tech. Support:.........................800-323-0601
Sales:.....................................800-323-0601
Customer Service:...................800-532-0600
Tech. Support FAX: 510-490-6745
FAX: 510-623-1112
CompuServe:......................GO HERCULES
E-Mail:......................support@hercules.com
BBS:..510-623-7449
FTP: ftp.hercules.com
Web: www.hercules.com

Herring Way Technologies
6816 Herring Way
Charlotte, NC 28211-3579
Main: 704-364-3346
Sales:.....................................800-946-4277
FAX: 704-364-5676
E-Mail:................................info@ability.com
BBS:.......................................704-364-2049
Web: www.ability.com

Heurikon Corp.
Computer Products
8310 Excelsior Dr.
Madison, WI 53717
Main: 608-831-5500
Sales:.....................................800-356-9602
Tech. Support FAX: 608-831-8844
FAX: 608-831-4249
E-Mail:..............................sales@heuikon.com
FTP: ftp.heuikon.com
Web: www.heurikon.com

Hewlett-Packard (HP)
3000 Hanover St.
Palo Alto, CA 94304
Main:......................................415-857-1501
Tech. Support:.........................208-323-2551
Sales:.....................................800-243-9812
Customer Service:...................800-752-0900
CompuServe:.......................................GO HP
America Online:......................... Keyword HP
BBS:.......................................208-344-1691
Web: www.hp.com

Hi-image, Inc.
1820 Gateway Dr. Ste. 370
San Mateo, CA 94404
Main:.....................................800-345-3540
Tech. Support FAX:.................415-358-9535
CompuServe:...........................GO IMAGEIN
BBS:.......................................415-358-9795
Web: www.hi-image.com

Hi-Tech Advisers
PO Box 129
Ravena, NY 12143-0129
Main:.....................................518-756-3800
Tech. Support:.........................518-756-6666
Sales:.....................................800-882-4310
Customer Service:...................518-756-3800
CompuServe:............................ 70313,1720

Hi-Tech Media, Inc.
445 5th Ave.
New York, NY 10016
Main:.....................................212-293-3900
Sales:.....................................800-696-9646
FAX:......................................212-293-7979
E-Mail:..............................msb@l-2000.com
Web: www.mmsource.com

Hi-Tech USA
1562 Centre Pointe Dr.
Milpitas, CA 95035
Main:.....................................408-262-8688
Tech. Support:.........................408-262-8688
Customer Service:...................408-956-8285
Tech. Support FAX:.................408-262-8772

Hibbs Henle Nelson Corp.
1115 Foothill Blvd.
La Canada, CA 91011
Main: 818-952-1000
Tech. Support:.........................714-363-7244

High Level Design Systems
E-Mail:...............................support@hlds.com
Web: www.hlds.com

High Res Technologies, Inc.
PO Box 76
Lewiston, NY 14092
Main: 416-497-6493

Hilgraeve, Inc.
111 Conant Ave. Ste. A
Monroe, MI 48161
Main: 313-243-0576
Tech. Support:.........................313-243-0576
Tech. Support FAX: 313-243-0645
E-Mail:.......................support@hilgraeve.com
BBS: 313-243-5915
Web: www.hilgraeve.com

HiQuality Systems, Inc.
740 N Mary Ave.
Sunnyvale, CA 94086
Main: 408-245-5836
Tech. Support:.........................408-245-5836
Tech. Support FAX: 408-245-3108
BBS: 408-245-3108
Web: www.hiq.com

Hirschman, Richard GmbH & Co.
Industrial Row
PO Box 229
Riverdale, NJ 07457
Main: 201-835-5002
Tech. Support FAX: 201-835-8354

Hitachi Data Systems
750 Central Expressway
Santa Clara, CA 95050-0996
Main:......................................408-970-1000
Tech. Support FAX:.................800-348-4357
FAX:.......................................408-727-8036
Web: www.hdshq.com

Hokkins Systemation
131 E Brokaw Rd
San Jose, CA 95112
Main:......................................408-436-8303
Tech. Support:........................408-436-8303
FAX:.......................................408-436-3021
E-Mail: ....hht@hokkins.com
BBS:......................................408-436-1820

Home Page Software
Santa Monica, CA
E-Mail: ....tanny@netcom.com
FTP: ftp.netcom.com/pub/ta/tanny
Web: www.vpm.com/trafalmador/

Honeywell
3800 W 80th St.
Minneapolis, MN 55431
Main:......................................800-328-5111
E-Mail: ....info@corp.honeywell.com
Web: www.honeywell.com

Hooleon Corp.
411 S 6th St.
Cottonwood, AZ 86326
Main:......................................800-937-1337
Tech. Support:........................520-634-7515
Tech. Support FAX:.................520-634-4620

Horan Data Services
708 Walnut St.
Cincinnati, OH 45202
Main: 800-677-8885
Tech. Support:.......................800-677-8885
Sales:.....................................800-677-8885
Customer Service:...................800-677-8885
Tech. Support FAX: 800-929-3423
FAX: 800-929-3423
E-Mail:...........................infor@horandata.net
FTP: ftp.horandata.net
Web: www.horandata.ner

Horizons Technology, Inc.
3990 Ruffin Rd.
San Diego, CA 92123-9644
Main: 619-292-8331
Tech. Support:.......................619-292-8320
Sales:.....................................800-828-3808
Tech. Support FAX: 619-565-1175
FAX: 619-292-9439
E-Mail:............................info@horizons.com
BBS:......................................619-268-0380
Web: www.horizons.com

Horstmann Software Design Corp.
1035 S. Saratoga-Sunnyvale Rd. Ste. 5A
San Jose, CA 95129
Main: 408-366-1222
Tech. Support FAX: 408-366-0822
E-Mail:.....................support@horseman.com

Houghton Mifflin Interactive
222 Berkeley St.
Boston, MA 02116
FAX: 617-351-1110
E-Mail:.................................hmi@hmco.com
Web: www.hmco.com/hmco/trade/newmedia/
index.html

Human Designed Systems
3945 Freedom Circle 4th floor
Santa Clara, CA 95054
Main: 408-748-3456
FAX: 408-748-3499
Web: www.hlds.com

Hummingbird Communications
480 San Antonio Rd.
Mountain View, CA 94040
Web: www.hummingbird.com

HyperAct, Inc.
3437 335th St.
West Des Moines, IA 50266
Sales: 515-987-2910
FAX: 515-987-2909
E-Mail: ....rloewy@hyperact.com
Web: www.hyperact.com/

Hyundai Electronics America
510 Cottonwood Dr.
Milpitas, CA 95035
Main:.....................................408-232-8000
Tech. Support:........................408-232-8191
Customer Service:...................408-232-8191
Tech. Support FAX:.................408-232-8121
BBS:......................................800-955-5432
Web: www.hea.com

I-Boy Software Company
770 S. Acco Plaza
Wheeling, IL 60090-6070
Main:.....................................312-541-9500
Sales: 800-222-6462
FAX: 312-541-9638

IBM Corp.
Rt. 100 PO Box 100
Somers, NY 10589
Main:.....................................800-436-7658
Tech. Support:........................800-772-2227
Sales: 800-426-3333
Customer Service:...................800-772-2227
E-Mail: ....askibm@info.ibm.com
BBS:......................................919-517-0001
Web: www.ibm.com

IDEAssociates, Inc.
70 Oak Park
Bedford, MA 01730
Main: 617-275-2800
Tech. Support:........................800-343-0056
Sales:.....................................617-275-2800
Customer Service:...................800-257-5027
Tech. Support FAX: 617-533-0505
BBS: 617-533-0514
Web: www.idea.com

IDG Books Worldwide, Inc.
919 E. Hillsdale Blvd. Ste. 400
Foster City, CA 94404
Main: 415-655-3000
Tech. Support:........................800-762-2974
Sales:.....................................800-434-3422
Customer Service:...................800-434-3422
FAX: 415-655-3299
E-Mail:............................info@idgbooks.com
Web: www.idgbooks.com

IDS
12800 Garden Grove Blvd. E
Garden Grove, CA 92643
Main: 714-530-8677
Tech. Support:........................714-530-8697
Tech. Support FAX: 714-530-0817
BBS: 714-530-0815

IET
1250 Bixby Dr.
City of Industry, CA 91745
Main: 818-336-1003
Tech. Support:........................818-336-1003
Tech. Support FAX: 818-330-0052
E-Mail:.................................letusa@aol.com
BBS: 818-330-0052

IMC Networks Corp.
16931 Millikan Ave.
Irvine, CA 92714
Main:.....................................800-624-1070
Tech. Support:.........................714-724-1070
Sales:.....................................800-624-1070
Customer Service:...................800-624-1070
Tech. Support FAX:.................714-724-1020
BBS:.......................................714-724-1020
Web: www.imcnetworks.com

IMSI
1895 Francisco Blvd. East
San Rafael, CA 94901
Main:.....................................415-257-3000
Sales:.....................................800-833-4674
Customer Service:...................800-833-8082
FAX:.......................................415-257-3565
BBS:.......................................415-454-2893
Web: www.imsisoft.com

IONA Technologies
201 Broadway 3rd floor
Cambridge, MA 02139-1955
Main:.....................................617-679-0906
Sales:.....................................800-672-4948
Customer Service:...................617-668-6522
FAX:.......................................617-679-0910
E-Mail: ....sales@iona.com
Web: www.iona.ie:8000/www/index.html/

IOtech, Inc.
25971 Canon Rd.
Cleveland, OH 44146
Main:.....................................216-439-4091
FAX:.......................................216-439-4093
E-Mail: ....sales@iotech.com
BBS:.......................................216-439-5754
Web: www.iotech.com

IPS Publishing, Inc.
12606 NE 95th St. Ste. C-110
Vancouver, WA 98682
Main: 800-933-8378
Tech. Support:........................ 800-933-8378
Sales:..................................... 800-933-8378
Customer Service:................... 800-933-8378
Tech. Support FAX: 360-944-9156
FAX: 360-944-9156
America Online:......................... Keyword IPS
E-Mail:.........................examinacan@aol.com
Web: www.primenet.com/~examncan

ITI Software
France
Sales:..................................... 514-597-1692
FAX: 514-835-4772
BBS:....................................... 514-835-5945

IVI Publishing
7500 Flying Cloud Dr. Ste. 400
Minneapolis, MN 55344-3739
Main: 612-996-6000
Tech. Support:........................ 612-996-6301
Sales:..................................... 612-996-6000
Customer Service:................... 612-996-6350
Tech. Support FAX: 612-996-6001
E-Mail:.................................support@ivi.com
Web: www.heathnet.ivi.com

Iconovex Corp.
Innovex, Inc
7900 Xerxes Ave. South   Ste. 550
Bloomington, MN 55431
Main: 612-896-5100
Tech. Support:........................ 800-943-0292
Sales:..................................... 800-943-0292
Customer Service:................... 800-943-0292
Tech. Support FAX: 612-896-5101
FAX: 612-896-5101
E-Mail:............................ fyi@iconovex.com
Web: www.iconovex.com

Icot Corp.
3801 Zanker Rd.
San Jose, CA 95134-1402
Main:.....................................800-762-3270
Tech. Support:.......................408-433-3300
Tech. Support FAX:...............408-433-9466
BBS:.....................................408-432-3148

id Software, Inc.
18601 LBJ Freeway Ste. 615
Mesquite, TX 75150
Main:.....................................214-613-3589
Tech. Support:.......................970-522-1791
FAX: 214-686-9288
E-Mail: ....info@idsoftware.com
Web: www.idsoftware.com

Ideal Engineering
#29 8560 162nd St.
Surrey, BC V4N 1B4
Canada
Sales:.....................................604-572-8614
E-Mail: ....david_bailey@mindlink.bc.ca

Ikegami Electronics (USA), Inc.
37 Brook Ave.
Maywood, NJ 07607
Main:.....................................201-368-9171
Tech. Support:.......................201-368-9171
Sales:.....................................201-368-9171
Customer Service:..................201-368-9171
Tech. Support FAX:...............201-569-1626

Ilog Inc.
1901 Landings Dr. Building G
Mountain View, CA 94043
Main:.....................................800-367-4564
Tech. Support:.......................415-390-7137
Sales:.....................................800-367-4564
Customer Service:..................415-390-9000
Tech. Support FAX:...............415-390-0946
FAX: 415-390-0946
E-Mail: ....info@ilog.com
Web: www.ilog.com/ilog/home.html

imageFX
3021 Brighton-Henrietta Rd.
Rochester, NY 14623
Main: 800-229-8030
Tech. Support:.......................716-272-8030
Sales:.....................................800-229-8030
FAX: 716-272-1873
CompuServe: ....GO IMAGEFX
BBS: 716-272-1707
Web: www.imagefx.com

Imagers Overnight Digital Services
1575 Northside Dr.Building 400 Ste. 490
Atlanta, GA 30318
Main: 404-351-5800
Sales:.....................................800-398-5821
E-Mail:.......................imagers@imagers.com
Web: www.imagers.com

ImageSoft, Inc.
2 Haven Ave.
Port Washington, NY 11050
Main: 718-767-5181
Tech. Support:.......................718-767-5181
E-Mail:......................ecurrie@ix.netcom.com
BBS: 718-756-1860

Imagine Software Solutions, Inc.
7136 Summit Ave.
Cincinnati, OH 45243
Sales:.....................................800-453-4722
FAX: 513-984-2170

Imperial Computer Corp.
318 S San Gabriel Blvd. Ste. B-C
San Gabriel, CA 91776
Main: 818-285-1256
Tech. Support:.......................818-285-1256
Customer Service:..................818-285-1256
Tech. Support FAX: 818-285-9488
E-Mail:............................dalai2@gnn.com
BBS: 818-285-9488

In Focus Systems, Inc.
27700 B SW Pkwy.
Wilsonville, OR 97070
Main:......................................503-685-8888
Tech. Support:........................800-294-6400
Sales:....................................800-294-6400
Customer Service:..................800-327-7231
Tech. Support FAX:................503-685-8887
CompuServe:...........................GO INFOCUS
BBS:......................................503-692-4476
Web: www.infs.com

Independent Technology Service
4495 Runway St.
Simi Valley, CA 93063
Main:......................................818-882-7747
Tech. Support:........................805-526-1555
Sales:....................................818-882-7747
Customer Service:..................818-882-7747
Tech. Support FAX:................805-526-2590
E-Mail:...............................intech@msn.com
BBS:......................................818-718-8748

Index Stock Photography
126 Fifth Ave.7th Floor
New York, NY 10011
Main:......................................212-929-4644
Web: www.indexstock.com

Individual Software Inc.
5870 Stoneridge Dr.
Pleasanton, CA 94588
Main:......................................510-734-6767
Tech. Support:........................800-331-3313
Sales:....................................800-822-3522
Customer Service:..................800-822-3522
Tech. Support FAX:................510-734-8337
CompuServe:...........................76366,3213
E-Mail:..........76366,3213@compuserve.com

Industrial Video, Inc.
1601 N. Ridge Rd.
Lorain, OH 44055
Main:......................................800-362-6150
Sales:....................................216-233-4000
E-Mail:..............af741@cleveland.freenet.edu

Inet
260 Chatman Rd Ste. 208
Newark, NJ 19702
Main: 302-454-1780
FAX: 302-454-1718
E-Mail:...................................sales@inet.net
FTP: ftp.inet.net
Web: www.inet.net

Infinitext Software Inc.
7 Marsh Hawk Rd.
Irvine, CA 92714
Main: 714-651-0640
FAX: 714-651-0640

Infoflex, Inc.
840 Hinckley Ste. 107
Burlingame, CA 94010
Main: 415-6976045

InfoNable Corporation
6340 Geary Blvd. Ste. 4
San Francisco, CA 94121
Sales:..................................... 415-666-3345
FAX: 415-666-3065

Information Builders, Inc.
1250 Broadway
New York, NY 10001
Main: 212-736-4433
Tech. Support:........................ 212-736-4433
Tech. Support FAX: 407-727-7615
CompuServe:............................ GO FOCUS
Web: www.ibi.com

Information Machines
20219 Chapter Dr.
Woodland Hills, CA 91364
Main: 818-884-5779

Informix Software, Inc.
4100 Bohannon Dr.
Menlo Park, CA 94025
Main:.....................................800-331-1763
Tech. Support:........................415-926-6300
Sales: 415-926-6300
E-Mail: ....info@informix.com
BBS:.....................................415-322-2805
Web: www.informix.com

Ingenius
4 Inverness Ct. East
Englewood, CO 80112
Main:....................................303-705-8800
Sales: 800-772-6397
Customer Service:..................800-435-7688
E-Mail: ....info@ingenius.com
Web: www.ingenius.com

Ingram Micro
PO Box 25125
Santa Ana, CA 92799-5125
Main:....................................714-566-1000

Inherent Technologies
2110 SW Jefferson St.
Portland, OR 97201
Main:....................................503-224-6751
FAX: 503-224-8872
E-Mail: ....webmaster@inherent.com
Web: www.inherent.com

Inner Media
60 Plain Rd.
Hollis, NH 03049
Sales: 800-962-2949
FAX: 603-465-7195

Innovative Technology, Ltd.
PO Box 726
Elk City, OK 73648
Main: 800-253-4001
Tech. Support:........................405-243 0030
Sales:....................................800-253-4001
Customer Service:..................800-253-4001
Tech. Support FAX: 405-243-2810
E-Mail:.................................tech@itlnet.net
BBS: 405-243-2810
Web: www.itlnet.net

Inscape
1933 Pontius Ave.
Los Angeles, CA 90025
Main: 310-312-5705
FAX: 310-312-6677
E-Mail:..........................inform@inscape.com
Web: www.pathfinder.com/inscape

Inset Labs
Quarterdeck
150 W. Pico Blvd.
Santa Monica, CA 90405
Tech. Support:........................310-309-4250
Sales:....................................310-309-3700
Customer Service:..................800-354-3222
Web: www.insetusa.com

Insight Development Corp.
2420 Camino Ramon Ste. 205
San Ramon, CA 94583
Main: 800-825-4115
Tech. Support:........................510-244-2000
Sales:....................................800-825-4115
Tech. Support FAX: 510-244-2020
E-Mail:...........................info@insightdev.com
Web: www.insightdev.com

Insight Enterprises
1912 W 4th St.
Tempe, AZ 85281
Main: 800-776-7600
Tech. Support:........................800-927-7848
Sales:....................................800-927-7848
BBS: 602-829-9193
Web: www.insignia.com

Insignia Solutions
2200 Lawson
Santa Clara, CA 95054
Main:......................................408-327-6000
Tech. Support:.......................408-327-6500
Customer Service:..................800-848-7677
Tech. Support FAX:................408-627-6343
FAX:......................................408-627-6105
Web: www.insignia.com

Inso Corp.
330 N. Wabash15th Floor
Chicago, IL 60611
Main:......................................312-329-0700
Tech. Support:.......................312-527-4357
Sales:....................................800-333-1395
Customer Service:..................312-329-0700
Tech. Support FAX:................312-670-0820
FAX:......................................312-670-0820
E-Mail: ....saleschi@inso.com
BBS:......................................312-670-0820
Web: www.inso.com

InstallShield Corp/Demo Shield
1100 Woodfield Rd. Ste. 108
Schaumburg, IL 60173-9946
Main:......................................847-240-9111
Tech. Support:.......................847-240-9135
Sales:....................................800-374-4353
Tech. Support FAX:................847-240-9138
FAX:......................................847-240-9120
E-Mail: ....info@installshield.com
BBS:......................................847-240-9137
Web: www.support@installshield.com

Integra Technologies Corp.
132 Calvary St.
Waltham, MA 02154
Main:......................................617-899-0012
Sales:....................................800-225-1616

Integra Technology
411 108th Ave. NE Ste. 1600
Bellevue, WA 98004
Main:......................................206-637-5600
Sales:....................................800-842-8395
FAX:......................................206-637-5607
Web: www.integra.net

Integrand Research Corp.
8620 Roosevelt Ave.
Visalia, CA 93291
Main: 209-651-1203
Tech. Support FAX: 209-651-1353
E-Mail:............................ integrand@aol.com
BBS:.................................... 209-651-1353

Integrated Computer Solution, Inc.
201 Broadway
Cambridge, MA 01239
Main: 617-621-0060
Tech. Support:....................... 617-621-0060
Sales:.................................... 617-621-0060
Customer Service:.................. 617-621-0060
Tech. Support FAX: 617-621-9555
FAX: 617-621-9555
E-Mail:..................................... info@ics.com
Web: www.ics.com

Integrated Device Technology
2975 Stender Way
Santa Clara, CA 95054
Main: 408-727-6116
Sales:.................................... 800-345-7015
Customer Service:.................. 800-345-7015
FAX: 408-492-8674
E-Mail:..................................... info@idt.com
FTP: ftp.idt.com
Web: www.idt.com

Intel Corp.
2200 Mission College Blvd.
Santa Clara, CA 95052
Tech. Support:....................... 503-264-7000
Sales:.................................... 800-538-3373
Customer Service:.................. 800-264-7000
Web: www.intel.com

Intellicom
20415 Nordoff
Chatsworth, CA 91311
Main: 818-407-3900
FAX: 818-882-2404
Web: www.intellicom.com

IntelliCorp, Inc.
1975 El Camino Real West
Mountain View, CA 94040
Main:......................................415-965-5700
Tech. Support:.........................415-965-5500
Sales:.....................................415-965-5700
Tech. Support FAX:.................415-965-5608
FAX: 415-965-5647
E-Mail: .... dispatcher@intellicopr.com
BBS:......................................415-965-5644
FTP: ftp.intellicorp.com
Web: www.intellicorp.com

IntelliGenetics Inc.
2105 S Bascom Ave. Ste. 200
Campbell, CA 95008
Main:......................................408-879-6300
FAX: 408-879-6302
E-Mail: .... products@ig.com
Web: www.ig.com

Interactive Development Environment
595 Market St.10th Floor
San Francisco, CA 94105
Main:......................................415-543-0900
Tech. Support:.........................800-444-7871
Tech. Support FAX:.................415-543-0145
FAX: 415-543-0145
E-Mail: ....info@ide.com
Web: www.ide.com

InterActive, Inc.
204 N Main
Humboldt, SD 57035
Tech. Support:.........................605-363-5117
Tech. Support FAX:.................605-363-5102
BBS:......................................605-363-5102
Web: www.iact.com

Interactive Software Engineering, Inc.
270 Storke Rd. Ste. 7
Goleta, CA 93117
Main: 805-685-1006
FAX: 805-685-6869
E-Mail:.....................................info@eiffel.com
Web: www.eiffel.com

Intercon Systems Corp.
950 Herndon Pkwy. Ste. 420
Herndon, VA 22070
Main: 703-709-9890
Sales:..................................... 703-709-5500
Tech. Support FAX: 703-709-5559
FAX: 703-709-5555
E-Mail:............................ info@intercon.com
BBS: 703-709-9896
Web: www.intercon.com

Interface Technology
67 Poland St.
Bridgeport, CT 06605
Main: 800-523-3199
Tech. Support:........................ 203-384-0400
Tech. Support FAX: 203-331-9719

Intergraph Corp.
1 Madison Industrial Park
Huntsville, AL 35894
Main: 800-763-0242
FAX: 800-730-6188
Web: www.intergraph.com

Intergraph Software Systems
1 Madison Industrial Park
Huntsville, AL 35894
Main: 800-763-0242
Web: www.intergraph.com

Interleaf, Inc.
62 Fourth Ave.
Waltham, MA 02154
Main: 617-290-0710
Sales:..................................... 800-955-5323
FAX: 617-290-4943
Web: www.ileaf.com

Interlink Computer Sciences
47370 Fremont Blvd.
Fremont, CA 94538
Main:.....................................800-422-3711
Tech. Support:.......................415-657-9800
FAX:......................................510-659-6381
E-Mail: ....info@interlink.com
BBS:......................................415-659-6381
Web: www.interlink.com

International Data Sciences, Inc.
501 Jefferson Blvd.
Warwick, RI 02886-1317
Tech. Support:........................401-737-9900
Sales: 401-737-9900
Tech. Support FAX:................401-737-9911
E-Mail: ....idsdata@businesson.com
Web: www.idsdata.com/

International Instrument, Inc.
2282 Townsgate Rd.
Westlake Village, CA 91361
Main:....................................800-543-3475
Tech. Support:.......................805-495-7673
Tech. Support FAX:................805-379-0701

International Software Engineering
Haja
57 M-35
Negaunee, MI 49866
Main:....................................906-475-4713
Tech. Support FAX:................906-475-0085
FAX:......................................906-475-9576
E-Mail: ....ise@up.net
Web: www.haja.com

International Technologies & Software
655-K N Berry St.
Brea, CA 92621
Main:....................................714-990-1880
Tech. Support FAX:................714-990-2503
E-Mail: ....its@ix.netcom.com

Internet Infinity, Inc.-SiteRating
2707 Plaza Del Amo
Torrance, CA 90503
Main: 310-533-4800
Tech. Support:.......................310-533-4800
Customer Service:..................310-533-4800
Tech. Support FAX: 310-533-1993
Web: www.internetinfinity.com

InterPlay Productions
17922 Fitch Ave.
Irvine, CA 92714
Main: 714-553-6655
Tech. Support:.......................714-553-6678
Customer Service:..................714-553-6678
FAX: 714-252-2820
CompuServe:.........................GO GAMEPUB
America Online:...............Keyword Interplay
E-Mail:.......................support@interplay.com
BBS:.....................................714-252-2822
FTP: ftp.interplay.com
Web: www.interplay.com

Intersect
1571 Whitmore Ave.
Ceres, CA 95307
Main: 800-326-6548
Tech. Support:.......................408-954-8038
Tech. Support FAX: 209-541-1401
Web: www.intrsect.com

InterSolv
1700 NW 167th Pl.
Beaverton, OR 97006
Main: 503-645-1150
Tech. Support:.......................800-443-1601
Sales:....................................800-547-4000
Customer Service:..................800-443-1601
Tech. Support FAX: 503-645-4576
FAX:......................................503-645-4576
Web: www.intersolv.com

Intersolve, Inc.
9420 Key West Ave.
Rockville, MD 20850
Main: 301-838-5000
FAX: 301-838-5065
Web: www.intersolv.com

Intex Solutions, Inc.
35 Highland Circle
Needham, MA 02194
Main:......................................617-449-6222
Tech. Support FAX:.................617-444-2318

Intracorp Entertainment, Inc.
INTRACORP
501 Brickell Key Dr. Ste. 600
Miami, FL 33131
Main:..305-373-7700
Tech. Support:.........................305-373-7700
Sales:......................................305-373-7700
Customer Service:...................800-468-7226
Tech. Support FAX:.................305-577-9875
CompuServe:........................ GO INTRACORP
E-Mail: ....Info@intracorp.com
FTP: ftp.gate.net/pur/users/intracor
Web: www.intracorp.com

Intuit
PO Box 3014
Menlo Park, CA 94026
Main:......................................415-944-6000
Tech. Support:.........................800-624-8742
Sales:......................................415-322-0573
Customer Service:...................800-624-8742
Web: www.intuit.com

Inventory Locator Service, Inc.
Aviall Inc.
3965 Mendenhall Rd.
Memphis, TN 38115
Main:......................................800-233-3414
Tech. Support:.........................901-794-4784
Tech. Support FAX:.................901-794-1760
Web: www.go-ils.com

Invisible Software, Inc.
1162 Chess Dr.
Foster City, CA 94404
Main:......................................415-570-5967
Customer Service:...................407-260-5007
Tech. Support FAX:.................407-260-5007
BBS:.......................................415-345-5509
Web: www.invissof.com

Iomega Corp.
1821 W Iomega Way
Roy, UT 84067
Main: 801-778-1000
Tech. Support:........................801-778-1000
Sales:.....................................801-778-1920
Customer Service:...................801-778-1465
Tech. Support FAX: 801-778-3461
FAX: 801-778-3190
America Online:.................. Keyword Iomega
BBS: 801-778-5888
Web: www.iomega.com

Isaacson Software, Eric
416 E University Ave.
Bloomington, IN 47401
Main: 812-339-1811
Tech. Support FAX: 812-335-1611
CompuServe: ....GO ZIPKEY
Web: www.eji.com

Island Graphics
80 E Sir Francis Drake Blvd. Ste. 2-B
Larkspur, CA 94939
Main: 415-464-3800
Sales:.....................................800-598-8118
Customer Service:...................415-491-1000
Tech. Support FAX: 415-464-3838
E-Mail:...........................islandgfx2@aol.com
FTP: ftp.island.com
Web: www.island.com

Isogon Corp.
330 7th Ave. 7th Floor
New York, NY 10001
Main: 212-376-3200
Tech. Support:........................212-376-3260
Sales:.....................................212-376-3200
Tech. Support FAX: 212-376-3280
FAX: 212-376-3260

Iterated Systems
3525 Piedmont Rd.Seven Piedmont Ctr. Ste.
600
Atlanta, GA 30305
Main: 800-437-2285
FAX: 404-264-8300
E-Mail:............................. info@iterated.com

Ivan Levison Direct Mail Copywriting
14 Los Cerros Dr.
Greenbrae, CA 94904
Main:.....................................415-461-0672
FAX:.......................................415-461-7738
E-Mail: ....ivan@levison.com
Web: www.levison.com

JDR Microdevices
1850 S. 10th St.
San Jose, CA 95112-4108
Main:.....................................800-538-5003
Tech. Support:........................800-538-5002
Sales: 800-538-5000
Tech. Support FAX:................800-538-5005
BBS:.......................................408-559-0250
Web: www.jdr.com

JP Software, Inc.
PO Box 1470
East Arlington, MA 02174
Main:.....................................617-646-3975
Tech. Support:........................617-646-3975
Sales: 800-368-8777
Customer Service:...................617-646-3975
Tech. Support FAX:.................617-646-0904
CompuServe:..............................GO JPSOFT
E-Mail: ....support@jpsoft.com
BBS:.......................................617-354-3230
FTP: ftp. Std.com/vendors/jpsoft
Web: www.jpsoft.com

JSB
108 Whispering Pines Dr. Ste. 115
Scotts Valley, CA 95066-4785
Main:.....................................408-438-8300
Sales: 800-359-3408
FAX:.......................................408-438-8360
Web: www.jsbus.com

JYACC, Inc.
116 John St.
New York, NY 10038
Main:.....................................800-458-3313
Tech. Support:........................212-267-7722
Tech. Support FAX:.................212-608-6753
Web: www.jyacc.com

Jade Eye
PO Box 10423
Burke, VA 22009
Main: 800-932-8009

Jakarta Media Storage
265 Winn St.
Burlington, MA 01803-2616
Main: 617-273-5383
Sales:.....................................800-288-5383
FAX: 617-273-3053

Jameco Electronic
1355 Shoreway Rd.
Belmont, CA 94002
Main: 415-592-8097
Tech. Support:........................415-592-8097
Customer Service:...................800-831-4242
Tech. Support FAX: 415-595-2664
E-Mail:.............................info@jameco.com
BBS:.......................................415-637-9025
Web: www.jameco.com

James River Group, Inc.
125 N 1st St.
Minneapolis, MN 55401
Main: 612-339-2521
Tech. Support:........................612-339-2521
Sales:.....................................612-339-2521
Customer Service:...................612-339-2521
Tech. Support FAX: 612-339-4445
FAX: 612-339-7056
FTP: ftp.jriver.com/pub/
Web: www.jriver.com

Jamestown Software
2508 Valley Forge Dr.
Madison, WI 53719
Main: 608-271-2090
Tech. Support FAX: 608-271-8959
CompuServe:.............................. 74275,745

Jasmine Multimedia Publishing
6746 Valjean Ave. Ste. 100
Van Nuys, CA 91406
Main:.......................................818-780-3344
Tech. Support:........................800-798-7535
Sales: 818-780-3344
Customer Service:..................818-780-3344
Tech. Support FAX:................818-780-8705
E-Mail: .... jasmine@jasmine.com
FTP: ftp.jasmine.com
Web: www.jasmine.com

Jay Pee Tech Distributors
915 Bridgeport Ave.
Shelton, CT 06484
Main:.......................................203-929-0790
Tech. Support FAX:................203-929-6948
E-Mail: ....ramesh@acorgis.com
BBS:.......................................203-929-6948

JenHolland Corporation
18872 MacArthur Blvd. Ste. 400
Irvine, CA 92715
Main:.......................................714-442-4400
FAX: 714-253-6712

JetForm Corp.
PO Box 606
Leominister, MA 04153
Main:.......................................800-267-9976
Tech. Support:........................613-594-3026
Sales: 800-267-9976
Customer Service:..................613-594-8886
Tech. Support FAX:................613-751-4808
BBS:.......................................613-563-2894
Web: www.jetform.com

Jinco Computers
5122 Walnut Grove Ave.
San Gabriel, CA 91776
Main:.......................................818-309-1108
Tech. Support:........................818-309-1103
Sales: 800-253-2531
Tech. Support FAX:................818-309-1107
E-Mail: .... jinco@wavenet.com
Web: www.jinco.com

Joe Berde & Associates
10875 Rancho Bernardo Rd. Ste. 101
San Diego, CA 92127
Main: 619-673-5057
Sales:.....................................619-673-5057
Customer Service:..................619-673-5057
Tech. Support FAX: 619-673-5054
FAX: 619-673-5054
Web: www.digitalstyle.com

Johnson-Grace Co. (div of America Online, Inc.)
2 Corporate Plaza
Newport Beach, CA 92660-7929
Main: 714-759-0700
FAX: 714-729-4643
Web: www.jgc.com

Jostens Learning Corp.
9920 Pacific Heights Blvd. Ste. 500
San Diego, CA 92121
Main: 800-521-8538
Tech. Support:........................800-548-8372
Sales: 800-422-4339
Customer Service:..................800-548-8372
Tech. Support FAX: 619-622-7877
FAX: 619-587-1629
E-Mail:........................... sdsupport@jlc.com
Web: www.jlc.com

JourneyWare Media, Inc.
550 Center St. Ste. 123
Moraga, CA 94556
Main: 510-254-4520
Tech. Support:........................510-254-4520
Sales: 510-254-4520
Customer Service:..................510-254-4520
Tech. Support FAX: 510-284-2619
FAX: 510-284-2619
E-Mail:.....................david@journeyware.com
Web: www.journeyware.com

Jovian Logic
47929 Fremont Blvd.
Fremont, CA 94538
Main:.....................................510-651-4823
Tech. Support:........................510-651-4823
Customer Service:...................510-651-4823
Tech. Support FAX:................510-651-1343
CompuServe:.............................75300,221
E-Mail:.........................info@jovianlogic.com
BBS:.....................................510-651-6989
Web: www.jovianlogic.com

Joy Systems
2144 Bering Dr.
San Jose, CA 95131
Tech. Support:........................408-435-0980
Sales:....................................408-435-0980

K-Talk Communications, Inc.
1287 King Ave. Ste. 203
Columbus, OH 43212
Main:.....................................614-488-8818
FAX:......................................614-488-9505
E-Mail:...................................lisa@ktalk.com
Web: www.ktalk.com

KDS/Korea Data Systems Co., Ltd.
12300 Edison Way
Garden Grove, CA 92641
Main:.....................................714-379-5599
FAX:......................................714-379-5595
Web: www.kdusa.com

Kadak Products, Ltd.
206-1847 W Broadway
Vancouver, BC V6J 1Y5
Canada
Main:.....................................604-734-2796
Tech. Support:........................604-734-2796
BBS:.....................................604-734-8114

Kalglo Electronics Co., Inc.
5911 Colony Dr.
Bethlehem, PA 18017
Main: 610-837-0700
Tech. Support:........................ 610-837-0700
Sales:.................................... 800-524-0400
FAX: 610-837-7978

Kaplan InterActive
444 Madison Ave. Ste. 803
New York, NY 10022
Main: 212-751-1877
Web: www.kaplan.com

Kay Elemetrics
2 Bridgewater Lane
Lincoln Park, NJ 07035
Main: 800-289-5297
Sales:.................................... 201-628-6200
FAX: 201-628-6363
BBS:..................................... 201-227-7760
Web: www.kayelemetrics.com

Keithley MetraByte Corp.
Keithley Instruments
440 Miles Standish Blvd.
Tauton, MA 02780
Main: 508-880-3000
FAX: 508-880-0179
BBS:..................................... 508-880-3602

Kennedy Networking Solutions
1023 Lendee Dr.
Nisswa, MN 56468
Main: 800-932-5216

Kenosha Computer Corp.
2133 91st St.
Kenosha, WI 53143
Main: 800-255-2989
Tech. Support:........................ 414-697-9595
Tech. Support FAX: 414-697-0620

Kensington Microware, Ltd.
251 Park Ave. S
New York, NY 10010
Main:.....................................800-535-4242
Tech. Support:........................212-475-5200
BBS:......................................212-475-5996
Web: www.kensington.com

Kensington Technologies
2855 Campus Dr.
San Mateo, CA 94403
Main:.....................................800-535-4242
Sales: 415-572-2700
Web: www.kensington.com

Kentrox Industries, Inc.
14375 NW Science Park Dr.
Portland, OR 97229-9886
Main:.....................................800-232-5879
Tech. Support:........................503-643-1681
Sales: 503-643-1681
Tech. Support FAX:.................503-641-3341
Web: www.kentrox.com

Key Power, Inc.
9214 S. Norwalk Blvd.
Santa Fe Springs, CA 90670
Customer Service:...................800-535-4242

Keypoint Technology
20480 E. Business Pkwy.
Walnut, CA 91789
Main:.....................................909-444-8800
Tech. Support:........................800-888-8383
Sales: 800-888-8583
FAX: 909-468-3756
BBS:......................................909-468-1241

Keystone Technology
7510 N. Broadway Extension Ste. 205
Oklahoma City, OK 73116
Main:.....................................405-848-9902
Customer Service:...................800-364-7820
E-Mail: ....service@keytech.com
Web: www.keytech.com

Keytronics Corp.
North 4424 Sullivan Rd.
Spokane, WA 99214
Main: 509-928-8000
Tech. Support:........................800-262-6006
Tech. Support FAX: 509-927-5252
E-Mail:......................jmurray@keytronic.com
BBS: 509-927-5288

Kidsoft, L.L.C.
10275 N. De Anza Blvd.
Cupertino, CA 95014-2237
Main: 408-255-3434
Tech. Support:........................408-255-1328
FAX: 408-342-3500
Web: www.kidsoft.com

Kimtron Corp.
4181 Business Ct. Dr.
Fremont, CA 94538
Main: 800-777-8755
Tech. Support:........................510-623-8900
Tech. Support FAX: 510-623-8945
BBS: 408-436-1380

Kinetic Software
8404 Swathmore Court
Knoxville, TN 37919
Web: www.esper.com/kinetic

Kingston Technology
17600 Newhope St.
Fountain Valley, CA 92708
Main: 714-435-2600
Tech. Support:........................714-435-2639
Customer Service:...................714-435-2600
Tech. Support FAX: 714-437-3310
CompuServe: ....GO KINGSTON
E-Mail:............. tech_support@kingston.com
BBS: 714-435-2636
Web: www.kingston.com

Kipp Visual Systems
360-C Christopher Ave.
Gaithersburg, MD 20878
Main: 301-670-7906
E-Mail:......................kipp@rasputin.umd.edu

Knight-Ridder Info Inc.
Knight-Ridder, Inc.
2440 El Camino Real
Mountain View, CA 94040-1400
Main:.....................................800-334-2564
Tech. Support FAX:.................415-254-7070
Web: www.krinfo.com

Knowledge Adventure
1311 Grand Central Ave.
Glendale, CA. 92101
Main:.....................................800-482-0215
Tech. Support:.......................818-246-4811
Sales: 800-542-4240
Customer Service:..................800-542-4240
Tech. Support FAX:................818-246-5604
E-Mail: .... support@adventure.com
Web: www.adventure.com

Knowledge Dynamics Corp.
PO Box 780068
San Antonio, TX 78278-0068
Main:.....................................800-331-2783
Tech. Support:.......................210-979-9424
Sales: 210-979-9424
Tech. Support FAX:................210-979-9004
BBS:......................................212-979-8837
Web: www.install.com

Knowledge Garden, Inc.
5116 Hartwick Lane
West Palm Beach, FL 33415
Main:.....................................407-615-8209
Sales: 407-615-8209
Tech. Support FAX:.................407-615-8461
E-Mail: .... info@kgarden.com
FTP: ftp.kgarden.com
Web: www.kgarden.com

Knowledge Point, Inc.
1129 Industrial Ave.
Petaluma, CA 94954
Main:.....................................707-762-0333
Tech. Support:.......................707-762-0383
FAX:......................................707-762-0802

Knozall Systems, Inc.
375 E Elliot Rd. Ste. 10
Chandler, AZ 85225-1130
Main: 800-333-8698
Tech. Support:........................ 602-545-0006
Tech. Support FAX: 602-545-0008
FAX: 602-545-0008
CompuServe:...........................GO KNOZALL
E-Mail:.............................. sales@knozall.com
Web: www.knozall.com/www.knozall

Kolod Research, Inc.
1898 Techny Ct
Northbrook, IL 60062
Main: 708-291-1586

Konica Business Machines USA
Konica
500 Day Hill Rd.
Windsor, CT 06095
Main: 800-456-6422
Sales:.................................... 860-683-2222
Tech. Support FAX: 860-285-7601
FAX: 860-285-7452
Web: www.kbm.com

Koss Corp.
4129 N Port Washington Ave.
Milwaukee, WI 53212
Main: 414-964-5000
Tech. Support:........................ 800-872-5677
Sales:.................................... 414-964-5000
Customer Service:.................. 800-872-5677
Tech. Support FAX: 414-964-8615
FAX: 414-964-8615

Krash Computer Consultants
200 Hembree Park Dr.
Roswell, GA 30076-3890
Main: 770-751-9473
Sales:.................................... 800-221-4767
FAX: 770-475-4659

Kuck & Associates
1906 Fox Dr.
Champaign, IL 61820-7334
Main:.......................................217-356-2288
Sales: 217-356-5184
FAX: 217-356-5199
Web: www.kai.com

Kuehl Systems
11339 Sorrento Valley Rd
San Diego, CA 92121
Main:.......................................619-587-0787
Sales: 800-934-3345

Kurtiniferrous
PO Box 1477
Fremont, CA 94539
Main:.......................................415-623-7899

KurtVision
12201 Texas Ave. Ste. 4
Los Angeles, CA 90025
Main:.......................................310-207-8223
Tech. Support:.........................310-207-8223
Web: www.kurt.com

Kwery
Sales:......................................206-644-7830
FAX: 206-644-8409

LG Semicon America Inc.
3003 N 1st St.
San Jose, CA 95134
Main:.......................................800-777-1192
Tech. Support:.........................408-432-1331
Tech. Support FAX:.................408-432-6067
FAX: 408-432-6067
BBS:...408-432-6068

Labtec Enterprises
3801 NE 109th Ave. Ste. J
Vancouver, WA 98682
Main:.......................................360-896-2000
Tech. Support FAX:.................360-896-2020
E-Mail: ....feedback@labtec.com
Web: www.labtec.com

Lan-Link Corp.
944 Goddard
PO Box 4098
Chesterfield, MO 63006
Main: 314-537-9800
Tech. Support:........................314-394-9723
FAX: 314-394-6659

Lan Times
1900 O'Farrell St. Ste. 200
San Mateo, CA 94403
Main: 415-513-6800
Customer Service:...................415-513-6849
Web: www.wcmh.com

LANCAST/Casat Technologies
12 Murphy Dr.
Nashua, NH 03062
Main: 603-880-1833
Tech. Support:........................800-952-6227
Sales:.....................................800-952-6227
Customer Service:...................800-952-6227
Tech. Support FAX: 603-881-9888
FAX: 603-881-9888
E-Mail:...............................lancast1@aol.com

Lancity
200 Bullfinch
Andover, MA 01810
Main: 508-682-1600
Tech. Support FAX: 508-682-3200
E-Mail:................................lcb@lancity.com

Lanex Corp.
Ideas, Inc.
10727 Tucker St.
Beltsville, MD 20705
Main: 800-638-5969
FAX: 301-595-9145

Lantronix
15353 Baranca Pkwy.
Irvine, CA 92718-2216
Main:......................................800-422-7015
Tech. Support:........................800-422-7044
Sales:.....................................714-453-3990
Customer Service:...................714-453-3990
Tech. Support FAX:.................714-453-3995
Web: www.lantronix.com

Lapsoft Inc.
8402 Laurel Fair Cir. Ste. 207
Tampa, FL 33610
Main:......................................800-767-3279
Tech. Support:........................813-684-8291
Tech. Support FAX:.................813-622-7046

Larscom Incorporated.
4600 Patrick Henry Dr.
Santa Clara, CA 95054
Main:......................................408-988-6600
Tech. Support FAX:.................408-986-8690
BBS:.......................................408-986-8690
Web: www.larscom.com

Laser Communications, Inc.
1848 Charter Lane Ste. F
Lancaster, PA 17605-0066
Main:......................................717-394-8634
Tech. Support:........................800-527-3740
Sales:.....................................800-527-3740
Customer Service:...................800-527-3740
Tech. Support FAX:.................717-396-9831
FAX:.......................................717-396-9831
E-Mail: ....lasercom@epix.net
Web: www.lasercomm.com/lasercomm

Laser Master
7092 Shady Oak Rd.
Eden Praire, MN 55344
Main:......................................612-944-9457
Tech. Support:........................619-941-4919
Tech. Support FAX:.................612-941-8652

LaserGo, Inc.
9715 Carroll Center Rd. Ste. 107
San Diego, CA 92126
Main: 619-578-3100
Tech. Support:........................ 619-578-3100
FAX: 619-578-4502
E-Mail:............................lasergo@lasergo.com
BBS:...................................... 619-578-3818
Web: www.lasergo.com

Lattice, Inc.
3020 Woodcreek Dr. Ste. D
Downersgrove, IL 60515
Main: 800-444-4309
Tech. Support:........................ 214-516-1888
FAX: 708-769-4083

Lazarus Data Recovery
381 Clementina St.
San Francisco, CA 94103
Main: 800-765-9292
Tech. Support:........................ 800-765-9292
FAX: 415-495-5553
Web: www.lazarus.com

Lead Technologies Inc.
900 Baxter St
Charlotte, NC 28204
Sales:...................................... 800-637-1837
FAX: 704-372-8161
Web: www.leadtools.com

Leading Design
3417 Fremont Ave. North Ste. 221
Seattle, WA 98103
Main: 206-547-5985
Sales:...................................... 800-355-9845
FAX: 206-547-5988
CompuServe:.......................... 76306,343
Web: www.ldesign.com

Leading Edge
14 Brent Dr.
Hudson, MA 01749
Main: 508-562-3322
Tech. Support:........................ 800-245-9868
FAX: 508-568-3618

Leading Spect

1025 Segovia Cir.
Placentia, CA 92670
Main:.....................................714-666-2626
Tech. Support:........................714-666-8608
Sales: 800-234-0688
Customer Service:..................714-666-8608
Tech. Support FAX:................714-666-2900
FAX: 714-666-2900

Legacy Storage Systems, Inc.

138 River Rd. Ste. 204
Andover, MA 01810
Main:.....................................800-966-6442
Tech. Support:........................800-996-6442
Sales: 508-681-8400
FAX: 508-689-9004
BBS:......................................800-361-5685

Legato Systems, Inc.

3145 Porter Dr.
Palo Alto, CA 94304
Main:.....................................415-812-6000
FAX: 415-812-6032
Web: www.legato.com

Lenen Systems International Inc.

290 Woodcliff Office Park
Fairport, NY 14450-4212
Sales: 800-225-3635
FAX: 716-248-9185
CompuServe:............................713-33,622
Web: www.lenel.com/lenel/

Leo Electronics

PO Box 11307
Torrance, CA 90501-1307
Main:.....................................800-421-9565
Tech. Support:........................310-212-6133
Sales: 310-212-6133
Tech. Support FAX:................310-212-6106
Web: www.excess.com

Letraset Graphic Design Software

40 Eisenhower Dr.
Paramus, NJ 07653
Main: 201-845-6100
Tech. Support:........................201-845-6100
Sales: 201-845-6100
Customer Service:..................201-845-6100
Tech. Support FAX: 201-845-5047
FAX: 201-845-5047

Level Five Research

Information Builders
1335 Gateway Dr. Ste. 2005
Melbourne, FL 32901
Main: 407-729-6004
Tech. Support:........................407-729-6004
Sales: 407-729-6004
Customer Service:..................407-729-6004
FAX: 407-727-7615
Web: www.L5R.com

Leviton

2222 222ND St. SE
Bothell, WA 98021
Main: 206-486-2222
Tech. Support:........................800-722-2082
Sales: 800-722-2082
Customer Service:..................800-722-2082
Tech. Support FAX: 206-483-5270
FAX: 206-483-5270

Lexmark International, Inc.

55 Railroad Ave.
Greenwick, CT 06836
Main: 606-232-2000
Tech. Support:........................606-232-3000
Sales: 800-438-2468
Customer Service:..................800-879-2755
Tech. Support FAX: 606-232-2873
FAX: 606-232-6725
CompuServe: ....GO LEXMARK
BBS: 606-232-5238
FTP: ftp.lexmark.com
Web: www.lexmark.com

Liberty
120 Saratoga Ave. Ste. 82
Santa Clara, CA 95051
Main:......................................408-983-1127
Tech. Support FAX:.................408-243-2885
Web: www.libertyinc.com

Liebert Corp.
Emerson Electric
1050 Dearborn Dr.
PO Box 29186
Columbus, OH 43229
Main:......................................614-888-0246
Sales:.....................................800-877-9222
Tech. Support FAX:.................614-841-6973
E-Mail:............................Pulsed@liebert.com
Web: www.liebert.com

Lifeboat Publishing
1163 Shrewsbury Ave.
Shrewsbury, NJ 07702
Sales:.....................................908-389-0037
FAX:.......................................908-389-9227
BBS:.......................................908-389-9783

Lind Electronic Design
6414 Cambridge St.
Minneapolis, MN 55426
Main:......................................800-659-5956
Tech. Support:.......................612-927-6303
Sales:.....................................612-927-6303
Customer Service:..................612-927-6303
FAX:.......................................612-927-7740

Lindo Systems, Inc.
PO Box 148231
Chicago, IL 60622
Main:......................................800-441-2378
Tech. Support:.......................312-248-0465
Sales:.....................................312-871-2524
FAX:.......................................312-871-1777
Web: www.lindo.com

Link Technologies
Wyse Technology
3471 N First St.
San Jose, CA 95134
Main: 408-473-1700
Tech. Support:.......................800-448-5465
Customer Service:..................800-448-5465
FAX: 408-922-4390
BBS:.......................................408-922-4400
Web: www.wyse.com

Linksys Group, Inc., The
17401 Armstrong Ave.
Irvine, CA 92713
Main: 714-261-1288
Tech. Support:.......................714-261-1288
Sales:.....................................800-546-5797
Customer Service:..................714-261-1288
Tech. Support FAX: 714-261-8868
BBS:.......................................714-261-2888
Web: www.linksys.com

Linotype-Hell Co.
425 Oser Ave.
Hauppage, NY 11788
Main: 516-434-2000
Tech. Support:.......................800-633-1900
Sales:.....................................800-842-9721
Customer Service:..................800-633-1900
Tech. Support FAX: 516-434-2748
FAX: 516-434-2748
E-Mail:...........................info@linotype.com
Web: www.linotype-hell.com

Litespeed Software
1800 19th St.
Bakersfield, CA 93301
Main: 805-324-4291
Tech. Support FAX: 805-324-1437
Web: www.litespeed.net

Lively Computer, The
8314 Pkwy. Dr.
La Mesa, CA 91942
Main: 619-589-9455
FAX: 619-589-5230
E-Mail:.....................tlively@connectnet.com

Living Books
160 Pacific Avenue Mall Ste. 201
San Francisco, CA 94111
Main:.....................................415-352-5200
FAX: 415-352-5213

Logal Software, Inc.
125 Cambridge Park Dr.
Cambridge, MA 02140
Main:..............................617-491-4440-111
Sales:.............................617-491-4440-103
FAX: 617-491-5855
Web: www.logal.com

Logitech
6505 Kaiser Dr.
Fremont, CA 94555
Main:.....................................510-795-8500
Tech. Support:.......................510-795-8100
Sales: 800-231-7717
Customer Service:..................800-231-7717
Tech. Support FAX:................510-505-0978
CompuServe:......................... GO LOGITECH
E-Mail: ....tech_support@logitech.com
BBS:.....................................510-795-0408
Web: www.logitech.com

Lomas Data Products
420 Maple St. Ste. 2
Marlboro, MA 01752
Main:.....................................508-460-0333
Tech. Support FAX:................508-460-0616

Looking Glass Software, Inc.
1222 La Cienega Blvd. Ste. 305
Inglewood, CA 90304
Sales: 310-348-8240
FAX: 310-348-8240

Lorax, The
PO Box 1471
Minot, ND 58701
Main:.....................................701-838-4686
Sales: ....,..........800-992-0616
FAX: 701-838-4932

Lotus Development - cc: Mail
55 Cambridge Pkwy.
Cambridge, MA 02142
Main: 617-577-8500
Tech. Support:........................ 508-988-2500
Sales:..................................... 800-343-5414
Customer Service:................... 800-343-5414
Tech. Support FAX: 617-693-7811
CompuServe: ....GO LOTUS
BBS: 415-691-0401
FTP: ftp.support.lotus.com/pub
Web: www.lotus.com

Lotus Word Processing
5600 Glenridge Dr.
Atlanta, GA 30342
Tech. Support:........................ 508-988-2500
Sales:..................................... 800-343-5414
CompuServe: .... GO LOTUSWP
BBS: 770-395-7707
Web: www.support.lotus.com

Lucas Learning Ltd.
PO Box 10667
San Rafael, CA 94912
Main: 415-444-8800
FAX: 415-444-8898
Web: www.glef.org

LucasArts
PO Box 10307
San Rafael, CA 94912
Tech. Support:........................ 415-507-4545
Sales:..................................... 800-985-8227
Tech. Support FAX: 415-507-0300
FAX: 818-587-6629
CompuServe: ....GO GAMAPUB
America Online:............... Keyword Lucasarts
BBS: 415-507-0400

Lucent Technologies
2701 Maitland Center Pkwy. Ste. 200
Maitland, FL 32751
Main:......................................800-448-6727
Tech. Support:........................407-662-7100
Sales:.....................................800-448-6727
Customer Service:...................800-448-6727
FAX:.......................................800-826-5399
BBS:......................................407-662-7171
Web: www.att.com/mss

MCBA, Inc.
330 N Brand Blvd. Ste. 350
Glendale, CA 91203
Main:.....................................818-242-9600
Tech. Support FAX:.................818-500-4805

MCI Communications Corp.
1801 Pennsylvania Ave. NW
Washington, DC 20006
Main:.....................................202-872-1600
Sales:.....................................800-955-5195
Web: www.mci.com

MECC
6160 Summit Dr. N
Minneapolis, MN 55430-4003
Main:.....................................612-569-1500
Tech. Support:........................612-569-1678
Sales:.....................................800-685-6322
Customer Service:...................612-569-1678
Tech. Support FAX:.................612-569-1531
FAX:.......................................612-569-1551
BBS:......................................612-569-1710
Web: www.mecc.com

MEI/Micro Center
1100 Steelwood Rd.
Columbus, OH 43202
Sales:.....................................800-634-3478
FAX:.......................................614-486-6417

MIDI Land, Inc.
440 S. Lone Hill Ave.
San Dimas, CA 91773
Main:.....................................909-592-1168

MIPS Technologies, Inc.
2011 North Shoreline Blvd.
MS9l-925
Mountain View, CA 94039-7311
Main: 415-933-3121
FTP: ftp.sgigate.sgi.com
Web: www.mips.com

MIS Computer Systems
45395 N Port Loop W
Fremont, CA 94538
Main: 800-733-9188
Tech. Support FAX: 510-226-0230

MMI
1001 Millersville Rd
PO Box 4547
Lancaster, PA 17604
Main: 717-872-6567
Tech. Support:........................717-872-2442
Sales:.....................................800-334-2722
FAX: 717-871-9959
Web: www.mmi.com

MW Media
60 South Market St. Ste. 720
San Jose, CA 95113
Main: 408-286-4200
Tech. Support:........................408-286-4200
Sales:.....................................408-286-4200
Customer Service:...................408-286-4200
FAX: 408-288-4728
Web: www.mwmedia.com

Mabry Software
PO Box 31926
Seattle, WA 98103
Sales:.....................................206-634-1443
FAX: 206-632-0272
CompuServe:..........................71231,2066
FTP: ftp.halcyon.com/local/mabry/files/
Web: www.halcyon.com/mabry/welcome.html

MacMillan Publishing

201 W 103rd St.
Indianapolis, IN 46290-1094
Main:......................................317-581-3500
Tech. Support:.......................317-581-3833
Sales:....................................800-716-0044
Customer Service:.................800-858-7674
Tech. Support FAX:................317-581-4773
FAX:......................................317-581-3550
CompuServe:.....................GO MACMILLAN
America Online:........... Keyword Superlibrary
BBS:......................................317-581-4771
FTP: ftp.mcp.com
Web: www.mcp.com

Macola Software

333 E Center St.
PO Box 1821
Marion, OH 43301-1824
Main:....................................800-468-0834
Tech. Support:.......................614-382-5999
Tech. Support FAX:................614-387-6149

Macromedia

600 Townsend St.
San Francisco, CA 94103
Main:....................................415-252-2000
Tech. Support:.......................415-252-9080
Sales:....................................800-328-2126
Customer Service:.................415-252-2000
Tech. Support FAX:................415-703-0924
FAX:......................................415-626-0554
CompuServe:...................GO MACROMEDIA
America Online:.......... Keyword Macromedia
E-Mail: ....sales@macromedia.com
FTP: ftp.macromedia.com
Web: www.macromedia.com

Macronix, Inc.

1338 Ridder Park Dr.
San Jose, CA 95131
Main:....................................408-453-8088
Sales: 800-858-5311
BBS:......................................408-453-8488
Web: www.modems.com

Macros Solutions Ltd.

Main: 403-922-5514
FAX: 403-922-2859
Web: www.bittco.com

Macrosn's New Media

20 Academy St.
Arlington, MA 02174
Main: 617-646-4550
FAX: 617-646-3161
E-Mail:....................................info@macsym
Web: www-elc.gnn.com/gnn

Madge Networks, Inc.

Madge Network
2310 N First St.
San Jose, CA 95131-1101
Main: 408-955-0700
Tech. Support:.......................800-876-2343
Sales:....................................408-955-0700
Customer Service:.................800-876-2343
Tech. Support FAX: 408-955-0970
BBS: 408-955-0262
Web: www.madge.com

Madison Cable

AMP
125 Goddard Memorial Dr.
Worcester, MA 01603
Main: 508-752-7320
FAX: 508-752-4230

Mag InnoVision

2801 S Yale St.
Santa Ana, CA 92704
Main: 714-751-2008
Tech. Support:.......................800-827-3998
Sales:....................................800-827-3998
Customer Service:.................800-827-3998
Tech. Support FAX: 714-751-5522
Web: www.maginnovision.com

Magee Enterprises, Inc.
PO Box 1587
Norcross, GA 30091
Main:....................................800-662-4330
Tech. Support:.......................770-446-6611
Tech. Support FAX:................770-368-0719
CompuServe:............................ GO MAGEE
E-Mail:.............................. sales@magee.com
Web: www.magee.com

Magellan Geographix
6464 Hollister Ave.
Santa Barbara, CA
Main:....................................800-929-4627
FAX:.....................................805-685-3330
CompuServe:........................GO MAGELLAN
Web: www.magellangeo.com

Magic Page
3043 Luther St.
Winston-Salem, NC 27127
Main:....................................910-785-3695
E-Mail:.........................spiff@cup.portal.com

Magic Software
1624 Kaiser Ave.
Irvine, CA 92714
Main:....................................800-3456244
Tech. Support:.........................714-2501720
Sales:....................................714-2501718
Tech. Support FAX:.................714-2507404
FAX:.....................................714-2507404
CompuServe:............................. 70521,645
BBS:....................................714-250-8945
Web: www.magic-sw.com

Magnavox
1 Philips Dr.
Knoxville, TN 37914
Main:....................................423-521-4316
Tech. Support:.......................800-835-3506
Sales:...................................800-292-6066
Customer Service:...................800-835-3506
Tech. Support FAX:.................423-475-0387
Web: www.magnavox.com

Malkovich MultiMedia
12707 N. Freeway Ste. 140
Houston, TX 77060
Main: 800-448-0601
FAX: 713-872-4908

Management Systems Designers
131 Park St. NE
Vienna, VA 22180
Main: 703-281-7440
FAX: 703-281-7636

Manhattan Electric Cable
CDT
203 Progress Dr.
Manchester, CT 06040
Main: 800-228-6322
Tech. Support:........................ 860-643-3547
Tech. Support FAX: 860-643-3556

Mannesmann Tally Corp.
8301 S 180th St.
Kent, WA 98064
Main: 206-251-5500
Tech. Support:........................ 206-251-5532
FAX: 206-251-5520
E-Mail:..........................webmaster@tally.com
Web: www.tally.com

Mansfield Software Group
PO Box 532
Storrs, CT 06268
Main: 860-429-8402
Tech. Support FAX: 860-487-1185
CompuServe:............................ GO PCVENA
E-Mail:............................ support@kedit.com
Web: www.kedit.com

MapInfo Corp.
One Global View
Troy, NY 12180
Main: 518-285-6000
Tech. Support:........................ 518-285-6327
Sales:................................... 800-327-8627
FAX: 518-285-6060
Web: www.mapinfo.com

Mark of the Unicorn, Inc.
1280 Massachusetts Ave.
Cambridge, MA 02138
Main:.......................................617-576-2760
Tech. Support:........................617-576-3066
Sales:......................................617-576-2760
Customer Service:...................617-576-2760
Tech. Support FAX:................617-354-3068
FAX:..617-576-3609
CompuServe:...........................713-33,3666
America Online:....................Keyword Motu
E-Mail:.................................info@motu.com
Web: www.motu.com

MarketSmart
2175 De La Cruz Blvd. Ste. 9
Santa Clara, CA 95050
Main:......................................408-236-2266
E-Mail:.....................sales@marketsmart.com
Web: www.marketsmart.com

Mathematica, Inc.
100 Trade Center Dr.
Champaign, IL 61820-7237
Main:......................................217-398-0700
Tech. Support:........................217-398-6500
Sales:......................................800-441-6284
Customer Service:...................217-398-5151
Tech. Support FAX:................217-398-0747
FAX:..217-398-0747
CompuServe:...........................76702,1400
E-Mail:.......................support@wolfram.com
BBS:.......................................217-398-1898
Web: www.wolfram.com

MathSoft
101 Main St.
Cambridge, MA 02142-1521
Main:......................................617-577-1017
Tech. Support:........................970-339-7119
Sales:......................................800-628-4223
Customer Service:...................800-628-4223
Tech. Support FAX:................617-577-8829
FAX:..617-577-1778
E-Mail:......................support@mathsoft.com
Web: www.mathsoft.com

Mathtype
Main:......................................310-433-0685
FAX:..310-433-6969
E-Mail:.................mtsupport@mathtype.com
Web: www.mathtype.com/mathtype

MathWorks, Inc., The
Cochituate Pl.
24 Prime Park Way
Natick, MA 01760
Main:......................................508-647-7000
FAX:..508-647-7001
Web: www.mathworks.com

MatrixSoft - SWAG
E-Mail:...............................larsh@ionsys.com
Web: www.ionsys.com/~larsh/ms.html

Matrox Electronic Systems
1025 St. Regis
Dorval, PQ H9P 2T4
Canada
Main:......................................514-969-6320
Tech. Support:........................514-685-2630
Sales:......................................800-361-1408
Customer Service:...................514-685-2630
Tech. Support FAX:................514-685-2853
FAX:..514-969-6363
E-Mail:...............graphics.sales@matrox.com
BBS:..514-685-6008
FTP: ftp.matrox.com/pub/mga
Web: www.matrox.com

Maxim Technology
3930 W 29th S Ste. 35
Wichita, KS 67217
Main:......................................316-941-9797
Tech. Support:........................316-941-9797
FAX:..316-941-9883
E-Mail:......................maxim@southwind.net

Maximum Computer Technologies Inc.
Building 200 Ste. 210
1000 Cobb Pl. Blvd.
Kennesaw, GA 30144-3684
Main:......................................800-582-9337
FAX:...770-428-5009
E-Mail: .... info@maxtech.com
Web: www.maxtech.com

Maximum Strategy
801 Buckeye Court
Milpitas, CA 95035
Main:......................................408-383-1600
Tech. Support:.........................800-352-1600
FAX:...408-383-1616
E-Mail: .... support@maxstrat.com
Web: www.maxstrat.com

Maxis
2121 N California Blvd. Ste. 60
Walnut Creek, CA 94596-3572
Main:......................................510-933-5630
Tech. Support:.........................510-927-3905
Sales:......................................800-336-2947
Customer Service:...................800-336-2947
Tech. Support FAX:.................510-927-3581
CompuServe:...........................GO GAMPUB
America Online:....................maxis@aol.com
E-Mail: ....support@maxis.com
BBS:...510-254-3869
FTP: ftp 199.182.213.85
Web: www.maxis.com

Maxpeed Corp.
1120 Chess Dr.
Foster City, CA 94404
Main:......................................415-345-5447
FAX:...415-345-6398
BBS:...415-345-8512
Web: www.maxspeed.com

MaxTech
1000 Cobb Pl. Blvd. Ste. 240
Kennesaw, GA 30144
FAX:...404-428-5009
Web: www.maxtech.com

Maxtor Corporation
211 River Oaks Pwky
San Jose, CA 95134
Main: 408-432-1700
Tech. Support:..................... 800-262-9867
Customer Service:................... 800-262-9867
Tech. Support FAX: 303-678-2260
FAX: 408-432-4510
E-Mail: .... technicalassistance@maxtor.com
BBS:....................................... 303-678-2222
Web: www.maxtor.com

McAfee Associates
2710 Walsh Ave.
Santa Clara, CA 95051
Main: 408-988-3832
Tech. Support:....................... 408-988-3832
Sales:..................................... 408-988-3832
Customer Service:................... 408-988-3832
Tech. Support FAX: 408-970-9727
CompuServe:............................ GO MCAFEE
America Online:...................Keyword Mcafee
E-Mail:.........................support@mcafee.com
BBS:....................................... 408-988-4004
FTP: ftp.mcafee.com
Web: www.mcafee.com

McCarty Associates, Inc.
455 Boston Post Rd.
Old Saybrook, CT 06475-9949
Main: 860-388-6994
FAX: 860-388-6826
E-Mail:.....................tmccarthy@connix.com

McData
310 Interlocken Pkwy.
Bloomfield, CO 80021
Main: 800-545-5773
Tech. Support:....................... 303-460-9200
BBS:....................................... 303-465-4996

McDonnell Douglas Network Systems
18881 Von Karman Ste. 1800
Irvine, CA 92715
Main: 714-724-5604

McKinley Group, The
Sausalito, CA
Web: www.mckinley.com

Media Architects, Inc.
1075 NW Murray Rd. Ste. 230
Portland, OR 97229
Sales: 503-639-2505
FAX: 503-297-6744
CompuServe:.............................. 74774,707

Media Cybernetics, Inc.
8484 Georgia Ave. Ste. 200
Silver Spring, MD 20910
Main:.....................................301-495-3305
Tech. Support:.......................301-495-3305
Sales: 800-992-4256
Customer Service:...................800-992-4256
Tech. Support FAX:.................301-495-5964
FAX: 301-495-5964
E-Mail: .... techsupport@mediacy.com
BBS:......................................301-495-2986
Web: www.mediacy.com

Media Factory
1930 Junction Ave.
San Jose, CA 95131
Main:.....................................800-879-9536
Tech. Support:.......................800-879-9536
Sales: 408-456-8848
Customer Service:...................408-456-8848
Tech. Support FAX:.................408-456-9337
FAX: 408-456-9298
CompuServe:............................ 75467,1560
E-Mail: .... sales@mediafactoryinc.com
Web: www.mediafactoryinc.com

Media Mosaic
520 NW Davis St.
Portland, OR 97209-3620
Main:.....................................800-972-3766
Sales: 503-225-1988
FAX: 503-225-1987
Web: www.media-mosaic.com

Media Source
2197 Canton Ste. 210
Marrietta, GA 30066
Main: 800-356-2553
Tech. Support:.......................800-356-2553
Sales:....................................800-356-2553
Customer Service:...................800-356-2553
Tech. Support FAX: 770-919-9228
FAX: 770-919-9228
E-Mail:.................sales@mediasourceinc.com
Web: www.com/mediasource

Media Synergy Inc.
260 King St. East Ste. 403
Toronto, ONT M5A 1K3
Canada
Main: 416-369-1100
FAX: 416-369-9037
CompuServe: 76201,444
Web: www.media-mosaic.com

Media Vision
107 Bonaventura Dr.
San Jose, CA 95134
Main: 510-770-8600
Tech. Support:.......................503-882-1177
Sales:....................................408-428-9355
Customer Service:...................800-638-2807
FAX: 408-428-9346
BBS: 510-770-0968
Web: www.mediavis.com

MegaHaus
2201 Pine Dr.
Dickenson, TX 77539
Main: 713-534-3919
Tech. Support:.......................713-534-2630
Web: www.megahaus.com

Megahertz
US Robotics
605 North 5600 West
Salt Lake City, UT 84116
Main:.....................................800-527-8677
Tech. Support:........................801-320-7777
Sales:....................................800-527-8677
Customer Service:...................801-320-7777
Tech. Support FAX:................801-320-6020
CompuServe:......................GO MEGAHERTZ
America Online:.............Keyword Megahertz
E-Mail:......................techsupport@mhz.com
BBS:......................................801-320-8841
FTP: ftp.megahertz.com
Web: www.megahertz.com

Megatel Computer Corp.
125 Wendell Ave.
Weston, ONT M9N 3K9
Canada
Main:.....................................416-245-2953
E-Mail:......................megatel@patcom.com
BBS:......................................416-245-6505
Web: www.emj.com

Memorex Telex
Irving, TX
Web: www.mtc.com

Mendelson Electronics
340 E 1st St.
Dayton, OH 45402
Main:.....................................800-422-3525
Tech. Support:........................513-461-3525
FAX:......................................513-461-7020
E-Mail:...............................maci@maci.com
Web: www.maci.com

Meridian Data, Inc.
5615 Scotts Valley Dr.
Scotts Valley, CA 95066
Main:.....................................408-438-3100
Sales:....................................800-767-2537
FAX:......................................408-438-6816
Web: www.meridian-data.com

Merisel, Inc.
200 Continental Blvd.
El Segundo, CA 90503
Main:....................................310-615-3080
Tech. Support:........................900-737-8324
Sales:...................................800-637-4735
Customer Service:...................708-595-6714
FAX:......................................310-535-4214
E-Mail:....................webmaster@merisel.com
Web: www.merisel.com

Meta Software Corp.
125 Cambridge Park Dr.
Cambridge, MA 02140
Main:....................................800-227-4106
Tech. Support:........................617-576-6920
FAX:......................................617-661-2008

Metagraphics Software Corp.
200 Clock Tower Pl . Ste. 201E
Carmel, CA 93923
Main:....................................800-332-1550
Tech. Support:........................408-622-8940
FAX:......................................408-622-8955
CompuServe:............................GO METAGR
BBS:......................................408-622-8945
Web: www.metagraphics.com

MetaTools Digital Theatre, The
6303 Carpinteria Ave.
Carpinteria, CA 93013
Main:....................................805-566-6200
Tech. Support:........................805-566-6200
Customer Service:...................805-566-6200
FAX:......................................805-566-6385
Web: www.metatools.com

MetaTools, Inc.
Web: www.hsc.com

Methode Electronics
7444 W Wilson Ave.
Chicago, IL 60656
Main:....................................800-323-6858
Tech. Support:........................708-867-9600
FAX:......................................708-867-9130
Web: www.methode.com

Metra Information Systems
45395 N Loop West
Fremont, CA 94538
Main:.....................................510-226-9188
Sales:....................................510-651-2300
Tech. Support FAX:................510-226-0231
BBS:.......................................408-730-5933

Metrics Inc.
465 Phillips St.
Waterloo, ONT N2L 6C7
Canada
Main:.....................................519-855-2458
Web: www.metrics.com

Mextel Corp.
159 Beeline Rd.
Bensenville, IL 60106
Main:.....................................800-888-4146
Tech. Support:.......................708-595-4146
Tech. Support FAX:................708-595-4149

Micom Communications
4100 Los Angeles Ave.
Simi Valley, CA 93063
Main:.....................................805-583-8600
Tech. Support:.......................805-583-8600
Sales:....................................800-642-6687
Tech. Support FAX:................805-583-1997
Web: www.micom.com

Micro Computer Systems Inc.
Main:.....................................214-659-1514
FAX: 214-659-1624
E-Mail:...........................info@mcsdallas.com
Web: www.mcsdallas.com

Micro Design International
6985 University Blvd.
Winter Park, FL 32792
Main:.....................................407-677-8333
Tech. Support FAX:................407-677-8365
E-Mail:...........................sales@microdes.com
BBS:.......................................407-677-8365
Web: www.microdes.com

Micro Dynamics
8555 16th St., Ste. 700
Silver Springs, MD 20910
Main: 301-589-6300
Tech. Support FAX: 301-589-3414
Web: www.mdl.com

Micro Express, Inc.
1801 Carnegie Ave.
Santa Ana, CA 92705
Main: 800-989-9900
Tech. Support:........................800-762-3378
Sales:....................................714-852-1400
Tech. Support FAX: 714-852-1225

Micro Integration
1 Science Park
Frostburg, MD 21532
Main: 800-832-4526
Tech. Support:........................800-642-5888
Sales:....................................301-369-0800
Tech. Support FAX: 301-689-0808
BBS: 301-689-0848

Micro Logic Corp.
PO Box 70
S Hackensack, NJ 07602
Main: 800-342-5930
Tech. Support:........................201-342-7468
Sales:....................................201-342-6518
Tech. Support FAX: 201-342-0370
Web: www.miclog.com

Micro Sense
320 Andrew Ave.
Leucadia, CA 92024
Main: 800-544-4252
Tech. Support:........................619-632-8621
Tech. Support FAX: 619-753-6133
E-Mail:................. docdrive@microsense.com
Web: www.microsense.com

Micro Sim Corporation
20 Fairbanks
Irvine, CA 92718
Main:.....................................714-770-3022
Tech. Support:........................714-837-0790
Sales:.....................................800-245-3022
Tech. Support FAX:................714-455-0554
E-Mail:..............tech.support@microsim.com
BBS:.......................................714-830-1550
Web: www.microsim.com

Micro Smart, Inc.
200 Homer Ave.
Ashland, MA 01721
Main:.....................................800-370-9090
Tech. Support:........................508-872-9090
Tech. Support FAX:................508-881-7708
FAX:.......................................508-881-1520
BBS:.......................................508-881-1520

Micro Solutions Computer Products
132 W Lincoln Hwy.
DeKalb, IL 60115
Main:.....................................815-756-3411
FAX:.......................................815-756-6417
Web: www.micro-solutions.com

Micro Source
801 Clanton Rd
Charlotte, NC 28217
Web: www.msi-online.com

Micro Sports
2255 Center St. Ste. 107
Chattanooga, TN 37421
Tech. Support:........................615-877-7815
Customer Service:...................800-937-7737
E-Mail:.................support@microsports.com
BBS:.......................................615-870-5694
Web: www.microsports.com

Micro Star Software Ltd.
3775 Richmond Rd.
Nepean, ONT K2H 5B7
Canada
Main: 800-267-9975
Tech. Support:........................ 619-436-0493
Sales:..................................... 613-596-2233
FAX: 613-596-5934
E-Mail:......................... cade@microstar.com

Micro System Options
21052 NE 91St.
Redmond, WA 98053
Sales:..................................... 206-868-5418
FAX: 206-868-7780

Micro Technology, Inc.
4905 E La Palma
Anaheim, CA 92807
Main: 800-999-9684
Tech. Support:........................ 714-970-0300
Tech. Support FAX: 714-693-2202
Web: www.mti.com

MicroBiz
300 Corporate Dr.
Mahwah, NJ 07430
Main: 800-637-8268
Tech. Support:........................ 201-512-1221
Sales:..................................... 201-512-0900
Tech. Support FAX: 201-512-1919
BBS:....................................... 201-512-0801
Web: www.microbiz.com

Microcal Software, Inc.
1 Roundhouse Plaza
Northampton, MA 01060
Main: 800-969-7720
Tech. Support:........................ 413-586-2013
FAX: 413-585-0126
E-Mail:............................info@microcal.com
BBS:....................................... 413-586-0149
FTP: ftp.microcal.com
Web: www.microcal.com

Microchip Technology Inc.
2355 W Chandler Blvd.
Chandler, AZ 85224
Main:......................................508-480-9990
Sales:.....................................508-480-9990
Web: www.ultranet.com/biz/mchip/

Microcom Systems, Inc.
500 River Ridge Dr.
Norwood, MA 02062
Main:......................................800-822-8224
Tech. Support:........................617-551-1999
Sales:.....................................617-551-1745
FAX:.......................................617-551-1021
BBS:.......................................617-255-1125
Web: www.microcom.com

Microcomputer Concepts
15200 Transistor Ln.
Huntington Beach, CA 92649
Main:......................................800-772-3914
Tech. Support:........................714-898-3002
Sales:.....................................714-898-3002

Microdyne Corp.
3601 Eisenhower Ave. Ste. 300
Alexandria, VA 22304-9703
Main:......................................800-255-3967
Sales:.....................................703-329-3700
FAX:.......................................703-329-3722
BBS:.......................................703-960-8509
Web: www.mcdy.com

Microfield Graphics, Inc.
9825 SW Sunshine Ct
Beaverton, OR 97005
Main:......................................800-334-4922
Tech. Support:........................503-626-9393
Tech. Support FAX:................503-641-9333
E-Mail:..............................sb-info@mfg.com
Web: www.softboard.com

MicroGate Corp.
9501 Capital of Texas Hwy.
Austin, TX 78759
Main: 800-444-1982
Tech. Support:........................ 512-345-7796
Sales:..................................... 512-345-7791
FAX: 512-343-9046
E-Mail:.......................... sales@microgate.com
Web: www.microgate.com

Micrografx
1303 E Arapaho Rd.
Richardson, TX 75081
Main: 800-671-0144
Tech. Support:........................ 800-733-3729
Sales:..................................... 214-234-1769
Customer Service:.................... 800-733-3729
E-Mail:........................ sales@micrografx.com
BBS: 214-234-2694
Web: www.micrografx.com

MicroHelp
4359 Shallowford Industrial Pkwy.
Marietta, GA 30066
Main: 770-516-0899
Tech. Support:........................ 770-591-6448
Sales:..................................... 800-922-3383
Customer Service:.................... 770-516-0899
Tech. Support FAX: 770-516-1099
FAX: 404-516-1099
CompuServe: 74774,55
E-Mail:.......................... tech@microhelp.com
BBS: 404-516-1497
FTP: ftp.microhelp.com
Web: www.microhelp.com

Microleague Multimedia Inc.
1001 Millersville Rd.
PO Box 4547
Lancaster, PA 17604-4547
Main: 717-872-6567
Tech. Support:........................ 717-872-2442
Sales:..................................... 800-334-2722
Customer Service:.................... 800-334-2722
Tech. Support FAX: 717-871-9959
E-Mail:.......................... techsupp@mmi.com
BBS: 717-872-6179
Web: www.mmi.com

Microlite Corp.
2315 Mill St.
Ali Quippa, PA 15001-2228
Main:.......................................412-375-6711
Tech. Support:........................412-375-6711
Tech. Support FAX:.................412-375-6908
E-Mail: .... info@microlite.com
Web: www.microlite.com

Microlytics, Inc.
2 Tobey Village Office Park
Pittsford, NY 14354
Main:.......................................800-828-6293
Tech. Support:........................716-248-9150
Sales: 716-248-9150
FAX:..716-248-3868
Web: www.microlytics.com

Micron Technology, Inc.
900 E Karcher Rd
Nampa, ID 83687
Main:.......................................800-423-5891
Tech. Support:........................800-438-3343
Sales: 800-438-3343
Customer Service:...................800-438-3343
Tech. Support FAX:.................800-270-1232
FAX:..208-893-3424
CompuServe:............................ 76450,1645
E-Mail: .... techsupport.meis@micron.com
BBS:..800-270-1207
Web: www.mei.micron.com

MicroNet Technology
80 Technology
Irvine, CA 92618
Main:...................................... 714-453-6100
Tech. Support:........................714-453-6060
Tech. Support FAX:.................714-453-6061
FAX:..714-453-6101
E-Mail: .... tech@micronet.com
BBS:..714-837-7164
Web: www.micronet.com

Micronics
221 Warren Ave.
Fremont, CA 94539
Main:......................................510-651-2300
Web: www.micronics.com

Micropolis
21211 Nordhoff St.
Chatsworth, CA 91311
Main: 818-709-3300
Tech. Support:........................ 818-709-3325
Sales:..................................... 800-395-3748
Customer Service:................... 818-709-3325
Tech. Support FAX: 818-709-3497
FAX: 818-709-3497
BBS:.. 818-709-3310
Web: www.micropolis.com

MicroProse Software, Inc.
Spectrum-Holobyte, Inc
180 Lakefront Dr.
Hunt Valley, MD 21030
Main: 510-522-3584
Sales:..................................... 510-522-3584
FAX: 510-522-3587
CompuServe:.......................... GO GAMBPUB
America Online:.............Keyword Microprose
E-Mail:...................... support@holobyte.com
BBS:.. 510-522-8909
Web: www.hollobyte.com

Microrim, Inc.
Abacus Acct. Systems
15395 SE 30th Pl.
Bellevue, WA 98007
Main: 800-248-2001
Tech. Support:........................ 206-649-9500
Tech. Support FAX: 206-746-9350
CompuServe:.......................... GO MICRORIM
E-Mail:...................... support@microrim.com
BBS:.. 206-649-9836
Web: www.microrim.com

MicroSearch
Houston, TX
Main: 713-988-2818
FAX: 713-995-4994

MicroSim Corp.
20 Fairbanks
Irvine, CA 92718-9905
Main:.....................................714-770-3022
Tech. Support:.........................714-770-3022
FAX: 714-455-0554
BBS:.......................................714-830-1550
Web: www.microsim.com

Microsoft Corp.
1 Microsoft Way
Redmond, WA 98025-6399
Main:.....................................206-882-8080
Sales: 800-426-9400
Customer Service:...................800-936-3500
Tech. Support FAX:.................800-727-3351
FAX: 206-936-7329
BBS:.......................................206-936-6735
FTP: ftp.microsoft.com
Web: www.microsoft.com

Microsoft Corp. -Access
See main listing under Microsoft Corp.
Tech. Support:.........................206-635-7050

Microsoft Corp. - Automap
See main listing under Microsoft Corp.
Tech. Support:.........................206-635-7146

Microsoft Corp. - BASIC
See main listing under Microsoft Corp.
Tech. Support:.........................206-635-7053

Microsoft Corp. - Bob
See main listing under Microsoft Corp.
Tech. Support:.........................206-635-7044

Microsoft Corp. - Bookshelf
See main listing under Microsoft Corp.
Tech. Support:.........................206-635-7172

Microsoft Corp. - Cinemania
See main listing under Microsoft Corp.
Tech. Support:.........................206-635-7172
FTP: ftp.microsoft.com
Web: www.microsoft.com

Microsoft Corp. - Developer Support
See main listing under Microsoft Corp.
Tech. Support:.........................206-635-7053

Microsoft Corp. - DOS 5 & 6
See main listing under Microsoft Corp.
Tech. Support:.........................206-646-5104

Microsoft Corp. - DOS Support
See main listing under Microsoft Corp.
Tech. Support:.........................206-646-5104

Microsoft Corp. - Encarta
See main listing under Microsoft Corp.
Tech. Support:.........................206-635-7172

Microsoft Corp. - Excel for Windows
See main listing under Microsoft Corp.
Tech. Support:.........................206-635-7070

Microsoft Corp. - Hardware
See main listing under Microsoft Corp.
Tech. Support:.........................206-635-7040

Microsoft Corp. - Language Support
See main listing under Microsoft Corp.
Tech. Support:.........................206-635-7053

Microsoft Corp. - Magic School Bus & Kids Products
See main listing under Microsoft Corp.
Tech. Support:.........................206-635-7140

Microsoft Corp. - Money
See main listing under Microsoft Corp.
Tech. Support:.........................206-635-7131

Microsoft Corp. - Multimedia Products
See main listing under Microsoft Corp.
Tech. Support:.........................206-635-7172

Microsoft Corp. - Office for Windows
See main listing under Microsoft Corp.
Tech. Support:.........................206-635-7056

Microsoft Corp. - OS/2
See main listing under Microsoft Corp.

Microsoft Corp. - Plus
See main listing under Microsoft Corp.

Microsoft Corp. - PowerPoint
See main listing under Microsoft Corp.
Tech. Support:.........................206-635-7145

Microsoft Corp. - Profit
See main listing under Microsoft Corp.
Tech. Support:.........................800-723-3333

Microsoft Corp. - Project
See main listing under Microsoft Corp.
Tech. Support:.........................206-635-7155

Microsoft Corp. - Publisher
See main listing under Microsoft Corp.
Tech. Support:.........................206-635-7140

Microsoft Corp. - Scenes and Games
See main listing under Microsoft Corp.
Tech. Support:.........................206-637-9308

Microsoft Corp. - Schedule+
See main listing under Microsoft Corp.
Tech. Support:.........................206-635-7049

Microsoft Corp. - Video for Windows
See main listing under Microsoft Corp.
Tech. Support:.........................206-635-7172

Microsoft Corp. - Windows 3.1, 3.11
See main listing under Microsoft Corp.
Tech. Support:.........................206-637-7098

Microsoft Corp. - Windows 95
See main listing under Microsoft Corp.
Tech. Support:.........................206-635-7000

Microsoft Corp. - Windows Entertainment Products
See main listing under Microsoft Corp.
Tech. Support:.........................206-637-9308

Microsoft Corp. - Word for MS-DOS
See main listing under Microsoft Corp.
Tech. Support:.........................206-635-7210

Microsoft Corp. - Word for Windows
See main listing under Microsoft Corp.
Tech. Support:.........................206-462-9673

Microsoft Corp. - Works for MS-DOS
See main listing under Microsoft Corp.
Tech. Support:.........................206-635-7150

Microsoft Corp. - Works for Windows
See main listing under Microsoft Corp.
Tech. Support:.........................206-635-7130

MicroSpeed
5005 Brandin Ct.
Fremont, CA 94538
Main: 510-490-1403
Tech. Support:.........................800-232-7888
Sales:......................................800-232-7888
Customer Service:...................800-232-7888
Tech. Support FAX: 510-490-1665
BBS:...510-490-1664
FTP: ftp.microspeed.com
Web: www.microspeed.com

Microstar Labs
2265 116th Ave. NE
Bellevue, WA 98004
Main: 206-453-2345
FAX: 206-453-3199
E-Mail:.............................info@mstarlabs.com
Web: www.mstarlabs.com/mstarlabs/

MicroSystems Development
4100 Moorpark Ave. M/S 104
San Jose, CA 95117
Main: 408-296-4000
Web: www.msd.com

Microsystems Software, Inc.
600 Worcester Rd.
Framingham, MA 01701
Main:......................................508-879-9000
Sales:....................................800-489-2001
Customer Service:...................508-879-9000
Tech. Support FAX:................508-626-8515
FAX: 508-626-8515
E-Mail: .... support@microsys.com
BBS:.....................................508-875-8009
Web: www.microsys.com

MicroTech
7304 15th Ave. NE
Seattle, WA 98115
Main:....................................206-526-7989
Tech. Support:.......................206-526-7989
Sales:...................................800-521-9035
Customer Service:..................206-526-7989
Tech. Support FAX:................206-522-6727

MicroTech Solutions, Inc.
1885 N. Farnsworth Ave. Ste. 6-7-8
Aurora, IL 60506-1162
Main:....................................708-851-3033
FAX: 708-851-3825
E-Mail: ....info@mt-inc.com
BBS:....................................708-851-3929
Web: www.mt-inc.com

Microtek Lab, Inc.
3715 Doolittle Dr.
Redondo Beach, CA 90278
Main:....................................310-297-5000
Tech. Support:.......................310-297-5100
Sales:...................................800-694-4160
Customer Service:..................310-297-5000
FAX: 310-297-5050
CompuServe:........................GO GRAPHSUP
America Online:......................Keyword MGR
E-Mail: .... support@mteklab.com
BBS:....................................310-297-5102
Web: www.mteklab.com

Microtest, Inc.
4747 N 22nd St.
Phoenix, AZ 85016
Main: 800-526-9675
Tech. Support FAX: 602-952-6660
E-Mail:..........................sales@microtest.com
BBS: 602-957-7716
Web: www.microtest.com

MicroUnity
255 Caspian Dr.
Sunnyvale, CA 94089
FAX: 408-734-8136
Web: www.microunity.com

MicroVideo Learning Systems
250 Park Ave. S
10th Floor
New York, NY 10003
Main: 800-231-4021
Tech. Support:.......................212-777-9595
Tech. Support FAX: 212-777-9597
E-Mail:.........................info@microvideo.com
BBS: 212-7779633
Web: www.plaza.interport.net/pc-training

Microwave Filter Company, Inc.
6743 Kinne St.
East Syracuse, NY 13057
Main: 800-448-1666
Tech. Support:.......................315-437-3953
Tech. Support FAX: 315-463-1467
America Online:........................mfc@ras.com
Web: www.ras.com/mwfilter/mwfilterhtm

MicroWay, Inc.
PO Box 79
Kingston, MA 02364
Main: 508-746-7341
Tech. Support FAX: 508-746-4678
E-Mail:......................... tech@microway.com
BBS: 508-746-4678
Web: www.microway.com

MicroWest Software Systems
10992 San Diego Mission Rd. Ste. 110
San Diego, CA 92108
Main:.....................................619-280-0440
Tech. Support:.......................800-969-9699
Tech. Support FAX:................619-280-0467
BBS:.......................................619-280-0467

Microwork, Inc.
47 W St. Andrews Ln
Deerfield, IL 60015
Main:.....................................847-940-8979
Tech. Support:.......................847-940-8979
Sales: 847-940-8979
CompuServe:............................ 76247,2351

Microx
9821 Katy Frwy Ste. 260
Houston, TX 77024
Main:.....................................713-467-7000

Midern Computer
18005 Cortney Ct.
City of Industry, CA 91748
Main:.....................................818-964-8682
Tech. Support:.......................818-964-4849
Sales: 800-741-2219
Tech. Support FAX:................818-964-2381
BBS:.......................................818-964-0682

Midisoft Corp.
PO Box 1000
Bellevue, WA 98009
Main:.....................................206-391-3610
Tech. Support:.......................206-313-3495
Sales: 800-776-6434
Customer Service:..................206-391-3610
Tech. Support FAX:................206-313-3491
FAX:.......................................206-391-3422
CompuServe:.......................... GO MIDISOFT
America Online:.................midisoft@aol.com
E-Mail: ....techsup@midisoft.com
BBS:.......................................206-391-7966
FTP: ftp.midisoft.com
Web: www.midisoft.com

Midwest Micro-Peripheral Corp.
6910 US Rte 36 E
Fletcher, OH 45326
Main: 800-423-8215
Tech. Support:.......................800-262-6622
Sales:....................................800-423-8215
Customer Service:..................800-423-8215
Tech. Support FAX: 800-643-6622
FAX:.......................................800-643-6622
BBS:.......................................513-368-2299
Web: www.mwmicro.com

Midwestern Diskette
509 W Taylor Hwy 34
Creston, IA 50801
Main: 800-332-3035
Tech. Support:.......................800-221-6332
Tech. Support FAX: 515-782-4166
BBS:.......................................515-782-4166

Miltape Business Products
500 Richardson Rd. S
Hope Hull, AL 36043
Main: 334-284-8665
FAX: 334-613-6302

Mindscape-The Software Toolworks
Pearson
88 Rowland Way
Novato, CA 94945
Main: 415-897-9900
Tech. Support:.......................415-898-5157
Customer Service:..................415-897-9900
FAX: 415-897-2747
America Online:.................mscape@aol.com
Web: www.mindscape.com

Mitsubishi Electronics, America, Inc.
5665 Plaza Dr.
Cypress, CA 90630
Main: 800-843-2515
Tech. Support:.......................800-344-6352
Customer Service:..................800-344-6352
Tech. Support FAX: 714-229-6566
E-Mail:...................tsupport@msm.mea.com
BBS:....................................714-236-6286
Web: www.mela-itg.com

Mitsubishi International Corp.
520 Madison Ave.
New York, NY 10022
Main:......................................212-605-2000
Tech. Support FAX:................212-605-1847
FAX: 212-605-2597
E-Mail:.........................support@milusa.com
BBS:......................................212-605-1847
Web: www.milusa.com

Mitsumi Corp.
2019 Saturn St.
Monterrey Park, CA 91754
Main:......................................213-727-5096
Customer Service:...................213-727-5096
FAX: 213-727-5985
Web: www.mitsumi.com

Mitten Software Corp.
10709 Wayzata Blvd.
Minnetonka, MN 55305
Main:......................................800-825-5461
Tech. Support:........................612-593-5019
Sales:.....................................800-825-5461
Customer Service:...................612-593-5019
Tech. Support FAX:................612-593-5028
FAX: 612-593-5028
CompuServe:...........................72371,2444
E-Mail: ....mitten@gnn.com
BBS:......................................612-593-1050
Web: members.gnn.com/mitten

Modgraph
60 Gill St.
Woburn, MA 01801
Main:......................................800-327-9962
Tech. Support:........................617-938-4488
Sales:.....................................800-327-9962
Customer Service:...................800-327-9962
Tech. Support FAX:................617-938-4455
FAX: 617-938-4455

Modular Avcom Systems
513 Maude Ct.
Sunnyvale, CA 94086
Main:......................................408-733-5000
Tech. Support FAX:................408-733-5329
Web: www.avcom.com

Molex Incorporation
2222 Wellington Ct.
Lisle, IL 60532
Main: 708-969-4550
Tech. Support:......................708-964-2321
Sales:...................................708-969-4550
Customer Service:..................708-969-4550

Moller & Huth
Solmsstr, 23
Berlin, D-10961
Germany
Sales:...................................493-069-24495
FAX: 493-069-23555

Momentum Software Corp.
401 S Van Brunt St.
Englewood, NJ 07631
Main: 201-871-0077
Tech. Support:......................800-767-1462
Tech. Support FAX: 201-871-0807
E-Mail:.................comments@momsoft.com
Web: www.momsoft.com

Money Smith Systems Inc.
PO Box 333
Converse, TX 78109
Sales:...................................800-242-4775
FAX: 505-281-0498
CompuServe: 70324,1077
Web: www.nmia.com:80/~monsmith/

Monotype Typography
150 S Wacker Dr.
Chicago, IL 60606
Main: 312-855-1440
Tech. Support:......................800-666-6897
Sales:...................................800-666-6897
Customer Service:..................800-666-6897
Tech. Support FAX: 312-855-9475
E-Mail:...................tech@monotypeusa.com
Web: www.monotype.com

Montrose Products
28 Sword St.
Auburn, MA 01501
Main:......................................800-346-6626
Tech. Support:.........................508-791-3161
Sales:....................................800-346-6626
Customer Service:...................800-346-6626
Tech. Support FAX:................508-793-9862
FAX:.......................................508-793-9868

Morning Star Technologies
3518 Riverside Dr. Ste. 101
Columbus, OH 43221-1754
Main:......................................614-451-1883
Sales:....................................800-558-7827
FAX:.......................................617-459-5054
E-Mail:......................sales@morningstar.com
FTP: ftp.morningstar.com:pub/
Web: www.morningstar.com

Morningstar
225 W. Wacky Dr. Ste. 4
Chicago, IL 60606
Main:......................................312-696-0700
Tech. Support:.........................312-696-0070
Sales:....................................312-696-0700
Tech. Support FAX:................312-696-6001
FAX:.......................................312-696-6001
BBS:.......................................312-427-9215

Morris Consulting
1052 Doreen Pl. Ste. 2
Venice, CA 90291
Main:......................................310-399-7351
FAX:.......................................310-399-7351
E-Mail: ....bmorris@1x.netcom.com
Web: www.ix.netcom.com

Mortice Kern Systems
185 Columbia St. West
Waterloo, ONT N2L 5Z5
Canada
Main: 519-884-2251
Tech. Support:.......................519-884-2270
Sales:...................................800-265-2797
Customer Service:...................519-884-8861
E-Mail:............................support@mks.com
BBS:......................................519-884-2861
Web: www.mks.com

Moses Computers
15466 Los Gatos Blvd.
Los Gatos, CA 95032
Main: 408-358-1550
Sales:....................................800-306-6737
FAX: 408-356-9049

Motion Works
524 Second St.
San Francisco, CA 94107
Sales:....................................415-541-9333
FAX: 415-541-0555

Motorola, Inc.
10700 N De Anza Blvd.
Cupertino, CA 95014
Main: 708-576-5000
Tech. Support:.......................800-365-3694
BBS:......................................408-366-4804
Web: www.motorola.com

Mountain Lake Software
298 Fourth Ave. Ste. 401
San Francisco, CA 94118-2468
Main: 800-669-6574
Tech. Support:.......................415-752-6515
Sales:....................................800-669-6574
Tech. Support FAX: 415-752-6506
E-Mail:..................techsupport@mtlake.com
Web: www.mtlake.com

Mouse Systems Corp.
47505 Seabridge Dr.
Fremont, CA 94538
Main:.....................................510-656-1117
FAX: 510-770-1924
BBS:.......................................510-770-1924
Web: www.mousesystems.com

Mozart Systems Corp.
1350 Bayshore Hwy. Ste. 630
Burlingame, CA 94010
Main:.....................................415-340-1588
FAX: 415-340-1648
CompuServe:............................GO MOZART
Web: www.mozart.com

Mr. Hardware Computers
PO Box 148
Central Islip, NY 11722
Main:.....................................516-234-8110
FAX: 516-234-8110
BBS:.......................................516-234-6046

Multi-Industry Tech
16717 Norwalk Blvd.
Cerritos, CA 90703
Main:.....................................800-366-6481
Tech. Support:........................310-921-6669
Tech. Support FAX:.................310-802-9218

Multi Soft, Inc.
4262 US Rte. 1
Monmouth Junction, NJ 08852
Sales:.....................................908-329-9200
FAX: 908-329-1386

Multi-Tech Systems, Inc.
2205 Woodale Dr.
Mounds View, MN 55112
Main: 800-328-9717
Tech. Support:.......................800-972-2439
Sales:.....................................800-328-9717
Customer Service:...................800-328-9717
Tech. Support FAX: 612-785-9874
FAX: 612-785-9874
E-Mail:....................mtssales@multitech.com
BBS: 612-785-9874
FTP: ftp.multitech.com
Web: www.multitech.com

Multicom Publishing Inc.
1100 Olive Way Ste. 1250
Seattle, WA 98101
Main: 206-777-5300
Tech. Support:.......................206-622-5530
Sales:.....................................206-622-5530
Customer Service:...................206-622-5530
FAX: 206-622-4380
Web: www.multicom.com

Murata Business Systems
5560 Tennyson Pkwy.
Plano, TX 75024
Main: 800-543-4636
Tech. Support:.......................214-403-3300
Sales:.....................................214-403-3300
Customer Service:...................214-403-3300
Tech. Support FAX: 214-403-3465
FAX: 214-403-3400

Mustang Software, Inc.
6200 Lake Ming Rd.
Bakersfield, CA 93306
Main: 800-999-9619
Tech. Support:.......................805-873-2550
FAX: 805-873-2430
BBS: 805-873-2400
Web: www.mustang.com

Mustek
Tech. Support:.........................714-247-1300
Customer Service:...................714-247-1300
BBS:.......................................714-247-1330
Web: www.mustek.com

Mylex
34551 Ardenwood Blvd.
Fremont, CA 94555
Main:.....................................510-796-6100
Tech. Support:.........................510-796-6100
Sales: 510-796-6100
Customer Service:...................510-796-6100
Tech. Support FAX:.................510-745-7715
BBS:.......................................510-793-3491
Web: www.mylex.com

NCE Storage Solutions-Mountain
NCE Computer Group
9717 Pacific Heights Blvd.
San Diego, CA 92121
Main:.....................................619-658-9720
Tech. Support:.........................619-628-9720
Sales: 800-767-2587
Customer Service:...................619-658-9720
Tech. Support FAX:.................619-658-9733
CompuServe:.......................GO MOUNTAIN
BBS:.......................................619-626-8550
Web: www.ncegroup.com

NCR Corp.
1700 S Patterson Blvd.
Dayton, OH 45479
Main:.....................................513-445-5000
Tech. Support:.........................800-531-2222
Sales: 800-531-2222
Customer Service:...................800-531-2222
BBS:.......................................513-445-4184
Web: www.ncr.com

NDC Communications
265 Santa Ana Court
Sunnyvale, CA 94086
Main: 408-730-0888
Tech. Support:....................... 800-323-7325
Sales:................................... 408-730-0888
Customer Service:.................. 408-730-0888
Tech. Support FAX: 408-730-0889
FAX: 408-730-0889
Web: www.ndc.lan.com

NEBS Software (One-Write Plus)
500 Main St.
Groton, MA 01471
Main: 800-225-6380
Sales:................................... 800-882-5254
Customer Service:.................. 603-880-5100
Tech. Support FAX: 603-880-5102
FAX: 800-234-4324
E-Mail:...............................info@nebs.com
BBS:.................................... 800-937-9951
Web: www.nebs.com

NEC Technologies, Inc.
1414 Massachusetts Ave.
Boxborough, MA 01719
Main: 508-264-8000
Tech. Support:....................... 800-632-4525
Sales:................................... 800-632-4636
FAX: 508-264-8673
Email: ....tech-support@nectech.com
BBS:.................................... 508-635-4706
Web: www.nec.com
Web: www.nulogic.com

NHC Communications
5450 Cote de Liesse
Mt Royal, PQ H4P 1A5
Canada
Main: 800-361-1965
Tech. Support:....................... 514-734-4251
FAX: 514-735-8057

NRI
4401 Connecticut Ave. NW
Washinton, DC 20008
Main: 202-244-1600
FAX: 202-966-5074

Nakamichi America Corp.
955 Francisco St.
Torrance, CA 90502
Main:.................................310-538-8150
Sales:................................800-421-2313
FAX: 310-324-7614

Nanao USA Corp.
23535 Telo Ave.
Torrance, CA 90505
Main:.................................800-800-5202
Tech. Support:.......................310-325-5202
Tech. Support FAX:.................310-530-1679
BBS:..................................310-530-1679
Web: www.traveller.com/nanao/

National Braille Press, Inc.
88 St. Stephen St.
Boston, MA 02115
Main:.................................617-266-6160
Tech. Support:.......................617-266-6160
Sales:................................917-266-6160
Customer Service:...................617-266-6160
Tech. Support FAX:.................617-437-0456
FAX: 617-437-0456

National Instruments Corp.
6504 Bridge Point Pkwy.
Austin, TX 78730-5039
Main:.................................800-433-3488
Tech. Support:.......................512-794-0100
Sales:................................512-794-0100
Customer Service:...................800-433-3488
Tech. Support FAX:.................512-794-5678
FAX: 512-794-8411
BBS:..................................512-794-5422
FTP: ftp.natinest.com
Web: www.natinst.com

National Radio Institute
4401 Connecticut NW
Washington, DC 20008
Main:.................................202-244-1600
Tech. Support:.......................202-244-1600
Customer Service:...................202-244-9805
FAX: 202-244-2047

National Semiconductor
2900 Semiconductor Dr.
Santa Clara, CA 95052
Main: 408-721-5000
Tech. Support:.......................800-272-9959
Sales:................................408-721-8412
Customer Service:...................408-721-5000
Tech. Support FAX: 800-428-0065
FAX: 800-428-0065
Web: www.nsc.com

Natural Speech Technologies
Main: 619-457-2526

Needham's Electronics
4630 Beloit Dr. Ste. 20
Sacramento, CA 95838
Main: 916-924-8037
Tech. Support:.......................916-924-8037
Sales:................................916-924-8037
Customer Service:...................916-924-8037
Tech. Support FAX: 916-924-8065
FAX: 916-924-8065
E-Mail:.....................needhams@quick.com
BBS: 916-924-8094
Web: www.needham.com

Nerve Internet Services, The
134 Maple Grove Dr.
Oakville, ONT L6J 4VJ
Canada
Sales:................................905-845-2570
FAX: 905-845-8245
E-Mail:.........................web@thenerve.com
Web: www.he.net/~thenerve/

Net Manage Inc.
2340 130th Ave. NE
Bellevue, WA 98005-1754
Main:......................................206-869-9600
Tech. Support:.......................206-885-0559
Sales:....................................206-885-4272
Customer Service:..................206-885-4272
Tech. Support FAX:.................206-885-0127
FAX:......................................206-885-0127
CompuServe:................................GO ECHO
E-Mail: .... eccsupport@netmanage.com
BBS:......................................206-881-0905
FTP: ftp.netmanage.com
Web: www.netmanage.com

Netcom
800 Saginaw Dr.
Redwood City, CA 94063-4740
Main:......................................415-366-4400
Sales:....................................800-234-4638
FAX:......................................415-366-5675
Web: www.netcom.com

NetFrame Systems, Inc.
1545 Barber Ln.
Milpitas, CA 95035
Main:......................................408-474-1000
Tech. Support:.......................408-434-4194
Sales:....................................800-737-8377
Tech. Support FAX:.................408-474-4228
FAX:......................................408-434-4190
Web: www.netframe.com

Netis Technology, Inc.
1606 Century Point Dr.
Milpitas, CA 95035
Main:......................................408-263-0368
Tech. Support:.......................408-263-0395
Sales:....................................408-263-0368
Customer Service:..................408-263-0368
Tech. Support FAX:.................408-263-4624
FAX:......................................408-263-4624
E-Mail: ....support@netis.com
FTP: ftp.netis.com
Web: www.netis.com

Netlink
1881 Worcester Rd.
Framingham, MA 01701
Main: 508-879-6306
Tech. Support:....................... 800-638-5465
Sales:................................... 800-638-5465
Customer Service:.................. 800-638-5465
Tech. Support FAX: 508-872-8136
FAX: 508-872-8136
E-Mail:...............................info@netlink.com
BBS:.................................... 508-872-8136
Web: www.netlink.com

NetManage, Inc.
10725 N. DeAnza Blvd.
Cupertino, CA 95014
Sales:................................... 408-973-7171
FAX: 408-257-6405
E-Mail:...................... sales@netmanage.com
FTP: ftp.netmanage.com/pub
Web: www.netmanage.com/

NeTpower, Inc.
545 Oakmead Pkwy.
Sunnyvale, CA 94086
Main: 800-801-0900
Tech. Support FAX: 408-720-8558
BBS:.................................... 408-522-2690
Web: www.netpower.com

NetPro Computing
7150 E. Camelback Rd. Ste. 100
Scottsdale, AZ 85251
Main: 602-998-5008
Sales:................................... 602-941-3600
Customer Service:.................. 602-941-3600
FAX: 602-941-3610
E-Mail:.............................Info@NetPro.com
Web: www.netpro.com

Netscape Communications Corp.
501 E. Middlefield Rd.
Mountain View, CA 94043
Main:....................................415-254-1900
Tech. Support:........................800-320-2099
Sales:...................................415-937-2555
Customer Service:...................415-937-2555
Tech. Support FAX:................415-528-4121
FAX:....................................415-528-4124
E-Mail:.........................client@netscape.com
Web: home.netscape.com

NetSoft
Sales:...................................714-768-4013
FAX:....................................714-768-5049

Network Access Services Inc.
PO Box 28085
Bellingham, WA 98228-0085
Main:....................................360-733-9279
FAX:....................................360-676-0345
E-Mail:...............................info@nas.com
Web: www.nas.com

Network Appliance
319 North Bernardo Ave.
Mountain View, CA 94043
Main:....................................415-428-5100
FAX:....................................415-428-5151
Web: www.netapp.com

Network Communications Corp.
5501 Green Valley Dr.
Bloomington, MN 55437-1003
Main:....................................800-333-1896
Tech. Support:........................800-451-1984
Sales:...................................800-333-1896
Customer Service:...................800-333-1896
Tech. Support FAX:................612-844-0487
FAX:....................................612-844-0421
BBS:....................................612-844-0487
Web: www.netcommcorp.com

Network Computing Devices
350 N Bernardo Ave.
Mountain View, CA 94043
Main: 415-694-0650
Tech. Support:........................415-694-0650
Tech. Support FAX: 405-961-7711
BBS: 415-961-7711
Web: www.ncd.com

Network Connection
1324 Union Hill Rd.
Alpharetta, GA 30201
Main: 800-327-4853
Tech. Support:........................404-751-0889
Customer Service:..................800-327-4853
Tech. Support FAX: 404-751-1884
Web: tnc.www.com

Network Enhancement Tools
20218 Bridgedale Ln.
Humble, TX 77338
Main: 713-446-2154
Tech. Support:........................713-446-2154
Tech. Support FAX: 713-540-3045

Network Equipment Technologies
800 Saginaw Dr.
Redwood City, CA 94063
Main: 800-234-4638
Tech. Support:........................415-366-4400
Tech. Support FAX: 415-366-5675
Web: www.net.com

Network Integrators
PO Box 1909
Salem, VA 24153
Main: 540-389-9844
FAX: 540-389-4408

Network Peripherals, Inc.
1371 McArthur Blvd.
Milpitas, CA 95035
Main:.....................................800-674-8855
Tech. Support:........................408-321-7375
Sales:....................................800-674-8855
Customer Service:..................800-674-8855
Tech. Support FAX:................408-321-9218
FAX:......................................408-321-9218
E-Mail: ....support@npix.com
Web: www.npix.com

Network Products Corp.
1440 W Colorado Blvd.
Pasadena, CA 91105
Main:....................................818-440-1850
Tech. Support:........................818-440-1973
Sales:....................................818-440-1850
Customer Service:..................818-440-1973
Tech. Support FAX:................818-440-0879
CompuServe:............................ 75300,1105
E-Mail: ...techsupport@networkproducts.com
BBS:.......................................818-440-9030
Web: www.networkproducts.com

Network Software Associates, Inc.
Sales:....................................703-875-0444
FAX:......................................703-875-0451

Network Solutions
505 Huntmar Park Dr.
Herndon, VA 22070
Main:....................................703-742-0400
Sales:....................................703-742-4740
FAX:......................................703-742-4811
BBS:......................................703-742-0846
Web: www.netsol.com

Network Systems
7600 Boone Ave. N
Minneapolis, MN 55428
Main:....................................612-424-4888
BBS:......................................612-424-2853
Web: www.network.com

Network Systems Corp.
Storage Tech
2430 Camino Ramon Ste. 240
San Ramon, CA 94583
Main: 510-275-1550
FAX: 510-275-1599
Web: www.Network.com

Network Wizards
PO Box 343
Menlo Park, CA 94026
Main: 415-326-2060
FAX: 415-326-4672
E-Mail:................................ info@nw.com
Web: www.nw.com

NeuralWare, Inc.
202 Park West Dr.
Pittsburgh, PA 15275
Main: 412-787-8222
Tech. Support FAX: 412-787-8220
E-Mail:.......................sales@neuralware.com
Web: www.neuralware.com

Neuron Data, Inc.
1310 Villa St.
Mountain View, CA 94041
Main: 415-528-3450
Web: www.neurondata.com

Nevrona Designs
2581 E. Commonwealth Cir.
Chandler, AZ 85225-6019
E-Mail:......................jgunkel@primenet.com
FTP: ftp.primenet.com/users/j/jgunkel/dephi

New Brunswick Information Technolgy Alliance
Frederickton, NB
Canada
Main: 506-457-1164
E-Mail:-..................................guyr@nbita.org
Web: www.discribe.ca/nbita

New MMI Corp.
2400 Reach Rd.
Williamsport, PA 17701
Main:......................................800-221-4283
Tech. Support:........................800-221-4283
FAX: 717-327-1217
BBS:.......................................717-327-9952
Web: www.newmmi.com

New Media
1 Technology
Building A
Irvine, CA 92718
Main:......................................714-453-0100
Tech. Support:........................714-453-0314
Sales: 714-453-0100
Customer Service:..................714-453-0100
Tech. Support FAX:................714-453-0114
CompuServe:........................GO NEWMEDIA
E-Mail:nmctechsupport@newmediacorp.com
BBS:.......................................714-453-0214
Web: www.newmediacorp.com

New Riders
Simon & Schuster, Paramount, Viacom
201 W. 103rd St.
Indianapolis, IN 46290
Main:......................................317-581-3500
Sales: 800-428-5331
FAX: 317-581-3550
CompuServe:......................GO MACMILLAN
Web: www.mcp.com

Newbridge Networks
593 Herndon Pkwy.
Herndon, VA 22070-5421
Main:......................................703-834-3600
Tech. Support:........................703-834-5300
E-Mail: .... info@newbridge.com
BBS:.......................................703-471-7080
Web: www.newbridge.com

Newer Technology
4848 W. Irving
Wichita, KS 67209
Main:......................................800-678-3726
Tech. Support:........................316-943-0222
FAX: 316-943-4515

NewGen
3545 Cadillac Ave. Ste. A
Costa Mesa, CA 92626
Main: 714-641-8600
Sales:.................................... 800-756-0556
Customer Service:.................. 714-436-5150
Tech. Support FAX: 714-641-0900
E-Mail:........................support@newgen.com
BBS: 714-641-3869
FTP: ftp.newgen.com
Web: www.newgen.com

NewTek, Inc.
1200 SW Executive Dr.
Topeka, KS 66615
Main: 800-843-8934
Tech. Support:........................ 913-228-8282
BBS: 913-354-1584
Web: www.newtek.com

NeXT Computer, Inc.
900 Chesapeake Dr.
Redwood City, CA 94036
Main: 415-366-0900
FAX: 415-780-3714
Web: www.next.com

Next Move, The
INTRACORP
501 Brickell Key Dr. Ste. 600
Miami, FL 33131
Main: 305-373-7700
Tech. Support:........................ 305-373-7700
Sales:.................................... 305-373-7700
Customer Service:.................. 305-373-7700
Tech. Support FAX: 305-577-9875
CompuServe: ....GO THREESIXTY
America Online:.............. Keyword Capstone
E-Mail:............................ info@intracorp.com
FTP: ftp.gate.net/pur/users/intracor
Web: www.intracorp.com

Nico Mak Computing, Inc.
PO Box 919
Bristol, CT 06011
Web: www.winzip.com/winzip/

Nikon Electronic Imaging
1300 Walt Whitman Rd
Melville, NY 11747
Main:...800-645-6687
Tech. Support:........................516-547-4355
Sales:.......................................800-526-4566
Customer Service:...................800-645-6678
FAX:...516-547-0299
Web: www.klt.co.jp/nikon

Niles & Associates, Inc.
800 Jones St.
Berkeley, CA 94710
Main:...510-559-8592
Tech. Support:........................510-559-8592
Sales:.......................................510-559-8592
Customer Service:...................510-559-8592
Tech. Support FAX:.................510-559-8683
FAX:...510-559-8683
E-Mail: ....info@niles.com
FTP: ftp.niles.com
Web: www.niles.com

Nintendo of America
PO Box 957
Redmond, WA 98073
Main:.......................................206-882-2040
Tech. Support:........................800-255-3700
Sales:.......................................800-255-3700
Customer Service:...................800-255-3700
America Online:.....................................NOA
E-Mail: ....codes@nintendo.com
Web: www.nintendo.com

Nissho Electronics USA Corp.
18201 Von Karmen Ave. Ste. 350
Irvine, CA 92715
Main:.......................................800-233-1837
Tech. Support FAX:.................714-261-8819

NitWit Software, Inc.
17280 Newhope St. Ste. 1
Fountain Valley, CA 92708
Sales:.......................................714-444-3964
FAX:...714-444-3954

Niwot Networks
1880 S Flatiron Crt. Unit M
Boulder, CO 80301
Main: 303-444-7765
E-Mail:........................niwotnet@aol.com
Web: members.aol.com/niwotnet

Nohau Corp.
51 E. Campbell Ave.
Campbell, CA 95008
Main: 408-866-1820
FAX: 408-378-7869
E-Mail:..................... nohau@shell.portal.com
BBS:... 408-378-0940
Web: www.nohau.com

Nokia
1505 Bridgeway Blvd. Ste. 128
Sausalito, CA 94965
Main: 415-331-4244
Tech. Support:....................... 800-483-7952
Sales:..................................... 800-296-6542
FAX: 415-331-0424
America Online:.............. bynokia@aol.com
E-Mail:................................info@nokia.com
Web: www.nokia.com

Nolo Press
950 Parker St. Ste. 4
Berkeley, CA 94710
Main: 510-549-1976
Tech. Support:....................... 510-549-1973
Sales:..................................... 510-549-1976
Customer Service:.................. 800-992-6656
Tech. Support FAX: 510-548-5902
America Online:..................... nolo@aol.com
Web: www.nolo.com

Nonstop Networks
20 Waterside
New York, NY 10010
Main: 212-481-8488
Customer Service:.................. 212-738-1819
Tech. Support FAX: 212-779-2956
E-Mail:.......... 71603,1751@compuserve.com
BBS:... 212-779-2956
Web: www.borg.com/~nonstop

NoRad Corp.
1160 E Sandhill Ave.
Carson, CA 90746
Main:......................................310-605-0808
Tech. Support:........................800-262-3260
Sales:....................................800-262-3260
Customer Service:..................800-262-3260
Tech. Support FAX:................310-605-5051
E-Mail:......................norad@noradcorp.com
BBS:......................................310-458-6397
Web: www.noradcorp.com

Norda Technologies, Inc.
PO Box 645
Andover, NJ 07821
Main:......................................201-786-6878
Tech. Support FAX:................201-786-5868

North Bay Technical
PO Box 1052
Fairfax, CA 94978-1052
Main:......................................415-883-1717
Tech. Support FAX:................415-457-7253

Northeast Data Corp.
2117 Buffalo Rd. Ste. 290
Rochester, NY 14624
Sales:....................................716-247-5934
FAX: 716-247-5934
E-Mail: ....pkingned@msn.com

Norton-Lambert
PO Box 4085
Santa Barbara, CA 93140
Main:......................................805-964-6767
Tech. Support:........................805-964-6767
Sales:....................................805-964-6767
Customer Service:..................805-964-6767
Tech. Support FAX:................805-683-5679
CompuServe:.......................... GO CLOSEUP
BBS:......................................805-683-2249

Novell Groupware Division
Nobel, Inc.
1555 N. Technology Way
Orem, UT 84057
Main: 801-226-6000
Tech. Support:........................800-861-2146
Sales:....................................800-395-7135
Customer Service:..................800-792-7170
BBS: 801-224-0920
Web: www.novell.com

Novell, Inc.
1555 N Technology Way
Orem, UT 84057-2399
Main: 800-453-1267
Tech. Support:........................800-638-9273
Sales:....................................800-451-5151
Customer Service:..................801-429-7000
Tech. Support FAX: 801-429-5200
BBS: 801-373-6999
Web: www.novell.com

Novellus
3970 N. 1st St.
San Jose, CA 95134
Main: 408-432-5254

Now Software, Inc.
921 SW Washington St. Ste. 500
Portland, OR 97205
Main: 503-274-2810
Tech. Support:........................206-654-7929
Sales:....................................503-274-2810
Customer Service:..................800-237-2078
FAX: 503-274-0670
America Online:....................Keyword Now
E-Mail:............................info@nowsoft.com
FTP: ftp.nowsoft.com
Web: www.nowsoft.com

Noyes Fiber Systems
PO Box 398, Rt. 106
Laconia, NH 03247
Main:....................................603-528-7780
Tech. Support:.......................800-321-5298
Sales:...................................800-321-5298
Customer Service:..................800-321-5298
Tech. Support FAX:...............603-528-2025
BBS:....................................603-528-2025

Ntergaid, Inc.
60 Commerce Park
Milford, CT 06460
Main:....................................800-254-9737
Sales:...................................203-783-1280
FAX:.....................................203-882-0850
BBS:....................................203-882-0848
Web: www.ntergaid.com

nuLogic, Inc.
475 Hillside Ave.
Needham, MA 02194
Main:....................................617-444-7680
FAX:.....................................617-444-2803
E-Mail:............................sales@nulogic.com

Number Nine Visual Technology
18 Hartwell Ave.
Lexington, MA 02173
Main:....................................800-438-6463
Tech. Support:.......................617-674-0009
Sales:...................................800-438-6463
Customer Service:..................617-674-0009
BBS:....................................617-862-7502

NuMega Technologies, Inc.
PO Box 7780
Nashau, NH 03060-7780
Main:....................................603-889-2386
FAX:.....................................603-889-1135
CompuServe:..........................GO NUMEGA
E-Mail:............................info@numega.com
BBS:....................................603-595-0386
FTP: ftp.numega.com
Web: www.numega.com

Numonics
101 Commerce Dr.
Montgomeryville, PA 18936
Main: 800-247-4517
Tech. Support:.......................800-523-6716
Sales:...................................215-362-2766
Tech. Support FAX: 215-361-0167

ON Technology
72 Kent St.
Brookline, MA 02146
Main: 800-767-6683
BBS:....................................617-734-4160
Web: www.on.com

OPENetwork, Inc.
215 Berkeley Pl.
Brooklyn, NY 11217
Main: 718-398-3838
FAX: 718-638-2240
BBS:....................................718-638-2239

Oak Tree Publications
3800 S. W. Cedar Hills Blvd. Ste. 251
Beaverton, OR 97005
Main: 503-644-3824
Sales:...................................800-644-3824
FAX: 503-644-3919
E-Mail:............................contact@otp.com
Web: www.otp.com

Oaz Communications
44920 Osgood Rd.
Fremont, CA 94539
Main: 800-638-3293
Tech. Support:.......................510-226-0171
Tech. Support FAX: 510-226-7079
E-Mail:........................oaz@ix.netcom.com
BBS:....................................510-226-7084

Object Management Group, The
492 Old Connecticut Path
Framingham, MA 01701
Main: 508-820-4300
FAX: 508-820-4303
Web: www.omg.org

Ocean Information Systems Inc.
688 Arrow Grand Circle
Covina, CA 91722
Main:......................................818-339-8888
FAX: 818-859-7668
E-Mail: .... webmaster@ocean-usa.com
BBS:......................................818-859-7639
Web: www.ocean-usa.com/ocean/

Odyssey Technologies, Inc.
PO Box 62733
Cincinnati, OH 45262-0733
Sales: 800-293-7893
FAX: 513-777-8026
E-Mail: .... odyssey@eos.net
Web: www.eos.net/odyssey/

Okidata
532 Fellowship Rd.
Mount Laurel, NJ 08054
Tech. Support:.......................609-235-2600
Customer Service:..................800-654-3282
BBS:......................................609-778-4184
Web: www.okidata.com

Olduvai Corp.
9200 S Dadeland Blvd. Ste. 525
Miami, FL 33156
Main:.....................................800-822-0772
Tech. Support:.......................305-670-1112
Tech. Support FAX:................305-670-1992
CompuServe:.........................GO MACBVEN
America Online:.................Keyword Olduvai
E-Mail: .... olduvaigy@aol.com
Web: www.shadow.net/~olduvai

Olicom USA
900 E Park Blvd. Ste. 250
Plano, TX 75074
Main: 800-625-4266
Tech. Support:....................... 800-654-2661
Sales:................................... 800-625-4266
Customer Service:.................. 800-654-2661
Tech. Support FAX: 214-516-0640
CompuServe: .... GO OLICOM
E-Mail:.........................support@olicom.com
BBS: 214-422-9835
FTP: ftp.olicom.com
Web: www.olicom.com

Olivetti Office USA
765 US Hwy 202
PO Box 6945
Bridgewater, NJ 08807-0945
Main: 800-527-2960
Tech. Support:....................... 908-526-8200
FAX: 908-218-5677
BBS: 908-526-8405
Web: www.olivetti.com

Olympus Image Systems, Inc.
2 Corporate Center Dr.
Melville, NY 11747
Main: 800-347-4027
Sales:................................... 516-844-5000
FAX: 516-844-5353
Web: www.olympusamerica.com

Omega Engineering, Inc.
1 Omega Dr.
PO Box 4047
Stamford, CT 06907-0047
Main: 203-359-1660
Tech. Support FAX: 203-359-7700
E-Mail:.............................. info@omega.com
Web: www.omega.com

Omen Technology, Inc.
10255 Old Corn Pass Rd.
Portland, OR 97231
Main: 503-614-0430
BBS: 503-621-3735

Omni-Data Communications
906 N Main Ste. 3
Witchita, KS 67203
Main:......................................316-264-5068
Tech. Support:........................316-264-5589
Tech. Support FAX:................316-264-5589
FAX:.......................................316-264-7031
E-Mail: .... odcom@aol.com
BBS:.......................................316-264-7031
Web: www.omnidata.com

OmniSoft
1723 Westbrook Ave.
Los Altos, CA 94024
Sales: 415-917-1395
E-Mail: .... bchandra@omnisoft.com
FTP: FTP: //via.net/pub/omnisoft
Web: www.omnisoft.com/~omnisoft

Ontrack Computer Systems
6321 Bury Dr.
Eden Prairie, MN 55346
Main:......................................800-752-1333
Tech. Support:........................612-937-2121
Sales: 800-752-1333
Customer Service:...................612-937-2121
Tech. Support FAX:................612-937-5815
FAX:.......................................612-937-5815
CompuServe:..........................GO ONTRACK
E-Mail: .... tech@ontrack.com
BBS:.......................................612-937-0860
FTP: FTP: //ftp.ontrack.com
Web: www.ontrack.com

Opcode Systems Corp.
3950 Fabian Way
Palo Alto, CA 94303
Main:......................................415-856-3333
Tech. Support:........................415-856-3331
Sales: 415-856-3333
Customer Service:...................415-812-3274
Tech. Support FAX:................415-856-3332
FAX:.......................................415-856-3332
CompuServe:...... GO MIDIVENO (Section 7)
America Online:.................Keyword OPCode
E-Mail: .... support@opcode.com
Web: www.opcode.com

Open Systems, Inc.
7626 Golden Triangle Dr.
Eden Prairie, MN 55344
Main: 800-328-2276
Tech. Support:........................612-829-0011
Sales:......................................612-829-0011
FAX: 612-829-1493
E-Mail:...............................info@osas.com
Web: www.osas.com

Opis Corp.
1101 Walnut St. Ste. 350
Des Moines, IA 50309
Main: 800-395-0209
Tech. Support:........................515-284-0209
Tech. Support FAX: 515-284-5147
CompuServe:...............................GO OPIS
BBS:.. 5152847006
Web: www.opis.com

Optelecom
9300 Gaither Rd.
Gaithersburg, MD 20877
Main: 301-840-2121
Sales: 800-293-4237
Tech. Support FAX: 301-948-6357
BBS:....................................... 301-948-6357
Web: www.spidermedia.com//optelcem.html

Optical Cable
5290 Concourse Dr.
Roanoke, VA 24019
Main: 800-622-7711
Tech. Support:........................540-265-0690
FAX: 540-265-0725
BBS:.......................................703-289-9846
Web: www.occfiber.com

Optical Data Systems (ODS)
1101 E Arapaho Rd.
Richardson, TX 75081-9990
Main: 214-234-6400
Tech. Support FAX: 214-234-4059
Web: www.cds.com

Optima Technology Corp.
17062 Murphy Ave.
Irvine, CA 92714
Main:......................................714-476-0515
Tech. Support FAX:.................714-476-0613
E-Mail: ....techsupport@optimatech.com
BBS:......................................714-476-0626
Web: www.optimatech.com/optima/

Optisys
9250 N 43rd Ave. Ste. 12
Glendale, AZ 85302
Main:......................................800-327-1271
Tech. Support:......................602-997-9699
Tech. Support FAX:.................602-944-4051
E-Mail: ....support@optisys.com
BBS:......................................602-997-9786
FTP: ftp.optisys.com
Web: www.optisys.com

Optus Software
PO Box 101
Highlands, NJ 07732
Tech. Support:......................908-271-9568
Tech. Support FAX:.................908-271-9572
BBS:......................................908-271-4239

Ora Electronics
9410 Owensmouth
Chatsworth, CA 91311
Main:......................................818-772-2700
Tech. Support:......................818-772-2700
Sales: 818-772-2700
Customer Service:...................818-772-2700
Tech. Support FAX:.................818-718-8626
E-Mail: ....info@orausa.com
Web: www.orausa.com

Oracle Corp.
20 Davis Dr.
Belmont, CA 94002
Main:......................................800-345-3267
Tech. Support:......................415-506-7867
Sales: 800-633-0651
Customer Service:...................800-578-4672
BBS:......................................415-598-9216
Web: www.oracle.com

Orange Micro, Inc.
1400 N Lakeview Ave.
Anaheim, CA 92807
Main: 714-779-2772
Tech. Support:........................714-779-2772
Tech. Support FAX: 714-779-9332
E-Mail:.............ed_garcia@orangemicro.com
Web: www.orangemicro.com

Orbit Enterprises, Inc.
PO Box 2875
Glen Ellyn, IL 60138
Main: 800-767-6724
Tech. Support:........................708-469-3405
Tech. Support FAX: 708-469-4895

Orchid Technology, Inc.
232 E Warren Ave.
Fremont, CA 94539
Main: 510-683-0300
Tech. Support:........................510-661-3000
Sales:....................................800-767-2443
Customer Service:...................800-767-2443
Tech. Support FAX: 510-683-0355
FAX: 510-490-9312
CompuServe: ....GO ORCHID
BBS: 510-683-0327
Web: www.orchid.com

Orchird Technology
Micronics
221 Warren Ave.
Fremont, CA 94539
Main: 510-683-0428
Tech. Support:........................510-661-3000
Sales:....................................800-577-0977
Customer Service:...................800-577-0977
Tech. Support FAX: 510-651-6982
BBS: 510-651-6837
Web: www.micronics.com

Origin Systems, Inc.
Main: 512-434-4357
Web: www.origin.ea.com

Orissa Inc.
12 W 31st St.
New York, NY 10001
Main:....................................212-279-6060
Sales: 212-279-6060
Tech. Support FAX:................212-268-0885
FAX:.....................................212-268-0885
E-Mail: ....sales@orissa.com
BBS:.....................................212-268-0885

Ornetix
Main:....................................800-965-6650
E-Mail: ....tech@ornetix.com
Web: www.ornetix.com

Osborne/McGraw Hill
McGraw Hill Inc.
2600 10th St.
Berkeley, CA 94710
Main:....................................800-227-0900
Sales: 510-549-6600
Tech. Support FAX:................510-549-6603
E-Mail: ....customer.service@mcgraw-hill.com
Web: www.osborne.com

OsoSoft
1472 Sixth St.
Los Osos, CA 93402
Main:....................................805-528-1759
CompuServe:.......................... GO OSOSOFT
America Online:.................Keyword Ososoft
BBS:.....................................805-528-3753
Web: ourworld.compuserve.com/homepages
   /ososoft

Oswego Software
PO Box 310
Oswego, IL 60543
Main:....................................708-554-3567
FAX:.....................................708-554-0200
E-Mail: ....oswego@att.mail.com
BBS:.....................................708-544-3573

Other Guys, The
PO Box H
Logan, UT 84321
Main: 800-942-9402
Tech. Support FAX: 801-753-7620

Output Enablers
1678 Shattuck Ave. Ste. 247
Berkeley, CA 94709
Sales:....................................510-841-4883
Web: www.io.com/user/oe/

Output Technology Corp. (OTC)
2310 N Fancher Rd.
Spokane, WA 99212-1381
Main: 509-536-0468
Tech. Support:.......................509-536-0468
Sales:....................................800-468-8788
FAX: 509-533-1285
BBS:.....................................509-533-1217
Web: www.output.com

OverByte Industries, Inc.
661 Blanding Blvd. Ste. 391
Orange Park, FL 32073-5048
Main: 904-858-3348
E-Mail:......................overbyte@jax.gttw.com
Web: www.jkcg.com/webmaster/overbyte
   /index.thml

PC America
3232 Rio Mirada Dr., Building 3
Bakersfield, CA 93308
Main: 805-323-0707
Tech. Support FAX: 805-323-9747

PC Connection
6 Mill St.
Marlow, NH 03456
Main: 800-243-8088
Tech. Support:.......................603-446-3383
Sales:....................................800-243-8088
FAX: 603-446-7791

PC Consultants
11026-B Villa Ridge Ct.
Reston, VA 22091-4841
Tech. Support:........................703-860-0108
CompuServe:.............................76147,346

PC Designs
2504 N Hemlock Cir.
Broken Arrow, OK 74012
Tech. Support:........................918-251-5550
Sales:.....................................800-251-5665
Tech. Support FAX:.................918-251-7057

PC Docs, Inc.
PC Docs Group International
25 Burlington Mall Rd.
Burlington, MA 01803
Main:.....................................617-273-3800
Tech. Support:........................904-942-3627
Sales:.....................................800-933-3627
FAX:.......................................617-272-3693
BBS:.......................................904-942-1517
Web: www.pcdocs.com

PC Dynamics
31332 Via Colinas Ste. 102
Westlake Village, CA 91362
Tech. Support:........................818-889-1742
Customer Service:..................818-889-1741
Tech. Support FAX:.................818-889-1014
E-Mail: ....info@pcdynamics.com
FTP: ftp.pcdynamics.com
Web: www.pcdynamics.com

PC Guardian
1133 E. Francisco Blvd. Ste. D
San Rafael, CA 94901
Main:.....................................415-459-0190
Sales:.....................................800-288-8126
Tech. Support FAX:.................415-459-1162
BBS:.......................................415-995-2487

PC - Kwik
3800 SW Cedar Hills Blvd. Ste. 260
Beaverton, OR 97005
Main: 800-274-5945
Tech. Support:........................503-644-8827
Sales:.....................................800-284-7259
Customer Service:..................503-644-5644
Tech. Support FAX: 503-646-8267
FAX: 503-646-8267
CompuServe: 76004,151
Web: www.teleport.com//~gnome//
   pckwik.htm

PC Portable Manufacture
1431 Potrero Ave. Ste. E
South El Monte, CA 91733
Main: 800-966-7237
Tech. Support:........................818-444-7606
Tech. Support FAX: 818-444-1027
BBS: 818-444-1027

PC Power & Cooling, Inc.
5995 Avenida Encidas
Carlsbad, CA 92008
Main: 800-722-6555
Tech. Support:........................619-931-5700
Sales:.....................................619-931-5700
Tech. Support FAX: 619-931-6988
BBS: 619-931-6988

PC Time Data Corp.
40563 Encyclopedia Cir.
Fremont, CA 94538
Main: 800-878-3868
Tech. Support:........................415-623-8864
Sales:.....................................800-878-3868
Customer Service:..................800-878-3868
Tech. Support FAX: 415-623-8863
FAX: 415-623-8865

PC Video Conversion
1340 Tully Rd. Ste. 309
San Jose, CA 95122
Main: 408-279-2442
FAX: 408-279-6105
E-Mail:..........................sales@pcvideo.com
Web: www.pcvideo.com

PC&C Research Corp.
5251 Verdugo Way Ste. J
Camarillo, CA 93012
Tech. Support:.........................805-484-1685
Tech. Support FAX:.................805-987-8088
E-Mail: ....mintronix@interamp.com

PCVoice Inc.
Sales: 404-343-8201
FAX:..404-442-3156

PF Micro
3598 Cadiliac Ave.
Costa Mesa, CA 92626
Main:......................................800-999-7713
Tech. Support:.........................714-549-4669
FAX:..714-545-7294

PKWare, Inc.
9025 N Deerwood Dr.
Brown Deer, WI 53226
Main:......................................414-354-8699
FAX:..414-354-8559
CompuServe:............................GO PKWARE
America Online:..................Keyword PKWare
BBS:..414-354-8670
FTP: ftp.pkware.com
Web: www.pkware.com

PNY Electronics
200 Anderson Ave.
Moonachie, NJ 07074
Main:......................................201-438-6300
Tech. Support:.........................800-234-4597
Sales: 800-769-7079
Customer Service:..........800-769-7079-4450
Web: www.pny.com

PR Newswire
810 Seventh Ave.35th Floor
New York, NY 10019
Main:......................................212-832-9425
Sales: 800-832-5522
FAX:..800-793-9313
Web: www.prnewswire.com

PSDI
20 University Rd
Cambridge, MA 02138
Main: 617-661-1444
Customer Service:...................800-366-7734
FAX: 617-661-1642
Web: www.psdi.com

PSI Animations
17924 SW Pilkinton Rd.
Lake Oswego, OR 97035
Main: 503-624-8185
E-Mail:....................psianim@agora.rain.com

Pacific Data Products
9855 Scranton Rd.
San Diego, CA 92121
Main: 619-552-0880
Tech. Support:.........................619-587-4690
Sales:......................................800-737-7117
Customer Service:...................619-587-4690
Tech. Support FAX: 619-552-0889
CompuServe:...........................GO PACDATA
E-Mail:............................tech@pacdata.com
BBS:..619-452-6329
FTP: ftp.pacdata.com
Web: www.pacdata.com

Pacific Image Co.
919 S Fremont Ave. Ste. 238
Alhambra, CA 91803
Main: 818-457-8880
Tech. Support:........................818-457-9684
Tech. Support FAX: 818-457-8881
E-Mail:............................pacimage@aol.com
BBS:..818-457-9189
Web: www.pacimage.com

Pacific Micro Data, Inc.
16751 Millikan Ave.
Irvine, CA 92714
Main: 800-933-7575
Tech. Support:........................714-955-9490
Sales:......................................714-955-9090

Pacific Microelectronics, Inc.
201 San Antonio Cir., Ste. 250
Mountain View, CA 94040
Main:.....................................415-948-6200
Tech. Support:.......................415-948-6200
Sales:...................................415-948-6200
FAX: 415-948-6296

Pacific Softwork
4000 Via Pecscador
Camarillo, CA 93012
Main:....................................800-541-9508
Sales:...................................805-484-2128
Tech. Support FAX:................805-484-3929
E-Mail:.........................sales@pacificsw.com
BBS:....................................805-485-8204
Web: www.pacificsw.com

Packard Bell
8285 West 2500 S
Magna, UT 84044
Tech. Support:.......................800-733-4411
Sales:...................................800-733-4411
CompuServe:...................GO PACKARD BELL
E-Mail: ....support@packardbell.com
BBS:....................................801-250-1600
FTP: ftp.packardbell.com/pub
Web: www.packardbell.com/gfx/
  gfxhome.html

Pages Software, Inc.
9755 Clairemont Mesa Blvd.
San Diego, CA 92124
Main:....................................619-492-9124
Web: www.pages.com

Palisade Corp.
31 Decker Rd.
Newfield, NY 14867
Main:....................................800-432-7475
Tech. Support:.......................607-272-5228
Sales:...................................607-277-8000
FAX: 607-277-8001
Web: www.palisade.com

Panacea, Inc.
600 Suffolk St.
Lowell, MA 01854
Main: 508-937-1760
Tech. Support:.......................508-937-1760
Sales:...................................800-729-7420
Tech. Support FAX: 508-970-0199

Panamax
150 Mitchell Blvd.
San Rafael, CA 94903
Main: 415-499-3900
Tech. Support:.......................800-472-5555
Sales:...................................800-472-5555
Customer Service:..................800-472-5555
Tech. Support FAX: 415-472-5540
FTP: ftp.panamax.com
Web: www.panamax.com

Panasonic Communications
Matsushita Corp Of America
1707 N Randall Rd. Ste. E10
Elgin, IL 60123-7847
Main: 708-468-4600
Tech. Support:.......................800-222-0584
Sales:...................................800-742-8086
Customer Service:..................800-854-4536
Tech. Support FAX: 708-468-4555
Web: www.panasonic.com

Paperback Software International
2830 9th St.
Berkeley, CA 94710
Main: 800-255-3242
Tech. Support:.......................415-644-2116
Sales:...................................800-255-3242
Tech. Support FAX: 415-644-8241
BBS:....................................415-644-0782

PaperDirect, Inc.
100 Plaza Dr.
Seacaucus, NJ 07094
Main: 800-272-7377
Tech. Support:.......................201-271-9300
FAX: 800-443-2973

Papyrus Design Group, Inc.
35 Medford St.
Somerville, MA 02143
Main:......................................617-926-0700
Tech. Support:.......................617-868-3103
Sales:....................................800-836-1829
FAX:......................................617-926-7585
E-Mail: ....papyrus@world. Std.com
Web: www.papy.com

Para Systems, Inc.
1455 LeMay Dr.
Carrollton, TX 75007
Main:....................................800-238-7272
Tech. Support:.......................214-446-7363
Sales:....................................214-446-7363
FAX:......................................214-446-9011

Paradigm Software
908 Edann Rd.
Oreland, PA 19075
Main:....................................215-572-0758

Paradigm Systems, Inc.
2821 Hurstbourne Pkwy. Ste. 11
Louisville, KY 40220
Main:....................................502-495-5960
FAX:......................................502-495-5980
Web: www.paradigmsys.com

Paradise
800 E. Middlefield Dr.
Mountainview, CA 94043
Main:....................................800-444-3617
Tech. Support:.......................800-978-3079
Sales:....................................415-960-3353
Customer Service:...................800-444-3617
FAX:......................................415-335-2515
E-Mail: ....support@paradise.com
BBS:......................................714-753-1234
FTP: ftp.paradise.com/pub
Web: www.paradise.com

Parallax Graphics, Inc.
2500 Condensa St.
Santa Clara, CA 85051
Main: 408-727-2220
FAX: 408-980-5139
Web: www.parallaxinc.com

Parana Supplies
3625 Del Amo Blvd. Ste. 260
Torrance, CA 90503
Main: 310-793-1325
Tech. Support:...................... 800-472-7262
Customer Service:................... 800-472-7262
FAX: 310-793-1343

Parcplace Digitalk Inc.
999 East Arques Ave.
Sunnyvale, CA 94086
Main: 408-481-9095
Sales:..................................... 800-922-8255
Tech. Support FAX: 408-481-9095
E-Mail:.......................... infor@parcplace.com
Web: www.parcplace.com

Parkplace/Digitalk
5 Hutton Center Dr.
Santa Ana, CA 92707
Main: 714-513-3000
Tech. Support:...................... 714-513-3000
Sales:..................................... 800-759-7272
Customer Service:................... 714-513-3000
Tech. Support FAX: 714-513-3100
CompuServe:...................... GO PDDFORUM
E-Mail:..........................bugs@parkplace.com
FTP: ftp.parkplace.com
Web: www.parkplace.com

Parsons Technology, Inc.
1 Parsons Dr.
PO Box 100
Hiawatha, IA 52233-9904
Main:.....................................319-395-9626
Tech. Support:........................319-395-7314
Sales:....................................800-223-6925
Customer Service:..................800-223-6925
FAX: 319-395-7449
E-Mail: ....tsupport@parsonstech.com
BBS:.....................................319-393-1002
Web: www.parsonstech.com

Parsytec
Parsytec, GMBH
245 W Roosevelt Rd., Building 9, Unit 60
W Chicago, IL 60185
Main:.....................................708-293-9500
Tech. Support FAX:.................708-293-9525
E-Mail: ....sales@parsytec.com
Web: www.parsytee.com

Passport Designs
1151 D Triton Dr.
Fremont, CA 94404
Main:.....................................415-349-6224
Tech. Support:........................415-349-8090
Customer Service:..................800-443-3210
Tech. Support FAX:.................415-349-8008
FAX: 415-349-8008
Web: www.passport@aol.com

PathLink Technology
Sales:....................................408-720-7620
Web: www.pathlink.com

Patton Electronics Co.
7622 Rickenbacker Dr.
Gaithersburg, MD 20879
Main:.....................................301-975-1000
Tech. Support:........................301-975-1007
Tech. Support FAX:.................301-869-9293
E-Mail: ....sales@patton.com
Web: www.patton.com

Paul Mace Software
400 Williamson Way
Ashland, OR 97520
Main: 800-944-0191
Tech. Support:........................503-488-0224
Sales:....................................541-488-2322
FAX: 541-488-1549
BBS: 503-482-7435
Web: www.pmace.com

Pause and Recover
4901 W Rosecrans
PO Box 5046
Hawthorne, CA 90251-5046
Main: 800-421-5500
Tech. Support:........................213-973-7707

Paxtron Corp.
28 Grove St.
Spring Valley, NY 10977
Main: 914-576-6522
Sales:....................................800-815-3241
FAX: 914-624-3239

Peachtree Software
1505 Pavilion Pl. Ste. C
Norcross, GA 30093
Main: 800-228-0068
Tech. Support:........................770-279-2099
Sales:....................................800-247-3224
Customer Service:..................770-564-5800
Tech. Support FAX: 404-925-2777
FAX: 770-564-6000
CompuServe: ....GO PEACHTREE
America Online:...............Keyword Peachtree
E-Mail:.................. paw_support@peach.com
BBS: 770-564-8071
Web: www.peach.com

Penril Datacomm Networks, Inc.
14 Commerce Dr.
Danbury, CT 06813
Main: 203-748-7001
Tech. Support:........................800-453-3111
Sales:....................................800-348-8797
FAX: 203-797-9285
Web: www.penril.com

Pentax Technologies Corp.
100 Technology Dr.
Broomfield, CO 80021
Main:.......................................303-460-1600
Tech. Support:.........................303-460-1820
Sales: 303-460-1600
Customer Service:...................800-543-6144
Tech. Support FAX:................303-460-1628
BBS:.......................................303-460-1637

PeopleSoft
4440 Rosewood Dr.
Pleasanton, CA 94588
Main:.......................................510-225-3000
Sales: 800-947-7753
FAX:.......................................510-225-3100
Web: www.peoplesoft.com

Perceptive Solutions, Inc. (PSI)
2700 Flora St.
Dallas, TX 75201
Main:.......................................800-486-3278
Tech. Support:.........................214-954-1774
Sales: 214-954-1774
Tech. Support FAX:................214-953-1774
BBS:.......................................214-954-1856

Percon
1720 Willow Creek Cir. Ste. 530
Eugene, OR 97402
Main:.......................................800-873-7266
Tech. Support:.........................800-929-7899
Sales: 541-344-1189
Customer Service:...................800-929-7899
Tech. Support FAX:................541-344-1399
FAX:.......................................541-344-1399
E-Mail: ....tech@percon.com
BBS:.......................................541-344-1399
Web: www.percon.com

Performance Computing
15050 SW Knoll Pkwy. Ste. 2B
Beaverton, OR 97006
Main:.......................................503-641-1221
Tech. Support FAX:................503-641-3344
FAX:.......................................503-641-3344
E-Mail: ....info@perf.com
Web: www.teleport.com/~pciwww/

Performance Technology
Bay Networks
7800 IH 10 W Ste. 800
San Antonio, TX 78230
Main: 210-979-2000
Tech. Support:.........................210-979-2010
FAX: 210-979-2002
BBS:.......................................210-979-2012
FTP: ftp.perftech.com
Web: www.perftech.com

Performix
6618 Daryn Dr.
Westhills, CA 91307
Sales: 800-337-2448
FAX: 818-347-9455

Peripheral Repair Corp.
9233 Eton Ave.
Chatsworth, CA 91311
Main: 800-627-3475
Tech. Support:.........................818-700-8482
Tech. Support FAX: 818-700-0533

Perisol Technology
Silicon Electronics
1148 Sonora Court
Sunnyville, CA 94086
Main: 800-447-8226
Tech. Support:.........................408-738-1311
FAX: 408-738-0698
Web: www.perisol.com

Persoft
465 Science Dr.
Madison, WI 53711
Main: 608-273-6000
Tech. Support:.........................608-273-4357
Sales: 800-368-5283
Customer Service:...................800-368-5283
E-Mail:........................support@persoft.com
BBS:.......................................608-273-6595
FTP: ftp.persoft.com
Web: www.persoft.com

Personal Bibliographic Software, Inc.
PO Box 4250
Ann Arbor, MI 48106-4250
Main:......................................313-996-1580
FAX: 313-996-4672
Web: www.pbsinc.com

Personal Composer
PO Box 33016
Tulsa, OK 74153-1016
Main:......................................918-742-3488
FAX: 918-742-1232
CompuServe:........................... 103300,3702

Personal Tex
12 Madrona St.
Mill Valley, CA 94941
Main:......................................415-388-8853
Sales: 800-808-7906
Tech. Support FAX:................415-388-8865
E-Mail: ....pti@crl.com
Web: www.crl.com/~pti

Personal Training Systems
CBT Systems
173 Jefferson Dr.
Menlo Park, CA 94025
Main:....................................800-832-2499
Tech. Support:......................800-832-2499
Sales: 800-832-2499
Customer Service:..................800-832-2499
Tech. Support FAX:................415-462-2101
FAX: 415-462-2101
E-Mail: ....ptssales@ptst.com
FTP: ftp.ptst.com
Web: www.ptst.com

Phar Lap Software, Inc.
60 Aberdeen Ave.
Cambridge, MA 02138
Main:......................................617-661-1510
Tech. Support:......................617-876-2972
BBS:.....................................617-661-1009

Philips Consumer Electronics Corp.
1 Philips Dr.
Knoxville, TN 37914-1810
Main: 423-521-4499
Sales:....................................423-521-4316
Customer Service:..................423-475-1053

Phillips Laser Magnetic Storage
Phillips Electronics
4425 Arrows West Dr.
Colorado Springs, CO 80907
Main: 719-593-7900
Tech. Support:......................800-777-5674
Sales:....................................800-777-5674
FAX: 719-593-4597
E-Mail:.........susan_wright@lmsmail.lms.com
BBS: 719-593-4081

Phillips Media
1313 W Sepulveda Blvd.
Torrance, CA 90501
Main: 310-325-5999
Tech. Support:......................800-876-6679
Sales:....................................310-325-5999
Customer Service:..................310-444-6100
Tech. Support FAX: 310-539-9784

Philtek Power
4320 Sweet Rd. Unit B
Blaine, WA 98230
Main: 800-727-4877
Tech. Support:......................360-332-7252
Tech. Support FAX: 360-332-7253

Phoenix Division of Micro Firmware, Inc.
330 W. Gray St.
Norman Oklahoma 73069-7111
Tech Support 405-321-8333
Sales..800-767-5465
Tech Support Fax 405-321-8342
Main 405-321-8333
EMail:- .... support@firmware.com
Web: www.firmware.com

Phoenix Technologies Ltd.
2770 De La Cruz
Santa Clara, CA 95050
Main.. 408-654-9000
Fax 408-452-1985
Web: www.ptltd.com

Photonics Corp.
1515 Center Point Dr.
Milpitas, CA 95035
Main:...................................... 800-282-5747
Tech. Support:........................ 408-262-7700
Sales: 800-997-2326
Tech. Support FAX:................. 408-955-7950
BBS:.. 408-370-3172
Web: www.datatechnology.com

PhotoSphere Software
380 W. 1st Ave. Ste. 210
Vancouver, BC V5Y 3T7
Canada
Main:...................................... 800-665-1496
Sales: 604-876-3206
FAX:.. 800-757-5558
Web: www.photosphere.com/photos

Physics Academic Software
American Institute of Physics
PO Box 8202
NC State University
Raleigh, NC 27695-8202
Main:...................................... 800-955-8275
Sales: 800-955-8275
Customer Service:................... 919-515-7447
Tech. Support FAX:................. 919-515-2682
E-Mail: .... pas@aip.org
Web: www.aip.org/pas

Piceon
1996 Lundy Ave.
San Jose, CA 95131
Main: 408-432-8030
Tech. Support:........................ 408-432-8030
Sales:..................................... 800-366-2983
Customer Service:.................. 800-366-2983
Tech. Support FAX: 408-943-1309
FAX: 408-943-1309
E-Mail:.................. fredrickson@.piiceon.com
BBS:....................................... 408-431-8998
Web: www.piiceon.com

Pictorius Inc.
2000 Barrington St. 4th Floor
Halifax, NS B3J 3K1
Canada
Main: 902-492-2880
Customer Service:............ 902-492-2880-265
FAX: 902-492-3409
CompuServe:........................... 73300,3460
America Online:................ Keyword Prograph
E-Mail:........................... sales@pictorius.com
FTP: ftp.pictorius.com
Web: www.pictorius.com

Pierce Ellery Designs
540 Madison Ave.
New York, NY 10022
Main: 212-755-3282
FAX: 212-755-3436
Web: www.wavesys.com

Piller, Inc.
Piller, Germany/Lumayer
Rt. 4, Box 194, S Plank Rd.
Middletown, NY 10940
Main: 914-355-5000
Customer Service:.................. 800-597-6937
Tech. Support FAX: 914-355-9005
Web: www.piller.com

Pinnacle Micro, Inc.
19 Technology
Irvine, CA 92718
Main:.....................................714-789-3000
Tech. Support:.......................714-789-3100
Sales:...................................800-553-7070
Customer Service:..................714-789-3100
Tech. Support FAX:................714-789-3097
FAX:....................................714-789-3150
CompuServe:........................... 70534,3026
BBS:....................................714-789-3048
Web: www.pinnaclemicro.com

Pinnacle Publishing, Inc.
PO Box 888
Kent, WA 98032
Main:....................................800-788-1900
Tech. Support:.......................206-251-3513
Sales:...................................800-231-1293
Customer Service:..................206-251-1200
FAX:....................................206-251-5057
BBS:....................................206-251-6218

Pioneer New Media Technologies-Optical Memory
2265 E 220th St.
Long Beach, CA 90810
Main:....................................800-444-6784
Tech. Support:.......................408-496-9140
Customer Service:..................310-952-2111
Tech. Support FAX:................310-952-2100
BBS:....................................310-835-7980

Pivar Computing Services, Inc.
165 Arlington Heights Rd.
Buffalo Grove, IL 60089
Main:....................................547-459-6010
Tech. Support:.......................847-459-6010
Sales:...................................847-459-6010
Customer Service:..................847-459-6010
E-Mail:............................... gary@pivar.com
Web: www.pivar.com

Plant Software, Inc., The
102 - 930 W 1st St.
North Vancouver, BC V7P 3N4
Canada
Main: 604-682-8424
Tech. Support FAX: 604-682-8425
E-Mail:............................ info@theplant.com
Web: www.theplant.com

Platinum Software Corp.
195 Technology Dr.
Irvine, CA 92718-2402
Main: 800-426-0469
Tech. Support:.......................800-333-5242
Sales:...................................800-477-3725
Customer Service:..................800-453-4000
Tech. Support FAX: 714-453-4091

Platinum Software International
17 Thornburn Rd.
North Potomac, MD 20878
Main: 301-309-9169
Sales:...................................800-442-6861
Customer Service:..................708-620-5000
Web: www.platinum.com

Platinum Solutions
9800 La Cienega Blvd.
Inglewood, CA 90301-4440
Main: 310-670-6500
Tech. Support:.......................310-337-5995
Customer Service:..................310-670-6500
Tech. Support FAX: 310-670-2980
BBS: 310-670-2980
FTP: //ftp.locus.com/pub
Web: www.locus.com

Platinum Technology Santa Barbara Lab
Platinum Technology
340 S Kellogg Ave.
Goleta, CA 93117
Main: 805-683-5777
FAX: 805-683-4105
Web: www.softool.com

Play Inc.
2890 Kilgore Rd.
Rancho Cordova, CA 95670
Main:.....................................916-851-0800
Tech. Support:........................916-851-0900
Sales: 800-306-7529
Customer Service:...................916-851-0800
Tech. Support FAX:................916-851-0801
E-Mail: ....comments@play.com
BBS:.....................................916-983-3288
Web: www.play.com

PlexCom, Inc.
2255 Agate Court
Simi Valley, CA 93065
Main:.....................................800-753-9526
Tech. Support:........................800-753-9526
Sales: 800-753-9526
Customer Service:...................800-753-9526
Tech. Support FAX:................805-583-4764
FAX:......................................805-583-4764
E-Mail: ....sales@plexcom.com
FTP: ftp.plexcom.com
Web: www.plexcom.com

Plextor
4255 Burton Dr.
Santa Clara, CA 95054
Main:.....................................408-980-1838
Tech. Support:........................408-980-1838
Sales: 800-886-3935
Customer Service:...................408-980-1838
FAX:......................................408-986-1010
BBS:.....................................408-986-1569
Web: www.plextor.com

Plotworks, Inc.
16440 Eagles Crest Rd.
Ramona, CA 92065-9674
Main:.....................................619-457-5090
Tech. Support FAX:................619-789-4923

Polaris Software
1928 Don Lee Pl.
Escondido, CA 92029
Main: 619-735-2300
Tech. Support:........................619-735-2300
Sales:...................................800-722-5728
Customer Service:...................800-338-5943
Tech. Support FAX: 619-738-0113
BBS:.....................................619-592-2674

Polygon
1350 Baur Blvd.
St. Louis, MO 63132
Main: 314-432-4142
Tech. Support FAX: 314-997-9696
FAX: 314-997-9696
CompuServe:...............................723,2201
E-Mail:.............................info@polygon.com
Web: www.polygon.com

Polywell Computers, Inc.
1461-1 San Mateo Ave.
South San Francisco, CA 94080
Main: 800-999-1278
Tech. Support:........................415-583-7222
Sales:...................................800-999-1278
Tech. Support FAX: 415-583-1974
E-Mail:...................polywell@lx.netcom.com
BBS:.....................................415-583-1974
Web: www.polywell.com

Pony Computer, Inc.
32333 Aurora Rd.
Solon, OH 44139
Main: 216-498-4888
Tech. Support:........................216-498-0297
Sales:...................................216-498-4888
Tech. Support FAX: 800-246-7669

Popkin Software & Systems, Inc.
11 Park Pl. 15th Floor
New York, NY 10007
Main: 212-571-3434
Sales:...................................800-732-5227
FAX: 212-571-3436
Web: www.popkin.com

Portrait Display Inc.
6665 Owens Dr.
Pleasanton, CA 94588
Main:......................................800-858-7744
Tech. Support:.......................510-227-2721
Sales:....................................510-227-2700
FAX: 510-227-2705
BBS:......................................510-227-2744
Web: www.portrait.com

Positive Software Co.
1300 Columbia Ctr Blvd.
Richland, WA 99352
Main:.....................................509-735-9194
FAX: 509-735-6299
E-Mail: ....psc@pointofsale.com
BBS:......................................509-736-9544
Web: www.pointofsale.com

Positron Publishing, Inc.
1915 N. 121st St. Ste. D
Omaha, NE 68154
Main:.....................................402-493-6280
Sales:....................................800-365-1002
FAX: 402-493-6254
BBS:......................................402-493-4695

Power Computing Corp.
12337 Technology Blvd.
Austin, TX 78727-6104
Main:.....................................800-999-7279
Sales:....................................512-258-1350
FAX: 512-250-3390
Web: www.powercc.com

PowerPlus
4100 Caven Rd.
Austin, TX 78744
Main:.....................................800-878-5530
Tech. Support:.......................514-443-3372
Tech. Support FAX:................512-443-3518
E-Mail: ....pplus@io.com
BBS:......................................214-631-8697

Powersoft
561 Virginia Rd.
Concord, MA 01742
Main: 508-287-1500
Tech. Support:.......................800-937-7693
Sales:....................................800-395-3525
Customer Service:..................508-287-1500
BBS: 508-287-1850
FTP: ftp.powersoft.com/pub/
Web: www.powersoft.com

Power-Up Software Corp.
Global
1 Misco Plaza
Holmdel, NJ 07733
Main: 800-851-2917
Tech. Support:.......................908-264-8324
Sales:....................................908-246-1000
Customer Service:..................800-647-2699
Tech. Support FAX: 908-264-5955
FAX: 908-264-5955
E-Mail:......................misco@IX.netcom.com
Web: www.misco.netcom.com

Practical Peripherals, Inc./ Hayes
5854 Peachtree Corners East
Norcross, GA 30348
Main: 800-442-4774
Tech. Support:.......................770-840-9966
Sales:....................................770-840-9966
Customer Service:..................770-840-9966
FAX: 770-734-4601
BBS: 770-734-4600
Web: www.practinet.com

Prairie Group, The
PO Box 65820
West Des Moines, IA 50265-5820
Main: 515-225-3720
Tech. Support:.......................515-225-4122
Sales:....................................800-346-5392
Customer Service:..................515-225-3720
Tech. Support FAX: 515-225-2422
America Online:..................... Keyword Prairie
FTP: ftp.members.aol.com/prairieftp
Web: www.members.aol.com/prairiesft

Precision Computer Graphics
634 N. Glenoaks Blvd. Ste. 367
Burbank, CA 91502
Main:......................................818-842-6542
FAX:......................................818-842-1085

Precision Data Products
PO Box 8367
Grand Rapids, MI 49518
Main:......................................616-698-2242
Tech. Support:........................616-698-2242
Sales:.....................................800-968-2468
E-Mail: ....sales@precision.com
BBS:......................................616-698-7058

Preferred Solutions, Ltd.
34268 Xanadu Terrace
Fremont, CA 94555
Sales:.....................................510-713-9152
FAX:......................................510-713-9152
E-Mail: ....russf@netcom.com
Web: www.maui.net/~russf/ps.html

Premia Corporation
Sales:.....................................503-641-6000
FAX:......................................503-641-6001
BBS:......................................503-646-1374

Price Waterhouse
1251 Ave. of the Americas
New York, NY 10020
Main:......................................212-819-4833
FAX:......................................212-790-6638

Prima International
PCPI
3350 Scott Blvd. Building 7
Santa Clara, CA 95054
Main:......................................408-727-2600
Tech. Support FAX:.................408-727-2435
E-Mail: ....sales@prima-intl.com
Web: www.prima-intl.co.uk

Primatech
2041 Rosecrans Dr. Ste. 297
El Segundo, CA 90245
Main: 800-633-3113
Tech. Support:........................213-322-4440
BBS:......................................213-322-5522
Web: www.aescon.com/asti/index.htm

Primavera Systems, Inc.
2 Bala Plaza
Bala Cynwyd, PA 19004
Main: 800-423-0245
Tech. Support:........................610-668-3030
Sales:.....................................610-660-5825
Customer Service:...................610-667-8600
FAX: 610-667-7894
BBS:......................................610-660-5833
Web: www.primavera.com

Princeton Graphic Systems
2801 S. Yale St.
Santa Ana, CA 92704
Main: 714-751-8405
Tech. Support:........................800-747-6249
Sales:.....................................800-747-6249
Customer Service:...................800-747-6249
Tech. Support FAX: 714-751-5522
FAX: 714-751-5522
Web: www.maginnovision.com

Princeton Review Publishing
2315 Broadway
New York, NY 10024-4332
Main: 212-874-8282
Tech. Support:........................800-546-2102
Customer Service:...................800-546-2102
Tech. Support FAX: 800-546-2102
America Online:....Keyword prince & student
Web: www.review.com

Printer Connection
PO Box 927240
San Diego, CA 92192-7240
Main: 800-479-6090
Sales:.....................................800-479-6090
Customer Service:...................800-479-6092
Tech. Support FAX: 619-587-9001
Web: www.printercon.com

Printer Works, The
3481 Arden Rd.
Hayward, CA 94545
Main:......................................510-670-2700
Tech. Support:........................510-887-0324
Sales:.....................................800-225-6116
FAX: 510-786-0589
E-Mail:........................info@printerworks.com
Web: www.printerworks.com

Pro CD, Inc.
Acxiom
222 Rosewood Dr.
Danvers, MA 01923
Main:......................................508-750-0000
Tech. Support:........................508-777-7766
Customer Service:...................508-750-0055
Tech. Support FAX:.................508-750-0070
E-Mail: ....technical.support@procd.com
BBS:.......................................508-750-0077
Web: www.procd.com

Process Software
959 Concord St.
Framingham, MA 01701
Main:......................................800-722-7770
Tech. Support:........................508-879-6994
Tech. Support FAX:.................508-879-0042
E-Mail: ....support@process.com
Web: www.process.com

Procom Technology, Inc.
2181 Dupont Dr.
Irvine, CA 92715
Main:......................................714-852-1000
Tech. Support:.................800-800-8600-611
Sales:.....................................800-800-8600
CompuServe:............................ 75300,2312
E-Mail:............................info@procom.com
BBS:.......................................714-549-0527
Web: www.procom.com

Procomp USA, Inc.
6777 Engle Rd.
Cleveland, OH 44130
Main: 216-234-6387
Tech. Support:........................ 216-234-6387
FAX: 216-234-2233
BBS: 216-234-6581

Prodigy Services Co.
445 Hamilton Ave.
White Plains, NY 10601
Main: 914-448-8000
Sales:.................................... 800-776-3449
Web: www.prodigy.com

Professor Jones
1940 W State St.
Boise, ID 83702
Main: 800-553-2256
Tech. Support:........................ 208-342-6948
BBS: 208-342-2177

Programmer's Paradise
1163 Shrewsbury Ave.
Shrewsbury, NJ 07702
Main: 800-445-7899
Tech. Support:........................ 201-389-9228
BBS: 201-389-9227
Web: www.pparadise.com

Programmer's Shop
Software Developers
33 Riverside Dr.
Pembrooke, MA 02359
Main: 800-421-8006
Tech. Support:........................ 617-829-2036
Tech. Support FAX: 617-829-2096
BBS: 617-749-2018

Progress Software Corp.
14 Oak Park
Bedford, MA 01730-9960
Main:......................................800-477-6473
Tech. Support:........................617-280-4999
Tech. Support FAX:.................617-280-4025
FAX:.......................................617-275-4595
E-Mail: ....crescent@progress.com
BBS:.......................................617-275-4595
Web: www.progress.com

Project Software & Development
20 University Rd.
Cambridge, MA 02138
Main:......................................617-661-1444
Tech. Support FAX:.................617-661-1642
Web: www.psdi.com

Prometheus Products
9440 Tualatin-Sherwood Rd.
Tualatin, OR 97062
Main:......................................503-692-9600
Tech. Support:........................503-692-9601
Sales:.....................................800-477-3473
Customer Service:...................800-477-3473
FAX:.......................................503-691-1101
CompuServe:.............................. 76004,527
America Online:...........prometheus@aol.com
E-Mail: ....prometh@teleport.com
BBS:.......................................503-691-5199

Promptus Communications, Inc.
207 High Point Ave.
Portsmouth, RI 02871
Main:......................................401-683-6100
FAX:.......................................401-683-6105

Pronexus
Sales:.....................................613-839-0035
CompuServe:.............................. 74777,406
BBS:.......................................613-839-0034

Proteon, Inc.
2 Technology Dr.
Westborough, MA 01581-1799
Main: 800-545-7464
Tech. Support:........................508-898-3100
Sales:.....................................508-898-2800
Customer Service:...................508-898-3100
FAX: 508-366-8901
BBS:.......................................508-366-7827
Web: www.proteon.com

Proto View Development Corp.
2540 Route 130
Carnbury, NJ 08512
Main: 609-655-5000
Tech. Support:........................609-655-5000
Sales:.....................................609-655-5000
Customer Service:...................609-655-5000
Tech. Support FAX: 609-655-5353
FAX: 609-655-5353
E-Mail:..........................linfo@protoview.com
BBS:.......................................609-655-4441
Web: www.protoview.com

ProWorks
2371 NW Maser Dr.
Corvalis, OR 97330
Main: 541-752-9885
Tech. Support FAX: 503-567-8820
FAX: 800-232-5962
BBS:.......................................541-752-9886
Web: www.proworks.com

Proxima Corp.
9440 Carroll Park Dr.
San Diego, CA 92121
Main: 800-447-7692
Tech. Support:........................619-457-5500
FAX: 619-457-9647
Web: www.prxm.com

Proximity Technology, Inc.
Franklin Electronic Publishers, Inc
One Franklin Plaza
Burlington, NJ 08016-4907
Main:.....................................609-386-2500
Sales:............................609-386-2500-4054
Tech. Support FAX:.................609-239-5952
FAX: 609-387-0148
E-Mail: ....patti_bradshaw@franklin.com

PseudoCorp
2597 Potter St.
Eugene, OR 97405
Main:.....................................541-683-9173
Sales:.....................................541-683-9173
Customer Service:...................541-683-9173
Tech. Support FAX:.................541-683-9186
FAX: 541-683-9186
E-Mail: ....rhowden@teleport.com
BBS:.......................................804-873-2154
Web: www.teleport.com/~rhowden

Publishing Perfection
PO Box 307
Menomonee Falls, WI 53051
Main:.....................................800-782-5974
Tech. Support:........................414-252-5000
Tech. Support FAX:.................414-252-9120
E-Mail: ....sales@perfection.com
BBS:.......................................414-255-2071

Pure Data Ltd.
180 W Beaver Creek Rd.
Richmond Hill, ONT L4B 1B4
Canada
Main:.....................................905-731-6444
Tech. Support:........................905-731-4533
Sales:.....................................800-661-8210
Customer Service:...................905-731-4533
Tech. Support FAX:.................905-731-7017
FAX: 905-731-7017
CompuServe:......................... GO PUREDATA
E-Mail: ....support@puredata.com
BBS:.......................................905-731-4679
Web: www.puredata.com

Pure Software
1309 South Mary Ave.
Sunnyvale, CA 94087
Main: 408-720-1600
FAX: 408-720-9200
E-Mail:......................................info@pure.com
Web: www.pure.com

Pyramid
Covington, KY
Main: 606-292-2540
FAX: 606-292-2555
Web: www.pyramid.com

QLogic Corp./Emulex
3545 Harbor Blvd.
PO Box 5001
Costa Mesa, CA 92626
Main: 714-438-2200
Tech. Support:........................714-668-5037
Sales:.....................................800-867-7274
Customer Service:...................800-662-4471
Tech. Support FAX: 714-668-5008
E-Mail:...............tech_support@emulex.com
BBS: 714-708-3170
FTP: ftp.emulex.com
Web: www.emulex.com

QMS, Inc.
1 Magnum Pass
Mobile, AL 36618
Main: 334-633-4300
Tech. Support:........................334-633-4500
Tech. Support FAX: 334-633-3716
CompuServe: ....GO QMSPRINT
BBS: 334-633-3632
FTP: ftp.qms.com
Web: www.qms.com

Qplus, Inc.
2020 Beechwood Blvd.
Pittsburgh, PA 15217
Main: 412-521-9525
America Online:................Keyword Nutrition

Quadralay Corp.
3925 W. Braker Lane Ste. 337
Austin, TX 78759
Main:.......................................512-305-0240
Tech. Support FAX:.................512-305-0248
Web: www.quadralay.com

Qualcomm, Inc.
6455 Lusk Blvd.
San Diego, CA 92121-2779
Main:.......................................619-658-1291
Sales: 800-238-3672
FAX:.......................................619-658-1500
Web: www.qualcomm.com

Qualitas, Inc.
7101 Wisconsin Ave. Ste. 1024
Bethesda, MD 20814
Main:.......................................301-907-6700
Tech. Support:........................301-907-7400
Sales: 800-733-1377
Customer Service:..................800-676-0386
Tech. Support FAX:................301-907-0905
CompuServe:...........................GO PCVENA
America Online:................ Keyword Qualitas
E-Mail: ....tech@qualitas.com
BBS:....................................301-907-8030
FTP: ftp.qualitas.com/pub
Web: www.qualitas.com

Quality America, Inc.
PO Box 18896
Tucson, AZ 85731-8896
Tech. Support:........................800-722-6154
FAX:.......................................520-722-6705
E-Mail: ....qa-inc@qa-inc.com
Web: www.qa-inc.com/qa-inc

Quality Software Products
5711 W Slauson Ave. Ste. 240
Culver City, CA 90230
Main:.......................................800-628-3999
Tech. Support:........................213-410-0303
Sales: 800-628-3999
FAX:.......................................213-410-0124
BBS:....................................213-410-0124

Qualix Group Inc.
1900 S Norfolk St. Ste. 224
San Mateo, CA 94403
Main: 415-572-0200
Tech. Support:.......................800-245-8649
Tech. Support FAX: 415-572-1300
Web: www.qualix.com

Qualstar Corp.
6709 Independence Ave.
Canoga Park, CA 91303
Main: 818-592-0061
Tech. Support:.......................818-592-0061
Sales:....................................800-468-0680
Tech. Support FAX: 818-592-0116
E-Mail:................ sales@qualstar.attmail.com
BBS:....................................818-592-0116
Web: www.qualstar.com

Quantex Micro Systems Inc.
400 B. Pierce St.
Somerset, NJ 08873
Main: 908-563-4166
Tech. Support:.......................800-864-8650
Sales:....................................800-836-0566
Tech. Support FAX: 908-563-0407
BBS:....................................201-563-4999

Quantum Corp.
500 McCarthy Blvd.
Milpitas, CA 95035
Main: 408-894-4000
Tech. Support:.......................800-826-8022
Sales:....................................408-894-5200
Customer Service:.................800-345-3377
Tech. Support FAX: 408-894-3282
FAX: 408-894-3218
BBS:....................................800-472-9799
Web: www.quantum.com

Quantum Films Software Division
8230 Beverly Blvd. Ste. 17
Los Angeles, CA 90048
Main: 213-852-9661
FAX: 213-655-6745
Web: www.qedinc.com/qed/qed.html

Quantum Software Systems, Ltd.
175 Terrence Matthews Crescent
Kanata, ONT K2M 1W8
Canada
Main:.....................................613-591-0931
Sales:..........................800-676-0566 #3000
FAX: 613-591-3579
Web: www.qnx.com

Quark
1800 Grant St.
Denver, CO 80203
Main:....................................303-894-8888
Tech. Support:.......................303-894-8899
Sales:...................................800-788-7835
Customer Service:..................303-894-8888
Tech. Support FAX:................303-894-3399
CompuServe:........................... 70414,2101
America Online:...........WINQUARK@aol.com
E-Mail:..........................wintech@quark.com
Web: www.quark.com

Quarterdeck
13160 Mindanao Way
Marina Del Rey, CA 90292
Main:....................................310-309-3700
Tech. Support:.......................310-309-4250
Sales:...................................800-354-3260
Customer Service:..................800-354-3222
Tech. Support FAX:................310-309-3217
FAX: 310-309-5219
CompuServe:................. GO QUARTERDECK
E-Mail:...................... info@quarterdeck.com
BBS:.....................................310-309-3227
FTP: ftp.quarterdeck.com
Web: www.quarterdeck.com

Quest Tech
715 24th St. Ste. P
Paso Robles, CA 93446
Main:....................................805-237-6262
Tech. Support:.......................800-448-1184
Sales:...................................800-448-1184
Customer Service:..................800-448-1184
Tech. Support FAX:................805-237-6267
E-Mail:..jbarret@fix.net
BBS:.....................................805-237-6266
Web: www.fix.net/~jbarrett/questec.html

Questron
1011 Commerce Ct.
Buffalo Grove, IL 60089-2362
Main: 847-465-5000
Tech. Support FAX: 847-465-3770
E-Mail:.................................. info@ampli.com
Web: www.ampli.com

Quick Electronics, Inc.
10800 76th Court N
Largo, FL 34647
Main: 800-800-5500
Tech. Support:........................813-546-0311
Tech. Support FAX: 813-544-5500
BBS: 813-544-5500

QuickLogic Corp.
2933 Bunker Hill Lane
Santa Clara, CA 95054
Main: 408-987-2000
Tech. Support:........................800-842-3742
Sales:.....................................800-842-3742
FAX: 408-987-2012
Web: www.quicklogic.com

Quill Corp.
100 Schelter Rd.
Lincolnshire, IL 60069-3621
Main: 708-634-6650
Tech. Support:........................708-634-6650

Quinn-Curtis, Inc.
35 Highland Cir.
Needham, MA 02194
Main: 617-449-6155
Tech. Support FAX: 617-449-6109
BBS: 617-449-4783
Web: www.quinn-curtis.com/~quinn/

Quintus Corp.
47212 Mission Falls Court
Fremont, CA 94539
Main: 510-624-2800
Tech. Support:........................800-542-1283
FAX: 510-770-1377
BBS: 415-965-0551

RAD Data Communications
RAD, LTD
900 Corporate Dr.
Mahwah, NJ 07430
Main:......................................201-529-1100
Tech. Support:........................201-529-1100
Sales:....................................201-529-1100
Customer Service:..................201-529-1100
Tech. Support FAX:................201-529-5777
BBS:......................................201-512-1446
Web: www.rad.com

RAD Technologies, Inc.
745 Emerson St.
Palo Alto, CA 94301-9785
Main:......................................415-617-9430
Sales:....................................800-773-4723
FAX:......................................415-473-6826
Web: www.rad.com

RB Software
1109 Arnette Ave.
Durham, NC 27707

RG Software Systems, Inc.
6900 E Camelback Rd. Ste. 630
Scottsdale, AZ 85251
Main:......................................602-423-8000
FAX:......................................602-423-8389

RNS
Meret Communications, Inc..
7402 Hollister Ave.
Santa Barbara, CA 93117
Main:......................................805-968-4262
Tech. Support:........................800-262-2290
Sales:....................................800-262-8023
E-Mail:...............................support@rns.com
Web: www.rns.com

RYBS Electronics, Inc.
351 W Arapahoe
Boulder, CO 80302
Main: 303-444-6073
Tech. Support:........................303-444-7927
Tech. Support FAX: 303-449-9259
E-Mail:.................................sales@bybs.com
BBS:......................................303-443-7437
Web: www.rybs.com

Racal-Datacom, Inc.
PO Box 407044
Fort Lauderdale, FL 33340-7044
Main: 305-846-1601
Tech. Support:........................508-263-9929
Customer Service:..................800-526-8255
Tech. Support FAX: 508-635-9140
E-Mail:........ cust_service@rimail.interlan.com
FTP: FTP: //ftpserv.interlan.com/ftpserve/
Web: www.racal.com

Racore Computer Products
170 Knowles Dr. Ste. 206
Los Gatos, CA 95030
Main: 800-635-1274
Tech. Support:........................408-374-8290
FAX: 408-374-6653
BBS:......................................801-973-4228
Web: www.racore.com

Radiant Communications Corp.
5001 Hadley Rd.
South Plainfield, NJ 07080
Main: 800-969-3427
Tech. Support:........................908-757-7444
Sales:....................................908-757-7444
FAX: 908-757-8666
BBS:......................................908-757-8666

Radius/E-Machines

215 Moffett Park Dr.
Sunnyvale, CA 94089
Main:.......................................408-541-6100
Tech. Support:........................408-541-6100
Sales:.....................................800-227-2995
Customer Service:..................408-541-5750
Tech. Support FAX:................408-541-6150
CompuServe:........................... 760,042,155
America Online:............... Keyword RadiusTS
E-Mail:........................... infornet@radius.com
BBS:.......................................408-541-6190
FTP: ftp.radius.com
Web: www.radius.com

Raima Corp.

1605 NW Sammamish Rd. Ste. 200
Issaquah, WA 98027
Main:.......................................800-275-4724
Tech. Support:........................206-557-5333
Sales:.....................................206-557-0200
Tech. Support FAX:................206-557-5200
BBS:.......................................206-557-5337
Web: www.raima.com

Rainbow Technology

50 Technology Dr.
Irvine, CA 92718
Main:.......................................800-852-8569
Tech. Support:........................800-959-9954
Sales:.....................................714-450-7300
Tech. Support FAX:................714-450-7450
E-Mail:......................techsupport@rnbo.com
BBS:.......................................714-450-7485
Web: www.rnbo.com

Raindrop Software

833 E. Arapaho Ste. 104
Richardson, TX 75081
Sales:.....................................214-234-2611
FAX:.......................................214-234-2674
CompuServe:............................ 74431,1411

Rand McNally TDM, Inc.

8255 N. Central Park Ave.
Skokie, IL 60076
Main: 847-329-8100
Sales:.....................................800-333-0136
FAX:.......................................847-674-4496
Web: www.randmedia.ie/rand/

Raymond Commodore Amiga

898 Raymond Ave.
St. Paul, MN 55114-1521
Main: 612-642-9890
FAX: 612-642-9891

ReadySoft Inc.

3375 14th Ave., Units 7 & 8
Markham, ONT L3R 0H2
Canada
Main: 905-475-4801
FAX: 905-475-4802
E-Mail:................webmaster@readysoft.com
Web: www.readysoft.com

Real Time Devices, Inc.

200 Innovation Blvd.
PO Box 906
State College, PA 16804-0906
Main: 814-234-8087
Tech. Support FAX: 814-234-5218
BBS: 814-234-9427

Real World Corp.

PO Box 9516
Manchester, NH 03108-9516
Main: 800-678-6336
Tech. Support:........................603-641-0210
FAX: 603-641-0230
CompuServe: 103033,2154
BBS: 603-641-0220

RealAudio
1111 3rd St. Ste. 2900
Seattle, WA 98101
Main:.....................................206-674-2700
Tech. Support:........................206-674-2700
Sales: 800-230-5975
Customer Service:...................206-674-2700
Tech. Support FAX:................206-674-2699
FAX:..206-674-2699
Web: www.realaudio.com

Reality Online, Inc.
2200 Renaissance Blvd.
King of Prussia, PA 19406
Main:.....................................610-277-7600
FAX:..610-278-6115
E-Mail: ....info@reality-tech.com
Web: www.moneynet.com

Reasoning Systems, Inc.
3260 Hillview Ave.
Palo Alto, CA 94304
Main:.....................................415-494-6201
FAX:..415-494-8053
Web: www.reasoning.com

Recital Corp., Inc.
85 Constitution Ln. Ste. 200A
Danvers, MA 01923
Main:.....................................508-750-1066
Sales: 800-873-7443
FAX:..508-750-8097

Recreational Software Advisory
E-Mail: .... admin@rsac.org
Web: www.rsac.org

Red-Hawk
1405 S Milpitas
Milpitas, CA 95035
Main:.....................................408-945-1800
Customer Service:...................800-989-4295
FAX:..408-945-1396

Reed Technology and Information Services
20251 Century Blvd.
Germantown, MD 20874
Main: 800-922-9204
Tech. Support:........................301-428-3700
BBS:..301-428-2903

ReefNet Software
3610 Walnut Grove
Mississauga, ONT L5L 2608
Canada
Main: 905-820-3291
FAX: 905-820-1927
E-Mail:.................. reefnet@golo.interlog.com
Web: www.interlog.com/~reefnet

Reflection Technology
230 Second Ave.
Waltham, MA 02154
Main: 617-890-5905
Sales:.....................................800-670-4329
Customer Service:...................800-670-4329
FAX: 617-890-5918

Reliable Communications, Inc.
PO Box 816
Angelscamp, CA 95222
Main: 800-222-0280
Tech. Support:........................800-222-0042
Sales:.....................................800-222-8210
Tech. Support FAX: 209-736-0425
E-Mail:....................rcisystem@goldrush.com
Web: www.rcisystems.com

Reply Corp.
4435 Fortran Dr.
San Jose, CA 95134
Main: 408-942-4804
Tech. Support:........................800-473-7592
Sales:.....................................800-801-6898
FAX: 408-956-2793
BBS:..408-942-4897
Web: www.reply.com

Responsive Software
1901 Tunnel Rd.
Berkeley, CA 94705-1762
Main:....................................510-843-1034
Sales:...................................800-669-4611
FAX: 510-644-1013
Web: www.holonet.net/responsive

Retix
2401 Colorado Ave. Ste. 200
Santa Monica, CA 90404-3563
Main:....................................800-255-2333
Tech. Support:.......................310-828-7600
Sales:...................................310-828-3400
FAX: 310-828-2255
BBS:....................................310-828-2255
Web: www.retix.com

Reveal Computer Products, Inc.
6045 Variel Ave.
Woodland Hills, CA 91367
Main:....................................800-326-2222
Tech. Support:.......................818-702-6564
Sales:...................................818-704-6300
Customer Service:...................818-738-3252
Tech. Support FAX:................818-340-9957
FTP: ftp.reveal.com
Web: www.reveal.com

Revelation Software
Revelation Technologies, Inc.
201 Broadway
Cambridge, MA 02139
Main:....................................800-262-4747
Tech. Support:.......................800-262-4747
FAX: 617-494-0008
CompuServe:..................... GO REVELATION
E-Mail: ....info@revelation.com
Web: www.revelation.com

Rexon Software
2750 N Clovis Ave. Ste. 126
Fresno, CA 93727
Main:....................................800-228-9236
Tech. Support:.......................209-292-8888
Tech. Support FAX:................209-292-8908
BBS:....................................209-292-0541

Ricoh Corp.
5 Dedrick Pl
West Caldwell, NJ 07006
Main: 201-882-2000

Riser Bond Instruments
1207 M St.
PO Box 188
Aurora, NE 68818
Main: 402-694-5201
FAX: 402-694-2386

Riverbend Group-US Connect Baltimore/Washington
1430 Spring Hill Rd Ste. 600
McLean, VA 22102
Main: 703-883-0616
FAX: 703-893-9858

Roadwarrior International
AR Industries
16580 Harbor Blvd.
Fountain Valley, CA 92708
Main: 800-274-4277
Tech. Support:....................... 714-418-1400
Tech. Support FAX: 714-839-6282
E-Mail:........................... warrior@warrior.com
Web: www.warrior.com

Rockwell Software
2424 S. 102nd St.
West Allis, WI 53227
Main: 414-321-8000
Tech. Support:....................... 414-321-4266
Sales:................................... 414-321-1515
Customer Service:................... 800-223-5354
FAX: 414-321-2211
BBS: 414-321-0008
Web: www.rockwell.com

Rogue Wave Software
2065 Landings Dr.
Mountain View, CA 94043
Main:....................................800-487-3217
Sales:....................................415-691-9000
Customer Service:...................415-691-9000
FAX:......................................415-757-6650
E-Mail:.......................sales@roguewave.com
Web: www.roguewave.com

Roland Corp. U.S.
7200 Dominion Cir.
Los Angeles, CA 90040
Main:....................................213-685-5141
Tech. Support:.......................213-685-5141
Sales:....................................213-685-5141
Customer Service:...................213-685-5141
Tech. Support FAX:................213-726-8865
FAX:......................................213-722-0911
CompuServe:...........................GO ROLAND
Web: www.rolandus.com

Roland Digital Group
Roland Corp.
15271 Barranca Pkwy.
Irvine, CA 92718
Main:....................................714-727-2100
Tech. Support FAX:................714-727-2112
BBS:......................................714-975-0569

Rose Electronics
10707 Stancliff
Houston, TX 77099
Main:....................................800-333-9343
Tech. Support:.......................713-933-7673
Tech. Support FAX:................713-933-0044

Rosetta Technologies
9417 Princess Palm Ave.
Tampa, FL 33619
Main:....................................800-937-4224
Tech. Support:.......................800-937-4424
Customer Service:...................813-623-6205
FAX:......................................813-620-1107

ROSS Technology
5316 Hwy 290 W.
Austin, TX 78735
Main: 800-774-7677
Sales:....................................512-349-3108
FAX: 512-349-3101
E-Mail:.........................Webmaster@ross.com
Web: www.ross.com

Rugged Computer Systems Inc.
19407 Park Row Ste. 140
Houston, TX 77084
Main: 800-648-6262
Tech. Support:.......................713-578-2637
Sales:....................................800-648-6262
Customer Service:...................713-578-2637
Tech. Support FAX: 713-578-2750
FAX: 713-578-2750

Rupp Technology Corp.
2240 North Scottsdale Rd.
Tempe, AZ 85281
Main: 602-941-4789
Tech. Support:.......................602-941-4789
Sales:....................................800-844-7775
Customer Service:...................602-941-4789
Tech. Support FAX: 602-941-5505
CompuServe:..............................GO RUPP
America Online:................... dpa@aol.com
FTP: ftp.rupp.com
Web: www.rupp.com

S & S International, Inc.
1 New England Executive Park
Burlington, MA 01803
Main: 800-701-9648
FAX: 617-273-7474
CompuServe:.......................... 100443,3703
E-Mail:.................... info@us.drsolomon.com
Web: www.drsolomon.com

SAI Systems International, Inc.
915 Bridge Port Ave.
Shelton, CT 06484
Main: 800-331-0488
Tech. Support:.......................203-929-0790
Tech. Support FAX: 203-929-6948

SAS Industries
SAS Campus Dr.
Cary, NC 27513
Tech. Support:..........................919-677-8200
Sales:.....................................919-677-8200
FAX: 919-677-4444
E-Mail: ....datamation@sas.sascom
Web: www.sas.com

SBT Corp.
1401 Los Gamos Dr.
San Rafael, CA 94903
Main:......................................415-444-9900
FAX: 415-444-9901
CompuServe:..................GO ACCOUNTING
E-Mail: ....info@sbt.com
Web: www.sbt.com

SCO-The Santa Cruz Operation, Inc.
400 Encinal St.
PO Box 1900
Santa Cruz, CA 95061-1900
Main:......................................408-425-7222
Tech. Support:..........................800-347-4381
Sales:.....................................800-726-8649
Customer Service:...................800-347-4381
Tech. Support FAX:..................408-458-4227
CompuServe:.......................GO SCOFORUM
E-Mail: ....support@sco.com
BBS:.......................................408-426-9495
Web: www.sco.com

SCS Compute
3633 136th Pl. SE Ste. 300
Bellevue, WA 98006
Main:......................................206-643-2050
Tech. Support:..........................800-877-8297
Sales:.....................................800-326-1040
Customer Service:...................800-877-8297
Tech. Support FAX:..................206-562-1783
FAX: 206-562-1783
BBS:.......................................800-729-1040

SCT-Systems & Computer Technology, Inc.
4 Country View Rd.
Malvern, PA 19355
Main: 610-647-5930
Tech. Support:..........................800-223-7036
Sales:.....................................800-223-7036
Customer Service:...................800-223-7036
Web: www.sctcorp.com

SEEQ Technology
47200 Bayside Pkwy.
Freemont, CA 94538
Main: 510-226-2911
Sales:.....................................510-226-7400
Tech. Support FAX: 510-657-2837
FAX: 510-657-2837
Web: www.seeq.com

SPARC
Web: www.sparc.com

SPRY, Inc.
3535 128th Ave. SE
Belleview, WA 98006
Main: 800-447-2971
Tech. Support:..........................206-957-6000
Sales:.....................................206-957-8997
Customer Service:...................206-957-8996
Tech. Support FAX: 206-957-6000
FAX: 206-957-6000
BBS: 206-286-1722
Web: www.spry.com

SPSS, Inc.
444 N Michigan Ave.
Chicago, IL 60611
Main: 800-543-9262
Tech. Support:..........................312-329-2400
Sales:.....................................800-543-2185
Tech. Support FAX: 312-329-3410
FAX: 312-329-3668
BBS: 312-329-3668
Web: www.spss.com

STB Systems
1651 N Glenville Dr. Ste. 210
Richardson, TX 75081
Main:......................................214-234-8750
Tech. Support:.......................214-669-0989
Sales:....................................214-234-8750
Customer Service:..................214-234-8750
Tech. Support FAX:................214-669-1326
FAX:......................................214-234-1306
BBS:......................................214-437-9615
Web: www. Stb.com

Safe Harbor Computers
W226 N900 Eastmound Dr.
Waukesha, WI 53186
Main:......................................800-544-6599
FAX:......................................414-548-8130
Web: www.sharbor.com

Safeware, The Insurance Agency
5760 N High St.
PO Box 02211
Columbus, OH 43085-9990
Main:......................................800-781-1492
Tech. Support:.......................614-262-0559
FAX:......................................800-781-0559
CompuServe:................................ GO SAFE
BBS:......................................614-262-1714
Web: www.safeware.com

Sager Midern Computer, Inc.
18005 Cortney Ct.
City of Industry, CA 91748
Main:......................................818-964-8682
Tech. Support:.......................800-669-1624
Sales:....................................800-669-1624
FAX:......................................818-964-2381

Sageware Corp.
1282 Garner Ave.
Schenectady, NY 12309
Main:......................................518-377-1052

Sales Partner Systems, Inc.
770 W Granada Blvd. Ste. 116
Ormond Beach, FL 32174
Main: 904-672-8434
FAX: 904-673-4730
Web: www.spsi.com:8080

Samsonite
11200 E 45th Ave.
Denver, CO 80239
Main: 303-373-2000
Tech. Support:......................303-373-7343
Sales:....................................800-262-8282
Customer Service:..................800-223-7627
Tech. Support FAX: 303-373-6300

Samsung Information Systems America
3655 N 1st St.
Ledgewood, NJ 07852
Main: 800-446-0262
Tech. Support:......................800-446-0262
Sales:....................................201-229-4000
FAX: 201-347-8650
Web: www.sosimple.com

Samsung-Info. Systems Div.
Ridgefield Park, NJ 07660
Main: 201-229-4000
Tech. Support:.......................800-446-0262
Customer Service:..................800-726-7864
FAX: 201-229-4110
BBS:......................................201-691-6238
Web: www.samsung.co.kr/samsung.html

Samtron- Division of Samsung
18600 Broadwick St.
Rancho Dominguez, CA 90220
Main: 310-537-7000
Tech. Support:.......................714-522-1282
Customer Service:..................714-522-1282
FAX: 310-537-1300

Santorini Consulting & Design Inc.
2147 Union St.
San Francisco, CA 94123
Main:.......................................415-563-6398
Tech. Support FAX:.................415-563-0332
E-Mail: .... santorini@applelink.apple.com

Sapient Technology, Inc.
43855 Glenhazel Dr.
Ashburn, VA 22011
Sales:......................................703-729-5936
E-Mail: ....sapient@netrail.net
Web: www.xmission.com/~imagicom/sapient/
sapient.html

Saratoga Group, The
12930 Saratoga Ave. Ste. E
Saratoga, CA 95070
Main:......................................408-446-9115
FAX: 408-446-9134
Web: www.cyberwise.com

Saros
10900 NE 8th St.700 Plaza Ctr Building
Bellevue, WA 98004
Main:......................................206-646-1066
Sales: 800-827-2767
FAX: 206-462-0879
Web: www.saros.com

Sautter Group
935 E. 7220 S. Ste. D108
Midvale, UT 84047
Main:......................................801-255-0600
Sales: 800-766-7229
FAX: 801-255-0642

Sax Software
950 Patterson St.
Eugene, OR 97401
Main:......................................800-645-3729
FAX: 503-344-2459
E-Mail: ....mike@saxsoft.com
Web: www.saxsoft.com

Scala, Inc.
2323 Horse Pen Rd. Ste. 300
Herndon, VA 22071
Main: 703-713-0900
FAX: 703-713-1960
Web: www.scala.com

Scantron Corp.-Imaging Products Division
2082 Business Ctr. Dr. Ste. 150
Irvine, CA 92715
Main: 714-833-0333
Tech. Support:....................... 714-259-1076
Sales:............................ 800-722-6876-650
FAX: 714-833-2350
Web: www.scantron.com

Sceptre Technologies
16800 E. Gale Ave.
City of Industry, CA 91745
Main: 818-369-3698
Sales:..................................... 800-788-2878
FAX: 818-369-3488
BBS: 818-369-0607
Web: www.gus.com/emp/sceptre/sceptre.html

Scholastic New Media
568 Broadway
New York, NY 10012
Main: 212-343-7100
Customer Service:.................. 800-246-2986
E-Mail:................................... schcs@aol.com
Web: www.scholastic.com

Scientific Endeavors Corp.
508 N Kentucky St.
Kingston, TN 37763
Main: 423-376-4146
Sales:..................................... 800-998-1571
FAX: 423-376-1571
BBS: 615-376-1571

SciTech International
2525 N. Elston Ave.
Chicago, IL 60647-2003
Main:......................................312-486-9191
Sales: 800-622-3345
FAX:......................................312-486-9234
Web: www.scitechsoft.com

Scitex Corp.
6 Crosby Dr.
Bedford, MA 01730
Main:......................................617-275-8777
Tech. Support:........................617-276-5258
Sales: 800-947-4712
FAX:......................................617-275-8590
Web: www.pink2.scitex.com

Scitor Corp.
333 Middlefield Rd. 2nd Floor
Menlo Park, CA 94025
Main:......................................415-570-7700
Customer Service:...................415-462-4200
Tech. Support FAX:.................415-462-4300
FAX:......................................415-462-4201
E-Mail: ....sales@scitor.com
Web: www.scitor.com

Screen Play Systems
150 E Olive Ave. Ste. 203
Burbank, CA 91502
Main:......................................818-843-1627
Tech. Support:........................818-843-5557
Sales: 800-847-8679
Tech. Support FAX:.................818-843-8364
FAX:......................................818-843-8364
E-Mail: ....support@screenplay.com
Web: www.well.com/user/dramatic

Seagate Software
Seagate Technology
19925 Stevens Creek Blvd., Building 150
Cupertino, CA 95014
Main:......................................408-342-4500
Tech. Support:........................800-961-0501
Tech. Support FAX:.................408-342-4600
Web: www.sems.com

Seagate Software
37 Skyline Dr. Ste. 1101
Lake Mary, FL 32746
Main: 800-327-2232
Tech. Support:........................708-505-3300
Sales:....................................708-882-0067
Customer Service:...................708-505-3300
CompuServe:.....................GO PALINDROME
E-Mail:......................sales@smg.seagate.com
BBS:..708-505-3336
FTP: ftp.smg.seagate.com
Web: www.smg.seagate.com

Seagate Technology
920 Disc Dr.
Scotts Valley, CA 95066
Main: 408-438-3320
Tech. Support:........................408-438-8222
Sales:....................................408-438-8111
Customer Service:...................408-438-6550
Tech. Support FAX: 408-438-8137
CompuServe:...........................GO SEAGATE
America Online:..................seagate@aol.com
BBS:..408-438-8771
FTP: ftp.seagate.com
Web: www.seagate.com

Seagull Scientific Systems
15127 NE 24th Ste. 333
Redmond, WA 98052
Main: 206-451-8966
Sales:....................................800-758-2001
FAX: 206-451-8982

Secure-It, Inc.
18 Maple Ct.
East Longeadow, MA 01028
Main: 800-451-7592
Tech. Support:........................413-525-7039
Sales:....................................413-525-7039
FAX: 413-525-8807
Web: www.owls.com/secureit/index.html

Sega of America-Consumer Services
PO Box 8097
Redwood City, CA 94063
Main:....................................415-508-2800
Tech. Support:.......................800-872-7342
Sales:...................................888-734-2725
Customer Service:..................800-872-7342
CompuServe:...............................GO SEGA
America Online:..................... Keyword Sega
E-Mail:.......................webmaster@sega.com
FTP: ftp.sega.com
Web: www.sega.com

Segue Software, Inc.
1320 Centre St.
Newton Centre, MA 02159
Main:....................................617-969-3771
Tech. Support:.......................617-696-5323
Sales:...................................800-922-3771
FAX:.....................................617-969-4326
Web: www.segue.com

Seiko Instruments (USA), Inc.
1130 Ringwood Ct.
San Jose, CA 95131
Main:....................................800-888-0817
Tech. Support:.......................800-553-5312
Sales:...................................408-922-5900
Tech. Support FAX:................408-922-5835

Selfware, Inc.
8618 Westwood Ctr. Dr. Ste. S-450
Vienna, VA 22182-2222
Main:....................................703-506-0400
FAX:.....................................703-506-0580

SemWare
4343 Shallowford Rd. Ste. C3A
Marietta, GA 30062-5022
Main:....................................770-641-9002
FAX:.....................................770-640-6213
CompuServe:.......................GO SEMWARE
E-Mail:............. tech.support@semware.com
BBS:....................................770-641-8968
FTP: ftp.semware.com
Web: www.semware.com

Sequent Computer Systems
15450 SW Koll Pkwy.
Beaverton, OR 97006-6063
Main: 800-257-9044
Sales:...................................503-626-5700
FAX: 503-578-9890
Web: www.sequent.com

Sequiter Software, Inc.
PO Box 575
Newmarket, NH 03857-0575
Main: 403-437-2410
FAX: 403-436-2999
CompuServe: 713-21,1306
E-Mail:............................info@sequiter.com
BBS: 403-437-2229
Web: www.sequiter.com

Serif, Inc.
PO Box 803
Nashua, NH 03061-0803
Main: 603-889-8650
Sales:...................................800-489-6719
FAX: 603-889-1127
Web: www.serif.com

Server Technology, Inc.
1288 Hammerwood Ave.
Sunnyvale, CA 94089
Main: 408-745-0300
Tech. Support:.......................800-835-1515
Sales:...................................800-835-1515
Customer Service:..................800-835-1515
Tech. Support FAX: 408-745-0392
CompuServe: ....GO SERVER
FTP: ftp.servertech.com
Web: www.servertech.com

Shadow Cat Software
46712 Freemont
Freemont, CA 94538
Main: 800-998-4638
Tech. Support:.......................800-998-4646
Sales:...................................510-770-0220
Customer Service:..................510-770-0171
FAX: 510-770-0272
E-Mail:............. at-stanley-kan@addtron.com
Web: www.addtron.com

Shaffstall Corp.
7901 E 88th St.
Indianapolis, IN 46256
Main:....................................800-248-3475
Tech. Support:..............317-842-2077 #300
FAX:.......................................317-842-8294
E-Mail: ....sales@shaffstall.com
Web: www.shaffstall.com

Shape Electronics, Inc.
Wiremold
2105 Corporate Dr.
Addison, IL 60101
Main:....................................800-367-5811
Tech. Support FAX:.................708-620-0784
E-Mail: ....shape@earthlink.net

Sharp Electronics
Sharp Plaza
Mahwah, NJ 07430
Main:....................................201-529-8200
Tech. Support:........................800-237-4277
Customer Service:...................800-237-4277
BBS:......................................708-378-4007

Sharp's, Inc.
6018 Mechanicsville Turnpike
Mechanicsville, VA 23111
Main:....................................804-730-9697
Tech. Support:........................804-730-9697

Shea Technical Solutions
12201 Texas Ave. Ste. 4
Los Angeles, CA 90025
Main:....................................310-207-8223
Tech. Support:........................900-256-9968
Sales: 800-328-7448
Web: www.shea.com

SheAr Software
Gronausevoetpad 104
Enschede, BN 7511
Netherlands
Sales: 315-333-8184
E-Mail: ....vbx_dev@shear.iaf.nl

Shecom Computers
3981 E Mira Loma
Anaheim, CA 92806
Main: 800-366-4433
Tech. Support:........................ 714-634-4800
FAX: 714-579-7688
E-Mail:.............................. meher@msn.com
BBS:...................................... 714-637-6293
Web: www.bestsource.com/shecom

Sheridan Software Systems, Inc.
35 Pinelawn Rd. Ste. 206E
Melville, NY 11747
Sales:.................................... 516-753-0985
FAX: 516-753-3661
E-Mail:............................sales@shersoft.com
BBS:...................................... 516-753-5452
Web: www.shersoft.com

Sherwood
Inkel Usa
4181 Business Center Dr.
Fremont, CA 94538
Main: 510-623-8900
E-Mail:................. sales@sherwoodterm.com
Web: www.sherwoodterm.com

Shinko Technologies, Inc.
1497 Salmon Way
Hayward, CA 94544
Main: 800-997-4465
Sales:.................................... 510-441-1175
FAX: 510-441-2263

Ship Star Associates
36 Woodhill Dr.
Newark, DE 19711
Main: 302-738-7782
FAX: 302-738-0855
BBS:...................................... 302-738-0855

Shiva Corp.
28 Crosby Dr.
Bedford, MA 01730-1437
Main:......................................617-270-8300
Tech. Support:........................617-270-8400
Sales:.....................................800-977-4482
Customer Service:..................617-252-6300
FAX: 617-270-8599
BBS:.......................................617-273-0023
FTP: ftp.shiva.com
Web: www.shiva.com

Shopping Planet
5767 Uplander Way Ste. 206
Culver City, CA 90230
Main:......................................800-779-8461
FAX: 310-338-1396
Web: www.shoppingplanet.com

Shoreline Software
35-31 Talcottville Rd. Ste. 123
Vernon, CT 06066
Sales:.....................................800-261-9198
FAX: 203-870-5727
CompuServe:............................ 70541,2436

Shreve Systems
1200 Marshall St.
Shreveport, LA 71101
Main:......................................318-424-9791
Tech. Support:........................318-424-7987
Sales:.....................................800-227-3971
FAX: 318-424-9771
E-Mail: ....ssystems@softdisk.com
Web: www.shrevesystems.com

Siecor Corporation
800 17th St. NW
Hickory, NC 28601
Main:......................................800-743-2673
Tech. Support:........................704-327-5000
Tech. Support FAX:................800-634-9064
FAX: 704-327-5973
BBS:.......................................704-327-5488
Web: www.siecor.com

Siemens Components
10950 N. Tantau Ave.
Cupertino, CA 95014
Main: 408-777-4500
FAX: 408-777-4979
Web: www.siemens.com/business/comm.html

Siemens Components, Inc.
4900 Old Ironside Rd.
Santa Clara, CA 95054-1514
Main: 408-492-2000
Sales:..................................... 800-456-9229
Customer Service:................... 800-456-9229

Siemens Nixdorf Information System
200 Wheeler Rd.
Burlington, MA 01803
Main: 617-273-0480
Tech. Support FAX: 617-273-0480
FAX: 617-221-0231
Web: www.sni.de/public/sni_n.htm

Siemens Rolm Communications
4900 Old Ironside Rd.
Santa Clara, CA 95054
Main: 408-492-2000
Customer Service:................... 800-835-7656
FAX: 408-492-3430
Web: www.siemens.com

Siemon Co.
76 Westbury Park Rd.
Watertown, CT 06795
Main: 203-274-2523
BBS: 203-274-0940
Web: www.siemon.com

Sierra On-Line
3380 146th Pl. SE Ste. 300
Bellevue, WA 98007
Main:......................................206-649-9800
Tech. Support:.......................206-644-4343
Customer Service:................800-743-7725
Tech. Support FAX:................206-644-7697
FAX:.......................................206-641-7617
CompuServe:............................. GO SIERRA
America Online:.................... Keyword Sierra
BBS:..206-644-0112
Web: www.sierra.com

Sigma Data
17 Newport Rd.
New London, NH 03257-4567
Main:......................................800-446-4525
Tech. Support:.......................800-446-4525
Tech. Support FAX:................603-526-6915
E-Mail:......................sigma@sigmadata.com

Sigma Designs
46501 Landing Pkwy.
Fremont, CA 94538
Main:......................................510-770-0100
Tech. Support:.......................970-339-7120
Sales:.....................................800-845-8086
Customer Service:..................303-339-7120
Tech. Support FAX:................510-770-2640
FAX:.......................................510-770-2905
CompuServe:............................. GO SIGMA
BBS:..510-770-0111
FTP: ftp.realmagic.com
Web: www.realmagic.com

Silicon Graphics, Inc.
2011 N Shoreline Blvd.
Mountain View, CA 94043-1389
Main:......................................415-960-1980
Tech. Support:.......................415-960-1980
Sales:.....................................415-960-1980
Customer Service:..................415-960-1980
Tech. Support FAX:................800-800-4744
FAX:.......................................415-961-0595
BBS:..415-968-3579
Web: www.sgi.com

Silicon Valley Technologies
Silicon Valley Technologies
107 Bonaventura Dr.
San Jose, CA 95134
Tech. Support:....................... 408-428-9346
Customer Service:........... 408-428-9355-203
BBS:..................................... 510-770-8648

SilverPlatter Information Inc.
100 River Ridge Dr.
Norwood, MA 02062-5043
Main: 617-769-2599
Sales:.................................... 617-769-8763
Web: www.silverplatter.com

Silverware Inc.
3010 LBJ Freeway Ste. 740
Dallas, TX 75234
Sales: 214-247-0131
FAX: 214-406-9999
E-Mail:.........................jhalovan@onramp.net
BBS:..................................... 214-247-2177
Web: rampages.onramp.net/~silver/

Simpact Associates, Inc.
9210 Sky Park Ct.
San Diego, CA 92123
Main: 619-565-1865
Sales:.................................... 800-746-7228
Tech. Support FAX: 800-275-3889
FAX: 619-565-8196
E-Mail:................ techsupport@simpact.com
Web: www.simpact.com

Simple Technology
3001 Daimler St.
Santa Ana, CA 92705
Main: 714-476-1180
Tech. Support:....................... 714-476-1180
Sales:.................................... 714-476-1180
Customer Service:.................. 714-476-1180
Tech. Support FAX: 714-476-1209
FAX: 714-476-1209
E-Mail:.................. support@simpletech.com
BBS:..................................... 714-476-9034
FTP: ftp.simpletech.com
Web: www.simpletech.com

Simplicity Systems (Choice Computing)
1621 2nd Ave. NEPO Box 556
E. Grand Forks, MN 56721-0556
Sales: 218-773-8917
CompuServe:............................ 72163,3724
Web: www.iaccess.za/~pharper/choice.htm

Sirius Publishing
7320 E Butherus Dr. Ste. 100
Scottsdale, AZ 85260
Main:.....................................800-745-2747
Tech. Support:......................602-951-8405
Sales: 800-247-0307
Customer Service:..................602-951-3288
Tech. Support FAX:................602-951-3884
FTP: ftp.siriusnet.com
Web: www.siriusnet.com

Skillsbank Corp.
Baltimore, MD
Web: www.skillsbank.com

Sky Computers, Inc.
Analogic
27 Industrial Ave.
Chelmsford, MA 01824
Main:....................................508-250-1920
Tech. Support FAX:..................508-250-0036
E-Mail: ....info@sky.com
Web: www.sky.com

Slipped Disk
31044 John R
Madison Heights, MI 48071
Main:.....................................810-546-3475
BBS:.......................................810-399-1292

Smart Modular Technologies
4305 Cushing Pkwy.
Fremont, CA 94538
Main:....................................510-416-5656
Tech. Support:......................510-249-1605
Sales: 800-841-2729
Customer Service:..................800-841-2739
Tech. Support FAX:................510-249-1600
Web: www.apexdata.com.smartm

Smart Software, Inc.
4 Hill Rd.
Belmont, MA 02178
Main: 617-489-2743
FAX: 617-489-2748
CompuServe: 102021,2072
E-Mail:............... info@smartcorp.com

Soft Hard Systems
6324 Variel Ste. 313
Woodland Hills, CA 91367
Main: 818-999-9531
Tech. Support:......................818-999-9531
FAX: 818-999-9683
BBS: 818-999-9683

Softblox, Inc.
Sales:.....................................404-892-0202
FAX: 404-892-0981

Softbridge Group, The
125 Cambridge Park Dr.
Cambridge, MA 02140
Main: 800-955-9190
Tech. Support:......................617-576-2257
Sales:.....................................617-576-2257
Tech. Support FAX: 617-864-7747
E-Mail:..........................market@sbridge.com
Web: www.sbridge.com

SoftCop International, Inc.
935 Sheldon Ct.
Burlington, ONT L7L 5K6
Canada
Main: 905-681-3269
FAX: 905-681-8089
E-Mail:..........................softcop@hookup.net
Web: www.softcop.com

SoftCraft
Sales:..................................... 608-257-3300
FAX: 608-257-6733

Softdisk Publishing
606 Common St.
Shreveport, LA 71101
Main:......................................318-221-8718
Tech. Support:........................318-221-8718
Sales: 318-221-8718
Customer Service:..................318-221-8718
Tech. Support FAX:................318-221-8870
FAX:..318-221-8870
Web: www.softdisk.com

Sof-tek International, Inc.
1999 N. Amidon
Wichita, KS 67203
Sales: 316-838-7200
FAX:..316-838-3789
E-Mail: .... info@soft-tek.com

Softel VDM
11 Michigan Ave.
Wharton, NJ 07885
Sales: 201-366-9618
FAX:..201-366-3984
E-Mail: ....sales@softelvdm.com
BBS:..201-366-3940
Web: www.softelvdm.com

SoftInfo
E-Mail: ....softinfo@icp.com
Web: www.icp.com/softinfo/

Softkey International
1 Athenaeum St.
Cambridge, MA 02142
Main:......................................423-670-2020
Tech. Support:........................423-670-2020
Sales: 800-227-5609
E-Mail: .... support@softkey.com
Web: www.softkey.com

SoftKlone
Foretec
327 Office Plaza Dr. Ste. 100
Tallahassee, FL 32301
Main: 800-634-8670
Tech. Support:........................ 904-878-8564
Sales:..................................... 904-878-8564
Customer Service:................... 904-878-8564
Tech. Support FAX: 904-877-9763
BBS:....................................... 904-877-9763
Web: www.softklone.com

SoftLand, Inc.
610 Valley Stream Circle
Langhorne, PA 19053
Sales:..................................... 215-741-2030
FAX: 215-741-2030
E-Mail:............................. softland@msn.com

SoftMail Direct
Troy, NY
Main: 518-283-8444
FAX: 518-283-0830
E-Mail:.............................info@softmail.com
Web: www.softmail.com

Softoholic Computer Systems
4739 Driftwood Pl.
Burnaby, BC V5G 4E2
Canada
Customer Service:................... 604-451-1310
E-Mail:............................softoloic@bcit.bc.ca
Web: www.bcit.bc.ca/~fsimek

SoftQuad, Inc.
56 Aberfoyle Crescent, 5th Floor
Toronto, ONT M8X 2W4
Canada
Main: 416-239-4801
Sales:..................................... 416-239-4801
FAX: 416-239-7105
E-Mail:................................. sales@sq.com
Web: www.sq.com

Softronics Inc.
5085 List Dr.
Colorado Springs, CO 80919
Main:....................................800-225-8590
Tech. Support:........................719-593-9550
Sales: 719-593-9540
Customer Service:..................719-593-9540
Tech. Support FAX:.................719-548-1878
FAX: 719-548-1878
BBS:......................................719-548-1878
Web: www.softronics.com

SoftSource
301 W Holly St.
Bellingham, WA 98225
Main:....................................360-676-0999
FAX: 360-671-1131
Web: www.softsouce.com

Software AG of North America
11190 Sunrise Valley Dr.
Reston, VA 22091
Main:....................................703-860-5050
Tech. Support:........................800-525-7859
Sales: 800-423-2227
FAX: 703-391-8360
E-Mail: ....webmaster@sagus.com
Web: www.sagus.com

Software Architects, Inc.
19102 N Creek Pkwy Ste. 101
Bothell, WA 98011
Main:....................................206-487-0122
Sales: 206-487-0122
Customer Service:..................206-487-0122
Tech. Support FAX:.................206-487-0467
E-Mail: ....support@softarch.com
BBS:......................................206-489-0950

Software Developer
66 Simpson Rd.
Swanson, Auckland
New Zealand
Sales: 649-832-0088
E-Mail: ....sraike@iconz.co.nz

Software Development Systems
815 Commerce Dr. Ste. 250
Oak Brook, IL 60521
Main: 708-368-0400
Tech. Support:........................708-971-8170
Tech. Support FAX: 708-368-0400
FAX: 708-990-4641
E-Mail:....................................sales@sdi.com
BBS: 708-971-8513
Web: www.sdsi.com

Software Directions, Inc.
Parsippany, NJ
Main: 201-263-3990
Tech. Support:........................201-263-3990
Sales:....................................800-346-7638
BBS: 201-584-7771

Software FX, Inc.
2200 Corporate Blvd. NW Ste. 309
Boca Raton, FL 33431
Sales:....................................800-392-4278
FAX: 407-998-2383
CompuServe: 74777,3361

Software Interphase, Inc.
82 Cucumber Hill Rd. Ste. 140
Foster, RI 02825
Main: 800-542-2742
Tech. Support FAX: 401-397-6814
Web: www.sinterphase.com

Software Metrics
465 Phillip St. Ste. 1
Waterloo, ONT N2L 6C7
Canada
Main: 519-885-2458
Web: www.metrics.com

Software Packaging Associates
4650 Lake Forest Dr. Ste. 580
Cincinnati, OH 45242-3730
Main: 800-837-4399
Sales:....................................513-733-8800
FAX: 513-733-5599
E-Mail:............................info@softpack.com
Web: www.softpack.com

Software Partners, Inc.
1953 Landing Dr.
Mountain View, CA 94303
Main:......................................415-428-0160
Tech. Support FAX:.................415-428-0163
FAX:.......................................415-428-0163
E-Mail: ....sales@buckaroo.com
Web: www.buckaroo.com

Software Plus Chicago
Chicago, IL
Main:......................................312-878-7800

Software Productivity Centre
#450-1122 Mainland St.
Vancouver, BC V6B 5L1
Canada
Main:.............................604-662-8181 #108
FAX:.......................................604-689-0141
E-Mail: ....tools@spc.ca
Web: www.spc.ca/spc/Welcome.html

Software Products International
6620 Flanders Dr.
San Diego, CA 92121
Main:......................................800-937-4774
Tech. Support:.........................619-450-1526
FAX:.......................................619-450-1921
BBS:.......................................619-450-2179
Web: www.spii.com

Software Publishing Corp.
111 N Market St.
San Jose, CA 95113
Main:......................................408-537-3000
Tech. Support:.........................800-336-8360
Sales:.....................................800-562-9909
Customer Service:....................800-336-8360
Tech. Support FAX:.................408-537-3511
FAX:.......................................408-537-3500
BBS:.......................................408-977-0290
Web: www.spco.com

Software Science, Inc.
168 S Park Ste. 500
San Francisco, CA 94017
Main: 415-479-7286
Tech. Support:........................510-845-2110
Sales:.....................................800-468-9273
Customer Service:...................415-479-7288
Tech. Support FAX: 415-479-2563
CompuServe:............................ 72317,1673
E-Mail: ....ssi@well.com
BBS:.......................................415-479-1746
Web: www.well.com/user/ssi

Software Spectrum
2140 Merritt Dr.
Garland, TX 75041
Main: 214-854-5258
Sales:.....................................800-624-0503
Tech. Support FAX: 800-864-7878
Web: www.swspectrum.com

Software Ventures
PSI Net
2907 Claremont Ave.
Berkeley, CA 94705
Main: 510-644-3232
Tech. Support:........................510-644-1325
Sales:.....................................510-644-3232
Customer Service:...................510-644-3232
Tech. Support FAX: 510-848-0885
E-Mail:......................support@svcdudes.com
BBS:.......................................510-849-1912
FTP: ftp.svcdudes.com
Web: www.svcdudes.com

Software.Net
CyberSource Corp.
1050 Chestnut St. Ste. 202
Menlo Park, CA 94025
Main: 415-462-5522
Sales:.....................................800-617-7638
FAX: 415-473-3066
E-Mail:....................webmaster@software.net
Web: www.software.net

Softwave Technologies, Inc.
6501 Park of Commerce Blvd. Ste. 205
Boca Raton, FL 33487
Main:......................................800-763-8928
FAX: 407-998-6051
E-Mail: .... softwave@gate.net
Web: www.gate.net/~softwave

Solectek Corp.
6370 Nancy Ridge Dr. Ste. 109
San Diego, CA 92121
Main:......................................619-450-1220
Tech. Support:.........................619-450-1220
Sales:.....................................619-450-1220
Customer Service:...................619-450-1220
Tech. Support FAX:.................619-457-2681
BBS:.......................................619-450-6537
FTP: ftp.solecteck@cts.com
Web: www.solecteck.com

Solid Oak Software
PO Box 6826
Santa Barbara, CA 93160
Main:......................................805-967-9853
Tech. Support:.........................805-892-2557
Sales:.....................................805-967-9953
Customer Service:...................805-967-9953
Tech. Support FAX:.................805-967-1614
FAX: 805-967-1614
CompuServe:........................ GO SOLID OAK
E-Mail: .... infor@solidoak.com
Web: www.solidoak.com

Solomon Software
200 E Hardin St.
Findlay, OH 45840
Main:......................................419-424-0422
Tech. Support:.........................419-423-3688
Tech. Support FAX:.................419-424-3400
BBS:.......................................419-424-0763
Web: www.solomon.com

Solutions Engineering
2409 Linden Ln.
Silver Spring, MD 20910
Main:......................................800-635-6533
Tech. Support:.........................301-608-3001
Tech. Support FAX:.................301-608-3015

Sonic Systems Inc.
575 N Pastoria Ave.
Sunnyvale, CA 94086
Main: 408-736-1900
Tech. Support:.........................408-736-1900
Sales:.....................................408-736-1900
Customer Service:...................408-736-1900
Tech. Support FAX: 408-736-7228
E-Mail:............................tech@sonicsys.com
BBS: 408-736-7228
FTP: ftp.sonicsys.com
Web: www.sonicsys.com

Sony Electronics
10833 Valley View St.
Cypress, CA 90630
Main: 714-220-9100
Tech. Support:.........................714-229-4133
Sales:.....................................800-352-7669
Customer Service:...................714-229-4100
Tech. Support FAX: 800-883-7669
BBS: 408-955-5107
FTP: ftp.sony.com
Web: www.sel.sony.com

Sound Quest
West 13th Ave. Ste. 2131
Vancouver, BC VS4 1V8
Canada
Main: 800-667-3998
Sales:.....................................604-874-9499
Tech. Support FAX: 604-874-8971
FAX: 604-874-8971
CompuServe: 76702,2205
BBS: 604-874-8971

Sound Source Interactive

2985 E Hillcrest Dr., Unit A
Westlake Village, CA 91362
Main:......................................805-494-9996
Tech. Support:.......................805-494-9996
Sales:.....................................800-877-4778
Customer Service:..................805-494-9996
Tech. Support FAX:................805-495-0016
FAX:......................................805-495-0016
CompuServe:............................753611544
America Online:.........................ssi@aol.com
BBS:.....................................805-373-8589
FTP: ftp.chris.com
Web: www.chris.com/~ssi/

SourceMate Information Systems

20 Sunnyside Ave. Ste. E
Mill Valley, CA 94941
Main:......................................800-877-8896
Tech. Support:.......................415-381-1793
Sales:.....................................800-877-8896
Customer Service:..................800-877-8896
Tech. Support FAX:................415-381-6902
BBS:.....................................415-381-6902
Web: www.sourcemate.com

South Andrea Inc.

5370 52nd St. S. E.
Grand Rapids, MI 49508
Main:......................................616-698-0330
Sales:.....................................800-451-4319
FAX:......................................616-698-0325
BBS:.....................................616-698-8106

South Hills Electronics

760 Beechnut Dr.
Pittsburgh, PA 15205-9925
Main:......................................412-921-9000
Tech. Support:.......................412-921-0590
Sales:.....................................800-245-6215
FAX:......................................412-921-2254
Web: www.shillsdata.com

Southern Computer Systems

2732 7th Ave. S
Birmingham, AL 35233
Main: 800-533-6879
Tech. Support FAX: 205-322-4851
Web: www.scsinc.com

Soyo Tek Inc.

1209 John Reed Ct.
City of Industry, CA 91745
Main: 818-330-1712
Tech. Support:.......................818-968-4161
Sales:.....................................818-330-1712
Customer Service:..................818-330-1712
Tech. Support FAX: 818-968-4161
FAX: 818-968-4161
BBS:.....................................818-968-4161

Spectragraphics Corp.

9707 Waples St.
San Diego, CA 92121
Main: 619-450-0611
Tech. Support FAX: 619-450-0218
E-Mail:...................webmaster@spectra.com
Web: www.spectra.com

SpectraStar Products Division

General Parametrics Corp.
1250 Ninth St.
Berkeley, CA 94710-1545
Main: 510-524-3950
Sales:.....................................800-223-0999
FAX: 510-524-9954
Web: www.spectrastar.com

Spectrum

1021 S Wolfe Rd.
Sunnyvale, CA 94086
Main: 408-738-4387
Tech. Support:.......................408-738-4389
Sales:.....................................408-738-4387
Customer Service:..................408-738-4387
Tech. Support FAX: 408-738-4702
FAX: 408-738-4702
BBS:.....................................408-738-4702

Spectrum Human Resource System Corp.
1625 Broadway Ste. 2600
Denver, CO 80202
Main:..800-334-5660
Tech. Support:.........................303-534-8813
Sales:.......................................800-477-3287
Tech. Support FAX:.................303-595-9970
FAX:...303-595-9970
E-Mail:....................spect-info@specthr.com
BBS:...303-595-9970
Web: www.specthr.com

SpeechCraft, Inc.
10050 Ralston Rd. Ste. 2
Arvada, CO 80004
Sales:.............................303-940-6161-145
FAX:...303-940-9870
E-Mail:........................was@speechcraft.com

Speedware
3000 Executive Pkwy Ste. 111
San Ramon, CA 94583
Main:.......................................510-867-3300
FAX:...510-867-3300
Web: www.speedware.com

Spinoza Ltd.
11333 Iowa Ave.
Los Angeles, CA 90025
Sales:.......................................800-700-2217
FAX:...310-231-9773

Spiral Software
15 Auburn Pl.
Brookline, MA 02146
Main:.......................................617-739-1511
Tech. Support:.........................617-739-2730
Tech. Support FAX:.................617-739-4836
E-Mail:........................easyplot@spiralsw.com
Web: www.spiralsw.com/easyplot

Spirit of Performance
73 Westcott Rd.
Harvard, MA 01451
Main:.......................................508-456-3889
E-Mail:....................benmyers@ultranet.com

Spyglass, Inc.
PO Box 6388
Champaign, IL 61826
Main:......................................708-505-1010
Customer Service:..................708-245-6507
Tech. Support FAX:...............217-355-8925
Web: www.spyglass.com

Stac Electronics
12636 High Bluff Dr.
San Diego, CA 92130-2093
Main:......................................619-794-4300
Tech. Support:........................619-794-3700
Sales:.....................................800-522-7822
Customer Service:..................800-522-7822
Tech. Support FAX:...............619-794-3715
FAX:.......................................619-794-4572
E-Mail:...............software.support@stac.com
BBS:.......................................619-794-3711
FTP: ftp. Stac.com
Web: www. Stac.com

Stallion Technologies, Inc.
2880 Research Park Dr. Ste. 160
Soquel, CA 95073
Main:......................................800-347-7979
Tech. Support:........................408-395-5775
Tech. Support FAX:...............408-395-6396
BBS:.......................................408-395-6396
Web: www. Stallion.com

Standard Microsystems Corp.
80 Arkay Dr.
Hauppauge, NY 11788
Main:......................................516-435-6000
Tech. Support:........................800-992-4762
Sales:.....................................516-435-6255
Customer Service:..................516-273-3100
Tech. Support FAX:...............516-435-6107
FAX:.......................................516-273-5550
BBS:.......................................516-434-3162

Starcore/Apple Computer
Apple, Inc
1 Infinite Loop
Cupertino, CA 95014
Main:......................................408-996-1010
Tech. Support:.........................800-708-7827
FAX:..408-974-8910

Starfish Software
1700 Green Hills Rd
Scotts Valley, CA 95066
Main:......................................408-461-5800
Tech. Support:.........................800-953-9995
Customer Service:...................800-765-7839
CompuServe:........................... GO STARFISH
America Online:.................. Keyword Starfish
BBS:.......................................408-461-5930
Web: www. Starfishsoftware.com

StarPress, Inc.
425 Market St.
San Francisco, CA 94105
Main:......................................415-274-8383
FAX:..415-291-0225
E-Mail: ....starpress@dnai.com
Web: starpress.com/starpress

StarTech Computer Services
E-Mail: ....startech@neosoft.com
Web: www.neosoft.com/~startech/

Starwave Corp.
13810 Southeast Eastgate Way Ste. 400
Bellevue, WA 98005
Main:......................................206-957-2000
FAX:..206-957-2009
E-Mail: .... carriec@starwave.com
Web: www. Starwave.com

State of the Art
56 Technology
Irvine, CA 92718
Main: 714-753-1222
Customer Service:................... 800-854-3415
Sales:...................................... 800-447-5700
FAX: 714-753-0930
E-Mail: .... 72702,1605@compuserve.com
Web: www. Stateoftheart.com

StatSoft Corp.
2300 E 14th St.
Tulsa, OK 74104
Main: 918-749-1119
Tech. Support:........................ 918-749-1119
Sales:...................................... 918-749-1119
Customer Service:................... 918-749-1119
Tech. Support FAX: 918-749-2217
FAX: 918-749-2217
E-Mail: .... info@statsoftinc.com
BBS:.. 918-749-2217
Web: www. Statsoftinc.com

Steinberg North America
9312 Deering Ave.
Chatsworth, CA 91311
Main: 818-993-4091
Tech. Support:........................ 818-993-4161
Sales:...................................... 818-993-4091
Customer Service:................... 818-993-4091
Tech. Support FAX: 818-701-7452
FAX: 818-701-7452
CompuServe:........................... 713-33,2447
America Online:............... steinberg@aol.com
BBS:.. 818-701-7453
Web: www. Steinberg

Sterling Software, Inc.
200 W Lowe Ave.
Fairfield, IA 52556
Main: 515-472-7077
Tech. Support:........................ 800-533-6696
Sales:...................................... 800-522-4252
Customer Service:................... 800-444-8575
Tech. Support FAX: 515-472-7198
FAX: 515-472-7198
BBS:.. 515-472-7198

Stony Brook Software
187 E Wilbur Rd. Ste. 4
Thousand Oaks, CA 91360
Main:.....................................800-624-7487
Tech. Support:........................805-496-5837
Sales: 800-624-7487
Customer Service:...................800-624-7487
Tech. Support FAX:................805-496-7429
FAX: 805-496-7429

Storage Computer Corp.
11 Riverside St.
Nashua, NH 03062-1373
Main:.....................................603-880-3005
Tech. Support:........................603-880-3005
Sales: 603-880-3005
Customer Service:...................603-880-3005
Tech. Support FAX:................603-889-7232
FAX: 603-889-7232
Web: www. Storage.com

Storage Dimensions
1656 McCarthy Blvd.
Milpitas, CA 95035
Main:.....................................408-954-0710
Tech. Support:........................408-894-1325
Sales: 408-954-1331
Customer Service:...................408-894-1349
Tech. Support FAX:................408-944-1203
E-Mail: ....support@xstor.com
BBS:......................................408-944-1221
Web: www. Storagedimenions.com

Storage Technology
2270 S 88th St.
Louisville, CO 80028-4393
Main:.....................................303-673-5151
Tech. Support:........................800-735-2778
Sales: 303-673-5151
Customer Service:...................303-673-5151
Tech. Support FAX:................303-673-2869
Web: www. Stortek.com

Storm Primax Inc.
1861 Landings Dr.
Mountain View, CA 94043
Main: 415-691-6600
Tech. Support:........................ 415-969-9555
Customer Service:................... 800-275-5734
CompuServe: 73060,3227
America Online:............ easyphoto@aol.com
Web: www.easyphoto.com/storm/

Storm Software
1861 Landings Dr.
Mountain View, CA 94043
Main: 415-691-6600
FAX: 415-691-9825
E-Mail:.......................... info@easyphoto.com
Web: www. Stormpremax.com/storm/

StrandWare, Inc.
1529 Continental Dr.
Eau Claire, WI 54701
Main: 715-833-2331
FAX: 715-883-1995
E-Mail:................ mjstrand@strandware.com
Web: www.morsept.com/mmdoc/sw/
   standware.html

Strange Solutions Software
49 Mill St. Ste. 2
Randolph, MA 02368
Sales:..................................... 617-961-2464
CompuServe: 102123,3343

Strata, Inc.
2 W St. George Blvd.
Ancestor Sq. Ste. 2100
St. George, UT 84770
Main: 801-628-5218
Tech. Support:........................ 801-628-9751
Sales:..................................... 800-869-6855
Customer Service:................... 800-678-7282
FAX: 801-628-9756

Strategic Marketing Partners
4975 Preston Pk. Blvd. Ste. 775
Plano, TX 75093
Main:......................................214-985-4114
FAX:.......................................214-985-4188
E-Mail: ....smpnorcal@aol.com

Stream International, Inc.
105 Rosemont Rd.
Westwood, MA 02090
Main:......................................617-751-1000
Tech. Support:.........................617-251-6886
Sales: 617-751-1000
Customer Service:...................617-751-1000
Tech. Support FAX:.................617-751-7751
Web: www. Stream.com

Stylus Innovations, Inc.
One Kendall Sq. Building 300
Cambridge, MA 02139
Sales: 617-621-9545
FAX:.......................................617-621-7862
E-Mail: ....stylus@shore.net
FTP: ftp.shore.net
Web: www. Stylus.com/~stylus

Sub Systems, Inc.
11 Tiger Row
Georgetown, MA 01833
Sales: 800-447-6819
FAX:.......................................508-352-9019

SuftWatch Software, Inc.
105 Fremont Ave. Ste. F
Los Altos, CA 94022-3956
Main:......................................415-948-9500
FAX:.......................................415-948-9577
E-Mail: ....info@surfwatch.com

Sujit & Ranjit Inc.
2 Westboro Business Park
PO Box 1261
Westboro, MA 01581
Main: 508-898-2770
Sales:.....................................800-525-3577
Customer Service:...................800-525-3577
FAX: 508-898-9662
Web: www.accusoft.com

Summagraph ICS Corp.
8500 Cameron Rd.
Austin, TX 78754
Main: 512-776-9989
Tech. Support:.........................800-444-3425
Sales:.....................................800-444-3425
Customer Service:...................800-444-3425
Tech. Support FAX: 512-873-1368
E-Mail:.....techsupport@summagraphics.com
BBS:.......................................512-873-1477
FTP: ftp.summagraphics.com
Web: www.summagraphics.com

Summit Micro Design
149 Kifer Ct.
Sunnyvale, CA 94086
Main: 408-739-6348
Tech. Support:.........................408-739-6348
Sales:.....................................408-739-6348
Customer Service:...................408-739-6348
Tech. Support FAX: 408-739-4643
FAX: 408-739-6348
Web: www.smd-hq.com

Sun Micro Systems
2550 Garcia Ave.
Mountain View, CA 94043
Main: 415-960-1300
Tech. Support:.........................800-872-4786
FAX: 415-856-2114
E-Mail:...............webmaster@www.sun.com
Web: www.sun.com

Sun Moon Star
1941 Ringwood Ave.
San Jose, CA 95131
Main:.....................................408-452-7811
Tech. Support:.........................408-452-7811
FAX: 408-452-1411
BBS:.......................................408-452-8281
FTP: FTP: //www.sms.com
Web: www.sms.com

Sunburst Communications
101 Castleton St.
Pleasantville, NY 10570
Main:......................................914-747-3310
FAX: 914-747-4109
E-Mail: ....sunburst@aol.com

SunConnect
Sun Microsystems
2550 Garcia Ave.
Mountain View, CA 94043
Main:.....................................800-786-7638
Web: www.sun.com

SunStar Interactive
277 Chapel St. Ste. 4A
New Haven, CT 06513
Main:......................................800-660-4480
Sales: 203-785-8111
FAX: 203-785-8001
Web: www.sunstar.com

Super Computer
5980 Lakeshore Dr.
Cypress, CA 90630
Main:......................................714-826-9680
Tech. Support FAX:.................714-826-9681

SuperMac Technology
485 Potrero Ave.
Sunnyvale, CA 94086
Main:......................................408-541-6100
Sales: 800-541-7680
FAX: 408-541-6150
BBS:.......................................408-541-6190

Support Group, Inc.
PO Box 130
McHenry, MD 21541
Main: 800-872-4768
Tech. Support:.........................800-872-4768
Sales:.....................................800-872-4768
Customer Service:...................800-872-4768
Tech. Support FAX: 301-387-7322
E-Mail:..............74020,10@compuserve.com

Supra
312 SE Stonemill Dr. Ste. 150
Vancouver, WA 98684
Main: 360-604-1400
Tech. Support:.........................541-967-2490
Sales:.....................................800-727-8772
Customer Service:...................800-727-8772
Tech. Support FAX: 541-967-2401
CompuServe: ....GO SUPRA
America Online:.............SupraCorp@aol.com
E-Mail:............................pctech@supra.com
BBS: 541-967-2444
FTP: ftp.supra.com
Web: www.supra.com

Surfspot Software
42190 Madison Ave. #100
Culver City, CA 90230
FAX: 310-839-1240
E-Mail:.............surfspot@smpt.netvoyage.net
Web: www. surfspot.com

Survivor Software, Ltd.
11222 La Cienega Blvd. Ste. 450
Inglewood, CA 90304-1134
Main: 310-410-9527
Tech. Support:.........................310-338-0155
FAX: 310-338-1406
E-Mail:............................survivorsf@aol.com
Web: www.survivor.com

Sutrasoft
10506 Permian Dr.
Sugarland, TX 77478
Main:.....................................713-491-2088
Sales:....................................713-491-2088
Customer Service:...................713-491-2088
Tech. Support FAX:.................713-240-6883
CompuServe:............................ 76163,1164
E-Mail: ....info@sutrasoft.com
Web: www.sutrasoft.com

Swan Technologies
3075 Research Dr.
State College, PA 16801
Main:.....................................800-468-9044
Tech. Support:........................800-468-7926
Sales:....................................800-468-9044
Customer Service:...................800-468-9044
Tech. Support FAX:.................814-237-5416
FAX:......................................814-237-5416
BBS:......................................814-237-4450
Web: www.swantech.com

Swfte International, Ltd.
Stone Mill Office Park
724 Yorklyn Rd   Ste. 150
Hockessin, DE 19707
Main:.....................................800-237-9383
Tech. Support:........................305-567-9996
Customer Service:...................800-759-2562
FAX:......................................305-569-1350
CompuServe:............................ 76004,3520
America Online:...................Keyword Expert
E-Mail: ....expertsoft@aol.com
BBS:.................................. 302-234-1760
Web: www.expertsoftware.com

Swiss Telecom, NA
2001 L St. NW,
 Ste. 600
Washington, DC 20036
Main:.....................................800-966-1145
FAX:......................................202-429-0514

Switzer Communications
21 Tamal Vista Blvd. Ste. 135
Corte Madera, CA 94925
Main: 415-945-7070
FAX: 415-945-3235
E-Mail:.............................jessica@switz.com

Sybase, Inc.
6475 Christie Ave.
Emeryville, CA 94608
Main: 800-879-2273
Tech. Support:.......................800-879-2273
Sales:.....................................800-879-2273
Customer Service:...................800-879-2273
FAX: 508-287-4593
Web: www.sybase.com

Sybex, Inc.
2021 Challenger Dr.
Alameda, CA 94501
Main: 800-227-2346
CompuServe:............................... GO SYBEX
Web: www.sybex.com

Sydex Inc.
PO Box 5700
Eugene, OR 97405
Main: 541-683-6033
Sales:.....................................800-437-9339
Tech. Support FAX: 541-683-6033
FAX: 541-683-1622
BBS:......................................541-683-1385
Web: www.sydex.com

SyDOS-Division of SyQuest
47071 Bayside Pkwy.
Fremont, CA 94538
Main: 510-226-4137
Tech. Support:.......................800-249-2440
Sales:.....................................800-245-2278
Customer Service:...................800-437-9367
FAX: 510-226-1000
E-Mail:...................... support@syquest.com
Web: www.support@syquest.com

Sylvain Faust, Inc.
880 Boul De La Carriere Ste. 130
Hull, PQ J8N 2TB
Canada
Sales: 819-778-5045
FAX: 819-778-7943
E-Mail: .... info@sfi-software.com
BBS:......................................819-778-8556
FTP: ftp.sfi-software.com
Web: www.sft-software.com

Symantec Corp.
10201 Torre Ave.
Cupertino, CA 95014
Main:......................................408-253-9600
Tech. Support:........................541-465-8430
Customer Service:...................800-441-7234
CompuServe:........................ GO SYMANTEC
America Online:..............Keyword Symantec
BBS:......................................541-484-6669
FTP: ftp.symantec.com
Web: www.symantec.com

Symantec/Norton Product Group
2500 Broadway Ste. 200
Santa Monica, CA 90404
Main:......................................310-453-4600
Tech. Support:........................541-465-8420
Customer Service:...................800-441-7234
CompuServe:........................ GO SYMANTEC
America Online:..............Keyword Symantec
BBS:......................................541-484-6669
FTP: ftp.symantec.com
Web: www.symantec.com

Symmetry Development Systems
330 Townsend St. Ste. 202
San Francisco, CA 94107
Main:......................................415-512-0595
FAX: 415-512-0295
E-Mail: ....ssres@aol.com

Synario-Division of Data I/O
10525 Willows Rd. NE
Redmond, WA 98073-9746
Main: 206-881-6444
Tech. Support:....................... 800-247-5700
Sales:..................................... 800-332-8246
Customer Service:.................. 800-735-6070
Tech. Support FAX: 206-869-2821
FAX: 206-869-7423
E-Mail:.........................techhelp@data-io.com
BBS: 206-882-3211
FTP: ftp.data-io.com
Web: www.data-io.com

Synctronics Inc.
980 Buenos Ave. Ste. C2
San Diego, CA 92110
Main: 800-444-5397
Tech. Support:....................... 619-275-3525
Sales:..................................... 800-444-5397
Customer Service:.................. 800-444-5397
Tech. Support FAX: 619-275-3520
FAX: 619-275-3520

Syndesis Corp.
235 S. Main St.
Jefferson, WI 53549
Main: 414-674-5200
FAX: 414-674-6363

Synergy International
300 East 4500 South Ste. 100
Salt Lake City, UT 84107-3956
Main: 801-281-0237
Tech. Support:........................ 801-281-0237
Sales:..................................... 800-796-7491
FAX: 801-281-0238
Web: www.synergy1.com

Synergystex International
3065 Nationwide Pkwy.
Brunswick, OH 44212
Main: 330-225-3112
Tech. Support FAX: 330-225-0419

Synex Systems Corp.
Vancouver, BC
Canada
Main:.....................................604-688-8271
Sales: 800-663-8663
Web: www.synex.com

Synopsys Inc.
700 East Middlefield Rd. Building C
Mountain View, CA 94043
Main:.....................................415-962-5000
Tech. Support:........................415-245-8005
Sales: 800-388-9125
Customer Service:...................415-541-7737
FAX:......................................415-965-8637
E-Mail: ....designinfo@synopsys.com
Web: www.synopsys.com

Syntrex Inc.
2621 Van Buren Ave.
Valley Forge, PA 19484-3027
Main:.....................................800-526-2829
Tech. Support:........................610-650-3100
Sales: 800-526-2829
Customer Service:...................800-526-2829
Tech. Support FAX:.................610-650-3165
FAX:......................................610-650-3165

Syquest Technology
47071 Baseside Pkwy.
Fremont, CA 94538-6517
Main:.....................................510-226-4000
Tech. Support:........................415-490-7511
Sales: 800-245-2278
BBS:......................................415-651-3338

Syracuse Language Systems
719 E. Genesee St.
Syracuse, NY 13210
Main:.....................................800-688-1937
Sales: 315-478-6729
FAX:......................................315-478-6902

Sysper Technologies Inc.
362 S Abbott Ave.
Miltitas, CA 95035
Main: 800-441-5484
Tech. Support:.......................408-934-1500
Sales:.....................................800-441-5484
Customer Service:...................800-441-5484
Tech. Support FAX: 408-934-1900
FAX: 408-934-1900
BBS:......................................408-441-6609

System Connection
441 East Bay Blvd.
Provo, UT 84606
Main: 801-373-9800
Tech. Support:........................800-877-9143
Sales:.....................................800-877-8262
Customer Service:...................801-373-9800
Tech. Support FAX: 800-877-9143
FAX: 801-373-9847
E-Mail:.......................resaler@sconnect.com
BBS:......................................801-224-3334
FTP: ftp.sconnect.com
Web: www.sconnect.com

System Eyes Computer Store
730M Milford Rd. Ste. 345
Merrimack, NH 03054-4642
Main: 603-424-1188
Sales:.....................................603-424-3939
E-Mail:........ j_sauter@systemeye.ultranet.com

System Powerhouse, Inc.
911 Bunker Hill Ste. 180
Houston, TX 77024
Main: 800-999-3918
Tech. Support:........................713-827-1600
BBS:......................................713-827-7162

Systemetrics, Inc.
Main: 617-868-8308
FAX: 617-868-5906
Web: www.systemetrics.com

Systems & Computer Technology
4 Country View Rd.
Malvern, PA 19355
Main:.....................................610-647-5930
Tech. Support:.......................800-223-7036
Sales:...................................800-223-7036
Customer Service:..................800-223-7036
Web: www.sctcorp.com

TGV, Inc.
101 Cooper St.
Santa Cruz, CA 95060
Main:....................................800-848-3440
Tech. Support:.......................408-427-4366
Sales:...................................408-457-5200
Tech. Support FAX:................408-457-5205
BBS:.....................................408-427-4365
Web: www.tgv.com

T.H.E. Journal
150 El Camino Real Ste. 112
Tustin, CA 92680-3670
Main:....................................714-730-4011
Tech. Support:.......................714-730-4011
Sales:...................................714-730-4011
Customer Service:..................714-730-4011
FAX:.....................................714-730-3739
Web: www.thejournal.com

TIMC LTD.
20 York Mills Rd. Ste. 405
North York, ONT M2P 2C2
Canada
Sales:...................................416-222-5848
FAX:.....................................416-222-5844
E-Mail:.................timcmktg@netvision.net.il
Web: www.timc-gis.com

TM1 Software
513 Warrenville Rd.
Warren, NJ 07059
Main:....................................800-822-1596
Tech. Support:.......................908-755-9880
FAX:.....................................908-755-9230
BBS:.....................................908-755-4295

T/Maker Company
1390 Villa St.
Mountain View, CA 94041
Main: 415-962-0195
FAX: 415-962-0201
E-Mail:...............tech_support@Tmaker.com
Web: www.clickart.com

TPS Electronics
2495 Old Middlefield Way
Mountain View, CA 94043
Tech. Support:....................... 800-526-5920
Sales:................................... 415-988-0141
Customer Service:.................. 415-988-0141
Tech. Support FAX: 415-988-0289
FAX: 415-988-0289
Web: www.internet barcode@netcom.com

TSI Power Corp.
2836 Peterson Pl
Norcross, GA 30071
Main: 800-874-3160
Tech. Support:....................... 770-263-6063
Sales:................................... 800-874-3160
Customer Service:.................. 800-874-3160
Tech. Support FAX: 770-263-0638
FAX: 770-263-0638
E-Mail:.......tsipower.comsales@tsipower.com
Web: www.tsipower.com

TSR Systems, Ltd.
12121 Corporate Pkwy.
Mequon, WI 53092
Main: 414-243-5600
Sales:.............................. 414-243-5600-205
FAX: 414-243-5469
BBS: 516-331-6377

TSYP
1 Its a book Ln.
Santa Monica, CA 90405
Main: 310-581-4700
Web: www.cybermedia.com

TV One Multimedia Solutions

1445 Jamike Dr. Ste. 8
Erlanger, KY 41018
Main:......................................606-282-7303
Sales:....................................800-721-4044
FAX:......................................606-282-8225
E-Mail: ....sales@tvone.com
Web: www.tvone.com

T View, Inc.

7853 SouthWest Cirrus Dr.
Beaverton, OR 97008
Main:......................................503-643-1662
Tech. Support:.......................503-643-1662
Sales:....................................503-643-1662
Customer Service:..................800-356-3983
Tech. Support FAX:................503-671-9066
E-Mail: ....dougw@tview.com
FTP: ftp.tview.com
Web: www.tview.com

TYREX Manufacturing Group

1826 Kramer Lane Ste. M
Austin, TX 78758
Main:......................................800-772-7634
Sales:....................................512-837-6291
E-Mail: ....tyrex@btsweb.com
Web: www.btsweb.com/cable/tyrex/

Ta Engineering

PO Box 186
Moraga, CA 94556
Main:......................................510-376-8500
Tech. Support:.......................510-376-8500
Sales:....................................510-376-8500
Customer Service:..................510-376-8500
Tech. Support FAX:................510-376-4977
E-Mail: ....info@ta'eng.com
Web: www.ta'eng.com

Tactical Marketing Group

81 Norwood Ave.
Kensington, CA 94707
Main:......................................510-524-1356
FAX:......................................510-524-9141

Tadiran - CA

18400 Montevina Rd
Los Galtos, CA 95030
Main: 408-354-5473
Tech. Support:.......................408-354-5253
Customer Service:..................800-537-1368
FAX: 408-354-5253
BBS:......................................408-727-0560

Tadiran - NY

Tadiran Ltd - Israel
2 Seaview Blvd. Ste. 102
Port Washington, NY 11050
Main: 800-537-1368
Customer Service:..................516-621-4980
FAX: 516-621-4517
E-Mail:......................tadiran@village.ios.com
BBS:......................................516-621-4517
Web: www.echo-on.net/mob/tadiran

Tadpole Technology Inc.

12012 Technology Blvd.
Austin, TX 78727
Main: 512-219-2200
Tech. Support:.......................800-232-1881
Sales:....................................800-232-6656
Customer Service:..................800-232-1881
Tech. Support FAX: 512-219-2222
FAX: 512-219-2222
E-Mail:........................support@tadpole.com
Web: www.tadpole.com

Take to Anyone Computers

8816 A Reseda Blvd.
Northridge, CA 91324
Main: 818-700-9090
Tech. Support:.......................818-700-9090

Taligent

10355 N. DeAnza Blvd.
Cupertino, CA 95014
Main: 408-255-2525
FAX: 408-777-5181
Web: www.taligent.com

Tandberg Data
Tanberg Data/AS
2685-A Park Center Dr.
Simi Valley, CA 93065
Main:....................................805-579-1000
Tech. Support:........................805-579-1000
Customer Service:...................805-579-1000
Tech. Support FAX:................805-579-2555

Tandem Computers
191 Vallco Pkwy. Location 4-40
Cupertino, CA 95014-2595
Main:....................................408-285-6000
Sales:....................................800-482-6336
FAX: 408-285-0505
Web: www.tandem.com

Tandy Corp.
1800 One Tandy Ctr.
Ft Worth, TX 76102
Main:....................................817-390-3011
Tech. Support:........................817-878-6875
Tech. Support FAX:................817-878-6880
E-Mail: ....support@tandy.com
BBS:....................................817-390-2774
Web: www.tandy.com

Tangent Computer, Inc.
197 Airport Blvd.
Burlingame, CA 94010
Main:....................................800-800-5550
Tech. Support:........................800-800-5550
Sales:....................................415-342-9388
Tech. Support FAX:................415-342-9380
BBS:....................................415-342-7017

Tangram Enterprise Solutions, Inc.
Safeguard Scientifics
5511 Capital Center Dr. Ste. 400
Raleigh, NC 27606
Main:....................................800-245-7253
Tech. Support:........................919-851-6000
Sales:....................................800-482-6472
FAX: 919-851-6004
E-Mail: ....Infor@tesi.com
FTP: ftp.tesi.com
Web: www.tesi.com

Targus, Inc.
6180 Valley View St.
Buena Park, CA 90620
Main: 714-523-5429
Sales:....................................714-523-5429
Customer Service:...................714-523-5429
FAX: 714-523-0153

Tatung Co. of America
2850 El Presidio St.
Long Beach, CA 90810
Main: 800-827-2850
Tech. Support:........................213-979-7055
Sales:....................................310-637-2105
Tech. Support FAX: 310-637-8484
BBS: 310-635-9090
Web: www.tatung.com

Tatung Science & Technology
1840 McCarthy Blvd.
Milpitas, CA 95035
Main: 408-383-0988
Tech. Support:........................800-927-7880
Sales:....................................800-659-5902
FAX: 408-383-0886

Teac America, Inc.
7733 Telegraph Rd.
Montebello, CA 90640
Main: 213-726-0303
Tech. Support:........................213-727-4860
Sales:....................................213-726-0303
Customer Service:...................213-727-7694
Tech. Support FAX: 213-727-7629
FAX: 213-727-7652
BBS: 213-727-7660

Tech Hackers, Inc.
50 Broad St. Ste. 1737
New York, NY 10004
Main: 212-344-9500
FAX: 212-376-3280
Web: www.thi.com

Technical Aesthetics Operation
501 W 5th St.
Rolla, MO 65401
Main:.....................................800-264-1121
Tech. Support:........................573-364-4925
FAX:.......................................314-364-5631
CompuServe:...........................102677,1563

Technical Concepts
121 Hamburg St.
East Aurora, NY 14052
Main:.....................................800-344-2370
Tech. Support:........................716-655-0400
Sales:....................................716-655-2420
BBS:......................................716-655-2373

Technically Elite
6330 San Ignacia Ave.
San Jose, CA 95119
Main:.....................................800-543-8887
Tech. Support:........................408-370-4300
Tech. Support FAX:................408-370-4222
BBS:......................................408-370-4222
Web: www.tecelite.com

Technology Applications, Inc.
1350 Elbridge Payne Rd. Ste. 207
Chesterfield, MO 63017
Main:.....................................314-530-1981
Tech. Support FAX:................314-530-1788
Web: www.techapp.com

Technology Squared, Inc.
5198 W 76th St.
Edina, MN 55439
Main:.....................................612-832-5622
Tech. Support:........................800-685-7809
Sales:....................................800-762-3531
Customer Service:..................800-759-2133
Tech. Support FAX:................612-831-7770
FAX:......................................612-832-5709
Web: www.dtpdirect.com

Ted Gruber Software
PO Box 13408
Las Vegas, NV 89112
Main: 702-735-1980
Tech. Support:........................702-735-1980
Sales:....................................800-410-0192
Customer Service:..................702-735-1980
Tech. Support FAX: 702-735-4603
E-Mail:............................fastgraph@aol.com
BBS:......................................702-796-7134
FTP: ftp.accessnv.com/fg
Web: www.fastgraph.com

Tekelec
26580 W Agoura Rd.
Calabasas, CA 91302
Main: 800-835-3532
Tech. Support:........................818-880-5656
Sales:....................................800-835-3532
Customer Service:..................800-835-3532
Tech. Support FAX: 818-880-6993
FAX: 818-880-6993
E-Mail:...................webmaster@tekelec.com
BBS:......................................818-880-6993
Web: www.tekelec.com

Teknowledge Corporation
1810 Embarcadero Rd.
Palo Alto, CA 94303
Main: 415-424-0500
FAX: 415-493-2645
Web: www.teknowledge.com

Tektronix Corp.
PO Box 1000
Wilsonville, OR 97070-1000
Main: 503-682-3411
Sales:....................................800-832-9433
Web: www.tek.com

Telco Systems, Inc.
45550 Northport Loop E
Fremont, CA 94538
Main:......................................800-776-8832
Tech. Support:.......................800-227-0937
Sales:....................................800-776-8832
Customer Service:..................800-776-8832
FAX: 510-624-5680
BBS:......................................415-656-3031

Tele-Tech
500 Oakbrook Lane
Summerville, SC 29485
Main:......................................800-433-6181
Tech. Support:.......................800-537-8011
Sales:....................................800-433-6181
E-Mail: ....salessvc@tariffs.com

Telebit Corp.
1 Executive Dr.
Chelmsford, MA 01824
Main:......................................508-441-2181
Tech. Support:.......................508-441-2181
FAX: 508-441-9060
E-Mail: ....info@telebit.com
Web: www.telebit.com

Telebyte Technology, Inc.
270E Pulaski Rd.
Greenlawn, NY 11740
Main:......................................800-835-3298
Tech. Support:.......................516-423-3232
Sales:....................................800-835-3298
Customer Service:..................800-835-3298
Tech. Support FAX:.................516-385-8184
FAX: 516-385-8184
E-Mail: ....sale@telebyteusa.com
BBS:......................................516-385-8184
Web: www.telebyteusa.com

Teleconferencing Communication
152 Touay Court
DesPlaines, IL 60018
Main:......................................847-699-8431
Sales: 800-824-7283

Telect Co.
PO Box 665, or
2111 N Molter Rd
Liberty Lake, WA 99019
Main: 509-926-6000
Tech. Support:.......................800-551-4567
Sales:....................................800-551-4567
Customer Service:..................800-551-4567
Tech. Support FAX: 509-926-8915
FAX: 509-926-8915
BBS: 509-926-8915
Web: www.telect.com

Teledyne Kinetics
PO Box 939012
San Diego, CA 92193-9012
Main: 800-344-4334
Sales:....................................800-344-4334
Customer Service:..................800-344-4334

Telemate Software
4250 Perimeter Park So. Ste. 200
Atlanta, GA 30341
Main: 770-936-3700
Tech. Support:.......................770-936-3720
Tech. Support FAX: 770-936-3710
FAX: 770-936-3710
Web: www.telemate.com

Telematics International
ECI
1201 Cypress Rd.
Ft Lauderdale, FL 33309
Main: 800-833-4580
Tech. Support:.......................305-772-3070
BBS: 395-776-4127

TeleProcessing Products
4565 E Industrial St. Building 7-K
Simi Valley, CA 93063
Main: 805-522-8147
FAX: 805-581-6019
BBS: 805-581-6019
Web: www.teleprocessing.com

Telescape Communications
1965 West 4th Ave. Ste. 101
Vancouver, BC V6J 1M8
Canada
E-Mail: ....info@telescape.com
Web: www.telescape.com

Telesystems, Inc.
7501 Suzi Ln.
Westminster, CA 92683
Main:......................................714-898-2124

Teletech Systems
750 Birch Ridge Dr.
Roswell, GA 30076
Sales:....................................770-475-6985
FAX:......................................770-475-6985
CompuServe:............................. 72260,2217
E-Mail: .... techsupport@netcom.com
FTP: ftp.netcom.com/pub/vb/vb_helpwriter
Web: www.teletech-systems.com

Teletek
4600 Pell Dr.
Sacramento, CA 95838
Main:......................................916-920-4600
Tech. Support:........................916-920-4600
FAX:......................................916-927-7684
Web: www.tltkent.com

TeleVideo Systems, Inc.
2345 Harris Way
San Jose, CA 95131-1413
Main:......................................800-835-3228
Tech. Support:........................800-835-3228
FAX:......................................408-954-0622
BBS:......................................408-954-8231
Web: www.televideoinc.com

Templar Software
1125 Duke St.
Alexandria, VA 22314
Sales:....................................800-788-4794
FAX:......................................540-518-4480
CompuServe:............................. 72400,2345
Web: www.vbxtras.com/~templar/

Ten X Technology, Inc.
13091 Pond Springs Rd Ste. B200
Austin, TX 79729
Main: 512-918-9182
Sales:................................... 800-922-9050
FAX: 512-918-9495

Teneron Corporation
10540 Marty Ste. 170
Overland Park, KS 66212
Main: 913-385-2800
FAX: 913-385-0040
E-Mail:............................... teneron@aol.com
Web: www.teneron.com

Tera Computer Co.
2815 Eastlake Ave. East
Seattle, WA 98102
Main: 206-325-0800
Tech. Support FAX: 206-325-2433
E-Mail:.................................... info@tera.com
Web: www.tera.com

Teradyne, Inc. (Assembly test division)
321 Harrison Ave.
Boston, MA 02118
Main: 617-482-2700
Sales:................................... 800-777-2432
Tech. Support FAX: 617-422-3440
Web: www.teradyne.com

TeraTech
100 Park Ave. Ste. 360
Rockville, MD 20850-2618
Main: 301-424-3903
Tech. Support:....................... 301-762-8182
Sales:............................800-447-9120-517
FAX: 301-762-8185
E-Mail:........................... teratech@cpcug.org
BBS:.................................... 301-762-8184
FTP: ftp.teratech.com/pub/teratech/
Web: www.teratech.com/teratech

Terisa Systems
4984 El Camino Real
Los Altos, CA 94022
Main:.....................................415-919-1750
Tech. Support FAX:................415-919-1760
Web: www.rsa.com/rsa/pr/
   Terisa_Systems.html

Texas Instruments
PO Box 650311MS 3914
Dallas, TX 75265
Main:.....................................214-917-6278
Tech. Support:.......................800-848-3927
Sales:....................................800-848-3927
Customer Service:..................800-336-5236
FAX: 800-443-2984
BBS:......................................817-774-6809
Web: www.ti.com

Texas Microsystems, Inc.
5959 Corporate Dr.
Houston, TX 77036
Main:.....................................800-627-8700
Tech. Support:.......................800-627-8700
Sales:....................................800-627-8700
FAX: 713-541-8226
E-Mail: ....sales@texmicro.com
BBS:......................................713-541-8250
Web: www.texmicro.com

Think Software Corp.
1725 Duke St. Ste. 200
Alexandria, VA 22314
Main:.....................................703-518-2412
Sales:....................................703-518-2412
Customer Service:..................703-518-2412
Tech. Support FAX:................703-518-8190
FAX: 703-518-8190
CompuServe:.............................GO THINX
America Online:............. Keyword THINXINC
E-Mail: ....donn@paradigms.com

Thinking Machines Corp.
14 Crosby Dr.
Bedford, MA 01730
Main:.....................................617-276-0400
FAX: 617-276-0444
Web: www.think.com

Third Planet Publishing
17770 Preston Rd.
Dallas, TX 75252
Main: 214-713-2607
Tech. Support:.......................214-713-2630
Tech. Support FAX: 214-713-7613
E-Mail:...................digihelp@planeteers.com
FTP: ftp.planeteers.com
Web: www.planeteers.com

Third Planet Software
9911 W Pico Blvd. Ste. 1001
Los Angeles, CA 90035
Main: 310-553-2808
FAX: 310-553-1830
BBS:......................................310-553-2558

Three Card Flush
47-09 30th St.
Long Island City, NY 11101
Sales:....................................508-541-7100
BBS: 508-537-6761

Thunder Island, Inc.
PO Box 1034
Eau Claire, WI 54702
Sales:....................................715-835-8091
FAX: 715-835-5468

Thynx
619 Alexander Rd.
Princeton, NJ 08540
Main: 609-514-1600 235
Tech. Support:.......................201-808-2700
Customer Service:..................201-808-2700
Tech. Support FAX: 201-808-2676
FAX: 609-514-1818
CompuServe: ....GO CDVEN
America Online:.............thebureau@aol.com
BBS: 201-080-2676
Web: www.bep.com

TigerDirect
Global Direct
9100 S. Dadeland Blvd.
Miami, FL 33156
Main:.....................................800-888-4437
Sales:....................................800-477-8443
FAX:.......................................305-444-5010

Timberline Software
9600 SouthWest Nimbus Ave.
Beaverton, OR 97008
Main:.....................................503-626-6775
FAX:......................................503-641-7498

Time Warner Electronic Publishing
1271 Ave. of the Americas
New York, NY 10020
Main:.....................................212-522-7200
FAX:......................................212-522-1048
E-Mail: ......twep-webmaster@pathfinder.com
Web: www.pathfinder.com/twep

Timeline
23605 Telo Ave.
Torrance, CA 90505
Main:.....................................800-872-8878
Sales:....................................800-872-8878
Tech. Support FAX:................310-784-7590
FAX:......................................310-784-7590
BBS:......................................213-532-6304
Web: www.timeline.com

Timeplex Corp.
400 Chestnut Ridge Rd.
Woodcliff Lake, NJ 07675
Main:.....................................201-391-1111
Tech. Support:........................800-237-6670
Sales:....................................800-669-2298
FAX:......................................201-573-6470
Web: www.timeplex.com

Timeslips
Sage
17950 Preston Rd. Ste. 800
Dallas, TX 75252
Main: 800-285-0999
Tech. Support:........................ 508-768-7490
Customer Service:................... 800-285-0999
FAX: 214-248-9245
BBS:...................................... 508-768-7581
Web: www.timeslips.com

Tippecanoe Systems
5674 Stoneridge Dr. Ste. 119
Pleasanton, CA 94588
Main: 510-416-8510
Tech. Support:........................ 510-416-8510
Sales:..................................... 510-416-8510
Customer Service:................... 510-416-8510
Tech. Support FAX: 415-416-8516
FAX: 510-416-8516
E-Mail:.........................info@tippecanoe.com
Web: www.tippecanoe.com

Toner Etc.
124 Heritage Ave.
Portsmouth, NH 03801
Main: 800-370-8663
Tech. Support:........................ 800-639-9264
Sales:..................................... 800-370-8663
Customer Service:................... 800-370-8663
Tech. Support FAX: 603-431-0705
FAX: 603-431-0705
E-Mail:..................... toneretc@toneretc.com
BBS:..................................... 603-431-0705
Web: www.toneretc.com

Tool & Techniques, Inc.
2201 Northland Dr.
Austin, TX 78756
Main:.....................................800-444-1945
Tech. Support:........................512-459-1308
Sales:....................................800-444-1945
Customer Service:..................800-444-1945
Tech. Support FAX:................512-459-1309
FAX: 512-459-1309
CompuServe:............................76440,3346
E-Mail: ....djinfo@tnt.com
BBS:.....................................512-467-0206
FTP: ftp,//www.moontower.com/pub/tnt
Web: www.moontower.com/tnt

Top Microsystems Corp.
3320 Victor Court
Santa Clara, CA 95054
Main:.....................................408-980-9813
Tech. Support:........................408-980-9813
Sales:....................................408-980-9813
Customer Service:..................408-980-9813
FAX: 408-980-8626
Web: www.topmicro.com

Top Speed Corp.
150 E Sample Rd.
Pompano Beach, FL 33064
Main:.....................................954-785-4555
Tech. Support:........................954-785-4556
Sales:....................................800-354-5444
Customer Service:..................954-785-4555
Tech. Support FAX:................305-946-1650
CompuServe:.........................GO TOPSPEED
Web: www.topspeed.com

Torimaru Company
3841 N Freeway Blvd. Ste. 275
Sacramento, CA 95834
Main:.....................................916-646-1111
BBS:.....................................916-923-3447

Toshiba America Consumer Products
9740 Irvine Blvd.
PO Box 19724
Irvine, CA 92713-97248
Main: 800-334-3445
Tech. Support:........................800-999-4273
Sales:....................................800-959-4100
Customer Service:..................714-583-3000
BBS: 714-837-4408
Web: www.toshiba.com

Toshiba International Corp.
13131 W Little York Rd.
Houston, TX 77041
Main: 800-231-1412
Tech. Support:........................800-231-1412
Sales:..........................800-231-1412-#3604
Tech. Support FAX: 713-466-8773

Tosoh USA, Inc.
Tosoh Corp.
373 Vintage Park Dr. Ste. E
Foster City, CA 94404
Main: 415-286-2385
Tech. Support:........................415-286-2385
Tech. Support FAX: 415-286-2392
BBS: 800-238-6764

TouchStone Software
2124 Main St.
Huntington Beach, CA 92648
Main: 800-531-0450
Tech. Support:........................714-374-2801
Customer Service:..................714-969-7746
FAX: 714-969-1555
BBS: 714-969-0688

Tracer Technologies, Inc.
1600 Pennsylvania Ave. Ste. 101
York, PA 17404
Main: 717-843-5833
FAX: 717-843-2264
E-Mail:............................info@tracertek.com
Web: www.tracertek.com

Trans International
2120 East Howell Ave. Ste. 412
Anaheim, CA 92806
Main:......................................800-783-2120
Tech. Support:.......................714-634-1583
Sales:....................................800-783-2120
Customer Service:..................800-783-2120
Tech. Support FAX:................714-634-0409
BBS:.......................................714-634-0409

TransEra Corp.
345 E 800 South
Orem, UT 84058
Main:......................................801-224-6550
Tech. Support FAX:................801-224-0355

Transitional Technology, Inc.
5401 E La Palma Ave.
Anaheim, CA 92807
Main:......................................714-693-1133
Tech. Support:.......................714-693-1133
Sales:....................................714-693-1133
Customer Service:..................714-693-1133
Tech. Support FAX:................714-693-0225
FAX:......................................714-693-0225
E-Mail:..............................info@attech.com
Web: www.ttech.com

Transitions Networks, Inc.
North Star Universal
6475 City W Pkwy.
Eden Prairie, MN 55344
Main:......................................800-325-2725
Tech. Support:.......................800-260-1312
Tech. Support FAX:................612-941-2322
E-Mail:..........................info@transition.com
Web: www.transition.com

Traveling Software
18702 N Creek Pkwy.
Bothell, WA 98011
Main: 206-483-8088
Tech. Support:.......................206-483-8088
Sales:....................................800-343-8080
Customer Service:..................800-343-8080
Tech. Support FAX: 206-487-6786
CompuServe:.........................GO TRAVSOFT
BBS:.......................................206-485-1736
Web: www.travsoft.com

Trax Softworks, Inc.
5840 Uplander Way
Culver City, CA 90230-6620
Main: 310-649-5800
Tech. Support:.......................310-649-5800
Sales:....................................800-367-8729
Customer Service:..................310-649-5800
Tech. Support FAX: 310-649-6200
FAX: 310-649-6200
CompuServe:.................................GO TRAX
E-Mail:........................ support@traxsoft.com
Web: www.traxsoft.com/traxsoft/

Trend Micro Inc.
20245 Steven Creek Blvd. Ste. 101
Cupertino, CA 95014
Main: 800-228-5651
Tech. Support:.......................310-782-8190
Tech. Support FAX: 408-257-2003
E-Mail:...................... trend@trendmicro.com
BBS:.......................................310-328-5892
Web: www.trendmicro.com

Triangle Internet Co.
4909 Windy Hill Dr.
Raleigh, NC 27609
Main: 919-872-8435
FAX: 919-876-7064
E-Mail:...................................info@tico.com
Web: www.tico.com

Tribe Computer Works
2020 Challenger Dr.
Alameda, CA 94501-9941
Main:.....................................800-778-7423
Tech. Support:.........................510-814-3930
Sales:.....................................510-814-3900
FAX: 510-814-3980
Web: www.tribe.com

Tricord Systems, Inc.
2800 NorthWestern Blvd.
Plymouth, MN 55441
Main:.....................................612-557-9005
Tech. Support:.........................800-874-2673
Sales:.....................................800-874-2673
Tech. Support FAX:.................612-557-8403
BBS:.......................................612-557-1788

Trident Software
1001 Bridgeway Ste. 104
Sausalito, CA 94965-9949
Main:.....................................415-332-0188
Tech. Support FAX:.................415-332-0189
CompuServe:...........................102224,3610
BBS:.......................................415-332-7303
Web: www.tridentsoft.com

Tripp Lite
500 N Orleans
Chicago, IL 60610-4188
Main:.....................................312-755-5400
Tech. Support:.........................312-329-1602
Sales:.....................................312-755-5408
Customer Service:...................312-755-5401
Tech. Support FAX:.................312-644-6505
FAX: 312-644-6505
E-Mail: ....info@tripplite.com
BBS:.......................................312-644-6505
Web: www.tripplite.com

TriSoft Cyber Search
1825 E 38-1/2 St.
Austin, TX 78722
Main: 800-531-5170
Tech. Support:.........................512-472-0744
Sales: 512-472-0744
Tech. Support FAX: 512-473-2122
E-Mail:................................trisoft@bga.com
BBS: 512-473-2122
Web: www.zilker.net/~hydepark

Triticom
PO Box 444180
Eden Prairie, MN 55344
Main: 612-937-0772
FAX: 612-937-1998
BBS: 612-829-0135
Web: www.triticom.com

Triton Technologies/ Artisoft
200 Middlesex Tpke.
Iselin, NJ 08830
Main: 800-322-9440
Tech. Support:.........................908-855-9440
Customer Service:...................908-855-9440
FAX: 908-855-9608
BBS: 908-855-9609

Trompeter Electronics
31186 La Baya Dr.
Westlake Village, CA 91362
Main: 818-707-2020
Sales:.....................................818-707-2020
Customer Service:...................818-707-2030
Tech. Support FAX: 818-706-1040
BBS: 818-706-1040

True Data Products
PO Box 347
Uxbridge, MA 01569
Main: 800-635-0300
Tech. Support:.........................508-278-6556
Tech. Support FAX: 508-228-6748

Truevision
2500 Walsh Ave.
Santa Clara, CA 95051
Main:......................................408-562-4200
Tech. Support:........................800-729-2656
Sales:.....................................800-522-8783
Tech. Support FAX:.................317-576-7770
CompuServe:......................GO TRUEVISION
America Online:..............Keyword Truevision
E-Mail:.....................support@truevision.com
BBS:..317-577-8777
FTP: ftp.truevision.com
Web: www.truevision.com

Trusted Information Systems
3060 Washington Rd. (Rt. 97)
Glenwood, MD 21738
Main:.......................................301-854-6889
Sales:.....................................301-854-5335
Tech. Support FAX:.................301-854-5363
E-Mail:..tis@tis.com
Web: www.tis.com

Tulin Technologies
2156-H O'Toole Ave.
San Jose, CA 95131
Main:.......................................408-432-9025
Sales:.....................................408-432-9025
Customer Service:...................408-432-9025
Tech. Support FAX:.................408-943-0782
FAX:..408-943-0782
CompuServe:............................ 74264,3710

TurboPower Software
PO Box 49009
Colorado Springs, CO 80949
Main:.......................................719-260-9136
Sales:.....................................800-333-4160
FAX:..719-260-7151
CompuServe:............................ 76004,2611
BBS:..719-260-9726
FTP: FTP: rainbow.rmii.com:/pub2/
  turbopower
Web: www.tpower.com

Turtle Beach Systems
52 Grumbacher Rd.
York, PA 17402
Main: 717-767-0200
Tech. Support:........................ 717-764-5265
Sales:.....................................800-645-5640
Tech. Support FAX: 717-767-6033
BBS:... 717-767-0250
Web: www.tbeach.com

Turtle Beach Systems, Inc.
5690 Stewart Ave.
Fremont, CA 94538
Main: 510-624-6200
Tech. Support:........................ 510-624-6265
Customer Service:................... 510-624-6265
Tech. Support FAX: 510-624-6292
FAX: 510-624-6291
CompuServe:............................. GO TURTLE
America Online:...........Keyword Turtle Beach
E-Mail:......................... support@tbeach.com
BBS:... 510-624-6279
FTP: ftp.tbeach.com
Web: www.tbeach.com

Tut Systems
2495 Estand Way
Pleasant Hill, CA 94523
Main: 510-682-6510
Tech. Support:........................800-998-4888
Sales:.....................................800-998-4888
Customer Service:................... 800-998-4888
Tech. Support FAX: 510-682-4125
Web: www.tutsys.com

Twinhead Corp.
1537 Centre Pointe Dr.
Milpitas, CA 95035
Main: 800-545-8946
Tech. Support:........................408-945-0808
Sales:.....................................800-995-8946
Tech. Support FAX: 408-945-1532
FAX: 408-945-1080
BBS:..408-945-8334

Tyan Computer Corp.
1645 S Main St.
Milpitas, CA 95035
Main:.....................................408-956-8000
Tech. Support:........................408-956-8000
Sales:.....................................408-956-8000
Customer Service:..................408-956-8000
Tech. Support FAX:................408-956-8044
E-Mail:...........................support@tyan.com
BBS:.......................................408-956-8171
FTP: ftp.tyan.com
Web: www.tyan.com

UB Network
3900 Freedom Cir.
Santa Clara, CA 95054
Main:.....................................800-777-4526
Tech. Support:.........................408-562-5620
Customer Service:..................800-873-6381
Tech. Support FAX:................408-970-7337
BBS:.......................................408-970-7383
Web: www.ub.com

UCAR Unidata Program Center
PO Box 3000
Boulder, CO 80307
Main:.....................................303-497-8644
E-Mail:.................. support@unidata.ucar.edu
Web: www.unidata.ucar.edu/

UMAX Technologies, Inc.
3353 Gateway Blvd.
Fremont, CA 94538
Main:.....................................510-651-4000
Tech. Support:........................800-468-8629
Sales:....................................800-560-0311
Customer Service:..................800-562-0311
Tech. Support FAX:................510-651-3710
CompuServe:..............................GO UMAX
America Online:.................... umax@aol.com
E-Mail:...........................support@umax.com
BBS:.......................................510-651-2550
FTP: ftp.umax.com
Web: www.umax.com

US Robotics
8100 N McCormick Blvd.
Skokie, IL 60076-2920
Main: 708-982-5010
Tech. Support:........................708-982-5151
Sales:....................................800-550-7800
Customer Service:..................800-342-5877
Tech. Support FAX: 708-933-5800
E-Mail:.............................. support@usr.com
BBS: 708-982-5092
Web: www.usr.com

USA Flex
444 Scott Dr.
Bloomingdale, IL 60108
Main: 708-582-6206
Tech. Support:........................800-955-1488
Sales:....................................708-582-6202
Customer Service:..................800-777-2450
FAX: 708-351-7204
BBS: 708-351-6048

U-Tron Technologies, Inc.
47448 Fremont Blvd.
Fremont, CA 94538
Main: 800-933-7775
Tech. Support:........................510-656-3600
Tech. Support FAX: 510-650-1688
BBS: 510-656-1688

UUNET Communications Service
3060 Williams Dr.6th Floor
Fairfax, VA 22031-4648
Main: 703-206-5600
Sales:....................................800-488-6384
FAX: 703-206-5601
BBS: 703-876-5059
Web: www.alter.net

Ulead
970 W. 190th St. Ste. 520
Torrance, CA 90502
Main:.....................................310-523-9393
Tech. Support:........................310-523-9391
Customer Service:..................800-858-5323
Tech. Support FAX:.................310-523-9399
CompuServe:............................ GO ULEAD
America Online:............ Keyword UL Support
E-Mail: .... mkt@ulead.com
BBS:.......................................310-523-9389
FTP: ftp.ulead.com
Web: www.ulead.com

Unicom Electric, Inc.
11980 Telegraph Rd. Ste.103
Santa Fe Springs, CA 91792
Main:.....................................310-946-9650
Tech. Support:........................800-348-6668
Sales:.....................................310-946-9650
Customer Service:..................800-348-6668
Tech. Support FAX:.................310-946-9167
FAX:.......................................310-946-9167
E-Mail: ....jlo@interserv.com
Web: www.connectors.com/unicom/

Uniplex Business Software
1333 Corporate Dr. Ste. 240
Irving, TX 75038
Main:.....................................800-356-8063
Tech. Support:........................800-338-9940
Sales:.....................................800-356-8063
Customer Service:..................800-356-8063
Tech. Support FAX:.................214-756-8550
FAX:.......................................214-756-8550
E-Mail: ....uniplex.com
BBS:.......................................214-987-0303
Web: www.uniplex

UniPress Software, Inc.
2025 Lincoln Hwy. Ste. 209
Edison, NJ 08817
Main:.....................................800-222-0550
Tech. Support:........................201-985-8000
Sales:.....................................908-287-2100
FAX:.......................................908-287-4929
BBS:.......................................201-287-4929
Web: www.unipress.com

Unisys
2700 N 1st St.
PO Box 6685
San Jose, CA 95134
Main: 408-434-2848
Tech. Support FAX: 408-434-2131
Web: www.unisys.com

Unisys Corp.
PO Box 500
Blue Bell, PA 19424
Main: 215-986-6999
Tech. Support:........................ 215-986-4011
Customer Service:.................. 800-986-4797
Web: www.unisys.com

United Innovations
120 Whiting Farms Rd.
Holyoke, MA 01040
Main: 800-323-3283
Sales:..................................... 413-533-7500
Tech. Support FAX: 413-533-7755

Universal Data Systems (UDS)
5000 Bradford Dr.
Huntsville, AL 35805-1953
Main: 205-430-8000
Tech. Support:........................ 800-221-4380
FAX: 205-830-5657
BBS:....................................... 205-430-8926
Web: www.mot.com

Universal Technical Systems, Inc.
1220 Rock St.
Rockford, IL 61101-1437
Main: 815-963-2220
Tech. Support:........................ 815-963-2220
Sales:..................................... 800-435-7887
Customer Service:.................. 815-963-2220
Tech. Support FAX: 815-963-8884
FAX: 815-963-8884
CompuServe:..................... GO UTSSUPPORT
E-Mail:............................... support@uts.com
FTP: ftp.uts.com
Web: www.uts.com

Up Software
722 Lombard St. Ste. 204
San Francisco, CA 94133-2300
Main:......................................415-921-4691
Sales:.....................................800-959-8208
FAX: 415-921-0939
Web: www.upsoftware.com

Upsonic
29 Journey
Aliso Viejo, CA 92656
Main:......................................800-877-6642
Sales:.....................................714-449-9500
FAX: 714-448-9555
BBS:.......................................714-833-7164

User Group Connection
2840 Research Park Dr. Ste. 100
Soquel, CA 95073
Main:......................................408-477-4277
Tech. Support FAX:.................408-477-4290
America Online:.......................Keyword UGF
E-Mail: ....ugc@ugconnection.com
Web: www.ugconnection.com

V Communications, Inc.
432 Stevens Creek Blvd. Ste. 120
San Jose, CA 95129
Tech. Support:........................408-296-4385
Sales:.....................................408-296-4224
FAX: 408-296-4441
CompuServe:.......................... 103425,1241
Web: www.v-com.com

V_Graph Inc.
PO Box 105
Westtown, PA 19395
Main:......................................610-399-1521
Sales:.....................................800-852-6284
FAX: 610-399-0566
E-Mail: ....v_graph@zola.trend1.com
Web: www.v-graph.com

VNP Software
180 Franklin St.
Cambridge, MA 02139
Main: 802-496-7799
Tech. Support:........................617-661-4292
Sales:.....................................802-496-7799
Tech. Support FAX: 617-864-6768
E-Mail:...................................info@vnp.com
FTP: ftp.vnp.com
Web: www.vnp.com

Valitek, Inc.
100 University Dr.
Amherst, MA 01002
Main: 800-825-4835
Tech. Support:........................413-586-7408
Tech. Support FAX: 413-549-2900
Web: www.contagious.com/valitek/valitek.htm

ValueStor
1609 Regatta Ln.
Unit B
San Jose, CA 95112-1116
Main: 408-437-2300
Tech. Support:........................408-437-2310
Sales:.....................................800-873-8258
Customer Service:...................800-873-8258
Tech. Support FAX: 408-437-9333
BBS: 408-437-1616

Vanguard Inc.
777 Terrace Ave.5th Floor
Hasbrouck Heights, NJ 07604
Main: 201-288-1136
FAX: 201-288-0213
E-Mail:..............................contact@thru.net
Web: www.thru.net

Variant Microsystems
46520 Fremont Blvd. Ste. 614
Fremont, CA 94538
Main: 800-666-4227
Tech. Support:........................510-440-2870
Tech. Support FAX: 510-440-2873
BBS: 415-623-1372

Veldhuis Computer Company
39 Birchwood Ave.
Longmeadow, MA 01106
Sales: 413-827-9747
CompuServe:............................ 713563,533

Velocity Corp.
4 Embarcadero Center Ste. 3100
San Francsico, CA 94111-4106
Main:......................................415-776-8000
Tech. Support:........................415-392-4357
Sales: 415-776-8000
Customer Service:...................415-274-8840
Tech. Support FAX:.................415-776-8099
CompuServe:............................ 76660,2202
America Online:...........velocitydev@aol.com
E-Mail: .... info@velo.com
FTP: ftp.velocitygames.com
Web: www.velocitygames.com

Ven-Tel, Inc.
2121 Zanker Rd.
San Jose, CA 95131-2177
Main:......................................408-436-7400
Sales: 800-538-5121
FAX:.......................................408-436-7451
BBS:.......................................408-922-0988
Web: www.zoom.com/ventel

VenturCom, Inc.
215 1st St.
Cambridge, MA 02142
Main:......................................617-661-1230
FAX:.......................................617-577-1607
E-Mail: ....info@vci.com
Web: www.vci.com

Verbatim
1200 W.T. Harris Blvd.
Charlotte, NC 28262
Main:......................................704-547-6500
Tech. Support:........................800-538-8589
Sales: 888-837-2284
Customer Service:...................800-538-8589
Tech. Support FAX:.................704-547-6565
E-Mail: .... info@verbatimcorp.com
Web: www.verbatimcorp.com

Verilink
145 Baytech Dr.
San Jose, CA 95134
Main: 408-945-1199
Tech. Support:........................800-543-1008
Sales:.....................................800-837-4546
Customer Service:......... 408-945-1199 #359
FAX: 408-262-6260
BBS:.......................................408-262-6260

Verity, Inc.
1550 Plymouth
Mountain View, CA 94043
Main: 415-960-7600
FAX: 415-960-7698
E-Mail:..................................info@verity.com
BBS:.......................................415-960-7698
Web: www.verity.com

Vermont Creative Software
Pinnacle Meadows
Richford, VT 05476-2000
Main: 800-848-1248
Tech. Support:........................802-848-7571
Customer Service:...................802-848-7731
FAX: 802-848-3502
BBS:.......................................802-848-7581

Vermont Microsystems, Inc.
11 Tigan St.
Winooski, VT 05404-0236
Main: 800-354-0055
Sales:.....................................802-655-2860
FAX: 802-655-9058
BBS:.......................................802-655-7461

Versant
1380 Willow Rd. Ste. 201
Menlo Park, CA 94025
Main: 415-329-7500
Tech. Support:........................415-325-2380
Sales:.....................................800-837-7268
BBS:.......................................415-325-2380
Web: www.versant.com

Versitron
27 McCullough Dr.
New Castle, DE 19720
Main:.....................................800-537-2296
Tech. Support:.........................301-497-8600
Tech. Support FAX:.................302-323-8645

Vertex Technologies, Inc.
61 Executive Blvd.
Farmingdale, NY 11735
Main:.....................................800-248-3783
Tech. Support:.........................516-293-1610
FAX: 516-293-8033
E-Mail: ....info@vertextech.com
Web: www.vertextech.com

Vertisoft Systems, Inc.
4 Embarcadero Ct. Ste. 3470
San Francisco, CA 94111
Main:.....................................800-466-5875
Tech. Support:.........................803-295-5875
Sales: 415-956-5999
FAX: 415-956-5355
Web: www.vertisofsys.com

ViaCrypt a div of Lemcom Systems, Inc.
Lemcom Systems, Inc.
9033 N 24th Ave. Ste. 7
Phoenix, AZ 85201-2847
Main:.....................................602-944-0773
Tech. Support:.........................602-944-0773
Sales: 800-536-2664
Customer Service:...................602-944-0773
Tech. Support FAX:.................602-943-2601
CompuServe:..........................GO VIACRYPT
E-Mail: ....info@viacrypt.com
FTP: ftp.viacrypt.com
Web: www.viacrypt.com

Via-Grafix Corp.
1 American Way
Pryor, OK 74361
Main: 918-825-4844
Tech. Support:........................ 918-825-4844
Sales: 918-825-7555
Customer Service:................... 918-825-4844
Tech. Support FAX: 918-825-6359
CompuServe: ....GO DESIGNCAD
E-Mail:......................support@viagrafix,com
BBS: 918-825-4878
Web: www.viagrafix.com

Victory Enterprises
223 W Anderson Ln.
Austin, TX 78752
Main: 800-727-3475
Tech. Support:........................ 512-450-0801
Tech. Support FAX: 512-450-0869
E-Mail:...........................info@victoryent.com
Web: www.victoryent.com

VideoLogic, Inc.
1001 Bayhill Dr. Ste. 310
San Bruno, CA 94066
Main: 415-875-0606
Tech. Support:........................ 415-875-6862
Sales:.................................. 800-578-5644
FAX: 415-875-4167
CompuServe: ....GO VIDEOLOGIC
BBS: 415-875-7748
Web: www.videologic.com

VideoSoft
2625 Alcatraz Ave. Ste. 271
Berkeley, CA 94705
Sales:.................................. 510-704-8200
FAX: 510-843-0174
CompuServe: 74774,420
Web: www.videosoft.com

VideoTex of America, Inc.
5405 Morehouse Dr. Ste. 300
San Diego, CA 92121
Main: 619-452-8398
FAX: 619-452-0369
E-Mail:...................info@www.videotex.com
Web: www.videotex.com

Videotex Systems, Inc.
11880 Greenville Ave. Ste. 100
Dallas, TX 75243
Main:.....................................214-231-9200
Sales: 800-888-4336
FAX:.......................................214-231-2420
BBS:.......................................214-231-2432

Videx, Inc.
1105 NE Circle Blvd.
Corvallis, OR 97330-4285
Main:.....................................541-758-0521
FAX:.......................................541-752-5285
E-Mail: ....sales@videx.com
BBS:.......................................541-752-5285
Web: www.videx.com

Viewpoint DataLabs International, Inc.
625 S. State St.
Orem, UT 84058
Main:.....................................801-229-3000
Sales: 800-328-2738
Tech. Support FAX:.................801-229-3300
Web: www.viewpoint.com

ViewSonic
20480 Business Pkwy.
Walnut, CA 91789
Main:.....................................909-8697976
Tech. Support:........................909-8697976
Sales: 909-8697976
Customer Service:...................909-8697976
Tech. Support FAX:.................909-4683756
E-Mail: ....vstech@viewsonic.com
BBS:.......................................909-468-1241
Web: www.viewsonic.com

Viking Software Services
6804 S Canton Ave. Ste. 900
Tulsa, OK 74136
Main:.....................................918-491-2701
Sales: 800-324-0595
CompuServe:.............................71411,212
BBS:.......................................918-494-2701

Virgin Interactive Entertainment
18061 Fitch Ave.
Irvine, CA 92714
Main: 714-833-8710
Tech. Support:.......................714-833-1999
Sales:...................................800-874-4607
Customer Service:..................714-833-1999
Tech. Support FAX: 714-833-2001
FAX: 714-833-8717
E-Mail:.....................tech_support@vie.com
BBS:......................................714-833-8716
Web: www.vie.com

Visible Computer Supply
Wallace Computer Services
1750 Wallace Ave.
St. Charles, IL 60174
Main: 800-323-0628
Tech. Support:.......................800-323-0628
Customer Service:..................800-323-0628
Tech. Support FAX: 800-233-2016

Visio Corp.
520 Pike St. Ste. 1800
Seattle, WA 98101-4001
Main: 206-521-4500
Tech. Support:.......................206-521-4600
Sales:...................................800-446-3335
Customer Service:..................800-248-4746
Tech. Support FAX: 206-521-4501
CompuServe:.................................GO VISIO
Web: www.visio.com

Vision Software
2101 Webster St.8th Floor
Oakland, CA 94612
Main: 510-238-4100
Sales:...................................800-984-7638
FAX: 510-238-4101
Web: www.vision-soft.com

Visioneer, Inc.
2860 W Bayshore Rd.
Palo Alto, CA 94303
Main:.....................................415-812-6400
Tech. Support:.......................415-884-5548
Sales:....................................800-787-7007
Customer Service:..................800-787-7007
Tech. Support FAX:................503-884-8474
CompuServe:........................ GO VISIONEER
America Online:...............Keyword Visioneer
E-Mail: .... tech-support@visioneer.com
BBS:......................................415-493-0391
Web: www.visioneer.com

Visual Components, Inc.
15721 College Blvd.
Lenexa, KS 66219
Sales:....................................800-884-8665
FAX: 913-599-6597
E-Mail: ....sales@visualcomp.com
BBS:......................................913-599-6713
Web: www.visualcomp.com

Visual Numeric (VDA Division)
6230 Lookout Rd.
Boulder, CO 80301
Main:....................................303-530-9000
Sales:....................................800-447-7147
Tech. Support FAX:................303-530-9329
Web: www.vni.com

Visual Numerics (ADT Division)
9990 Richmond Ave. Ste. 400
Houston, TX 77042-4548
Main:....................................800-222-4675
Tech. Support:.......................713-954-6727
Sales:....................................713-954-6424
Tech. Support FAX:................713-781-9260
FAX: 713-781-9260
BBS:......................................713-781-9259
Web: www.vni.com

Visual Solutions, Inc.
487 Groton Rd.
Westford, MA 01886
Main: 508-392-0100
FAX: 508-692-3102
E-Mail:..................................info@vissol.com
BBS: 508-692-5714
Web: www.vissim.com

Vitec Multimedia
4366 Independence Ct. Ste. C
Sarasota, FL 34234
Main: 941-351-9344
FAX: 941-351-9423
E-Mail:........................vitechts@sprynet.com
Web: www.glimmer.com\vitec

VocalTec
35 Industrial Pkwy.
Northvale, NJ 07647
Main: 201-768-9400
Sales: 800-843-2289
Tech. Support FAX: 201-768-8893
E-Mail: ....info@vocaltec.com
Web: www.vocaltec.com

Voyetra Technologies
5 Odell Plaza
Yonkers, NY 10701-1406
Main: 800-233-9377
Tech. Support:.......................914-966-0600
Sales:....................................914-966-0600
Tech. Support FAX: 914-966-1102
E-Mail:...............................info@voyetra.com
BBS: 914-966-1216

Vtel Corp.
108 Wild Basin Rd.
Austin, TX 78746
Main: 512-349-3117
Tech. Support:.......................512-834-2700
Sales:....................................800-856-8835
FAX: 512-314-2792
Web: www.vtel.com

Vuong Systems
200 5th Ave.
Waltham, MA 02154
Main:.....................................617-890-1100
Sales:.....................................617-690-4543
Customer Service:..................617-890-4543
Tech. Support FAX:................617-672-4560

W.J. Shea & Associates
5310 W Camelback
Glendale, AZ 85301
Main:.....................................800-528-5567
Tech. Support:........................602-245-1050
Sales:.....................................800-528-5567
Customer Service:..................800-528-5567
Tech. Support FAX:................602-934-6605
BBS:.......................................800-344-6358

WRQ Inc.
1500 Dexter Ave. North
Seattle, WA 98109
Main:.....................................206-217-7500
Tech. Support:........................206-217-7000
Sales:.....................................800-872-2829
FAX:.......................................206-217-0293
CompuServe:......................GO REFLECTION
E-Mail:................................info@wrq.com
BBS:.......................................206-217-0145
Web: www.wrq.com

WYSIWYG Corp.
1900 S. Sepulveda Blvd. Ste. 208
Los Angeles, CA 90025
Main:.....................................800-489-6673
Sales:.....................................310-575-1991
FAX:.......................................310-575-3141
BBS:.......................................213-215-9668
Web: www.wysiwyg.com

Wacom Technology
Wacom Co. Ltd.
501 SE Columbia Shores Blvd. Ste. 300
Vancouver, WA 98661
Main: 360-750-8882
Tech. Support:........................ 360-750-8882
Sales:..................................... 800-922-6613
Customer Service:................... 800-922-6613
Tech. Support FAX: 360-750-8924
CompuServe:........................... GO WACOM
America Online:.................. wacom@aol.com
BBS:....................................... 360-750-0638
FTP: ftp.wacom.com
Web: www.wacom.com

Walker, Richer and Quinn, Inc.
1500 Dexter Ave. N
Seattle, WA 98109
Main: 206-217-7500
Sales:..................................... 800-872-2829
Tech. Support FAX: 206-217-0293
E-Mail:.................................... info@wrq.com
Web: www.wrq.com

Wall Data Inc.
11332 NE 122nd Way
Kirkland, WA 98034-6931
Main: 206-814-9255
Tech. Support:........................ 206-814-3400
Sales:..................................... 800-987-2572
Tech. Support FAX: 206-814-4300
CompuServe:........................GO WALLDATA
BBS:....................................... 206-558-0392
Web: www.walldata.com

Wall St. Directory, Inc.
PO Box 27740
Las Vegas, NV 89126
Main: 619-943-1936
FAX: 619-943-8768
E-Mail:............................wallst@wsdinc.com
Web: www.wsdinc.com

Walnut Creek CD Rom
4041 Pike Lane Ste. D
Concord, CA 94520
Main:.....................................510-674-0783
FAX: 510-674-0821
E-Mail: ....info@cdrom.com
Web: www.cdrom.com

Wandel & Goltermann Technologies
1030 Swabia Ct.
Research Triagle Park, NC 27709
Main:....................................919-941-5730
FAX: 919-941-5751
Web: www.wg.com

Ward Systems Group, Inc.
Executive Park West5 Hillcrest Dr.
Frederick, MD 21701
Main:....................................301-662-7950
Sales: 301-662-7950
FAX: 301-662-5866

Wasatch Computer Technology
123 E. 200 South
Salt Lake City, UT 84111
Main:....................................801-575-8043
Web: www.wasatchinc.com

Watcom Products, Inc.
415 Phillip St.
Waterloo, ONT N2L 3X2
Canada
Main:....................................800-265-4555
Tech. Support:........................519-884-0702
Tech. Support FAX:.................519-747-4971
E-Mail: ....sales@watcom.on.ca
BBS:....................................519-747-4971
FTP: ftp.watcom.com/pub/bbs
Web: www.watcom.com

Waterloo Maple, Inc.
450 Phillip St.
Waterloo, ONT N2L 5J2
Canada
Main: 519-747-2373
Sales:.................................... 800-267-6583
Tech. Support FAX: 519-747-5284
FAX: 519-747-5284
E-Mail:.....................support@maplesoft.com
FTP: ftp.maplesoft.com
Web: www.maplesoft.com

Wavetek Corp. Communications Division
5808 Churchman Bypass
Indianapolis, IN 46203
Main: 619-279-2955
Customer Service:................... 317-788-9351
Tech. Support FAX: 317-782-4607
Web: www.wavetek.com

Waypoint Technologies
Main: 205-539-2930
E-Mail:........................... waypoint@awa.com
Web: www.awa.com/waypoint/index.html

Waytek, Inc.
PO Box 690
Chanhassen, MN 55317-0690
Tech. Support:........................ 612-949-0765
Sales:.................................... 800-328-2724
Tech. Support FAX: 612-949-0965

Weaver Graphics
5165 S Hwy A1A
Melbourne Beach, FL 32951
Main: 407-728-4000
Tech. Support FAX: 407-728-5978

Webcom Communications Corp.
10555 E Dartmouth Ste. 330
Aurora, CO 80014
Main: 303-745-5711
FAX: 303-745-5712
E-Mail:.................. softpub@infowebcom.com
Web: www.infowebcom.com

Wedge Technology, Inc.
1657 McCandless Dr.
Milpitas, CA 95035
Main:......................................408-263-9888
Tech. Support:.........................408-263-0225
America Online:...........wedge1981@aol.com
BBS:..408-263-9958
Web: www.wedgetech.com

WeGotIt
1571 Whitmore Ave.
Ceres, CA 95307
Main:......................................800-326-6548
Tech. Support:.........................408-954-8038
Tech. Support FAX:.................209-541-1401
Web: www.wegotit.com

Weidemuller Inc., Paladin Tools
Weidmuller, Inc.
2150 Anchor Court
Newbury Park, CA 91320
Main:......................................800-272-8665
Tech. Support:.........................805-499-0318

Western Digital
8105 Irvine Center Dr.
Irvine, CA 92718
Main:......................................714-932-5000
Tech. Support:.........................800-832-4778
Sales:.....................................800-832-4778
Customer Service:...................800-832-4778
Tech. Support FAX:.................714-932-4012
FAX:.......................................714-932-7837
BBS:..714-753-1234
Web: www.wdc.com

Western Telematic, Inc.
5 Sterling
Irvine, CA 92718-9934
Main:......................................800-854-7226
Tech. Support:.........................714-586-9950
FAX:.......................................714-583-9514
Web: www.westtel.com

Westwood Studios
5333 S Arville Ste. 104
Las Vegas, NV. 89118-2226
Tech. Support FAX: 702-368-0677
E-Mail:.................... support@westwood.com
Web: www.westwood.com

WexTech Systems
310 Madison Ave. Ste. 905
New York, NY 10017
Main: 212-949-9595
Tech. Support:.........................212-949-0093
Customer Service:...................212-949-9595
Tech. Support FAX: 212-949-4007
CompuServe:..........................GO WEXTECH
BBS:..212-297-1862
Web: www.wextech.com

Whisk E Software
5370 52nd Ave. S.E.
Grand Rapids, MI 49508
Main: 616-698-0330
Sales:.....................................800-451-4319
FAX: 616-698-0325
BBS:..616-698-8106

White Pine Software
40 Simon St.
Nashua, NH 03060-3043
Main: 603-886-9050
Sales:..................................... 800-241-7463
FAX: 603-886-9051
E-Mail:.................................info@wpine.com
Web: www.whitepine.com

White Pine Software
1485 Saratoga Ave.
San Jose, CA 95129-4934
Main: 800-426-2230
Tech. Support:......................... 408-446-1919
Tech. Support FAX: 408-446-0666
E-Mail:.................................info@wpine.com
Web: www.whitepine.com

Whittaker Xyplex
Whittaker Corp.
295 Foster St.
Littleton, MA 01460
Main:......................................800-338-5316
Tech. Support:.......................800-435-7977
FAX: 508-952-4702
E-Mail: ....info@xyplex.com
Web: www.xyplex.com

Wilcom Products
PO Box 508
Laconia, NH 03247
Main:.....................................603-524-2622
Sales:....................................800-222-1898
Tech. Support FAX:................603-524-3735
BBS:......................................603-528-3804
Web: www.wilcominc.com

Wildside Press
154 W. 57th St. Studio 326
New York, NY 10019
Main:.....................................212-581-3000
Tech. Support:.......................212-757-8283
America Online:............rosebushco@aol.com
E-Mail: ....info@rosebush.com
Web: www.rosebush.com

Willoughby Internet Group
650 6th Ave.
New York, NY 10011
Main:.....................................212-639-2290
Tech. Support:.......................212-639-6807
Sales: 800-433-5499
Customer Service:..................212-639-2530

Wind River Systems, Inc.
1010 Atlantic Ave.
Alameda, CA 94501
Main:.....................................510-748-4100
Sales: 800-545-9463
Tech. Support FAX:................510-814-2010
E-Mail: .... inquiries@wrs.com
Web: www.wrs.com

WINGate Technologies
PO Box 327
Hope, NJ 07844
Main: 908-459-9293
Tech. Support FAX: 908-459-4001
CompuServe: 74407,2215
FTP: FTP: //ftp.digex.net/pub/access/wingate
Web: www.wingate.com

Wintek Corp.
1801 South St.
Lafayette, IN 47904-2993
Main: 800-742-6809
Tech. Support:.......................317-448-1903
FAX: 317-448-4823
E-Mail:..............................info@wintek.com
Web: www.wintek.com

Wintertree Software, Inc.
43 Reuter St.
Nepean, ONT K2J 3Z9
Canada
Sales:................................... 613-825-6271
FAX: 613-825-5521
E-Mail:..............................wsi@fox.nstn.ca
Web: fox.nstn.ca/~wsi

Wintronics
1316 Motor Pkwy.
Hauppauge, NY 11788
Main: 516-234-8040
FAX: 516-234-8321
Web: www.wintronics.com

Wol2Woll Software
1032 SummerPl. Dr.
San Jose, CA 95122
Sales:................................... 800-965-2965
FAX: 408-293-9369
E-Mail:.....................wol2wol@webcom.com
FTP: ftp.webcom.com/pub/wol2wol/ftp.
Web: www.webcom.com/~wol2wol/

Wolfram Research, Inc.
100 Trade Center Dr.
Champaign, IL 61820-7237
Main:.......................................217-398-0700
Tech. Support:.........................217-398-6500
Tech. Support FAX:.................217-398-0747
Web: www.wolfram.com

Word in Action
701 Cedar Lane Ste. 5
Knoxville, TN 37912
Sales:......................................800-699-6395
FAX:..423-693-5468
CompuServe:............................72037,2225
Web: www.wordinaction.com

WordPerfect
Corel,
1600 Carling Ave.
Ottawa, ONT K1Z 8R7
Canada
Main:.......................................613-728-8200
Tech. Support:.........................613-728-1010
Sales:......................................613-728-8200
Customer Service:...................800-772-6735
BBS:...613-728-4752
CompuServe:...................... GO CORELCORP
America Online:...................... Keyword Corel
FTP: ftp.corel.com
Web: www.wordperfect.com

Working Software
PO Box 1844
Santa Cruz, CA 95061
Main:.......................................408-423-5696
FAX:..408-423-5699
CompuServe:..........................GO MACBVEN
America Online:.................Keyword Working
E-Mail: .... info@working.com
Web: www.working.com

World Words, Inc.
2706 W. Avenue 32
Los Angeles, CA 90065
Sales:......................................213-343-0061
FAX:..213-343-0061
E-Mail: .... bookalle@earthlink.com

Worldata
5200 Town Center Cir.
Boca Raton, FL 33486
Main: 800-331-8102
Tech. Support FAX: 407-368-8345
E-Mail:............................mail@worldata.com
Web: www.worldata.com

Worthington Data Solutions
3004 Mission St. Ste. 220
Santa Cruz, CA 95060
Main: 800-345-4220
Tech. Support:.........................408-458-9938
Sales:......................................408-458-9938
Tech. Support FAX: 408-458-9964
Web: www.cruzio.com/~wds

Wyse
3471 N First St.
San Jose, CA 95134-1803
Main: 800-438-9973
Tech. Support:.........................800-800-9973
Sales:......................................408-473-1200
Customer Service:...................800-370-9973
FAX: 408-473-1222
BBS:...408-922-4400
Web: www.wyse.com

XcelleNet, Inc.
5 Concourse Pkwy Ste. 200
Atlanta, GA 30328
Main: 770-804-8100
Tech. Support:.........................770-804-2297
Sales:......................................800-322-3366
FAX: 770-804-8102
BBS:...770-804-8102

Xecom, Inc.
374 Turquoise St.
Milpitas, CA 95035
Main: 408-945-6640
FAX: 408-942-1346
E-Mail:................................info@xecom.com
Web: www.xecom.com/xecom

Xerox Palo Alto Research Center
3333 Coyote Hill Rd.
Palo Alto, CA 94304
Main:.....................................415-494-4000
Web: www.xsoft.com

Xicor, Inc.
1511 Buckeye Dr.
Milpitas, CA 95035
Main:......................................408-4328888
Tech. Support FAX:................617-899-6808
FAX: 408-432-0640
E-Mail: ....info@smtpgate.xicor.com
BBS:......................................800-258-8864
Web: www.xicor.com

Xilinx
2100 Logic Dr.
San Jose, CA 95124-3450
Main:.....................................408-559-7778
Tech. Support:.......................800-255-7778
Sales: 800-562-4647
Tech. Support FAX:................408-879-4442
E-Mail: ....webmaster@xilinx.com
BBS:......................................408-559-9327
FTP: FTP: //www.xilinx.com
Web: www.xilinx.com

Xinet
2560 Ninth St. Ste. 312
Berkeley, CA 94710
Main:.....................................510-845-0555
Tech. Support FAX:................510-644-2680
Web: www.xinet.com

Xinetron
3022 Scott Blvd.
Santa Clara, CA 95054
Main:.....................................800-345-4415
Tech. Support:.......................408-727-5509
Tech. Support FAX:................408-727-6499

Xing Technology
1540 W. Branch St.
Arroyo Grande, CA 93420-1818
Main: 800-294-6448
Sales:...................................805-473-0145
FAX: 805-473-0147
CompuServe: ....GO XINGSUPPORT
E-Mail:......................support@xingtech.com
BBS: 805-473-2680
Web: www.xingtech.com

Xircom, Inc.
2300 Corporate Center Dr.
Thousand Oaks, CA 91320
Main: 805-376-9300
Tech. Support:.......................805-376-9200
Sales:...................................800-438-4526
Customer Service:.................805-376-9200
Tech. Support FAX: 805-376-9100
CompuServe: ....GO XIRCOM
E-Mail:.................................cs@xircom.com
BBS: 805-376-9130
Web: www.xircom.com

Xpoint Corp.
3100 Medlock Bridge Rd. Ste. 370
Norcross, GA 30071
Main: 770-446-2764
FAX: 770-446-6129

Xxera Technologies
9665 E Las Tunas Dr.
Temple City, CA 91780
Main: 818-286-5569
Tech. Support:.......................818-286-5569
FAX: 818-286-5228

Xylogics
53 Third Ave.
Burlington, MA 01803-4491
Main: 800-225-3317
Tech. Support:.................617-272-8140-279
Sales:...................................800-892-6639
Tech. Support FAX: 617-273-5392
E-Mail:.......................support@xylogics.com
BBS: 617-273-1499
FTP: ftp.xylogics.com
Web: www.xylogics.com

Xyplex
Whittaker Corp.
295 Foster St.
Littleton, MA 01460
Main:......................................508-952-4700
Tech. Support:........................800-435-7997
Sales:....................................800-338-5316
Tech. Support FAX:................508-952-4702
E-Mail:..........................support@xyplex.com
Web: www.xyplex.com

Xyris Software, Inc.
Sales:....................................212-925-4388
FAX:......................................212-925-4929
CompuServe:............................ 71052,3172

Xyvision
101 Edgewater Dr.
Wakefield, MA 01880-1291
Main:......................................617-245-4100
Sales:....................................800-333-8947
Tech. Support FAX:................617-246-6209
Web: www.xyvision.com

ZFC
PO Box 15813
Amsterdam, Netherlands 1001NH
Main:....................................312-042-08248
E-Mail:...zfc@zfc.nl
Web: www.nl.net/~zfc/index.html

Zaphod Industries, Inc.
PO Box 442
Northwood, NH 03261
Main:......................................603-942-5077
Tech. Support FAX:................603-942-7466

Zenith Electronics
1000 Milwaukee Ave. Ste. 288
Glenview, IL 60025-2493
Main:......................................847-391-8000
FAX:......................................847-391-8919
BBS:......................................847-391-8919

Zenographics
34 Executive Park
Irvine, CA 92714
Main:......................................714-851-6352
Tech. Support:........................714-851-2191
Sales:....................................800-566-7468
Customer Service:.......... 714-851-6352 #290
Tech. Support FAX: 714-833-7465
FAX: 714-851-1314
CompuServe:.................................GO ZENO
E-Mail:.....esales@zeno.mhs.compuserve.com
BBS:...................................... 714-851-3860
FTP: ftp.zeno.com
Web: www.zeno.com

Zeos International, Ltd.
Micron Electronics
900 E Karcher Rd
Nampa, ID 83687
Main: 800-423-5891
Tech. Support:........................800-438-3343
Sales:....................................800-438-3343
Customer Service:...................800-438-3343
Tech. Support FAX: 800-270-1232
FAX: 208-893-3424
CompuServe:............................ 76450,1645
E-Mail:..........techsupport.meic@micron.com
BBS:......................................800-270-1207
Web: www.mei.micron.com

Zephyr Development Corp.
Summit Tower, 11 E. Greenway Plaza Ste. 520
Houston, TX 77046-1102
Main: 800-966-3270
Tech. Support:........................713-623-0089
Tech. Support FAX: 713-623-0091
E-Mail:...................bharris@zephyrcorp.com
BBS:......................................713-623-8979
Web: www.zephyrcorp.com

Zilog
210 E Hacienda Ave.
Campbell, CA 95008-6600
Main: 408-370-8000
Tech. Support FAX: 408-370-8056
E-Mail:...........................support@zilog.com
Web: www.zilog.com/

Zinc Software, Inc.
405 South 100 ESecond Floor
Pleasant Grove, UT 84062
Main:.....................................801-785-8900
Tech. Support:.......................801-785-8998
Sales:....................................800-638-8665
Tech. Support FAX:................801-785-8998
CompuServe:...............................GO ZINC
E-Mail:.................................tech@zinc.com
BBS:.....................................801-785-8997
FTP: ftp.zinc.com
Web: www.zinc.com

Zipperware
76 S. Main St.
Seattle, WA 98104
Main:.....................................206-223-1107
FAX: 206-223-9395
E-Mail: ....jon@nwlink.com

Zoom Telephonics, Inc.
207 South St.
Boston, MA 02111
Main:.....................................617-423-1072
Tech. Support:.......................617-423-1076
Sales: 800-631-3116
Tech. Support FAX:................617-423-4651
FAX: 617-423-3923
CompuServe:............................GO ZOOM
America Online:...............Keyword Zoomtell
BBS:.....................................617-423-3733
FTP: ftp.zoomtel.com
Web: www.zoomtel.com

Zylab Corp.
1130 W Lakehook Rd.
Buffalo Grove, IL 60069
Main:.....................................847-459-8000
Tech. Support:.......................800-544-6339
Sales: 800-544-6339
Customer Service:..................800-544-6339
FAX: 847-459-8054
BBS:.....................................847-459-8329

ZyXEL Communications
4920 E La Palma Ave.
Anaheim, CA 92807
Main: 714-693-0808
Tech. Support:.......................714-693-0808
Sales:....................................800-255-4101
Tech. Support FAX: 714-693-0705
CompuServe: 713-332734
E-Mail:.................................tech@zyxel.com
BBS: 714-693-0762
Web: www.zyxel.com

Glossary

Here are a few basic computer terms you'll see a lot. If you need help with your computer, be sure you understand these terms.

AUTOEXEC.BAT

A batch (.BAT) file used to give a PC basic DOS instructions when you turn it on. You can read and edit this file with any text editor. This and the CONFIG.SYS file are often used to analyze and troubleshoot problems with memory and other system problems.

boot disk

A disk containing the startup instructions for your computer. Usually this is the hard disk, but for safety, you should also create a floppy disk boot disk in case anything goes wrong with your hard disk, or there is problems with your computer in general. First Aid Deluxe has a feature to do this for you if you like.

browser

A software program that translates HTML (hypertext markup language) programming files into the pictures, text, and hypertext you see on the Internet. Netscape, Internet Explorer, Mosaic, and Lynx are examples of available browsers.

bug

A software mistake that is encountered when you try something the computer program you are running doesn't expect. One of the stories for the origin of this word is from the original ENIAC computer, when a moth was found lodged in one of the circuits.

byte

(*See also* megabyte) The second smallest measure of computer information. It is the equivalent of one alphabet letter or character.

cdev

cdev stands for *control panel device*. A software program that is installed, and must be accessed from, the Control Panels folder of a Macintosh computer.

clipboard

An area of system memory that hold information temporarily. When you *cut* information from a text or graphics file, it is held in the *clipboard* before you *paste* it to a new destination.

CONFIG.SYS

(*See also* AUTOEXEC.BAT) A configuration file used to give a PC basic DOS memory and system instructions when you turn it on. You can read and edit this file with any text editor. This and the CONFIG.SYS file are often used to analyze and troubleshoot problems with memory and other system problems.

components

(*See also* peripherals) Any hardware that is attached directly or indirectly to your computer.

crash

When your computer closes down the running program unexpectedly.

compression

Technology used to reduce the size of files for archiving, transfer, or storage. See *Zip files*.

disk storage

The number of bytes available for storing data or programs on a hard disk or floppy disk. The usual floppy disk size is 1.44 megabytes for 3.5" disks, (Macintosh, 1.6 or 2 MB) and a typical hard disk size for newer computers is 200 megabytes.

error message

A message from a computer program informing you that you cannot perform an action, or that something is wrong with the activity your computer is performing. When you need help, be sure to write down the error message -- and any associated code number, if one is displayed.

FTP

File Transfer Protocol. The necessary method to copy files over the Internet.

handshake

The agreement between two modems on the protocol to use when communicating. With faster modems (14.4 Kbps and faster) handshaking is done by the hardware, and you don't have to adjust the *protocols*.

hardware

Any physical part of the computer.

Hypertext

Any text that contains interactive, "hot" areas that you can select to go to another topic or location in a file.

icon

A small image on the desktop or in a software program that represents a program or a command within a program.

.INI files

Windows files that contain configuration information for applications or for Windows itself.

init

A program installed as a startup program on a Macintosh, for example, a clock. This program loads every time you restart the computer. One of the first trouble-shooting steps to take for a Macintosh is to restart the computer without loading the inits.

Internet

A collection of mainframe computers belonging to institutions and connected permanently. All other sites on the Internet are connected to this "backbone" of Internet sites.

kbps

A measurement of modem speed: kilobits per second. The current speeds are 14.4 kbps and 28.8 kbps.

kilobyte

One thousand megabytes -- actually, since all computing uses the binary system and is in multiples of 8 or 16, a kilobyte is actually 1024 bytes.

megabyte

(see also byte) One million bytes, or one thousand kilobytes. Megabytes have over-taken kilobytes as the standard measurement of disk storage and computer memory.

memory

The amount of random access memory (RAM) for your computer. Typical amounts are 4MB, 8MB or 16MB. DOS memory is a basic 640 K, with extended physical memory. Windows and DOS use memory differently. Windows creates a virtual memory file on your hard disk that enables it to perform faster by using the temporary storage area on your hard disk as if it were available memory. Occasionally, if your computer stops unexpectedly, this temporary storage area can be left on the disk. That's why it's a good idea to run a disk checking program.

modem

Stands for *modulator - demodulator*. A modem translates data into tones when sending it over the telephone lines, where the receiving modem translates the tones back into data. To do this, both modems must be *handshaking* and using the same *protocols*.

network

A group of computers joined by cabling and sharing information or other devices such as a printer.

offline/online

The condition of being actively connected to a printer, a network, or, through a modem, with a remote computer or network such as the internet.

operating system

The software that lets your computer work. It controls your keyboard, hard disk, and the messages you see on the screen. Examples include DOS, Windows 95, Macintosh, OS/2, and UNIX.

parallel

A type of port, generally used for printers, where multiple information is exchanged at once, or in *parallel*.

peripherals

(see also components): Any external equipment that you attach to your computer, such as a printer. (Strictly speaking, floppy disk drives (and CD-ROM drives) are also peripheral devices, because they are peripheral to the central processing unit.)

port

a physical location where you plug in *peripheral* equipment, such as a printer or a modem. The modem is usually connected to a COM (communications) port that you specify in the operating system. Ports can be *serial* (usually for modems but also for printers and other devices) or *parallel* (almost always for printers.)

preference files

Similar to .INI files in Windows, these Macintosh files list configuration information for programs.

print driver

A software file with specific instructions for a specific type of printer.

processor

The CPU, or central processing unit: is the chip that determines the processing capacity and speed for your computer. Performance is measured in number of computations per microsecond. The Pentium chip, for example, has 100 mHz - or megahertz, 120, 150, 166, and so on.

Program

A set of instructions that tell the computer what to do.

protocol

The speed, number of stop bits, and other data used by a modem to send information. The sending and receiving modems must be using the same protocol.

RAM

Random Access Memory. See Memory, above.

rebuild the desktop

A technique of restarting a Macintosh computer that forces it to reconfirm all its configuration information. It is usually done after new software is installed, or to help eliminate performance problems. To rebuild the desktop, hold down the Command key and Option keys at the same time.

software

Any program, usually stored on a disk and loaded into a computer's memory at a specific time, either when you start a program, or when the computer starts.

surge protector

An electrical outlet or power strip that has a built-in circuit protection from unusual power surges or spikes. It is recommended that you always use a surge protector for your computer and any equipment connected to your computer. Also, always use a grounded (3-prong) plug -- do not use an adapter unless it is properly grounded.

serial

A type of port (or communications method) used for sending information in a single stream. Modems use serial communications. Compare with *parallel*.

system files

Files that the computer loads on startup. They give instructions to the computer on how to use memory, where essential files are located on a hard disk, and what software and hardware is configured for your system.

TCP/IP

The protocol used to dial in over a telephone line and connect to a network server or to an Internet service provider. If you have a computer that is not connected to a network, you probably use this protocol to connect to the Internet.

virus

A computer program that behaves in an unauthorized, intrusive manner, often by attaching itself to other programs or to a system area (boot file) of a floppy disk, and then duplicating itself when actions such as copying files, loading file information, or running a program, are performed.

Web (or World-Wide Web)

The Internet's graphical files, accessible over the Internet if you have a *Web Browser*, such as Netscape, Mosaic, or Microsoft Internet Explorer. See also *Internet*.

Zip files

Abbreviation for a file containing other compressed files, probably created with the PKZIP shareware program. Zip files let you compress and transport files more efficiently. For example, you can compress 5MB of data into less then 1MB Zip file.

Index

T

Category Listings

accessories 70

audio/visual devices 71

BIOS

communications

services

user groups

utilities